Support for the second edition

'This second edition of Magic in Practice is a remarkable achievement. It is a dynamic, highly readable, well-referenced, practical guide to using Medical NLP in consultations, brought to life through the inclusion of numerous and wide-ranging fascinating case studies, all rooted in real life practice.

'It incorporates new and exciting material drawing on the latest findings from neuroscience and also on the experiences of a vast range of healthcare professionals who are further developing the applications of Medical NLP in their work.

'Since being trained by in this field more than a decade ago, I have used Medical NLP skills on a daily basis in my clinical work as a way of creating more powerful, rewarding consultations with patients. This new edition of the book is already energizing my work further, inspiring me to develop my skills to another level.'

Dr Arti Maini, General Practitioner, London, UK

'I would say the first edition of Magic In Practice gave us tools to better look after our patients and improve beyond the bare numbers. This second edition moves the game on, using better and more powerful concepts. Every healthcare professional should read this.

'We are in a position of great privilege where the needy seek our help. We owe it to them to maximize our impact on their wellbeing. For any treatment to work, one needs the patient to have belief that the intervention will work.

'These tools have made a big impact both clinically and beyond in both my professional and personal life. The more naturally they are used, the more effective they become. Since becoming a doctor, they are the most useful skills I have learnt. To improve oneself is a time-limited choice, so use your time wisely.'

Dr Khalid Hasan, Consultant Anesthiologist, Birmingham, UK

'Ever since I first attended a Medical NLP course run by Garner, I knew that his approach to wellbeing would change the way I practice.

'I have worked as a consultant psychiatrist for many years and can truly say that his approach has helped me become a holistic therapist in every sense of the word.... I approach my patients in a completely new wa
imagined possible.

'I was so pleased to see a second edition of M
clear and informative companion to my ever

'It will undoubtedly change the way you worl
The way you approach health, healing and 'dis
way you help your patients will never be the same.'

Dr Leon van Huyssteen, Consultant Psychiatrist,

‘One of the most exciting things for me as a physician is to see patients I have been treating for years have their lives transformed using the techniques described in this book.

‘They are now far too busy enjoying life to come and see me and I am so grateful to Garner for equipping me with the skills to do this.’

Dr Liz Croton, General Practitioner and GP Trainer, Birmingham, UK

‘The authors are shamefacedly altruistic in this second edition where their personal insights and sensitivity to the experiences of patients and clients are neatly woven throughout the text.

‘The healing value of Medical NLP to the patient, client and practitioner is articulated in such a way that the reader wants to learn more, develop skills and an array of tools they can access during any consultation or meeting to enhance the patient/client experience.

‘Many of the tools discussed within the book have wider application: the support of anxious learners and novice practitioners, and, as such, the book should be on the reading list for all those involved in care of others who are keen to ensure the wellbeing of those they care for and optimize their own ability to be effective and sensitive care givers.

Sandra Bannister, Director of Undergraduate Programmes, School of Health Sciences, University of Stirling, UK

‘This excellent and thought provoking second edition of Magic In Practice explores, among other things, the paradox of seemingly increasing ill health, or at least the reduced sense of well-being, despite the impressive technological advances made in medicine.

‘Although remarkable progress has been made in our understanding of, and the ability to manipulate, the genome, the metabolome, the microbiome etc, many people’s illnesses and symptoms leave the medical profession baffled. The authors explore the underlying causes of this phenomenon and offer practical solutions.

‘It is an impressive piece of work, exploring and linking the mind, the body, their interaction and encompassing a study of human behaviour in relation to health outcomes. This book is an essential read for anyone involved in healthcare, and will benefit the patient and practitioner alike.’

Dr Shahid A Khan, Consultant Physician & Adjunct Reader, Director of Clinical Studies, St Mary’s Hospital, London, UK

Magic in Practice

Introducing Medical NLP:
The Art and Science of Language
in Healing and Health

Second Edition
Revised and updated

Those who say it can’t be done
should not interrupt the person doing it

–Ancient Chinese proverb

Magic in Practice

Introducing Medical NLP: The Art and Science of Language in Healing and Health

Garner Thomson
with
Dr. Khalid Khan

Introduction by
Dr. Richard Bandler
Co-creator and Developer of Neuro-Linguistic Programming

Second Edition
Revised and updated

BOOKS
Hammersmith Health Books
London

First published in 2008 by Hammersmith Press Limited, London, UK.

This edition published in 2015 by Hammersmith Books Limited,
14 Greville Street, London EC1N 8SB, UK – www.hammersmithbooks.co.uk

Disclaimer
Please note that all information in this book is provided for educational purposes only and should not be construed as, nor replace, medical or psychiatric advice. If you are suffering from a physical or psychological problem, please seek the advice of the appropriately qualified health professional. If you wish to use Medical NLP in the treatment of others, either adjunctively or alone, you are required to undergo the appropriate training. See www.medicalnlp.com for details.

British Library Cataloguing in Publication Data: A CIP record of this book is available from the British Library.

Print ISBN: 978-1-78161-063-3
Ebook ISBN: 978-1-78161-064-0

Editor: Georgina Bentliff
Designed and typeset by: Bespoke Publishing Ltd
Production by: Helen Whitehorn, Path Projects Ltd
Rainbow image on cover: Copyright © Alekup/123rf.com
Index by: Dr Laurence Errington
Printed and bound by: TJ International Ltd

www.medicalnlp.com

Contents

IMPORTANT NOTE

Acknowledgments

Many people have contributed to both editions of this book in a variety of ways—but none more so than Dr. Richard Bandler, without whom it, quite literally, would have been inconceivable. His insight, intellectual honesty and wisdom have combined to create one of the most significant tools for human development in the past century.

Apart from his work, which continues to inspire our own, we are hugely grateful for the support and encouragement he has given to the foundation and development of The Society of Medical NLP. The number of doctors, students, and allied health professionals who have had the opportunity to experience and advance the power and potential of this extraordinary technology and to pass on the benefits to their patients is growing, and will, we hope, continue to do so as the years go by.

We thank those many doctors, students, and allied health professionals who have entrusted us with their training, and we applaud their courage in seeking to explore beyond the edges of their known maps. The discoveries and experiences they report back to us are a constant source of inspiration and delight. We are delighted to feature some of their experiences in this new edition. Of special interest to us are those health professionals who, armed only with the information in the first incarnation of *Magic in Practice*, went out, tried some of the patterns for the first time, and achieved notable—sometimes extraordinary—results.

Our appreciation goes to those researchers whose work we cite in this book. While they have inspired us in our search for explanations for the theories and principles we discuss, and the mysteries of the body-mind system, human relationships, and health, we emphasize that any interpretation placed upon their work is ours alone. Our thanks, too, to those writers and thinkers who granted our requests to quote their words or reproduce their diagrams. To those who have not and were, for whatever reason, unable to respond to our requests, we would appreciate it if they contacted us so we can include credits in later editions.

We would particularly like to thank Georgina Bentliff who originally commissioned *Magic in Practice* for Hammersmith Press, and who has so bravely taken on this second edition.

Finally, thanks to Dr. Naveed Akthar for his tireless help and meticulous approach in helping to proof-read this edition.

Comments on the Second Edition

From the earliest stage of publication, we have been touched by, and deeply grateful for, the unstinting encouragement, support, and recognition *Magic in Practice* has received from the vast majority of readers.

Reviews have been consistently enthusiastic in both online and print media; the book has found its way onto the reading lists of various universities and medical schools and we have been interviewed, and positively received, by some of the most respected publications in the world. We have been invited to address mainline institutions on the subject of 'the language of healing and health', and the subject matter has been validated for a number of continuing professional development programs for doctors and other health professionals in the United Kingdom and abroad.

Then there have been those people who attended Society of Medical NLP trainings, and went away to use and develop the principles and techniques they learned into new and even more effective interventions. Their experiences in applying the material have given rise to exciting results that are far beyond our original hopes.

Finally, there are our real teachers—the patients and clients who come to us for help, who challenge us by presenting complex and often extremely mystifying conditions. By accepting the Medical NLP tenet that every patient is unique, regardless of how much they or their illness resembles someone or something else, we find ourselves constantly pushed to the limits of our own understanding and experience. That is where we have learned to sit back and listen, watch and wait, and, sooner or later, the inner logic of the patient's experience often emerges to instruct us how to proceed.

This edition of *Magic in Practice* has been some time in preparation. Although it will be easily recognizable to those readers who know the first edition, much is new.

In some cases the emphasis has shifted. For example, where in the first edition we were hinting at looming disaster in healthcare, we now believe the crisis is upon us. An estimated one in 10 patients admitted to hospital in the European Union is a victim of medical error. A disproportionately large percentage (a further one in 10) of these accidents results in serious injury or death.[1]

Furthermore, according to a report by Dr. Barbara Starfield of the Johns Hopkins School of Hygiene and Public Health, medical errors are now the third leading cause of death in the United States, following cancer and heart disease.[2]

Some of the original chapters have been slightly edited to make them more self-contained, so the reader may dip in and out of the book according to her whim of the moment, while a number of sections have been added.

These include new chapters on priming; breathing; heart rate variability; cardiac chaos and coherence; and how a minor change in sleeping patterns can head off an abundance of health problems. Additional evidence is mounting that people's perception of their situation is at least as toxic as whatever condition they might actually be suffering—a real wake-up call to health-providers to pay attention to *how* the patient thinks about her problem, not just to what the problem allegedly 'is'.

Some of the scientific research has been updated, additional examples, anecdotes, and exercises have been introduced, and we have included new material on a number of topics, ranging from the stranglehold of 'WEIRD' science; the effect of relationships on the progression of cancer; 'lifestyle diseases': the West's newest export to the emerging world; how medicine can create or cure disease by the definitions it uses; how exposure to media reports can cause or worsen physical conditions; and even how the color of a cigarette pack can affect the taste of its contents.

We also include a seven-step, evidence-based guide to reducing the risk of death from any of the major circulatory or respiratory diseases by more than a third. Finally, at the request of many time-poor colleagues, we have included sure-fire techniques to control the wandering consultation and improve patient satisfaction.

Our only request to the reader is that he or she approaches this new edition with an open mind. We say this: explore the contents, then try them out for yourself and see what works for you and your patients or clients. Feel free to contact us with your questions and experiences at: info@medicalnlp.com or visit us on Facebook at: The Society of Medical NLP.

Foreword to the Second Edition

Dr. Richard Bandler
Co-creator and Developer of Neuro-Linguistic Programming

I am so glad to write this introduction to the second edition of *Magic in Practice* by Garner Thomson and Dr. Khalid Khan.

People often ask me if I am proud of what I have done by co-creating Neuro-Linguistic Programming. The answer is, I don't really think about it at all. I'm very proud of the effect it has had on the fields of psychology, education, sales training and business ... the list goes on.

However, at the top of my list are the authors of this book who bravely entered the field of medicine to provide doctors with new, easier ways to view their own research and draw on skills that would help thousands of patients.

I believe by updating their book they are responding to those they teach in the same way they ask doctors and healthcare professionals to update their views on communication in general.

Everything can be done better ... that is why I never stop. Hurrah to this second edition!!!!

Dr. Richard Bandler
2014

Foreword to the First Edition

Dr. Richard Bandler
Co-creator and Developer of NLP

All I can say is: it's about time. This is the kind of book I hoped one of my students would write. What Garner Thomson has done, with Dr. Khalid Khan, is to take my work further and, with great precision, present tools for healthcare professionals, while at the same time offering all those in NLP a solid understanding of how the technology of NLP works in the brain.

I have for years been very good at modeling successful healers, but have fallen short on providing the science. I have used Magnetic Resonance Imaging since it was available to understand the mysteries of the brain. Now, these gentlemen have gone so much farther. I say thank you—and recommend that any Neuro-Linguistic Programmer read this over and over and over.

It seems obvious to me that the more we know about the brain and how it works well, the better off we will be. And the two most important applications of my work will always be education and health. My work has been accepted by psychologists and therapists. Over the years, I have trained thousands of doctors, teachers, and healthcare professionals. The American Dental Society claimed that NLP had the only cure for dental phobia.

However, I doubt that myself: I believe there are as many ways for the brain to learn better behavior as there is imagination in the world. What this book represents is a startling step forward in filling in details and applying technology. Rigorous, yet easy to understand, this is a presentation of powerful patterns of human learning. I believe that, 50 years from now, you will find it on every healthcare professional's bookshelf.

So be one of those exceptional people who lead the pack and get it there now. I am proud to have been the inspiration for such an elegant and wonderful book. Having read it just once, I am now going to go back through it again. You should do the same.

The only other thing I can say is: Thank you!

Dr. Richard Bandler

Overview

Any sufficiently advanced technology is indistinguishable from magic.—
Arthur C. Clarke[3]

Why, in the most scientifically, economically and socially advanced time in the history of our species, do we seem to be suffering from more depression, anxiety, and psychophysical problems than ever before?

Medicine has defeated most of the infectious diseases that shortened our lives 100 years ago; we are living many more years, with greater access to healthcare. And yet, between 25 per cent and 50 per cent of the problems for which patients now seek help have no evident pathological cause.[4]

Despite the almost daily promises of medical 'cures' and 'breakthroughs' in the media, the list of 'functional' or 'somatoform' disorders is long and seems to be growing. At the moment, it includes chronic medically unexplained pain, irritable bowel syndrome, chronic fatigue syndrome, non-ulcer dyspepsia, headaches, premenstrual syndrome, temporomandibular joint disorder (TMJD), a wide range of autoimmune dysfunctions, and environmental illnesses, such as electromagnetic hypersensitivity, and allergies.

Add to that, the 'emotional' disorders, such as depression, anxiety, phobias, obsessive compulsive disorder (OCD), and post-traumatic stress disorder (PTSD), and we can see why the health services are in danger of being overwhelmed, health professionals are becoming frustrated, and patient dissatisfaction is growing.

The changing face of disease

Lifestyle diseases—sometimes referred to as 'diseases of civilization'—have taken over from communicable (infectious) diseases as the greatest health risk in the Western world.

These diseases, ranging from asthma and atherosclerosis, through certain forms of cancer, chronic liver, pulmonary and cardiac disease, to osteoporosis, obesity, stroke, and kidney failure, all have a strong behavioral component. In other words, the way many people are living in the 'civilized' world is now a major cause of chronic illness and early death.[5,6,7]

A research paper published by *The Lancet* points to the fact that diets in many Western countries changed dramatically in the second part of the 20th century, with significant increases in the consumption of meat, dairy products, vegetable oils, fruit juices, and alcohol. At the same time, large reductions in physical activity have been matched by a surge in obesity. An increase in many cancers, including colorectal, breast, prostate, endometrial, and lung, correlates strongly with diets high in animal products, sugar, and fat.

The fact that many people who move from one country to another acquire the cancer rates of the new host country suggests that environmental and behavioral factors are more significant than genetics.[8] Furthermore, as increasing numbers of developing countries adopt Western patterns of work, diet and exercise, the incidence of lifestyle diseases is spreading fast.

Smoking, high-calorie fast food, and lack of exercise are expected to cost India an accumulated loss of $236.6-billion within a decade, while the resultant toll of chronic disease—all of long duration and slow progression—will seriously affect people's earnings.

According to a report jointly prepared by the World Health Organization and the World Economic Forum, income loss to Indians as a result of these diseases, which was already high, at $8.7 billion in 2005, is projected, at the time of writing, to rise to $54 billion in 2015.[9]

Pakistan faces an accumulated loss of $30.7 billion, with income loss increasing by $5.5 billion to $6.7 billion by 2015, and China, the worst of all countries under review, is expected to suffer an accumulated loss of $557.7 billion. Loss of income will reach $131.8 billion, almost eight times what it was in 2005.

According to the report, 60% of all deaths worldwide in 2005—a total of 35 million—resulted from non-communicable (read, avoidable) diseases and accounted for nearly half the number of premature deaths.

Despite growing insight into the cause (and cost) of the mounting scourge of lifestyle disease, mainstream medicine's response—to tackle the effect, rather than the cause—is proving singularly ineffective.

However, all this means that many of these diseases and a large percentage of deaths can be avoided by relatively simple changes in lifestyle, including dietary changes; increased exercise; stress management; and early detection of, and response to, fluctuations in health and wellbeing. In fact, an extensive Europe-wide study by Cambridge University researchers clearly shows that comparatively minor lifestyle changes can add a decade or more to the average person's lifespan.

The study, part of the European Prospective Investigation and Nutrition (EPIC) study, involving more than 500,000 people in 10 European countries, reveals that

- adding fruit and vegetables to your daily diet can add three years to your life;
- not smoking turns the clock back by four to five years; and
- even moderate exercise can increase life expectancy by up to three years.[10]

A follow-up study at London's Imperial College has since confirmed that seven relatively simple changes to diet and lifestyle can reduce the risk of dying from any of the major circulatory or respiratory diseases, including stroke and angina, by up to 34%.[11]

These are:

1. Be as lean as possible without becoming underweight and by eating mainly a plant-based diet;
2. Be physically active for at least 30 minutes a day;
3. Limit consumption of energy-dense foods. These are foodstuffs and drinks high in sugar, fat, and refined carbohydrates;
4. Eat a variety of vegetables, fruits, whole grains, and pulses, such as lentils and beans;
5. Limit consumption of red meat to 17.5 oz (500 grams) cooked

weight a week, and avoid processed meats, such as bacon, ham, and salami;

6. Limit alcoholic drinks to two for men and one for women a day; and
7. New mothers should breastfeed their infants for up to six months.

Further studies confirm that as little as 15 minutes a day spent exercising can significantly reduce the incidence of both cancer and heart disease.[12]

Physicians are familiar with patients' resistance to 'doing the right thing' (quitting smoking, exercising more, stopping snacking on donuts), however much they are confronted with the challenge to their own mortality. It is therefore understandable that reliance on anti-smoking, fat- and cholesterol-busting drugs, and gastric-band surgery is on the rise, despite the risks and comparative ineffectiveness involved.

Our contention (and, the reason for writing this book) is that human behavior is more easily, and infinitely more safely, altered by the methods outlined in this book than by drugs, surgery, or well-intentioned advice. Our experience is that people's capacity to program and re-program their beliefs, behavior, and, by extension, possibly even their biology, is far greater than they are usually given credit for.

However, while most sufferers of chronic dysfunctions accept that some kind of change is necessary for their recovery, few, if any, know specifically how to make that change.

Just as importantly, many physicians are equally mystified as to how effectively to help their patients.

Part of the confusion may be simply explained: the reductionist, molecular, biomedical, cause-and-effect model that proved so spectacularly successful in defeating the microbe is failing to address the more complex psychosocial factors responsible for the current rise in chronic disease and early death.

Cartesian Dualism, the separation of 'mind' from body, still affects training and research. Although the hunt for 'causality' has shifted from germ to gene, and while the prognosis for a number of fairly rare genetic disorders is improving, no gene is likely to be found for each of the scores of medically unexplained dysfunctions with which practitioners and patients wrestle every day of their lives.

Failure to find the cause (what is 'the' cause of depression? what is 'the' cause of cancer?) means in practice that the focus of treatment falls on the symptom. Therefore, our dependence on the trillion-dollar pharmaceutical industry is growing, and is matched only by the hopes invested in technological innovation as the rescuer of humanity in what is perceived as an ongoing battle with the 'disease' of life.

The problem of 'mind'

The implication of all diagnoses of 'functional' or 'somatoform' disorders may be that they are all, or partly, 'in the mind'. And 'mind' is not widely considered a matter of concern for the average medical professional.

Current treatment guidelines offer two main options: psychotropic (mind-altering) medication, and outsourcing the problem to a 'talking cure' professional (where these are available). Either way, the integrity of the patient-as-a-whole is compromised, or, Cartesian Dualism is reinforced.

Pause here and reflect on which cultures, aside from Westerners, subscribe to the 'all-in-the-mind' explanation for chronic conditions for which no obvious organic cause can be found. As it happens, there aren't many. The reason? Possibly because they have no 'mind' in which 'all' can skulk.

English, as it happens, is one of the few languages that has a word for, and, therefore, a concept of, 'mind'. Other health systems might speak of problems with your energy meridia; *chi*; *prana*; humors; spells and evil spirits. Or, they might point to environmental or dietary deviations from what is required by your innate *prakruti*, or body-type—but almost never of your mind. Even René Descartes, at whom holists (including ourselves, we must admit) continue to sneer for single-handedly creating the mind-body split, never actually said the 'mind', as such, was irrelevant, or even separate from the body. It just didn't figure in the way of thinking at the time.

In his most famous works, Descartes spoke about *amê* and *corps* (and, sometimes, anima). *Corps* was easy enough to understand, but the translators ran into trouble with the French word, *amê*. The closest English equivalent to both *amê* and the Latin *anima* (which he also sometimes used), is 'soul'. Just about everyone who believes in the concept of an eternal soul would be happy to declare it separate from the finite physical body, even though Descartes himself regarded it as anchored during life to the pineal gland. But, the damage to the deep complexities of human thought and feeling had been done. *Body 1, Mind 0.*

What was missed at the time, and continues to be missed, is that 'mind' is not, and cannot be, an entity in the same way a body can. Nor are the thoughts and feelings, the experiences by which people 'know' they have a mind, discrete objects that can be isolated, identified, and studied in the same way as an organ, a germ or a gene.

All experience is process. People attach meaning to process. Meaning, in turn, affects biology. Therefore, any physical experience we have must affect, and, in turn, be affected by, both the physical and the mental, in an ongoing, dynamic feed-back loop.

To suggest that a problem is 'all in the mind' reduces process, and, therefore, lessens the possibility of change. It is as useless and as semantically skewed as to say 'the light is all in the wire'.

The delivery problem

Problems increase when we look at the 'delivery' of healthcare, as opposed to its application. For various reasons, some of them political, we have entered a period of cost-effectiveness, 'quality-adjusted life years', evidence-based medicine, and increasing bureaucracy.

As care becomes increasingly standardized—by the National Institute for Health and Clinical Excellence (NICE) in the United Kingdom, and insurance companies in the United States—the personal is giving way to the impersonal, compassion is surrendering to science and practitioners, patients and the economy are all paying the price. Doctors are increasingly required to practice medicine unquestioningly, according to a set of guidelines delivered from sources on high. If they don't, they can face highly punitive consequences. In our opinion, this is not science; this is theology. Patients' unhappiness with the care they receive is, in turn, reflected in the growing trend towards litigation.

It should be no surprise, then, that so many physicians retreat behind the barricades of professional detachment, from where they practice an essentially defensive form of medicine that places the effectiveness of the patient's treatment on the other side of a mountain of bureaucratic obligations, legal concerns, official guidelines, and targets, as well as restrictions on treatment modalities, resources, and time. And no surprise that so many patients are responding negatively towards what they regard as a lack of concern, interest, and sufficient information by emigrating towards 'alternative' healthcare, or to the offices of their legal advisors with an intention to sue.

A crisis in the making

In the first edition of this book, we hinted at the possibility of a crisis engulfing Western medicine. Now, and with no sense of satisfaction, we report our belief that today's healthcare is already in crisis. An estimated one in 10 patients admitted to hospital in the EU is a victim of medical error. A disproportionately large percentage (a further one in 10) of these accidents results in serious injury or death.[13]

Figures from elsewhere are even more worrying. According to a report by Dr. Barbara Starfield, MD, MPH, of the Johns Hopkins School of Hygiene and Public Health, medical errors are now the third leading cause of death in the United States, following cancer and heart disease.[14]

Under-reported statistics

Many researchers believe that the figures for medical errors may be significantly under-reported throughout the world, possibly for fear of litigation.[15] Since no effective, mandatory, official system of registration of medical errors, no mandatory root cause analysis, and no systems to prevent the occurrence of medical errors exist in Europe, the figures may be even higher than one in 10. In contrast, motor vehicle accidents have been for decades routinely and systematically registered along with the recording of deaths and injuries.

Various studies blame a number of factors, including work stress in hospitals, limited consultation time, and reduced financial resources. But one of the recurring problems revealed in successive studies is defective communication—between doctors and nurses and their patients, as well as among health professionals themselves. Effective leadership, as well as effective clinical outcomes, is highly dependent on accurate, targeted and mindful communication.

Health professionals, too, are victims of the situation. A large body of evidence shows many doctors suffer high levels of stress as a result of their work, impairing both their health and their ability to provide quality care to their patients. The main sources of work-related stress and burnout among doctors, in both primary and secondary care, have been identified as: workload; the resultant effect on their personal lives; organizational changes; poor management; insufficient resources; constant exposure to the suffering of their patients; medical errors; complaints and litigation.[16]

We believe both patient and practitioner can benefit from an expanded model of healthcare—the patient by being seen and treated as a 'whole person', and the practitioner by having a choice of non-invasive, non-pharmacological tools and principles that, in the consultative partnership, can help to meet that need.

Whole-person healing

In many ways, this is an idea whose time has come. The Center for Advancement of Health in Washington DC is one of several influential organizations currently lobbying for changes in the approach to healthcare.[17] Those organizations, and a growing number of individual campaigners, are broadly in agreement that:

- Attitudes, thoughts, feelings, and behaviors must be recognized as important aspects of healing and health;
- The mind and body flourish or perish together. Therefore patients should not be sent to one 'repair shop' for sick thoughts and feelings and to another for sick bodies;
- Scientific evidence is overwhelming that how and where we live, who we are, and how we think, feel, and cope, can powerfully affect our health and wellbeing. To ignore this is irresponsible; and
- Patient care must shift to treating the whole person. This will result in healthier individuals, healthier communities and healthier nations.[18]

Noble as these sentiments are, it is not enough simply to urge the health professional to begin practicing whole-person healthcare. What exactly is 'holistic patient management', and how might it be practically pursued in the context of the medical consultation? Indeed, although we have come to know a lot about disease, what exactly is 'health'? These are just some of the questions this book seeks to answer.

Health as process

Our first presupposition is that health is more than an absence of disease. Rather, it exists along an ever-changing continuum between order and chaos. Our body-mind system is in a state of constant, dynamic interaction with both the internal and external environment, which itself is changing rapidly. The degree to which we are able to respond to these changes and can restore body-mind systemic balance (see our thoughts about autonomic coherence on pages 25, 253, 254 and 255) reflects both our current health and our ability to heal.

One purpose of this book is to unravel (as far as is possible at this stage in our knowledge) those elusive qualities that make up a 'positive relationship' between doctor and patient—and to share with our colleagues in the healthcare professions some of the principles and techniques that we, and many of the doctors and medical students who have undergone our trainings, have found to help facilitate the healing process.

The development of NLP

Neuro-Linguistic Programming, as its name suggests, refers to language (words, as well as other symbol systems, such as physical posture, gestures and related non-verbal forms of communication) as a function of the nervous system and its transformation into 'subjective experience'.

Put more simply, it focuses on the way we use our five senses to create a 'map' of 'reality', which we then use to navigate our way through the world. It is a basic premise of NLP that the quality of our maps dictates the quality of our lives. In our opinion, NLP ranks as one of the most significant epistemological developments of our time. It developed—

and continues to develop—out of Dr. Richard Bandler's curiosity about the nature of subjective experience, especially that of individuals whose performance is outstanding in their fields. While most scientific research begins with investigation into how problems and deficiencies develop, Dr. Bandler's question has always been: *how do people achieve excellence?*

His first subjects were a group of therapists, unrelated in their approaches, but who were nonetheless achieving results well beyond those of their peers. These included Dr. Milton Erickson, a medical doctor and clinical hypnotist, Virginia Satir, now widely regarded as the founder of family therapy, Gestalt therapist Fritz Perls, and noted body-worker Moshe Feldenkrais. Bandler observed certain commonalities in their work. Interestingly, none of the subjects of his study appeared consciously aware of these patterns, and they had never met each other, and even when they later came together, they were reportedly unimpressed by one another.

Bandler and his colleague, John Grinder, began to experiment. By identifying each sequence of their subjects' approach, testing it on themselves and other eager volunteers, and refining the processes, they found that the effects could be replicated. Furthermore, these capabilities could easily be taught to others, with similar results.

These experiments led to one of the key presuppositions that have come to underpin NLP: *Subjective experience has a structure.* Following on from that is the corollary: *Change the structure, and the subjective experience will also change.*

It was widely believed at that time that, apart from drugs, interpretation and insight were the only means whereby effective emotional and behavioral change could be achieved, and that only with considerable effort and time. But Bandler continued to demonstrate, on a range of patients, including long-stay schizophrenic and psychotic patients, that changing the map could have a dramatic and immediate effect. In the introduction to his first book, *The Structure of Magic*, published in 1975, he wrote:

The basic principle here is that people end up in pain, not because the world is not rich enough to allow them to satisfy their needs, but because their representation of the world is impoverished.[19]

Two other key principles emerged from Richard Bandler's essentially pragmatic approach. The first was that human beings act largely out of various permutations of patterned responses, and, the second, that each person has a signature way of 'coding' his experience by the use of his five senses.

Medical NLP and health

Medical NLP—the development and application of the principles and techniques of NLP to the specific needs of health professionals and their patients—is an internationally recognized and licensed model that formally integrates non-invasive, non-pharmacological, and clinically effective approaches with the existing principles and techniques of the consultation process. Training and certification by The Society of Medical NLP is recognized and licensed by Dr. Richard Bandler, the co-creator and developer of NLP, and his Society of NLP. It has also been approved for continuing professional development programs in both the United Kingdom and the Netherlands.

Supported by extensive research and clinical experience, it offers, for the first time, explicit principles and techniques applicable to a wide range of complex, chronic conditions that have symptoms, but no readily identifiable cause. In holding, as a goal, the physical and psychological coherence of the patient, and integrating seamlessly with any aspect of healthcare, it functions as a practical and continually evolving 'salutogenic' (health promoting and affirming) model of 'whole-person' healing and health in the spirit envisioned and advocated by Aaron Antonovsky.[20]

One of the central messages of *Magic in Practice* is that a fundamental component of an effective consultation is an equal and proactive contract between doctor and patient. The relationship functions as a therapeutic agent in itself.

Many practitioners will admit to being mystified by the fact that two patients with apparently identical symptoms will respond entirely differently to the same treatment. And many patients can recall encountering a physician, who, somehow, by some indefinable means unrelated to any specific treatment, just 'made me feel better'.

Equally, some patients make unexpected, sometimes dramatic, recoveries against all the predictions of current medical knowledge... although these 'spontaneous remissions' still tend to be more of an embarrassment to orthodox science. 'Anecdotal' is the label usually attached to these events, which, sadly, tends to preclude any closer examination on the part of those people purportedly committed to unbiased scientific investigation.

If pressed, both patient and physician will agree that some factor, other than conventional medical treatment, is responsible for facilitating healing. The doctor may attribute this to the patient's 'attitude', the patient to the doctor's 'bedside manner'.

The underlying dynamic undoubtedly depends on effective communication. To focus our students' attention on the true process and purpose of communication, we draw attention to the origins of the word. It is derived from the Indo-European collective, *Ko*, meaning 'share', and *Mei*, meaning 'change'. Communication in Medical NLP, therefore, is a *Ko Mei* process—*a coming together, a sharing, in order to effect change.*

We would like to emphasize, too, that practitioners of NLP and Medical NLP are not de facto 'therapists'. As Dr. Bandler repeatedly asserts, practitioners don't strive to 'cure' problems, but to help their clients (or patients) re-learn more resourceful physical and/or psychological behaviors that allow them to function more effectively. In Medical Neuro-Linguistic Programming, our cry is: *treat the patient, don't try to cure the disease.* Therefore, a knowledge of, or adherence to, a particular school of 'psychology' or a specific medical specialization, is not necessary for effective intervention.

What is not in doubt is the fact that the *quality* of the relationship between practitioner and patient is at least as important as the treatment itself. Historical evidence exists that a number of treatments now discarded as 'unscientific' demonstrated a 50–70% cure rate when they were still regarded as mainstream.[21] More recent research, specifically in the area of 'emotional' disorders (increasingly falling within the provenance of general medicine), suggests that as little as 15% of effectiveness results from the therapeutic procedure alone.[22]

Physicians who have been in practice for more than a few decades will not be surprised by this. For much of the first part of the 20th century, the relational quality between doctor and patient was emphasized in medical training and explicit in practice, even as science was advancing the knowledge and expertise of the health practitioner. This original commitment to partnering wisdom, human values with technological innovation, and respect for the patient was reflected in the mottos adopted by a number organizations and associations around the world.

In 1952, Britain's Royal College of General Practitioners adopted the motto *Cum Scientia Caritas* (Science with Compassionate Care). The Canadian Orthopedic Association's motto is, *Pietate, Arte et Scientia Corrigere* (With compassion, skill and knowledge we set right), and the Association of Surgeons of Great Britain and Ireland's is, *Omnes Ab Omnibus Discamus* (Let us learn all things from everybody).

We applaud the sentiments, but are unsure, in this age of stringent financial targets and controls and purely 'evidence-based' treatment, to what extent they are actually practiced today. Many people, not least patients, hanker after a 'humanization' of science—especially medicine.

As a modest contribution to this end, *Magic in Practice* presents key 'mainstream' NLP techniques applied in the specific context of healthcare, as well as new approaches developed in real-world situations out of the principles of observation, information gathering, hypothesis-creation, and some considerable clinical experience.

Although the principles and techniques presented here are not intended to replace medical consultation and appropriate treatment, they will be of interest to doctors in both primary and secondary care, as well as nurses, psychologists, counselors, and therapists—anyone, in fact, interested in developing a more integrative and effective approach to patient care.

Why 'Magic'?

Since NLP's emergence in the mid-1970s, 'magic' has been a word often associated with its practice. Where it functions as a 'meta-psychology', it focuses on structure and process (how we create and maintain our model of 'reality'), rather than losing itself in detail and speculation. It demands behavioral flexibility on the part of the practitioner to accommodate the uniqueness of each individual's patterns, and provides a systematic means of generating techniques specifically tailored to the needs of each patient or client.

The speed with which an elegantly designed and applied intervention can result in change can often challenge and mystify. The mystery is intensified when we consider that the primary tools of these interventions are non-pharmacological, non-invasive, and non-toxic, something that cannot be said for virtually any other current treatment in the field of medical care.

More than 30 years ago, the idea that neurological processes could be impacted and re-routed by non-invasive processes was largely speculative. Richard Bandler was one of the first researchers to apply neural scanning by magnetic resonance imaging (MRI) technology to explore the impact of NLP on brain function. Since then, as we will show in this book, neuroscience and psychology have evolved dramatically, to cast even more light into the 'black box' of brain and behavior.

We now know—and ignore at our own peril and that of our patients—that the brain constantly moves in and out of complex, interrelating dynamic equilibria, responding to the context or 'meaning' of its experience,[23] is actively damaged by 'negative' data[24] and can even alter its physical architecture.[25] It follows then that communication within the practitioner-patient relationship is an important source of data for the meaning-making brain and the body with which it functions as an integrated whole.

Words can literally affect us for better or worse. It is surprising, then, that so little time and attention are paid to the quality and precision (what NLP calls the 'elegance') of the language we use. Substantial research supports the assertion that *how* a respected health professional says something can directly affect the patient's physical and psychological wellbeing at least as much as *what* he says.[26]

Of course, communication works in different ways. Not only can clinical outcomes be affected for better or worse by the quality of the patient-physician relationship, but, in the event of medical accident, the patient's decision to litigate has been shown in several studies to be based substantially more on the doctor's 'attitude' and the quality of the relationship between doctor and patient than on the accident itself.[27]

We believe that at least part of the apparent 'magic' of Medical NLP derives not from any mystical properties of the methodology, but from the narrowness of the paradigm it is seeking to expand. To take Arthur C. Clarke's Third Law further, it is not difficult to demonstrate that virtually any health technology would appear superior to one that regards the individual as merely:

1. a biomechanical 'object' whose thinking processes have little impact on his health or wellbeing;
2. a product of purely Newtonian cause-and-effect processes;
3. a closed system, largely uninfluenced by other 'closed systems';
4. equal in every way to every other individual, benefiting only from standardized treatments;
5. an organism that produces symptoms which require suppression or removal without any significant regard to the reason or reasons for the appearance of those symptoms; and
6. 'fixable' by the application of purely mechanistic rules in much the same way as a watchmaker fixes a watch.

The placebo effect—or, the neurophysiology of care?

Any change for the better that is unexplained by scientifically approved treatment is often dismissed by the medical establishment as the placebo response. We are not unduly perturbed by this. So prevalent is the response at all levels of research and treatment that we are utterly confident in the declaration that *something important is happening that deserves to be recognized and, wherever possible, incorporated into practical healthcare.*

Furthermore, we believe that a greater awareness of this apparently inbuilt psychophysiological capability can renew hope for millions of people whose complex chronic conditions remain inadequately addressed by Western scientific knowledge. By this, we are not proposing a reintroduction of dummy pills and sham treatments, but, rather, consideration of the psychological and biochemical substrates that underlie the human body–mind system to self-regulate under certain conditions, the mechanisms of which are just beginning to be understood.

The problem faced by medical orthodoxy, as pointed out by Gershom Zajicek in a seminal paper in the *Cancer Journal*, is that nothing in pharmacokinetic theory accounts for the placebo effect. Therefore, rather than abandon current belief, the placebo effect is dismissed as random error or noise which should be ignored.[28]

Regrettably, the word, 'placebo' (derived from the medieval prayer, *Placebo Domino*, 'I shall please the Lord') has acquired pejorative overtones, suggesting deception, weakness, and scientific irrelevancy. But this is a semantic rather than a scientifically grounded shift. As we will point out throughout this book, the word for a thing is not the thing itself. We should not confuse naming or defining with understanding or experiencing. *We do not make something invalid merely by labeling it as such.*

Here's another way of looking at the placebo effect (our way):

The placebo response doesn't mean that nothing important has happened; it simply means that something which we haven't been measuring has happened.

Indeed, so pervasive—and sometimes so dramatic—is the placebo response that some scientists have suggested reclassifying it. Suggestions include 'the healing response', 'remembered wellness', the 'human effect', and the 'meaning response', none of which suggests irrelevance or chicanery.

So powerful is the placebo effect that it is routinely employed (and abused) by the pharmaceutical industry. Placebos are routinely used as controls to test new drugs, and, once their purpose has been served, they are discarded.

Or, are they?

After claiming they have successfully eliminated the placebo effect, the pharmaceutical companies go on to market their products in carefully designed sizes, shapes, and colors, all of which are known to increase the placebo effect.[29] They know that cheaper generics are less effective than expensive brand names, and that highly advertised brand names perform best of all (and certainly sell billions of pills), especially if advertised by well-known and popular celebrities.

Still, all that shouldn't matter if the drug performs better than the placebo against which it has been tested, should it?

In theory, no. But, here are three important facts about placebos in research:

1. Most trials go through a 'washing' stage before they start in earnest. The purpose is to identify and remove the 'high placebo responders'. The control, therefore, is far from randomized and is already slewed in favor of the drug being tested;
2. While a placebo is described as 'an inert substance', no such

substance actually exists. Even sugar, or the fillers used in a placebo pill, could have an effect on the person taking them; and, possibly most important of all…

3. As pointed out in the *Wall Street Journal* health blog by Dr. Beatrice Golomb, associate professor of medicine in the division of general internal medicine at UCSD School of Medicine, *placebos are not standardized*, and *their contents are seldom made public.*[30] Therefore, the concept of a truly randomized, double-blind control test exists more in general mythology than in scientific fact.

In all its forms, the placebo is here to stay. Research into the effect is widespread. Taken together, the studies suggest that the placebo response is a product of a complex interaction of various processes that fall into three main classifications: 'expectancy', 'meaning', and 'conditioning'.[31]

Briefly, this suggests that both practitioner and patient expect a positive outcome, and that the patient is able to understand and attribute meaning to his experience. Conditioning refers to the adoption and perfection of new, health-related behaviors and responses; to the linking of a specific stimulus to a new and healthful response—and, even to the therapeutic effect of receiving advice or medication from a trusted expert.

It would be difficult to study, or even identify, the placebo response, except within the context of relationships—those of the patient and his world-view; the patient and his understanding; and, crucially importantly, the patient and his practitioner.

All treatment outcomes are, in large part, a result of relationships, and relationships are made or broken by communication. We therefore respectfully offer this book for the consideration of all practitioners, regardless of school or specialty, who believe there should be 'something more' to healthcare than standardized interpretations and treatments. Conditioning, expectancy, and meaning are all processes that can be modeled, developed, and transmitted through the principles and techniques of Medical NLP.

Whatever we choose to call it, there is a whole vista of healing and health beyond drugs, surgical procedures or psychological counseling. As we will show, there is an increasing body of research that suggests that the success of many currently accepted procedures (up to 75% in one recent review of 19 depression therapy studies[32]) is unrelated to the physical treatment itself.

Whether we call it the placebo response, the human effect or the healing response, it is both 'real' and a valuable component of good medicine. Dr. W. Grant Thompson, a noted consultant on clinical trials and author of *The Placebo Effect and Health*, observes that, whatever the view, the placebo effect is a reality and modern medicine can benefit from understanding it. Wise doctors, he adds, know that it is a factor in every treatment and an essential part of their daily work.[33]

We do not claim to have definitive answers; we certainly have many questions still unanswered that continue to spark our curiosity. But, even at this stage, we can point to a substantial body of theory and research currently excluded from 'evidence-based' medical decision-making. It is also interesting to note how much of this now supports the observation and reasoning that prompted Richard Bandler and his colleagues to develop NLP more than 30 years ago.

We also present explicit principles and techniques that we and our Medical NLP-trained colleagues have found useful in our practices, together with anecdotes and case studies —some of them new for this edition of *Magic in Practice*—to illustrate their practical application. Certain details, of course, have been changed to maintain confidentiality.

We encourage you to develop curiosity and behavioral flexibility, to explore these principles for yourself, and to reclaim the status of the practitioner as co-creator of his patients' health by actively enhancing and administering what Michael Balint referred to as the most powerful of all drugs—the practitioner himself.[34]

Or, as a senior consultant remarked at the end of one of our trainings, 'If all this is the placebo effect, I want to be the best placebo I possibly can.'

1

Towards Healing and Health: a solution-oriented approach

*We cannot solve problems with the same level of thinking that created them.—**Albert Einstein***

Problem-solving is an energy-intensive approach that focuses on deficiencies in the hope of identifying and removing them. Solution-orientation explores and develops options, choices, and possibilities with a view to re-orientating the individual or group towards flexibility and growth.

Problem-solving is reactive, remedial, and piecemeal. Solution-orientation is active, generative, and holistic.

Problem-solving looks at people as a collection of 'parts'. Solution-orientation sees the person-as-whole.

Problem-solving is external to the patient's experience (both 'cause' and symptom are regarded as alien invaders, disrupting the integrity of the patient's body–mind system). Solution-orientation is internal to the patient (the person who exhibits the problem is unique, and is as important as the problem itself).

Many of the current problems in healthcare derive from a reductionist, mechanistic view of humans and human nature that is several centuries old. Still largely committed to both a reductionist cause-and-effect model and the enduring myth of Cartesian Dualism, the separation of humans into mutually exclusive domains of body and mind, mainstream medicine has little power over the rising tide of complex, chronic, and inexplicable dysfunctions that can result in lifetimes of debility and pain.

People are living longer, mainly because of science's massive advances in the areas of infection and acute medicine, but they are not necessarily enjoying a consistently better quality of life. The nature of the problems we now face is changing. Disease itself is changing. But we—health providers and patients—are not.

Today, a doctor may go through his entire career without ever encountering a case of smallpox, diphtheria, or epiglottitis, but he will almost certainly feel overwhelmed by the sheer weight of the conditions that now characterize the majority of the problems patients present.

In Britain, the Royal Society of General Practitioners has been reported as estimating that around 50% of the problems seen by general practitioners are social, 25% psychological, and approximately half of the remaining 25% are psychosomatic.[35] In practice, physicians report that most of the remaining 12.5% of 'organic' disorders seen involve at least some aspects of the psychosocial dysfunctions mentioned above.

The cause-and-effect model, when routinely applied to some complex, chronic conditions, is contributing to a massive epidemic of new problems. Over-dependence on the 'magic bullet' approach contributes to tunnel vision; iatrogenic illness; antibiotic-resistant organisms; and reduction in treatment options for the practitioner. The complex, multi-factorial nature of illness and the inherent biological diversity of human beings are in serious danger of being ignored in the pursuit of a 'perfect' science.[36,37,38] Meanwhile, misdiagnosed and under-treated anxiety disorders alone cost the United States' economy $54 billion a year, with much of the economic burden resulting from patients seeking—and receiving—treatment for the physical symptoms of the dysfunctions.[39]

In England, the total cost of mental health problems has been estimated by the Sainsbury Centre for Mental Health at £77.4 billion, including £12.5 billion in care, £23.1 billion in lost output, and £41.8 billion in 'hidden' costs.[40] Despite the best intentions of its practitioners, medical practice is morphing from the provision of 'healthcare' into costly, and often inadequate, attempts to manage or contain 'dis-ease', including distressing and incapacitating, but not necessarily medical, conditions.

WEIRD science and empty evidence

The rise of evidence-based medicine (EBM)—the standardization of treatments based on randomized controlled trials (RCTs)—as the only acceptable basis for healthcare is also giving rise to problems. Its application, to the exclusion of human qualities such as instinct, experience, and common sense, diminishes artistry and compassion, both qualities long accepted as significant adjuncts to the practitioner's application of best available scientific knowledge.

Some researchers, including Professor John P.A. Ioannidis, of the Department of Hygiene and Epidemiology at Greece's Ioannina School of Medicine, believe that most published research findings are false, for a variety of reasons, including the fact that the researchers may simply be measuring accurately the 'prevailing bias'. This is another way of saying heuristical (rule of thumb) thinking predisposes people—even scientists—to verify what we already believe.[41]

Behavioral science has provided the basis for many drug-based treatments now accepted as gold-standard in Western medicine. The only problem is, when they are applied to an undifferentiated patient population, they often don't work ... perhaps because we're all just too WEIRD.

University of British Columbia psychologists have coined the acronym to help explain why results from behavioral studies on people in Western nations don't usually represent the rest of the world.

According to the study, research subjects are drawn entirely from Western, Educated, Industrialized, Rich, and Democratic (WEIRD) societies (probably around 12% or less of the world's population). Researchers—often implicitly—assume that all human populations respond identically to these 'standard subjects', whereas the comparative behavioral sciences database suggests that not only is there considerable variability in experimental results across populations, but that WEIRD subjects are particularly unusual compared with the rest of the species—what the researchers call 'frequent outliers'.[42]

Given that the volunteers used in these studies are often young male undergraduates in good health, the proportion of 'representative' subjects drops even more. However, the generalization from the few to the many—from a handful of WEIRD young men in good health to the human race as a whole—is a fundamental aspect of RC testing.

Treatments not easily validated by traditional research procedures are largely ignored—despite the fact that much of our historical success in defeating disease has arisen from trial and error, based on bold hypotheses, rather than from RCTs. Many treatments still in use, and unlikely soon to be abandoned, derive from 'another kind' of evidence. These include antibiotics, insulin, tracheostomy (to relieve tracheal obstructions), the draining of abscesses, vaccination, and even the use of aspirin.

Some scientists—even those from within the ranks of EBM—are beginning to suggest that certain classes of evidence, other than that provided by RCTs, warrant acceptance. Professor Paul Glasziou, Director of the Center for Evidence-Based Medicine at the University of Oxford, together with three colleagues, has developed a simple and elegant algebraic formula for measuring what they call the 'signal (treatment effect) to noise (natural outcome) ratio'. A high signal-to-noise ratio, they say, reflects a strong treatment effect, even in the presence of confounding factors, such as the natural progression of a disease.[43]

We continue to argue that an outcome that satisfies an individual patient's needs (and does no harm) should be the prime objective of every consultation. 'Flow' (a relatively unselfconscious day-to-day existence) and 'functionality' (the patient's own measure of her ability to operate effectively in her own world) are key objectives Medical NLP espouses.

Many studies now emerging help give direction and substance to the Medical NLP proposition that whole-person health is both possible and applicable—with some adjustment to current opinion. Some of these suggest that:

- 'health' does not necessarily follow from the removal of the symptom;
- many 'dysfunctions' are, in fact, adaptive responses that have helped humans survive and flourish as a species;
- a purely medical response to some of these may actually damage the individual's overall ability to resist and progress towards healing and health;
- bodies, brains, and especially immune systems, need to be challenged in order to function effectively. Removing challenge may impair the ability to respond and survive;
- while one gene may predispose the carrier to a particular disease,

many of the factors that influence gene expression—whether some conditions develop or not—lie within the way people live their lives, the attitudes they hold, the meaning they attribute to their situation and the relationships upon which they can, or cannot, rely;

- physical symptoms can often not only 'communicate' emotional or social distress, but can also provide the astute practitioner with highly specific guidance on how she can assist the patient to restore balance to his life;
- the *relationship* between practitioner and patient is an important (sometimes the *most* important) factor that precipitates healing; and
- the practitioner's communication—verbal and non-verbal—can bypass conscious processing and directly and measurably affect the functioning of the patient's neurological system … for better or worse.

Most practitioners may well feel overwhelmed in the face of the implications raised by all this and, quite understandably, revert to the first-line response of attempted symptom removal. However, a simple shift of perspective, from a purely problem-solving to a solution-oriented approach, helps us to make sense of it all.

More than 30 years ago, when Dr. Richard Bandler posed the paradigm-shifting question, *If knowing how people get ill doesn't always help them recover, how do people get better?*, he opened the way for the development of the methodology now known as Neuro-Linguistic Programming (NLP). This also alerted some leaders in other fields—humanistic, systemic, and family psychology, sports, and business, in particular—to the possibility that energy previously spent trying to remedy apparently intractable problems could be more profitably directed at exploring outcomes and solutions.

Regrettably, the approach seems to be defaulting back to the molecular, cause-effect approach favored by Big Pharma and those of a surgical bent. However, the astute and patient researcher will find that a more generative (as opposed to remedial) approach has since been strongly supported by numerous studies. As an example, several research projects have confirmed that expectation alone—the anticipation, of both health professional and patient, that something good and positive will result from treatment—can have a powerful, positive effect on clinical outcomes.[44,45,46]

Solutions: more than the removal of a problem

When medicine's essentially problem-solving approach fails to remedy a complaint, or constellation of complaints, a subtle transfer of responsibility to the patient takes place. Labels, such as 'functional', 'psychogenic', 'somatoform', 'psychosomatic', and 'medically unexplained' may carry implications of some degree of mental or emotional imbalance. Now, the label (and the patient) becomes the problem.

A problem-oriented approach easily confuses the removal or suppression of the symptom with its cure—but, as anyone who has been treated with antidepressants will confirm, 'not being depressed' is seldom the same thing as 'being happy'. According to the problem-oriented model, illness, in all its forms, is the result of some deficit or other, whether it is the failure of the individual to pursue sensible dietary advice, an immune system that ignores a cancer cell, or a brain that ceases to balance its uptake of serotonin. Problem-oriented medicine looks for 'proximal' causes and largely ignores factors such as the evolutionary or adaptive nature of the illness; the unconscious 'meaning' or value the dysfunction might have to that specific individual, and the entire psychological, social, and spiritual landscape within which the patient and his problem exist.

An expanded view

A solution-oriented approach recognizes the need for an expanded view of both illness and health. Although many organizations and individual practitioners recognize the need for a more 'holistic' approach, few suggest how this might be achieved.

Some attempt to accomplish this by randomly incorporating or recommending 'complementary' techniques, such as homeopathy, acupuncture, and aromatherapy. But although any of these may well add value for the patient, their piecemeal incorporation does not equate with a whole-person view of the patient.

In some countries, traditional medicine is gaining ground. In India, for example, leading 'alternative' approaches, lumped under the label AYUSH (standing for Ayurveda, Yoga, Unani, Siddha, Sowa Rigpa, and Homeopathy), are state-sanctioned and allopathic practitioners are encouraged to incorporate them into their equally popular Western-style treatments.

The Medical NLP approach presented in this book does not favor any particular 'alternatives' to Western medicine, but aims to help widen the practitioner's perspective, to include, along with her biomedical profile, insight into:

- the uniqueness of each patient;
- the emotional and psychological aspects of her situation;
- the 'meaning' of her illness, both personally and adaptively;
- the social context within which her problem has arisen;
- the as-yet untapped resources she brings to the consultation.

With this in mind, the practitioner is better equipped to explore with the patient her needs, resources, and endogenous potential for change.

The need for options

All patients seeking help from a health professional for any chronic problem are stuck and stressed. The problem has not yet resolved itself (if it is self-limiting), or all previous attempted actions and remedies have failed.

The inbuilt capacity for self-regulation (shared by all living systems) has been compromised. This either causes, or is a factor in, almost every major illness to which people fall prey.[47,48] Flexibility, responsiveness, adaptability—these biological necessities must all be restored if health is to be improved and maintained.

Medical NLP regards the human being as a biological system embedded in a succession of larger systems (psychological, social, spiritual, and evolutionary). To help an individual create options at any of these levels is to increase the flexibility of her functioning as an integrated whole. Practitioners themselves also benefit from having more options—especially those which have the potential to help their patients in the moment, without unnecessary recourse to drugs or outsourcing the problem to costly, time-consuming 'talking' therapies.

Seeking opportunities

The possibility of something positive emerging from the challenge of illness and dysfunction is surprisingly appealing to many patients. It is easy to understand how compelling (and sometimes how useful) such a belief might be when they are faced with the fear and chaos that can accompany chronic, inexplicable dysfunction, and dis-ease.

Some writers and psychologists, including Joseph Campbell and Carl Jung, have suggested that the metaphor of the individual's journey through crisis, challenge, and renewal is embedded in our cultural DNA. Certainly, the structure known as 'The Hero's Journey' is encountered throughout all story-telling societies, including in fairytales, movies, soap operas, and computer games.

The structure of The Hero's Journey involves a call to action (the crisis) and the protagonist's response to the call (seeking options, opportunities and guidance in an effort to resolve the crisis). A series of challenges and setbacks lead to a decisive—though often risky and frightening—final act, in a bid to gain healing, redemption, or reward. The hero then returns to her own world, renewed, healed or somehow transformed, with a message of deliverance to her people. (For a moving and inspiring contemporary non-fiction account that reflects this process in the context of healing and health, see *Choosing to Heal: Surviving the Breast Cancer System*, by musician and Medical NLP practitioner Janet Edwards. See also later chapters on the patient's story.)

Whether you and your patients choose to regard the consultation process as part of a symbolic journey or a partnership based on developing more choices, it is an opportunity to bring order out of chaos. To accomplish this, both need to explore the possibilities (other than the moderation or removal of the symptom) that can emerge when a previously stable situation suddenly destabilizes, and we embark on the complex, intriguing, and challenging process of change.

The qualities of change

Change can be easy, instantaneous, and lasting. Curiously, as family therapist Virginia Satir often observed, it is also something that many people fear more than anything else.

Experience shows that this fear is almost always based on the belief that gain can only arise out of pain, and on not knowing how—or, even that—a specific change can take place.

The opposing belief, that change can be relatively effortless, runs counter to the received 'wisdom' that suggests it should be a slow and painful process—or, as the old joke has it:

> *Q: How many psychiatrists does it take to change a light bulb?*
> *A: Only one—but, it'll be a long, difficult, and expensive process—and the light bulb really has to* ***want*** *to change.*

Certainly, change does not need to be hard work. As they were exploring the structure of the patterns they were observing, Richard Bandler and his colleagues began to question the belief that change is always incremental and takes place over an extended period of time. Dr. Bandler's suspicion, derived from the speed with which people learned to fear the object of a phobia, was that the brain was capable of rapid, or even 'one-pass', learning. Success with the now famous NLP fast phobia cure (also known as visual-kinesthetic dissociation, see page 300) bore this out. Since then, hundreds of thousands of people have benefited from this insight alone, in its wide range of applications.

This contrasts with slower, not necessarily equally effective, processes, including systematic desensitization, which gradually exposes the subject to the source of the phobic response, and flooding, which seeks to overwhelm the sufferer in a bid to 'blow out' the neurological circuits holding the responses in place.

Critics of these approaches (including ourselves) believe the first is too slow and, at best, only partly successful. The second carries a high risk that the subject may be unable to process the flooding, and be re-traumatized by the 'cure'. Bandler's approach by-passes both objections. 'It's easier to cure a phobia in 10 minutes than in five years,' he says:

[At first] I didn't realize that the speed with which you do things makes them last … I taught people the phobia cure. They'd do part of it one week, part of it the next, and part of it the week after. Then, they'd come to me and say, 'It doesn't work!' If, however, you do it in five minutes, and repeat it until it happens very fast, the brain understands. That's part of how the brain learns … I discovered that the human mind does not learn slowly.

Although, on the face of it, this might seem like a version of desensitization, the Phobia Cure differs in three other important respects. Its success depends on the effective dissociation of the subject from the experience; disruption of the process the sufferer has been unconsciously using in order to repeat the phobic response; and the creation of a solution frame into which the subject can associate. We will deal with the first two 'differences that make a difference' in later chapters. The third—developing outcome frames—is critical to the Medical NLP solution-oriented approach.

The requirements of change

In order to make change possible, the subject needs to:

1. *want* to change;
2. understand that she *can* change;
3. know *how* to change; and
4. notice *that* change has taken, or is taking, place.

Medical NLP regards the 'resistant' patient as a mythological creature. Perceived resistance usually stems from either a failure of the practitioner to uncover as yet unmet needs, or too little time being spent on trying to effect the change. Sometimes, the fear of changing is overwhelming, and this in turn we believe is based on the patient not understanding that change is possible, and not perceiving that both he and the physician have resources that have yet to be tapped.

It is the practitioner's responsibility to reduce the patient's anxiety level, identify unmet needs, and orientate the patient towards accepting the possibility of change. These will be discussed in detail later, but it can often be as simple as a form of verbal martial art:

Patient: *'I don't feel any better, and I've tried everything...'*
Practitioner: *'Everything? So, when do you get time to sleep?'*
Patient: *'Well, I mean I've tried a lot of things, and nothing has worked.'*
Practitioner: *'...yet.'*
Patient: *'Well, I can't see how this is going to help.'*
Practitioner (smiling): *'...yet.'*
Patient (smiles): *'Okay...yet.'*

Strategies such as this require good engagement and rapport with the patient. As you progress through this book, you will encounter (and, we trust, test and incorporate into daily practice) a number of principles and techniques to help increase motivation, change unresourceful beliefs and behaviors, and act directly on a wide range of chronic and 'functional' disorders.

Meanwhile, an important theme of this book, and the basis of any truly solution-oriented approach to medicine, is this: *the patient needs to know **how** to get (and remain) well.* As Albert Einstein observed, people can't solve their problems with the same level of thinking that created them.

In working within the Medical NLP systemic model, the practitioner evaluates and may intervene at all levels of the patient's experience: physical, mental, psychological, social, and spiritual. Since these operate as a Gestalt (an interactive system), and each Gestalt is unique to the individual, improvement or healing needs to be a bespoke process that the patient understands, and one which does not cause unnecessary concern or discomfort as it proceeds.

While a solution-oriented approach to consultation does not preclude the medico-legal requirements of due diligence, appropriate investigation, and best practice, undue focus on the problems has been shown sometimes to increase, rather than reduce, patients' distress. Consider the following: when investigating pain, most physicians are taught to ask a series of direct clinical questions as part of the decision-tree process known as the differential diagnosis. Questions, where cardiac problems are suspected, may include:

'Is it a crushing pain?'
'Does it radiate into your left arm?'

'Does it get worse if you exert yourself?'

Practitioners generally admit this is a problem-oriented approach, but consider it a necessary evil. At the same time, many suspect that even the mere suggestion of pain may in fact worsen patients' reporting, or their subjective experience, of pain. This turns out to be true, in certain cases at least.[50] Much more about this in later chapters.

In contrast, effective questioning can contribute substantially to the success of treatment. For example, the more general question, 'What's it like?' may elicit specific details about the problem without exposing the patient to excessive and potentially harmful synonyms for suffering. In many cases, the patient will provide specific information about location, onset, severity, aggravating factors, etc—most, if not all, the information needed—without any prompting or further suggestion.

If necessary, further gentle probing can fill in the details necessary for a full and appropriate diagnosis. And, when the time comes to re-orientate the patient towards improvement, the question, 'What will you be doing, and how will you feel, when this problem you've been having has been resolved?' is just one of the tools of the solution-oriented practitioner. The way the human brain is wired requires the patient to direct his attention away from her present, problematic state, towards a future-oriented solution-state, *in order for her to be able to provide an answer.*

Quite literally, the practitioner has begun to alter the firing of the neurons in the patient's brain. Purely conversationally, he is performing 'microsurgery', with language as his tools. (For more detailed suggestions for solution-oriented information-gathering, refer to the *Medical NLP Clinical Questioning Matrix* page 127.)

Knowing where to go

Solution-orientation is almost non-existent among existing consultation models. We have reviewed more than 15 frameworks, from the Calgary-Cambridge Comprehensive Clinical Method[51] to Usherwood's extensive model,[52] and have found only two that suggest, in part, that the patient's role may fruitfully extend beyond the end-point of merely understanding and following treatment advice.

The model advanced in this book supplements existing models with a number of elements, all of which have been demonstrated positively to influence the outcome of the healing relationship. These include: a proactive and equal partnership between doctor and patient;[53,54] recognition of and matching to the patient's unique world-view; the development of an increased sense of self-efficacy through manageable strategies;[55] a clear blueprint for further action; a shared expectation that progress is to some degree or other possible; and an agreed system whereby progress can be measured.

Furthermore, focusing on solutions rather than problems (developing health and healthy behaviors in place of removing 'sicknesses') helps the patient (and, in many cases, the physician) 'unstick' from a stuck situation, and begin to reduce frustration and stress. This, in turn, opens up room for hope and belief to enter the arena—both of these are now known to influence positively a number of health-supporting processes, including the functioning of the immune system, cellular activity, and even the expression of DNA.[56]

Our proposition here is simply this: if, as Western health professionals believe, 'psychosomatic illness' is a reality, they should be obliged also to accept and commit themselves to pursuing 'psychosomatic healing and health'.

EXERCISE

Begin to reframe problems in terms of possible solutions. By asking the right questions, you can orientate yourself, your patients, family, and friends towards choices and options, as well as help to create a future beyond the problem-state. Some suggestions for solution-oriented questions include:
'What will you be doing, [how will you be thinking, feeling, speaking, etc] when you have moved past this point?';
'What will be different or better when you are healthy again [have achieved your goal, etc]?';
'What have you not been able to do that you will really enjoy doing when this problem has been solved?'; and,
'What will you have learned from this experience?'
Notice any differences in your own, or your subject's, response. Keep notes of any particularly effective patterns you create.

2

Stress and Allostatic Load: the hidden factor in all disease

*My limbs tremble, my mouth is dry, my body shakes and my hair stands on end.—**Arjuna in The Bhagavad Gita***

A story we heard some time ago featured a gifted young medical student strolling along the banks of a river with his professor when they heard the cries of a drowning man. Being young and fit, the student leapt in and dragged the man to safety. A few meters further along, to their surprise, they spotted another man, swept up in the current and screaming for help. Again the student plunged in to the rescue. Only minutes later, the same thing happened.

The now drenched and exhausted student dragged the victim to safety, and gasped, 'I don't know how many times I can keep doing this'. The professor pondered for a moment and then said gently, 'Perhaps you should run ahead and stop whoever's pushing them in …'

With between a third and a half of all patients who seek medical attention suffering from symptoms that have no identifiable pathology or cause,[57,58,59] the time has come to move upstream and take another look at the factor or factors that all of them have in common.

'Stress' has been labeled a 'global epidemic' by the World Health Organization on the basis of studies showing that it can disrupt the functioning of almost every organ and system in the body, and is implicated to some degree in all cognitive and emotional dysfunctions.

And yet, despite evidence for the role of stress in human illness, no effective, comprehensive model or guidelines exist to give practitioners the tools and understanding to curb its effects.

The reductionist approach to illness has led inevitably to organizing presenting symptoms into sometimes arbitrary syndromes, which creates an illusion of discrete conditions, each of which has (or should have) a specific cause. Treatment here tends to be proximate, aiming to provide symptomatic relief, usually by pharmacological means.

In this chapter, we propose revisiting the deeply complicated and controversial subject of stress with a view to redefining its purpose and function. We are not suggesting that all illnesses can be 'cured' simply by 'managing' stress, but we, and many of our colleagues, can report considerable success in helping patients gain control over, or recover from, many chronic disorders using the working model we outline below and the approaches discussed elsewhere in this book (see pages 217 to 230).

In many ways, the history of the problems we face in diagnosing and treating stress parallels the history of the word itself. Linguistic Relativity (also known as the Sapir-Whorf Hypothesis—it suggests that the structure of our language affects the way we think), General Semantics (not to be confused with the field of semantics), and Neuro-Linguistic Programming all suggest that 'stress', like most other diagnostic terms, seeks to describe a process as if it were a concrete object or thing—as in 'I caught a cold', or 'My memory is bad', as if colds and memories have a physical reality separate from the process of 'cold-ing' or 'remembering'. (The shortage of verb-forms in English means that we sometimes have to invent them in order to restore process to the patient's experience.)

Most European languages share this tendency to 'reify', that is, to favor nouns over verbs. In NLP, this process is known as nominalization—reducing an experience, construct, concept or process to an object—and it can have a limiting effect on how we perceive and approach many emotional and physical problems. In medicine, this can lead to favoring biomedical explanations for ill-health over the processes they involve, ignoring social and psychological factors. This, in turn, can result in unnecessary pharmacological and surgical treatments.[60]

Psychologist Walter Cannon suggested nearly 100 years ago that stress could overwhelm the body's capacity for self-regulation, resulting in a breakdown of the body's integrity. The idea was largely ignored for several decades, until Hans Selye, then a young medical student, noticed that all the patients he observed being treated for infectious diseases shared certain symptoms apparently unrelated to the conditions being treated.

His observations were dismissed by the senior physicians he took them to as irrelevant to the diseases they had diagnosed and were treating. Only in the 1930s could Selye, now a qualified endocrinologist at McGill University, pursue his research into what he had begun to suspect was a 'generalized response' to the stress of systemic overload—a theory supported by further research which demonstrated that the same set of symptoms could be induced by virtually any stressors he applied to his subjects.

Despite continuing hostility from the medical profession, now firmly wedded to the belief that every symptom or disease should have a specific cause, Selye published his theory of a General Adaptation Syndrome in 1936.[61]

Since then, stress and its effects have driven hundreds of studies that unequivocally link it to most chronic disorders. But medical science's failure to develop an effective broad-spectrum approach has caused it to be co-opted by the 'complementary' therapies, where 'stress management' has become a multi-billion-dollar industry.

Why do we experience stress?

In evolutionary terms, it's easy to see that the fight-or-flight response is, as its name suggests, adaptive. Arjuna, in the historical description of the stress response quoted at the start of this chapter, was facing the prospect of violent death. Today, whether you're stepping into your morning shower, driving to work in the morning rush hour or facing a tiger that's escaped from the zoo, your brain is working at near light-speed to monitor for potential threats, mobilize your resources, and prompt you to action.

Responding to millions of years of natural selection, your brain 'remembers' the dangers of confronting a predator without full preparation. The protective regions of your brain are ancient and quick-tempered. They mistrust the slower calculating speed of the more 'reasonable' frontal cortex. The quarter-second or so that it takes to assess a situation rationally may mean the difference between life and death, so if the alarm is strident enough, it hijacks activity away from rational thought and trusts entirely to a primeval, entirely automated, response.

Simply put, when this happens, the hypothalamus fires the alarm to the adrenal glands, triggering thousands of simultaneous responses. Your adrenals flood your system with epinephrine (adrenaline), pushing your heart rate up, sending blood to your muscles and vital organs, and flooding your lungs and brain with oxygen. Glucose is released and fatty acids mobilized as a quick source of energy. Fibrinogen is released as the vessels near the surface of your skin contract, both actions intended to reduce bleeding and increase the clotting ability of your blood in the event of injury.

Endorphins—your body's natural opiates—lock into their receptors, blocking the sensations of pain. Nature doesn't want you to get hurt, but it also doesn't intend you to quit if the enemy draws first blood.

This is the classic fight-or-flight response. You are poised to move, either towards or away from a predator. You are hyper-alert, hyper-responsive. Time may seem to slow down as your synapses go into overdrive. Your vision alters, ready to detect any movement that may signal danger. The response is almost instantaneous and its purpose is to *prompt you into physical action* in order to keep you alive. Note that the majority of symptoms experienced by patients suffering from many 'functional' disorders are easily explained as natural, evolutionary responses to perceived threat. We find that patients are often deeply reassured when their beating hearts, tingling fingers and churning stomachs are explained in this way.

When the challenge has passed, your body-mind enters its second phase. Your body has suffered enormous chemical challenge, and it begins to generate other chemicals to neutralize the effect and to start repairs. One of the chief players here is cortisol. This steroid hormone, derived from cholesterol, has multiple functions: among other things, it exerts an anti-inflammatory action, helps the body restore your depleted energy sources, prompts the delivery of white blood cells to any site of injury, and, crucially, combines with other functions to fix the ordeal into your long-term memory for future reference.

This effect, reproducible under laboratory conditions, is known as stress-enhanced memory[62] and key centers in your brain will seek to match the pattern of the threat you've survived to those situations you encounter (or even imagine you'll encounter) in the future.

This is why we tend to remember exactly where we were and what we were doing when we encountered massive shock, such as the September 11th bombing of the Twin Towers in New York. This is also how phobias and post-traumatic stress disorders are seeded by traumatic events. All this is well and good; we would not have survived as a species had the system not been looking after us so efficiently. Like our prehistoric and animal ancestors, we are pretty well equipped to deal with acute stress.

The problem today

The problem today is twofold. First, the fight-or-flight response is still alive and well and responding to perceived threats. However, it cannot easily distinguish between the stresses of the modern world and real life-and-death confrontations of the kind played out on the savannahs of our past between predator and prey.

Second, the stress response is biphasic—that is, the system meets short-term stress by increasing certain responses, including immunological functions. Sustained stress, unresolved trauma, and failure to adapt can, however, all seriously impair cognitive functions, down-regulate immune responses and, eventually, create cellular and metabolic damage. In short, the very processes designed to save our lives in the short term become corrosive and damaging to both body and mind.[63]

It gets worse. Recent research suggests that even thinking about being stressed can double the chances of a heart attack.[64]

Furthermore, according to Dr. Hermann Nabi, head of the United Kingdom's Whitehall II study, which has followed several thousand London-based civil servants since 1985, risk of a heart attack is independent of biological factors, unhealthy behaviors, and other psychological factors.

In other words, just worrying about stress is as toxic as stress itself.

But, of course, not everyone is equally vulnerable, and what follows are some suggestions as to why this might be so.

Some definitions

To avoid confusion, we have adopted certain terms that we will use from here on. The words 'stress' and 'stressors' will refer to challenging events and experiences originating from outside the patient's body. These may include infections; the loss of a job or a loved one; or a daily drive to work on an overcrowded freeway.

Aside from the 'fight-or-flight response', the interplay of physiological and psychological responses that comprise the patient's autonomic reaction to challenge or perceived danger will be referred to in several different ways, including 'sympathetic arousal' or 'limbic arousal'.

The self-regulating mechanism that seeks to restore order after systemic shock or challenge is often referred to as 'homeostasis', a word that suggests the body has a set internal state to which it must return to maintain balance and health. Instead of this, we have borrowed the more recently coined word 'allostasis', defined as a process of achieving stability through psychological, physical, or behavioral flexibility.[65]

A growing body of research suggests that health is a product of dynamic equilibrium—ability to respond to challenge—rather than an absence of instability. The metaphor we sometimes use to explain allostasis to patients is that of riding a bicycle or learning to walk, both of which involve a constant interplay of losing and recovering balance. Without surrendering to the constant loss, and immediate recovery, of balance, we cannot move forward.

This corresponds with Richard Bandler's assertion that effectively applied NLP should *increase* the choices available to the subject, rather than simply remove the problem-response.

Finally, 'allostatic load' and 'systemic overload' refer to the point at which the patient is unable to process stress and maintain allostasis, and physical and/or psychological dysfunction occurs. Allostatic load may result not only from external stressors, but also from lifestyle, personal experience, meaning, unmet emotional needs, understanding, and attitude.

A more viable approach

From the above, it becomes apparent that increasing the individual's ability to achieve and maintain allostasis is a more viable approach to managing 'functional' disorders. We caution against medicating symptoms of allostatic load in all but the most serious situations.

Incautiously removing either the stressors or the symptoms of stress may actually reduce the ability fully to engage with and enjoy life, and disable the processes on which our physical and emotional survival depends. To put it another way, *we need stress.* And, under the right conditions, we even enjoy it.

The question persists, what makes the difference between the person who succumbs to stress and the one who not only survives, but may even thrive? Part of the answer may be genetic, although no conclusive evidence has yet appeared to support this premise. The rest may, in fact, lie deep in our evolutionary past. Research from two very different fields—ethology, the scientific study of animal behavior, and thermodynamics—opens a promising new direction, one we have found extremely useful in practical applications with patients suffering from a wide range of 'functional' disorders.

Connections with our animal past

Animal studies show that encounters with predators in the wild trigger much the same physiological response as humans experience when faced with an acute stress: a surge in stress chemicals accompanied by a rush of endorphins, presumably to deaden the pain of being torn apart. This is followed by immobility—the freeze alternative to fight or flight.

However, should the attack be aborted and the prey escape, something interesting occurs. Delivered from an untimely death, the animal stays frozen for a while, and then appears to be seized by a series of tremors. Sometimes these mimic the act of running away; at other times they seem more like uncontrollable muscle spasms. But they are always the consequence of a narrow escape.

After a few moments, the animal will right itself and make its escape. As far as we know, it does not develop ulcers or end up on a psychiatrist's couch. Ethologists now agree that the animal maintains allostasis by *dissipating*, or discharging, its stress.[66]

The significance of dissipation as a factor in allostasis also derives from the work of Russian-born, Nobel Prize-winner Ilya Prigogine, who argued that the Second Law of Thermodynamics—that increasing disorder and entropy are the inevitable result of expending energy—did not always hold true. Instead of collapsing into disorder, many systems move towards *increasing* order. Prigogine pointed out that science had thus far been focusing on closed systems, all of which tend towards an equilibrium state of maximum entropy. Open systems (those which take in energy in whatever form from outside themselves), however, maintain equilibrium when they are able effectively to dissipate entropy.

Allostasis, then, may be seen as being maintained, not in spite of entropy, but because of it. Failure to dissipate will inevitably result in increasing chaos and dysfunction. This led Prigogine to another extraordinary discovery: that energetic challenge (let's call this 'stress' for the moment) drives the system effectively enough until it reaches a point of maximum tolerance (called the bifurcation point), where the system either collapses in disorder or dissipates enough entropy to 'escape' (literally, a non-linear, quantum leap) to a higher level of organization (see **Figure 2.1**).

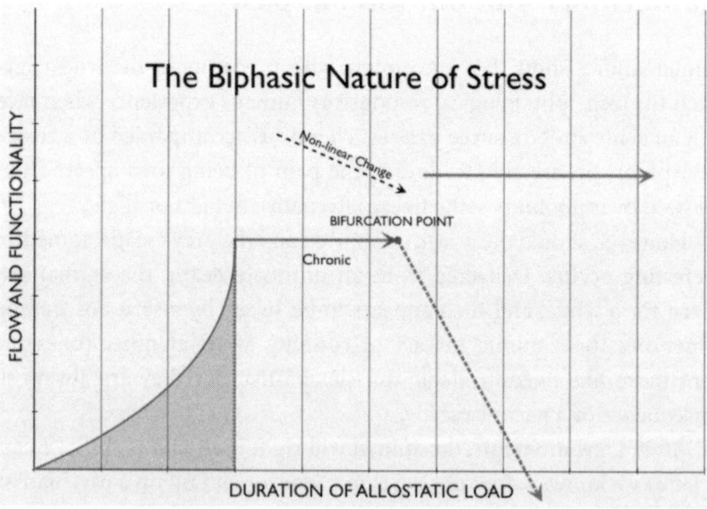

Figure 2.1 The biphasic nature of stress, bifurcation and escape to new order. Flow and functionality, including the immune response, initially improve in response to immediate challenge, but, when chronic stress approaches the bifurcation point, the subject either descends into increasing chaos, or 'escapes' to a new and higher level of neurological organization. Escape depends on effective dissipation of the excessive input of energy.

Further research has found that this model applies, not just to chemical systems, Prigogine's original focus, but also to traffic flow, companies, plants, animals, and human beings. In the case of human beings, our ideas, inventions, philosophy, even our brains, become more complex with use. Immune function is just one example of this process in action; the body is challenged by a pathogen and responds by reassembling its resources in order to meet a similar challenge in the future. The system does not become 'a little bit resistant', or 'gradually more resistant', but can escape to a level of more complex organization at which it operates until encountering the next challenge.

The important point to remember is that, as 'open, adaptive, dissipative structures', people function well in unstable environments and in the face of challenge, as long as (1) they retain the flexibility to respond, and (2) they have the capacity to dissipate entropy when it approaches the bifurcation point.

In other words, we have evolved to self-regulate and develop as a result of stress—*given the right circumstances*. Indeed, powerful new evidence of health as a constantly emerging property of challenge is appearing in a number of studies.

Routine obstruction of this evolutionary response—say, by overmedication of all symptoms of allostatic load—may, in the long run, act against our natural capacity to adapt and evolve.[67]

On the other hand, escape to a higher order of functioning corresponds with what we call 'flow and functionality'.

Both flow and functionality are characteristics of the individual in allostasis. It is not an 'absence of disease' or a 'sense of positivity and wellbeing' (both recent contributions to the definition of health). Rather, it is the capacity to function effortlessly and effectively, without much conscious thought, in everyday life. Flow is a present-tense state in which the individual is capable, both physically and cognitively, to respond to changing events, both internal and external to the individual.

Flow has inbuilt a paradoxical element: the fact that it occurs only when the potential for chaos and collapse is accepted and incorporated as a dynamic component of the experience of life.

Many approaches to 'healing' seek to ignore, avoid, or eliminate the possibility of a descent into chaos and disorder. But, as Ilya Prigogine suggested, excessive order can be as potentially dangerous to the individual as complete chaos. For humans, as dynamic, non-linear, complex systems, health, healing, and life itself—'functionality'—rely on the ability to operate, to flow, within a zone of responsive flexibility that lies between extreme order and utter chaos (see **Figure 2.2**).

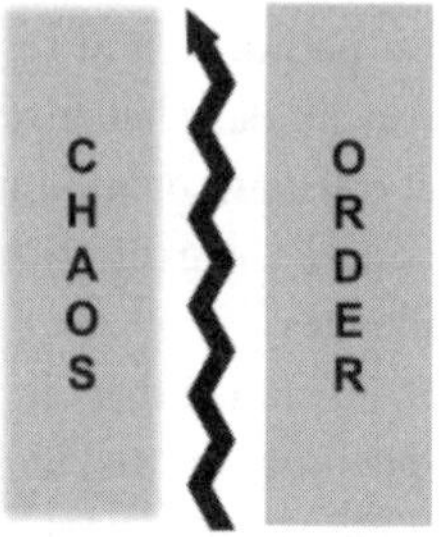

Figure 2.2 Flow is the ongoing ability to navigate between the extremes of order and chaos. Functionality in the individual is a dynamic process of constant responsiveness to change, both internal and external.

An analogy that appeals to the authors is the flow of traffic in certain parts of India. Roads, even in some towns and cities, are badly maintained by Western standards; traffic lights are non-existent in many areas; road rules exist in printed manuals but not on the highways and byways; the honk and roar and blare of motorists, cyclists, bikers, and *tuk-tuk* drivers are ceaseless. Among all this, stray dogs and sacred cattle weave their way unconcernedly through the mêlée. To the foreign eye and ear, this is pure, unadulterated anarchy.

And yet, even the most casual observation reveals a curious anomaly. Contrary to what Westerners—familiar with their own regimented modes of transport—might expect, accidents appear relatively rare. Native Indians are apparently highly skilled at reading the minimal cues and auditory signals of fellow road users.

Heart-stopping as it may sometimes be, experiencing the rush-hour flow of traffic on an Indian road is to be part of an extraordinarily complex improvisational dance in which every participant somehow seems to know when it's his time to move forward or fall back. To the newcomer, this may seem almost mystical in its complexity and creativity. (On the other hand, the national tendency of local residents to stone the vehicle perceived to be responsible for the accident and beat the hapless driver until such time as he escapes or is rescued by the police may provide a somewhat less arcane explanation of the Indian driver's extraordinary propensity for driving with extreme flamboyance, but also with a strong sense of survival.)

Prigogine would recognize this as a dynamic, non-linear, complex system in action. Mihály Csíkszentmihályi would certainly regard this as pure 'flow'.[68] In the opinion of the authors, all living systems have developed with this ability to navigate through the hoots and howls and racketing of everyday life, to detect, consciously and unconsciously, the signs of incipient breakdown and to take appropriate action. Ignorance, stress, inertia and, it must be said, even the iatrogenic effects of many currently accepted drug and surgical treatments, all conspire to disrupt the natural flow of effective physical and emotional function.

Figure 2.1 illustrates the biphasic nature of stress, together with bifurcation and escape to a new order. Most patients seeking help from a medical professional do so near or after the bifurcation point. Symptoms are indications that the system is struggling to dissipate entropy and move to a new, more flexible, or resistant order.

Whatever the specific cause or causes may be, this response, a loss of neurophysiological coherence, is readily observed by monitoring the subject's heart rate variability (HRV). Simply put, HRV, commonly used as a diagnostic tool in cardiology and obstetrics, provides a reliable measure of the functioning of the autonomic nervous system, which in turn reflects the overall psychophysical status of the subject.

HRV, one of the technologies we have adopted in Medical NLP and which we discuss in greater length later in this edition, may be seen as a real-time measurement of allostasis, the loss of which can be damaging or even fatal.[69]

The myth of 'somatization'

During any consultation, the patient and practitioner seek to bridge a gulf of subjective meaning. The events the patient notices and tries to describe are 'symptoms'; the doctor, meanwhile, is also looking for 'signs'—usually described as 'objective indications' of disease or disorder. In some cases, the disease is readily identifiable (say, jaundice) because the signs are evident.

However, where the practitioner favors signs to the exclusion of symptoms, problems can arise. In the absence of readily observable signs, due diligence and medico-legal concerns usually mean that the patient will be referred on to one or more specialists for further consultations and tests. Where no pathology is identified, the patient is at risk of being stigmatized as 'somatizing', suffering from 'psychosomatic', 'somatoform' or 'conversion' disorder, 'functional illness', or 'hypochondriasis'.

None of these nominalized terms is particularly helpful, because none of them provides insight into the problem. Moreover, they tend to exclude the patient's experience, the context within which his problem arises. Patients are quick to detect the underlying suggestion that what is ailing them is 'all in the mind'. If they do not medicate the patient, many doctors are quick to outsource the problem to psychologists, psychiatrists, or counselors (where available), reinforcing the picture of troublesome neurotics wasting the medical profession's valuable time.

Medical NLP regards 'somatization', with its overtones of neuroticism, as a fiction. Not only do imbalances within the body–mind system express themselves somatically, both as some kind of physical felt sense and in changes in cellular function or structure, but we cannot have any experience without some physical movement or manifestation.

As 'open adaptive systems', we humans are constantly processing billions of bits of data, both exteroceptive (from outside the body) and enteroceptive (from within), most of which are filtered out of our conscious awareness by mechanisms we will discuss in a later chapter. When these processes pass a certain threshold, they come into the subject's awareness as somatic events, which are then subjected to descriptions, inferences, and evaluations, by both the 'experts' reviewing the condition and the patient suffering from its effects.

However, we should not confuse the descriptions and inferences we use as convenient forms of classification with the event itself. The diagnosis is not the disease. The symptom is not the problem. The problem is the problem, and the symptom is the signal that the problem has not yet been recognized and resolved.

Closing unclosed 'loops'

In everyday experience, we are painfully aware of the stressful effects of 'unfinished business'. Uncompleted tasks remain in our conscious awareness, or just below, adding to the daily pressure of getting other jobs done.

This process was identified and studied by Russian psychologist Bluma Zeigarnik, who noticed that waiters tended to remember pending orders in exquisite detail, but immediately forgot them once those orders had been filled. Now known as the Zeigarnik Effect, its function, it is believed, is to create 'psychic tension' to drive us to complete an action.[70]

In Gestalt terms, we are hardwired to seek 'closure'. Many otherwise mysterious 'functional' disorders are now also thought to result from 'unfinished business'—that is, emotional or physical assaults on the system that were not effectively resolved at the time. Somatic memory—the 'psychic tension' held in the body's sensory, autonomic and somatic systems—seeks resolution, sometimes many years later.[71]

One possible manifestation of this, observed in fields as disparate as cardiology and ophthalmology, is known as the Anniversary Effect. Close inspection of patient records often reveals that some people return for consultations on or around the date of what turns out to be the anniversary of a particularly traumatic experience.[72]

Rather than investigate or revivify past traumas, it is our experience in a number of cases that some of the approaches we write about later create a context within which patients can safely and painlessly reintegrate and complete the experience, thus freeing themselves from the prison created, or perceived as created, by their history.

To restore allostasis and increase our capacity for healing and health, open loops need to be closed, whether by working through a backlog of unmade telephone calls, or by symbolically reclaiming the power that was stripped from us by overwhelming events from the past. We cannot, of course, change what happened in the past, but we can change the way we have been consciously or unconsciously responding to it.

EXERCISES

Carry out a three-day stress inventory on yourself and your patients as follows:

1. Five times each day (a) make a note of where you feel your stress levels are along a scale from 1-10 (1 being relaxed, 10 being massively over-stressed), and (b) identify and write down alongside each score what was happening in your immediate environment at the time.
2. Make a list of all the unfinished business (the open loops) in your life. These include tasks yet incomplete; projects unfinished; correspondence ignored; calls unmade, etc.
3. Notice how many of the stressors identified above are, in fact, responsible for creating and maintaining feelings of pressure. Now,
4. i. Go through your list, putting each item in order of importance.
   ii. After prioritizing your list, eliminate any items which are no longer important (you are almost certain to find a few).
   iii. Commit to taking from one to three items a day and close them off by completing the task. Continue until all your loops are closed.

Encourage your patients to complete this exercise as part of their healing journey.

3

Avoiding Compassion Fatigue: the dark side of empathy

*The minds of men are mirrors to one another, not only because they reflect each other's emotions, but also because those rays of passions, sentiments and opinions may be often reverberated…—**David Hume***

Stress and its impact on health and wellbeing do not begin and end with the patient. If patients can be at extreme risk from stress, health professionals of all specialties can be doubly so.

Physical and emotional wellbeing are dependent not just on the practitioner's capacity to achieve and maintain allostasis in his own life, but also on how resistant he may be to the daily, invisible risk of 'infection' by his patients' distress.

Patients expect the practitioners they consult to care about their problems. Doctors and other health professionals are encouraged—at least in their training—to display 'empathy' towards their patients. By understanding and sharing another person's feelings and ideas, it is widely believed we deepen our ability to help.

This is undoubtedly true. Empathy is a valuable tool for any health professional, and one deeply valued by patients. But unless it is understood and managed, it comes at a price.

We can be reasonably confident that empathy is necessary for the survival of our species. The ability to share feelings and experiences vicariously allows us to work together for the greater good of the group.

Conversely, the apparent inability of some people to care about the impact of their negative actions on others usually fills us with profound revulsion, as if some deep and sacred law has been violated.

Many training programs suggest that empathy is a learned skill. In fact, as many researchers are now beginning to suspect, people cannot *not* be empathetic, supposing they are free of any 'psychopathic' disorders that, for reasons not yet understood, prevent some individuals from even comprehending, much less experiencing, any of the emotions normally elicited by witnessing someone else's pain. Everyone has experienced wincing in sympathy when they see someone else stumble or trip. Even though they might laugh at the comedian who slips on a banana skin, they do so as a release of tension caused by seeing someone 'like us' suffer ignominy or pain. It is a natural, automatic response.

Medical students are given conflicting messages during training: be empathetic, but remain dispassionate when dealing with patients' pain and discomfort. Under pressure, many physicians take the second route, and understandably so. A doctor who has problems with blood or open wounds is of no use to the patient. But, it is important for health professionals to know that, while they might learn to conceal their feelings (even from themselves), millions of years of evolution have ensured that the response is wired into their neurology.

For example, when you see someone else's hand being pricked by a needle, the motor neurons in the same area on your own equivalent hand freeze as if you have received the needle-prick yourself. Using transcranial magnetic stimulation (TMS) for their studies, researchers have been able to establish that the 'social dimension' of pain extends to basic, sensorimotor levels of neural processing.[73] 'Somatic empathy'—the body's automatic response to the neurological state of another person[74]— is there, whether it is noticed or not.

The empathic 'mirror'

The discovery in the 1990s of a group of cells called 'mirror neurons' offers some explanation for how we translate exteroceptive information into internal, 'psychosomatic' experience. This brain-to-brain communication system synchronizes neural firing patterns so that the observer 'feels' someone else's experience as if it is happening to her. Mirror neurons probably also allow people to learn by observing, and neuroscientist V.S. Ramachandran has suggested they may have been the driving force of the 'great leap forward' in human cultural evolution 50,000 years ago.[75]

With the advent of language, the problem becomes more complicated. When the subject uses limited descriptions of his experience—often nominalized words such as 'depression', 'anxiety', 'relationship', 'anger'—the listener is required to plumb the depths of his own experience to attach meaning.

Known as a 'transderivational search' (TDS), this has its dangers. Unless the listener fills in the deleted part of the patient's communication, he is repeatedly re-entering and re-experiencing his own past experiences, and paying the price for reactivating the cascade of neurochemicals associated with pain and distress. He may 'understand' what the patient is going through, and he may 'feel for' her. He may think of himself, and be thought of, as a 'good person'. However, he not only reduces his ability to fully help the patient extricate herself from her problem, but also suffers the corrosive effects of the patient's distress.

Psychologist Daniel Stern warns of the risks of being 'captured'[76] by another person's nervous system; the result of this is what Elaine Hatfield and her colleagues at the University of Hawaii call 'emotional contagion'.[77]

Hatfield's theory—in line with NLP's earlier observation that physiology informs feeling, and vice versa—suggests that the listener's unconscious mimicry of the speaker's posture, facial expressions, tonality, breathing, etc, may 'infect' her with the speaker's emotions.

The Botox effect

Conversely, if the speaker's facial expressions are inhibited, say, by the use of Botox, his ability to read the emotions of other people is impaired. 'Embodied emotion perception' depends both on interpreting the non-verbal signals of others, and on being able to display emotions ourselves.[78] Like many of our animal cousins, humans are in a constant, dynamic, feedback-looped relationship with each other.

Hatfield suggests that emotional contagion is an unavoidable consequence of human interaction. Although we fully agree with the first part of Hatfield's conclusions, we question the inevitably of 'contagion'. Taking on the subject's experience 'as if' it is the practitioner's own is an example of association, well known in NLP. Put another way, she leaves her own subjective experience (dissociates) and 'steps into' the patient's (associates).

Even though this is an imaginal act, neuroscience can now demonstrate that there is little functional difference between a physical and an imagined action. You can even weaken or strengthen your muscles by simple mental rehearsal.[79] Your ability deliberately to associate into and dissociate from a patient's experience is the key to achieving engagement and emotional resonance, without suffering negative effects.

This capacity, as we will later demonstrate, can also be harnessed to therapeutic effect. Medical NLP recognizes three 'points of view' that allow us effectively to manage our relationships with others (**Figure 3.1**). However, failure to control these positions and the time we spend in them can lead to a number of undesirable consequences. (Please note that we may often observe mismanagement of these positions among patients. For example, someone who takes responsibility for spousal abuse because 'I make him mad' may be stuck in Position 2.)

Perspective	*Description*	*Positive effect*	*Negative effect*
1. Self	Associated into one's own body, engaged in subjective processing of data, feelings, behaviours	Allows us to apply learning and experience that the other may lack	To the exclusion of 2 or 3: single-mindedness, refusal to consider information that does not match own schema, 'selfishness', etc.
2. Other	Dissociated from self, associated into the other, sensing or imagining his feelings, responses, etc.	Open to other possibilities, increased understanding and empathy, increased social and emotional connectedness	To the exclusion of 1 and 3: Overinvolvement in the other's problems, loss of ego boundaries, physical and emotional overidentification, 'co-dependence', emotional contagion, burnout
3. Observer	Objective, 'as if' from physically and emotionally detached viewpoint	Yields information about the relationship between 1 and 2, open-mindedness, avoids bias and premature cognitive closure, reduces overemotionalism	To the exclusion of 1 and 2: Detached, uninvolved, uncaring, 'cold', machine-like

Figure 3.1 Perceptual positions

As we acquire flexibility in managing these aspects of our relationships with patients, we also learn how to avoid the defense mechanisms adopted by some health professionals to cope with daily exposure to illness, pain, and fear—withdrawal, dissociation, and alienation from the 'human connection' on which effective consultation should be based (permanently in Position 3).

When entropy prevails

Various authors have proposed different names for the negative risks practitioners face, including 'burnout', 'compassion fatigue', 'vicarious traumatization', and 'secondary traumatization'. We do not propose to discuss the differences between each of these models; it is enough to recognize that the signs and symptoms of allostatic load among practitioners are similar to those of patients.

These signs and symptoms are both communications of, and attempts to resolve, imbalance. How these are experienced and expressed may depend on the particular strategy or strategies the subject unconsciously adopts. Strategies are chains of internal actions (visualization, self-talk, feelings) that, when activated, in sequence, always result in the same behaviors and experiences. We discuss the subject in greater detail in later chapters, as well as in **Appendix D** (pages 367 to 369).

Figure 3.2 (below) demonstrates the effects of three behavioral responses to mounting allostatic load: Displacement, Obstruction, and Distraction.

We assume these coping strategies are learned during childhood, when they might have served a purpose. As we mature, however, they tend to become less socially acceptable and more detrimental to health and wellbeing.

Whether some effects, such as anxiety and aggression, result from sympathetic arousal, and others, including withdrawal and depression, from parasympathetic arousal, is still a subject of some contention among researchers. However, it is safe to assume that some or all these responses occur when the balance of the autonomic nervous system is disturbed. Rather than facilitating the flow of energy, these strategies all have the potential for spiraling down into more serious dysfunctions and disease.

Response	*Effect*
Displacement: Attempts to dissipate energy	Aggression, excitability, anxiety, crying, talking, physical activity, compulsive behaviour, etc.
Obstruction: Attempts to prevent energy entering the system	Withdrawal, depression, loss of energy and appetite, etc.
Distraction: Attempts to divert from feelings of disease	Dissociation, excessive use of food, alcohol, sex. Smoking and substance abuse, absorption in passive entertainment, such as television, etc.

Figure 3.2 Response to allostatic load

The stress-proof individual

Some people, however, undoubtedly have the ability to engage fully with the day-to-day challenges of work and life while somehow remaining impervious to stress and its effects. Although this may be partly genetic, research indicates that the ability to flourish in the face of challenge (in terms of the model outlined in the previous chapter, effectively to maintain allostasis) is marked by certain qualities usually ignored in orthodox medicine.

Hans Selye's largely reductionist approach (that the stress response is purely physiological) has been substantially modified by the discovery that perception of stress can both trigger and regulate allostatic load.

Known as psychological modulators, these fall into six main categories: social support/connectedness; a sense of control; predictability; outlook (optimistic vs. pessimistic); meaning or purpose; and the ability to dissipate frustration. All six are open to modification by the principles and techniques featured later in this book.

Although exploring how these psychosocial variables may be affecting patients with medically unexplained disorders could provide the practitioner with valuable insights, we urge you to use the following information and **Figure 3.1** to audit the psychological modulators that may be affecting your own allostatic load.

Note: Read the sections that follow, then record a score from 1 (meaning 'a little', or 'not at all') to 5 (meaning 'a lot', or 'extremely applicable') on each

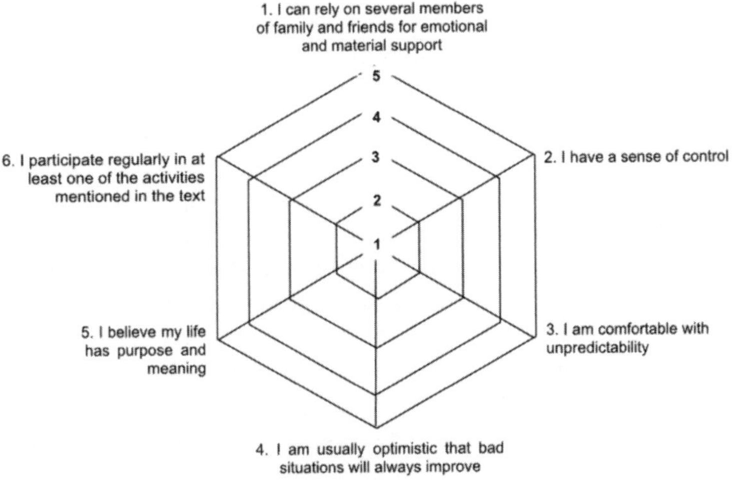

Figure 3.3 Life balance audit

corresponding segment of **Figure 3.3**. When you have finished, connect the dots to make a six-pointed shape which will provide a clear visual representation of your strengths and weaknesses.

1. Social support and connectedness

Researchers investigating strikingly low rates of myocardial infarction, reported in the 1940s from the little Pennsylvanian town of Roseto, where they expected to find a fit, tobacco- and alcohol-free community enjoying all the benefits of clean-living. When they arrived, they found as many smokers, drinkers, and couch potatoes as in the rest of the country, where heart disease was on the rise.

The difference between Roseto and other similar towns, the researchers discovered, was a particularly cohesive social structure. Somehow, the closeness Rosetans enjoyed inoculated them against cardiac problems. Predictably, as the community became steadily more 'Americanized', the protection disappeared.

A 50-year longitudinal study, published in 1992, categorically established that social support and connectedness had provided a powerfully salutogenic (health-promoting) effect on the heart.[80]

Nor was this a random fluctuation affecting a small, isolated community.

A number of studies have confirmed that host resistance to a wide range of illnesses is affected by the social context in which you live and the support you feel you receive. A recent study of 2,264 women diagnosed with breast cancer concluded that those without strong social bonds were up to 61% more likely to die within three years of diagnosis.

According to Dr. Candyce Kroenke, lead researcher at the Kaiser Permanente Research Center, California, the risk of death equals well-established risk factors, including smoking and alcohol consumption, and exceeds the influence of other risk factors such as physical inactivity and obesity.[81]

At least two major studies have suggested that loneliness can double the risk of elderly people developing Alzheimer-like diseases. Interestingly, the studies all suggest that feelings of loneliness, rather than social isolation itself, may cause the corrosive effects of dementia.[82,83]

Key factors in social integration have been identified as having someone to confide in, who can help with financial issues and offer practical support, such as baby-sitting, when you need it, and with whom you can discuss problems and share solutions.[84]

Some of the established benefits of social support and connectedness include: extended lifespan (double that of people with low social ties)[85]; improved recovery from heart attack (three times better for those with high social ties)[86]; reduced progression from HIV to Aids[87]; and even protection from the common cold.[88]

***Question 1** is: Do you feel supported by your family and friends?*

2. A sense of control

Feeling you are in control of your work and personal life is one of the best predictors of a long and healthy life. Conversely, feeling victimized by unpredictable forces outside of your control can be a killer. One large-scale study has revealed that people who feel they have little or no control over their lives have a 30% increased likelihood of dying prematurely than those who score highest in tests measuring a sense of power and control.[89]

Whether we look at rats or humans, the effect is the same. Where predictability and control are low, and environmental or occupational stress is high, the risk of cardiovascular and metabolic disease soars. However, for human beings there is hope. Happily for our survival in a stressful world, not only can health improve as control is restored, but even knowing that we have choices can significantly offset the effects of even major life-challenges[90], reduce our experience of pain and need for medication[91], and measurably increase longevity, even in later life.[92]

***Question 2** is: How much control do I feel I have in my life?*

3. Predictability

Our ability to predict events, such as pain and stressful situations, helps arm us against their effects. Habituation—the regularity with which stressful events occur—also helps us cope. Studies of urban populations in Britain who faced regular nightly air raids during World War 2 showed a greater level of resilience to stress diseases than their counterparts in the suburbs, where bombing was substantially more erratic.

Once again, perception is the key to how people respond. If your worldview is one of being at the mercy of random events—most of which are negative—allostatic load is inevitable. If you enjoy surprises (and there are many who do), the emotional response to the resultant surge in stress chemicals and endorphins is likely to be interpreted as excitement.

It must be emphasized that predictability, like control, can have its downside. Just as a misplaced sense of control over issues that are beyond our influence can be counter-productive, so can too much predictability. Studies of work-related stress have repeatedly shown that highly repetitive (read: boring) tasks can result in high levels of job dissatisfaction, absenteeism, and blood pressure. Less predictable work interspersed with the production-line activities reverses the effects.[93]

***Question 3** is: How comfortable am I with uncertainty?*

4. Positive expectancy

Positive expectancy (dismissed as 'hope' before social scientists decided to rebrand it to make mainstream scientists more accepting) has many health benefits. Multiple studies show that an optimistic outlook, by both the patient and the practitioner, can have a significant impact on clinical outcomes.[94,95,96]

Simply put, believing (and acting as if) the glass is half-full is good for your health. Even better is entertaining the possibility that the glass—or, any other vessel you choose to bring to the well—is full to over-flowing.

However, there is a caveat. Blind 'hope', as advanced by many self-help books, may have little impact on disease outcome, and exhorting someone to remain hopeful in difficult circumstances can prove taxing and lead to depression and self-blame. Realism, coupled with the anticipation of improvement, however small, can moderate the stress chemicals that an otherwise serious or critical situation can trigger.

A landmark study, referred to by Robert Sapolsky in his highly readable book on stress and coping, *Why Zebras Don't Get Ulcers*,[97] found that parents whose children had been diagnosed with cancer showed only a moderate rise in stress chemical levels when told there was a 25% risk of death.

The reason for this, the study concluded, was that odds of 75% of survival were perceived as miraculously high. As Sapolsky observes, it is not so much the 'reality' of the situation that affects our response, but the meaning we ascribe to it.

Question 4 *is: How much do I expect my situation, however challenging, to improve?*

5. Meaning, purpose, and spirituality

The way we evaluate past, and anticipate future, events can influence many aspects of our experience, including our health and wellbeing.

Large-scale and longitudinal studies, such as those carried out at Harvard University and Harvard School of Public Health, have demonstrated that explanatory styles—whether we apply an optimistic or a pessimistic spin to the meaning of our experience—are strong indicators of our future health status.[98,99]

Meaning is governed by many variables. Meta-analyses show that those people who are strongly committed to a religious belief and practice are nearly a third more likely to survive serious illness than those who hold no religious belief.[100]

A common factor of those with strong religious beliefs is an acceptance of events, positive or negative, as 'God's will'. Studies such as these arouse much controversy in scientific circles.

The most frequently encountered argument against a 'faith effect' is that religious people tend to follow healthier lifestyles and/or enjoy greater social integration than their non-religious counterparts. However, the 2000 study cited above (by Michael McCullough and colleagues) established that the highly engaged 'believers' lived significantly longer, even after the researchers accounted statistically for health behavior, physical and mental health, race, gender, and social support.

Discussing spirituality with their patients is something most practitioners avoid. And yet, holding some larger organizing belief in which we are a smaller, yet nonetheless important, part proves to be a significant part in achieving and maintaining allostasis. We (the authors) do not intend to equate 'spirituality' with 'religion', and we advise health professionals to be equally cautious. What we are more interested in, and what appears to have a greater impact on health, is a belief that the patient's life has some purpose or meaning as a part of a greater whole.

This may express itself as a deep commitment to an organized religion, or as an important goal or mission, such as 'being there for the children'. We are greatly inspired by the experiences of Austrian psychiatrist Viktor Frankl, who was arrested by the Nazis in 1942 and deported with his family to Theresienstadt, a notorious concentration camp set up by the Germans near Prague. During the following three years, incarcerated in the death camps of Auschwitz, Dachau, and Turkheim, Frankl lost his parents, his brother, and his wife, Tilly. Frankl himself survived, despite nearly succumbing to typhoid fever during the last months of the war.

His seminal work, *Man's Search for Meaning*,[101] recounts both his experiences and conclusions. Frankl spent his time at the very edge of annihilation observing his fellow prisoners, searching out the distinctions between those who survived and those who succumbed without struggle.

His observations suggested that those who looked for and found a sense of meaning in their lives—in other words, who believed they still had a mission to be fulfilled—and were free to choose their responses to whatever happened to them, were best equipped to transcend their circumstances and flourish, no matter how terrible those circumstances might be.

These two beliefs, in a mission or purpose, and the ability to choose our responses, are central to Medical NLP's therapeutic approach. Many of the principles and techniques later presented are aimed at achieving these ends.

***Question 5** is in two parts:*
The first part to consider (but not mark) is: What do you find helps you to cope when you have a problem or challenge? The second, which should be scored on the audit, is: How much does this help?

6. Dissipation

We draw a distinction between dissipation and displacement (yelling, crying, punching a wall, etc), none of which has been shown effectively to reduce chronic allostatic load, and may even worsen it.

As **Figure 3.2** (see page 34) indicates, displacement is usually counterproductive—physically, psychologically, and socially. Dissipation, on the other hand, may be incorporated into an ongoing program, designed to counter-balance, or even down-regulate, the fight-or-flight response. Some examples may be: regular exercise, especially light aerobic workouts, yoga, martial arts, and meditation (see Appendix A, pages 357 to 360). By 'regular', we mean at least four times a week for aerobic exercise and at least once a day for yoga, meditation, T'ai chi etc. Practiced correctly, these, and the resonant frequency breathing referred to elsewhere (see pages 258 to 259), will all improve heart rate regularity (HRV), which we also discuss in greater detail later in this book.

However, when making a lifestyle change to facilitate allostasis by dissipation, it is important to select an activity you find satisfying. The positive effects are directly related to perceiving your program as enjoyable. If it is not, find something else.

***Question 6** is: How much 'downtime' do you allow yourself (this should involve at least one regular practice selected from the suggestions above)?*

Now, unless you are a DC Comic™ superhero, you will have found areas of deficiency in your own life balance audit. This is valuable information, and we suggest you make a note of any area or areas open to improvement to use as material for later exercises. Of course, the audit can be used as a diagnostic tool with your patients, family, and friends.

EXERCISES

1. Practice 'mirroring' the posture, breathing patterns, and pitch, rhythm, and tonality of speech of a partner, and notice how this changes your internal 'state'. This is the effect of being in Position 2 in **Figure 3.1** on page 32. (Only do this with the agreement of your partner, or where you can be sure you can do it without drawing attention to yourself. Until you are proficient in mirroring, you need to be discreet to avoid giving offense.)
2. Now, step back into Position 1. Make sure you are fully associated, seeing through your own eyes, hearing through your own ears, and feeling with your own body.
3. Imagine floating out of your body and up into an 'observer' position. Notice the reduction or absence of emotions. Practice watching your interaction with your partner as if you were a neutral observer. Suspend comment or judgment.
4. Now, step back into Position 1. Make sure you are fully associated, seeing through your own eyes, hearing through your own ears, and feeling with your own body.
5. Practice these four steps as often as possible, until you can move easily and safely in and out of each position at will.
6. **Important note**: Always end the exercise by re-associating into your own 'self'. From this point on, make sure you are back in Position 1 after seeing each patient, and especially at the end of the day.

4

Words that Harm, Words that Heal: neurolinguistics in the consultation process

Words were originally magic, and to this day words have retained much of their ancient magical power.—***Sigmund Freud***[102]

Imagine for a moment that you, as a health professional, are given a tool that if used correctly could:

1. account for more than 50% of a successful clinical outcome—even using treatments that have been discarded as 'ineffective';
2. significantly reduce the need for painkillers, antihypertensives and anxiolytics; and
3. reverse many of the signs and symptoms of aging, all without medication.

Would you use it?

Now, imagine you have a tool that if used incorrectly could:

1. increase your patient's experience of pain and delay healing;
2. trigger attacks in diseases such as asthma; and
3. more than double your chance of being sued in the event of medical error.

Would you use it?

As you've probably guessed, it's one and the same tool. The good news is that it's a tool you already have. In fact, it came free in the genetic package you received at birth, along with the color of your eyes and the size of your feet. The bad news is: it didn't come with an instruction manual.

We're talking about language and its effects—what Professor Stephen Pinker calls that 'extraordinary collection of hisses and hums and squeaks and pops'[103] that not only transfers packets of information, simple and complex, between each other, but also binds us to others of our species.

Language, if some linguists are correct, is an innate capability in our species. We are born hardwired to communicate, to rapidly acquire the syntax (the rules) of our native tongue, and thereby connect with those around us in order to have them meet our needs. If we fail to bond, or lose those connections important to us, we may sicken and die.[104]

The challenge of communication

The suggestion that language can affect our health is the fundamental proposition of Medical NLP, and we are aware that it will be deeply challenging to some. To others, especially those at the receiving end of clumsy or malevolent communication, there's a visceral recognition that it's true.

Two anecdotes come to mind.

> **Case history**: *The 82-year-old mother of a friend had just been passed 'in pretty good condition' by the young intern who had examined her.*
>
> *As she got ready to leave with her husband, a sprightly four years her senior, the physician patted her arm and said, 'But, I want you to hold on to your husband's arm whenever you go out. You're pretty fragile, and if you don't you'll trip and fall and break a hip.'*
>
> *On the way out, her husband offered her his arm. The lady pulled away and said sharply, 'I haven't needed to hang on to you in 50 years of marriage, and I'm not going to start now.'*
>
> *As she stepped out of the front door of the clinic, she tripped and fell—and broke a hip.*

The story is true. And, unfortunately, so are many we hear from patients who have had similarly accidental, but negative, encounters with slipshod communicators. Some years ago, when Aids first made its appearance in the West, statistics indicated that mean survival from diagnosis to full-blown disease was roughly 2.5 years.

> ***Case history:*** *Two patients, both of whom were HIV-positive but uncharacteristically asymptomatic, were examined by the same attending physician, a newly fledged 'expert' in this new and mysterious disease. 'Technically', he said, 'you've passed the deadline. According to the statistics, you shouldn't even be alive now.'*
>
> *Within two weeks, both were dead. Nobody in the immediate vicinity was remotely surprised. After all, everyone knew a diagnosis of Aids was a death sentence. The only anomaly was that their symptoms had taken so long to develop.*

In both cases, the physicians acted with every positive intention, but little mindfulness. The intern's comments, intended to avoid accidents, contained a sub-text: 'If you don't do this, you will fall.' The Aids expert's comments not only emphasized that this terrible disease had a 'deadline', which the patients were flouting, but also implied the patients had no right to survive and upset the statistical equilibrium.

These comments—however well intentioned—may be seen as triggering a 'nocebo effect'. Even though the nocebo is more usually an inert substance that triggers adverse responses in the subject, communication at all levels, including the non-verbal, can negatively impact the listener. Even reading about diseases, or watching TV documentaries, can trigger adverse responses, new research has revealed.

Since the publication of the first edition of *Magic in Practice*, Dr. Michael Witthöft of Johannes Gutenberg University, Mainz (JGU), has completed an important new study in what has been dubbed the 'Wi-Fi syndrome' at London's King's College. 'The mere anticipation of possible injury may actually trigger pain or disorders. This is the opposite of the analgesic effects we know can be associated with exposure to placebos,' he says.

Curious about reports of an increase in 'electromagnetic sensitivity', Dr. Witthöft and his colleagues showed news reports about the purported health risks of Wi-Fi signals to one group of volunteers. A second, control group was shown a documentary on mobile phone security that included no reference to electromagnetic 'pollution'. Then, each participant in turn was exposed to dummy 'amplified Wi-Fi signals' and their responses were monitored.

Unlike the control group, more than half the participants who had viewed the report on the dangers of electromagnetic exposure reported experiencing characteristic symptoms, including agitation and anxiety, loss of concentration, or tingling in their fingers, arms, legs, and feet. Two participants quit the study because they were afraid to expose themselves to further 'radiation'.[105]

One man doubtlessly would be unsurprised by these findings. John Bargh is an American social psychologist, a gifted, respected, and unorthodox researcher in the field of language and influence.

One of his experiments stands as a warning to all those professionals entrusted with the health and wellbeing of others. Bargh gave two groups of subjects a collection of five-word sets with the instructions that they were to make grammatical four-word sentences out of each set. An example of these Scrambled Sentence Tests might include the words: a*pple, give, an, me, red*. The correct sentence would be '*give me an apple*', the word, *red* being redundant. One of Bargh's groups, however, was given sets that included words that might be associated with old age and its symptoms—*grey, wrinkled, tired*, etc—but never explicitly in that context.

The results were astonishing. The group exposed unconsciously to 'age' words were observed to move more slowly than before and reported that they were lacking energy and enthusiasm. The words they were exposed to literally made them temporarily older.[106]

Bargh and his colleagues have repeated the exercise in many different forms, always with the same results. The conclusions are inescapable: we unconsciously extract meaning from the words to which we are exposed and react according to the perceived meaning. This is known as priming.

Let's try a little experiment. Complete each step *before* moving on to the next.

Step 1

Stand, feet shoulder width apart, with your right arm and forefinger extended directly in front of you.

Without moving your feet, turn your upper body around to your right, following your pointed finger, as far as you can comfortably go. Find a mark that will let you know where your limit was. Return to the front and drop your arm to your side.

Now move on.

Step 2

Close your eyes, and in your imagination only, repeat the exercise without actually moving your body. Mentally follow your pointing finger around, right up to the point you last reached, and then *some considerable distance past.*

Pause for a moment before continuing.

Step 3

Now, open your eyes, extend your arm and forefinger again, and turn your body around to the right as far as you can, and notice this time how far your new limit has been re-set to.

The exercise is simple but enlightening. Although demonstrations like this often feature in business and self-development seminars as 'proof' of the 'power of the mind', the real wonder is in the mechanisms that underlie the phenomenon. Priming, the ability of the brain to recognize and respond to words and images smuggled in beneath the subject's perceptual radar, is one of the great curiosities of psychological and neurological research. If you found you could easily reach beyond your earlier attempt, you were effectively primed—in other words, your brain was set up by words alone to perform differently … and, your muscles, tendons, and joints unquestioningly obliged.

The words and phrases used to trigger this effect were presuppositional—that is, they assumed, without overtly stating, that your second performance would be an improvement on the first: *comfortably go, far, new limit, re-set* etc.

Nor should you be too embarrassed at the ease with which the effect is achieved. It simply means you're human.

Hypnotists, salespeople, and parents who use their offspring's full names to signal Something Very Serious Is About to Happen have all intuitively understood the power of priming for many years. Bargh and his colleague, Ohio State University psychologist Tanya Chartrand, estimate that around 95% of all behavior is automated, and have repeatedly demonstrated how easy it is to influence subjects to respond to certain unconsciously delivered cues, such as touching their elbows or scratching their noses.[107]

But pointing or touching your nose is entirely different from emotions, and emotions are distinct from physical health, are they not?

Well, not exactly.

Mending the body–mind split

For the past two centuries, the so-called Cartesian split between mind and body was unquestioned in scientific thought. Then, in 1985, Georgetown University School of Medicine psychopharmacologist Candace Pert published a ground-breaking paper, co-authored by Michael Ruff. It revealed the existence of an interactive 'psychosomatic network' buzzing with informational substances—peptides, hormones, and neurotransmitters—which acted in concert to maintain or impair the health and integrity of the individual.[108]

Pert, since credited as the discoverer of the opiate receptor, went on to extend her research into the multiple psychophysiological feedback loops modulated by what she has dubbed 'the molecules of emotion'. Furthermore, she found receptors for these molecules were not confined to the brain, but were distributed over almost every cell in the body.

Pert's discoveries were hugely challenging to the establishment. She endured criticism, marginalization, and even an attempt to hijack her research. But she held fast and has since been proved correct.

Her findings were largely responsible for transforming the newly emerging field of psychoneuroimmunology (PNI), the study of the relationship between the brain and health, from a little-known area of research into a fully fledged science. No longer could it be credibly argued either that the brain was merely a troublesome appendage to a mechanical body, or that the body was little more than a convenient perch for the patient's neck-top computer.

One problem, though, persisted in the field: if PNI could demonstrate the interaction of brain on body and body on brain, how did the brain acquire the information to trigger the process?

Operating outside the mainstream medical paradigm, thinkers, including Alfred Korzybski, Milton Erickson, and Richard Bandler and colleagues, had long concluded that communication was the key—permutations of the many ways in which we impart and process information, between each other and within ourselves. Since then, psychologists have largely concurred, but their evidence is often dismissed as 'soft' by their medical counterparts or, more commonly, is simply ignored.

Enter Dr. Richard Davidson and his team of researchers from the University of Wisconsin-Madison. Armed with the newly developed 'hard' research tool of functional magnetic resonance imaging (fMRI), which provides a convenient real-time 'window' on brain functions, they set out to discover whether 'emotion' was registered by the brain. They found more than this. Not only were specific areas of the brain seen to light up in response to certain emotion-laden words, but the body responded—just as Pert and her colleagues had been suggesting.

Davidson and his team monitored the responses of a group of asthmatics as they were exposed to three different categories of word: asthma-related words such as 'wheeze'; negative, but functionally unrelated words, such as 'loneliness'; and neutral words such as 'curtains'. At the same time, the subjects were given known allergens—dust-mite or ragweed extracts—to inhale. When the asthma-related words were encountered, not only did significant areas of the brain (the *anterior cingulate cortex* and the *insula*) show increased activity, but the volunteers promptly suffered asthma attacks.

The team, who have since embarked on large-scale studies, believe they have found hard evidence that certain emotions can cause flare-ups of the disease. This is something doctors have suspected for some time. However, and this is the important point, the 'allergen' inducing the asthma attacks was not simply the extract of dust-mite or ragweed, but one of those 'hisses and hums and squeaks and pops'. *The subjects had been physically harmed by a word.*[109]

Actually, even Sigmund Freud knew this was true. His comment, immediately following the one at the top of this chapter, is, '*By words one person can make another blissfully happy or drive him to despair.*'

Changing thoughts, changing minds

Any discussion about language and suggestibility would be incomplete without reference to two significant subjects: hypnosis and brainwashing.

Even after two centuries of effective application, hypnosis remains a controversial topic in mainstream medicine. This is a shame. We strongly believe that, in order to practice in the best possible interests of the patient, all health practitioners should understand hypnosis and hypnotic phenomena and regard them as unavoidable components of their daily consultations.

Hypnosis—if, by that, we mean states of increased suggestibility—occurs naturally, whether or not the practitioner has developed the sensory acuity to notice it. As we suggest later, spontaneous trance states can be utilized adjunctively in the treatment process. Meanwhile, practitioners need to be aware of the potential risks attached to unrecognized trance and trance phenomena when they occur during the consultation process.

Milton Erickson defined hypnosis in terms of a progressive narrowing of attention. The inference here is that the subject's ability to create new patterns of experience and function depends on eliminating the 'noise' of competing sensory data in favor of the 'signal' of the hypnotic suggestion. Erickson entertained certain presuppositions by which he operated and, as a result of which, many thousands of patients benefited.

Among these was the existence of an 'unconscious' mind. As a medical doctor and psychiatrist, he was fully aware that this was a metaphor—a convenient term for all the physical and psychological functions that operate below the level of immediate conscious awareness. Erickson also believed these 'other-than-conscious' functions exhibit intelligence (although not necessarily the deductive intelligence of the 'conscious' mind), metaphoric and analogical processing (much of his work was carried out obliquely, through stories and anecdotes), and also—in some cases—an almost child-like literal responsiveness to what it perceives as a 'command'.

In terms of outcome, there appears to be little distinction between hypnosis and priming, except that the latter occurs without the induction of 'formal' trance or through the medium of well-crafted suggestions. Either way, it is possible to deliver influential and potentially negative messages to the patient's unconscious—*whether or not they are intended by the speaker*. We explore this phenomenon, together with its antidote, in the chapter that follows.

Forcible or surreptitious 'thought-changing' is popularly regarded as brainwashing. Commonly associated with extreme political groups and cults, heightened suggestibility is also known to be induced by trauma, fear, and confusion. The late Margaret Thaler Singer and Janja Lalich identified a number of key prerequisites to successful thought-changing. Simply put, thoughts, values, behavior, allegiances, and beliefs may be substantially altered in conditions where the subject is deprived of his or her own clothing, familiar foods, timetable, and sense of control.

The effect is magnified when the victim is exposed to, but often excluded by, a highly specialized language, is required to submit to the 'wisdom' of a superior 'sacred' science, is discouraged from asking questions or making objections, and is constantly aware (or, at least believes) that the perceived authorities have the power of life or death.[110]

Now, compare these conditions to what can happen when a patient is facing a challenging consultation, has been admitted to hospital, or is facing a battery of complex tests.

Food, clothing, and contact with the outside world may be strictly controlled. The 'experts' use unfamiliar and distinctive terminology derived from an arcane science. Often the patient is kept in the dark about the significance of medical or surgical procedures. The doctors and nurses may be perceived as mysterious and powerful figures with the authority to decide who lives or dies. Questioning or criticism, especially of senior clinical personnel, is discouraged or ignored.

If it can be assumed that these conditions have the potential significantly to increase the patient's susceptibility to suggestion (and, we strongly suggest you take this as fact), consider the potential impact of some of the phrases collected by (real) patients from their practitioners:

> *'This is very serious surgery and there are risks attached to it. You will experience pain afterwards and it will be several weeks before you'll be able to move around comfortably.'* (A surgeon to a pre-surgical patient.)

> *'You can't possibly be ready to deliver. You're not in enough pain yet.'* (A midwife to a woman in labor.)

'People who take this medication often have dizziness or tingling in the hands and feet. Read the list of other side-effects inside the box and tell your doctor about any others you get.' (A druggist dispensing prescribed medication.)

'We'll get the results of the tests next week, but I can assure you, there's nothing to worry about yet.' (An ophthalmologist to a patient worried about anatomical changes to her retina.)

All the professionals above would argue that their intentions were impeccable and that they were obliged by law to deliver the information contained in their statements—and, we would agree. However, in the light of everything discussed so far, we would strongly caution all health practitioners to *assume that the patient in front of them is in an altered and highly suggestible state and proceed accordingly.*

All the medico-legal requirements of informed consent, 'safety netting' (instructions given to the patient for action to be taken should the condition worsen or persist), and discussion of side-effects, can be met and simultaneously tempered by the judicious use of positive semantic priming and 'hypnotic' suggestion.

Accomplishing this easily and elegantly requires planning and practice. We suggest you write out as many examples as possible; this makes it easier to tailor the language patterns to the individual patient and to deliver them confidently and effortlessly. Spend some time on the exercises at the end of this chapter before proceeding on to the next chapter. But, just before doing that, compare the statements above with the re-cast versions below:

The surgeon: *'This is serious surgery and there are risks, but we have a highly trained and experienced team looking after you. Some people have some discomfort afterwards, but it may well be less than expected, and we'll do everything we can to have you up and about as soon as possible.'*

The midwife: *'Not everybody's as relaxed as you seem to be when they're ready to deliver, and you seem really comfortable. Let's check and see how close you are now so we can make sure it continues to go smoothly.'*

The druggist: *'Some people who take this have dizziness or tingling in the hands and feet, but most people find it very easy to take. The drug companies have to list all possible side-effects, even when only a few people might have had them. Read the list and tell your doctor about any you might have, but most people only have good results.'*

The ophthalmologist: *'I'm sure from what I've seen that everything is fine. The tests you've had are very thorough and when we get the full results in a week, we'll know for sure if there's anything more that needs to be done.'*

All communication is an attempt to influence. When you say, 'Good morning' to a colleague, you expect some kind of response, preferably one that recognizes you as someone worthy of acknowledgement. A curt nod from the boss may leave you with a sense of annoyance, frustration—or, even concern about whether you're about to lose your job.

The problem with this is that most attempts to influence are done without clear purpose or design. Our intention is to focus your awareness on the process of communication—including unconscious and non-verbal communication—so that you can gain effectiveness and control.

The following section offers a number of powerful techniques of persuasion. The reader should bear in mind that these patterns are processed unconsciously by the listener, so it is important to adhere to the same ethical standards you would use in other areas of your practice.

Five patterns of positive influence

1. Semantic primes

Notice in the revised versions of instructions delivered above how many words implying success are used compared with the original examples, where the emphasis is on negative experiences. Some words and phrases used include: 'smoothly', 'looking after you', 'comfortable', 'relaxed', 'really helps', etc.

2. Presuppositions

Presuppositions are statements that assume something that is actually not verbalized. The subject must accept the presupposition in order to understand the statement, thereby 'bypassing' conscious resistance. An example is, 'When you take the medication regularly, you will find your symptoms come under control.' That the medication will be taken regularly is presupposed; the patient's attention is diverted on to the second part of the sentence.

3. Embedded commands

Embedded commands are self-standing 'orders' or 'instructions' hidden within a larger sentence. The example above also contains two embedded commands: 'Take the medication regularly', and 'Find your symptoms come under control'.

4. Primacy and recency

Since people tend to remember and respond to the first and/or the last of a set of statements, ensure that the most important instruction is delivered or repeated last.

5. Turning words

Words such as 'but' and 'however' are what we call 'turning words' (also sometimes known as 'exclusive words'), and have the effect of minimizing the impact of the clause immediately preceding it—for example, '*You're an intelligent and thoughtful person, but you need to pay more attention.*' Our natural response is to ignore the 'compliment' and focus on whatever qualifying statement follows. Even though we hear everything that is said, turning words make distinctions between what is to be regarded as in a class or category and what is not.

Another example: '*We've examined Johnny and we're confident he's fine, but if you have any worries during the night, you can always call our emergency number.*'

Doctors delivering instructions in this way often report an increase in unnecessary calls or visits by worried patients; therefore you should always be aware of the message that precedes the turning word and ensure that you wish to reduce its impact.

Here's a revised version, which conveys all the necessary information, meets all medico-legal requirements, and reassures the anxious parents: *'If you have any worries, you can call our emergency number at any time during the night, but we have examined Johnny and we're confident he's fine.'*

(**Note**: This is entirely contextual. Please do not turn into a linguistic fascist and call yourself, or everyone else, to task, every time the word 'but' is used. In ordinary conversation you need only to remain mindful of the effect your communication is having, and adjust if necessary.)

EXERCISES

Review and then write out as many patterns related to your specialty as you can. We advise keeping a file of your efforts and adding to it as new ideas and situations occur. See how many of these words you can introduce into your consultations without interrupting the flow.

Semantic primes

1. First, make a list of as many synonyms as you can for states of comfort, ease, peace, calm, relaxation, and relief, etc. Then, when you have at least 20, practice creating sentences that impart the required information but orientate the patient towards positive experiences and outcomes. Layer your synonyms for an amplified effect (for example, 'You'll notice how comfortably or easily or smoothly or effortlessly you can move your arm the more you exercise ...')
2. Now, create more sentences using these primes, only this time make sure the primes you use don't refer overtly to the patient's condition (for example, 'Since we refurbished the reception area, people can come and go more comfortably and easily and everything seems to work more smoothly or effortlessly ...')

Practice your priming with your patients and notice their response.

Presuppositions

Presuppositions most commonly start with words such as, 'when', 'after', 'before', 'as', 'during' etc. Immediately following these is the primary injunction you wish to deliver, followed by a phrase that diverts conscious attention away from the injunction. The intention is to smuggle the suggestion in under the radar of the left hemisphere's critical analysis.

Example:

'Before you start your new eating plan, make sure you've already bought all the food items you need.'

Starting the new eating plan is the more important part of the sentence, but conscious attention is directed towards shopping for the foods, prompting the unconscious mind to proceed as if the new plan is already a fact of life.

Embedded commands

Decide on your embedded command, and then create a secondary sentence within which it can be embedded while still making sense. When they are delivered, embedded commands should be analogically marked—that is, spoken slightly more loudly or softly, with a gesture or a slightly more emphatic tone, etc—to mark them out to the patient's unconscious processes as significant.

Example:

Command—*'Complete the full course of pills.'*

Secondary sentence—*'Everyone needs to make sure the infection is properly under control.'*

Analog marking—*'Everyone needs to* ***complete the full course of pills*** *to make sure the infection has been brought properly under control.'*

Primacy and recency

Summarize the main thrust of your message. Deliver the message, then repeat your summary. This will ensure that the most important point(s) will be more easily retained by the listener.

Turning words

List a number of instructions (especially 'safety netting' advice) that involve turning words. An example might be, 'This is an effective drug, but you might experience side-effects.'

In order to minimize overreaction to adverse but unlikely possibilities or experiences, place them first in the sentence, followed by a turning word, then a qualifier that presupposes a more positive outcome. Therefore, a revised version of the above examples might be, 'Some people have side-effects when taking this drug, but mostly we find it very effective.'

The formula is: ***Possibility + Turning word + Reassurance.***

5

Primes and Priming: the secret world of indirect influence

We're blind to what we don't expect.—***Professor Ellen Langer***

Even if none of the research mentioned in the previous chapter had been carried out, most people have an intuitive understanding, based on everyday experience, of the relationship between language and the 'gut response'. Think of how you feel when the boy racer on the freeway cuts you off in the fast lane, then winds down the window and yells obscenities at you. Or remember a heated argument with a spouse or a friend, or being reprimanded by your boss.

These are just words—except they have the power to light up the brain and set in motion a complex chain of neurochemical events, causing your palms to sweat and your gut to wrench, and which now have to be metabolized before your body can return to its default 'normal' state.

One of the concerns which the phenomenon opens up involves the possibility of negative and unintentional priming by means of the increasing number of patient questionnaires being introduced to 'assess' a wide variety of conditions, including pain, depression, anxiety, and obsessive compulsive disorder.

As we reported in the previous chapter, Davidson's team elicited an asthma attack with a single condition-specific word. What is happening inside the patient who is required to work his way through anything from 10 to more than 100 words related to illness, discomfort, and pain without being invited to offer his own words to describe his unique experience?

The quality of words is important, too, Richard Bandler often says, 'Your voice bathes the listener's entire body with the waveform. What you say and how you say it has a direct impact on the listener's nervous system.'

Candace Pert's recent research seems to bear this out. Words (like music), she says, affect the 'psychosomatic network' by causing certain ion channels to either open or close, thus regulating how a particular neural network works. 'You're literally thinking with your body,' she adds. 'The words…because sound is vibrating your receptors…actually (affect) the neural networks forming in your brain.'[111]

Building resilience

Wherever treatment derived from the molecular, cause-and-effect model has failed to bring the patient relief, we need to look more deeply into what else we can do. Since 'stress' is undeniably a factor in all 'functional' disorders, we have it within our powers to: reduce sympathetic arousal; help the patient learn to recover allostasis, not by blocking the symptoms of imbalance, but by helping him to raise the bar on his own physical-emotional resilience; and, wherever possible, alter the structure and process of his illness-behavior.

The medium is the word. Our ability as a species to influence and be influenced by language is an important contributory factor to restoring and maintaining health. The fact that we are enormously suggestible can and should be exploited—although, of course, with due and diligent care.

However, there is more. Much more. What researchers now understand is that the tone of someone's voice, the kind of pictures on the wall, the lay-out of the room, and even the temperature of a mug of coffee he is holding can powerfully influence someone's response...sometimes nearly at the speed of light.

Aileen sits at the computer console, staring intently at the screen. A senior who regards herself as 'mildly computer illiterate', she is slightly nervous to begin with. But the friendly researcher reassures her that all she has to do is to pay attention to the screen as a succession of words and phrases are flashed, faster then she, or anyone else, is able to read.

What she doesn't know is that all the words that are being presented to her unconscious mind are positive stereotypes about aging. Words and phrases such as, 'experienced', 'wise', 'good with children' are presented rapidly, each image lasting less than one hundredth of a second.
Sitting in the next booth is her friend Betty, almost the same age, with similar interests and in much the same state of health.
Betty's screen, however, features a stream of negative words and phrases, all related to aging: 'memory gets worse with age', 'aches and pains in the morning', 'need glasses to read'. Once again, the speed with which these images are presented prevents them from being read consciously.

Neither Aileen nor Betty know what the experimenters are looking for. But later, they are both given a memory test and a test to gauge their attitude towards aging.

The results are eye-opening, even to the researchers themselves. Aileen, and all the other elderly people involved in her group, demonstrate not only a significantly improved memory, but a markedly more positive attitude towards growing old.

Betty and her cohorts, on the other hand, do consistently worse. Their memory deteriorates, and they are significantly less inclined to regard growing older in a positive light.

Experiments along these lines were conducted by psychologist Becca Levy, who, together with Jeffrey Hausdorff, Rebecca Hencke, and Jeanne Wei, went on to show that presenting individuals with words and images related to health can trigger improved physical and psychological health, as well as healthier behavior. Likewise, words related to retention and recollection activated a healthier memory and increased cognitive abilities.[112,113]

It is particularly important to note that all of the words and images were presented to the test subjects *outside* of their conscious awareness. In other words, their physical and emotional states were buffeted by the winds and currents of the words the experimenters used, regardless of the meaning the latter intended to convey. Since the process functioned at an unconscious level, the speaker, not the listener, became responsible for the outcome of the conversation.

We have already discussed verbal (semantic) priming, and mentioned that it can take place outside the listener's conscious awareness. However, primes can occur in all senses, including sight, touch, taste, and smell.

Primes differ from anchors (discussed later in this book—see pages 145 to 157), in that the latter are simple stimulus-response (S-R) patterns, with one trigger setting off (firing) a specific state or response. Primes, on the other hand, are a function of implicit memory—cues that subliminally tell us what is expected of us: what to feel, how to behave, how to respond. Since they are usually embedded in our psyches during a lifetime of unconscious experience, they operate silently, consistently, and, all too often, to negative effect.

Harvard's Ellen J. Langer has demonstrated this phenomenon, elegantly and in many different ways. One study involved getting participants to role-play being air force pilots. A control group went through the same flight simulation as the 'pilots', but without any particular preparation. Both groups were asked to read eye charts both before and after the 'flight'. Since almost everyone knows that one of the conditions for qualifying as a pilot is excellent vision, Langer and her associates predicted that those participants who had been primed by listening to lectures, dressing in uniform, and adopting a 'pilot mindset' would show improved vision over those who were simply asked to read the eye chart from the same distance.

This, indeed, is precisely what happened. Simply pretending to be a pilot brought about a measurable improvement in the subjects' visual acuity.[114]

Langer's colleagues devised another intriguing test of the power of priming.

Identify the chart below and take a moment or two to explore the implications of this familiar image.

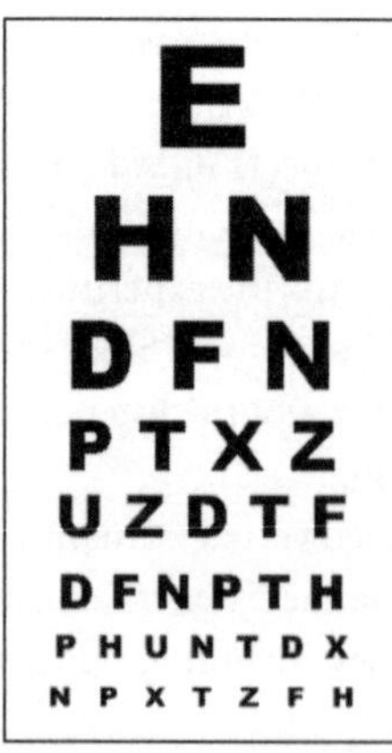

Most people in the West have had their eyes tested and will have no problem identifying the chart opposite.

However, the implications of this iconic image are profound. Implicit in the design of the chart, and the way eye tests are usually administered, is the assumption that the viewer will have increasing difficulty reading the letters from top to bottom, from larger to smaller. The subject in fact, is being primed to expect that his vision will worsen as he reads on.

Now, what would happen if the image changed so that the smaller letters were at the top and the larger ones were at the bottom as shown here?

In this case, the expectation is different. The reader starts with the anticipation that his vision will get better as he reads on...and, it does.

Langer notes, 'Participants tested indeed showed enhanced vision using the redesigned chart, and they were able to read lines they couldn't see before on a standard eye chart. In all but one case, subjects could read the same number of small letters on a line on the reverse chart that was only visible on a line 10 font sizes larger on the regular eye chart. Also interesting was that the subjects thought they did better on the normal chart. We're blind to what we don't expect.'[115]

Langer's most intriguing study, of course, is the one central to her book, *Counter Clockwise*, and repeated in the BBC documentary, *The Young Ones.* Here, Langer was able to reverse many of the signs and symptoms of aging by simply returning a group of elderly and infirm people to an environment that replicated a time in which they were in their prime. By recalling and 're-experiencing' health and wellbeing, the subjects experienced profound physical and emotional rejuvenation.[116]

The risk of negative priming

Now, let's see what happens when you visit your doctor's office.

Even though some effort might have been made to cheer up the environment, perhaps with a few bright pictures in the waiting room, or a vase or two of flowers, the main components will be implements and images associated with illness and disease.

Stethoscopes and sphygmomanometers jostle with kidney basins, tongue depressors, and syringes. Erudite volumes of diseases from A to Z line the shelves; a plastic skeleton—the ultimate mortality prime—hangs lifelessly in the corner. A poster of a flayed corpse, identifying the major muscle groups, dominates one wall.

Overseeing all this is your physician, smart and crisp in a clean white coat, a member of a profession dedicated to prolonging your time on the planet, but with fewer tools to help you achieve a better quality of life than he would care to admit.

Supposing you present with what the medical profession calls 'medically unexplained pain'. Of course, 'pain' is not a good enough word to explain one of the least understood phenomena in psychophysiology. So your physician gives you a form and invites you to fill it in. Along the top of the page is a scale, usually from 0 to 5, inviting you to rate the level of your pain.

If your ability to self-assess is in doubt, you may, instead, find five icons, ranging from the classic smiley-face to a particularly grouchy one, possibly with a tear spurting out of one eye.

The prime here is visual. For all people who read from left to right, the progression from bright and sunny to down, despondent and distressed means one thing: it's going to get worse (remember the eye chart experiments?).

Then, you're presented with a number of words allegedly helping the physician zone in on your particular malady.

These are words like: *pulsing; pounding; stabbing; cutting; wrenching;*

scalding; searing; aching; burning; throbbing; hammering; slicing; sharp; dull...usually 20 or more to choose from.

Similar tables exist for other conditions and dysfunctions, including depression, anxiety, and obsessive compulsive disorder (OCD). Their authors claim such metrics are 'evidence-based'. In fact, the 'evidence' is this: a certain number of patients are invited to choose a word describing their experience of their diagnosed condition. If a large enough number of people diagnosed with, say, rheumatoid arthritis, use the word 'burning' to describe their pain, 'burning' is considered to be an accurate representation of the experience of *all* sufferers of rheumatoid arthritis.

This generalization from the few to the many is specious, and endemic in medical research. Very quickly, the developers of such tables, as well as those who use them, forget that the word is not the experience it describes. Nor is there any way that it can be proved that all people who use the word 'burning' are actually sharing exactly the same experience. In fact, since part of the pain-message is interpreted by the module of the brain that attributes 'meaning' to the experience, we can be reasonably sure they are not. Meaning, almost by definition, is subjective. Nevertheless, diagnoses and treatments—sometimes quite invasive treatments—are based on the belief that all patients share the same experience, and that their experience establishes (proves) the existence of a particular condition.

Understanding means re-experiencing

But the problems run deeper than this. As we mention elsewhere (see pages 67 and 223), someone faced with a list of abstract words such as those found on the assessment tables is required to refer to his or her own experiential 'database' in order even to understand the words. To distinguish between 'throbbing' and 'aching' requires that they activate those neural networks where such experiences are stored and, activation and understanding, to varying degrees, means re-experiencing.[117]

Given the implications of Langer's extensive studies, and those of a growing number of independent researchers, it seems inarguable that by simply inviting an individual to review a list of pathological descriptors, the practitioner may be priming the patient to experience an even greater depth and breadth of pain. In fact, everything about the consultation—

from the posters on the walls of the reception room, through the smell of disinfectant and the instruments of investigation on the doctor's desk, to the dependence on technology-based test-results and the use of medical jargon—may be priming the patient to experience a greater degree of discomfort and ill-health than that with which he arrived.

In 2012, the Australian government sought to harness this effect by forcing tobacco companies to market their products in drab, olive-green packages with disturbing images of cancer sufferers, sick babies and diseased limbs.

Within days of the packages going on sale, smokers deluged consumer groups and advice centers, claiming the products had been tampered with in order to affect the taste. The implication was that smoking was no longer as pleasant a pastime as it had been when packages were adorned with colorful designs and text, albeit with smaller, less obtrusive images of the ravages of smoking. On the face of it, this was a victory for the anti-smoking brigade, although whether or not smokers might simply adapt to the 'new taste', as they have tended to when switching brands in the past, has yet to be determined.

For those who might doubt this effect, we refer you to the 1996 study by John Bargh and Tanya Chartrand. Assuming that goals and intentions are mental representations, Bargh and Chartrand replicated two well-known experiments, the results of which were well known. However, rather than explicitly delivering the goals, the experimenters primed the participants non-verbally. The results precisely matched those of the original experiments, in which the objectives were explicit, supporting their view that the outcome of a particular exchange can be the same whether the subject is activated unconsciously, or through an act of will.[118]

We urge the reader also to pay particular attention to both the patient's use of words related to body temperature, as well as to the ambient temperature of the room.

Recent research has found that subjects with weak social connectedness literally feel colder than their more social peers. They might signal this by using metaphors related to temperature, such as 'cold', 'cool', 'chilly', or 'frosty'.

Meanwhile, low ambient temperatures may actually deepen feelings of sadness and depression. Conversely, warmth—such as that experienced holding a cup of tea—has been shown significantly to improve the subject's mood.[119,120] A pleasant, warm atmosphere in your office, a cup of tea, or even larding your language with warmth-related words, such as 'thaw', 'heat', 'snug', and 'melt' may function as re-orientating primes.

Social psychologists have identified at least seven classes of priming.

1. **Semantic priming**, the most common form, uses words to create meaning that, in turn, influences later thoughts.
2. **Conceptual priming** uses ideas to activate a related response ('shoe', for example, may act as a prime for 'foot').
3. **Perceptual priming** describes the process whereby a fragment of an image is expanded to complete a more complex picture based on an image seen earlier.
4. **Associative priming** relies on 'collocation', the means whereby English words combine in predictable ways: 'chalk' and 'cheese', 'bread' and 'butter', 'distinguished' and 'career'. Freudian free association is based on associative priming.
5. **Non-associative semantic priming** links concepts, but less closely than semantic or conceptual priming. 'Orange', for example, may act as a non-associative prime for 'banana' (both fruit).
6. **Repetitive priming** refers to the way reiteration influences later thinking. Advertising motifs and jingles exploit this effect.
7. **Masked priming** occurs when words or images are presented too rapidly to be recognized consciously. Becca Levy's experiment, described above, is an example of masked priming.

Important points to remember:

- Priming relies on stimuli that influence future thoughts and actions, even though they may not seem to be connected;
- Priming increases the speed at which the primed subject responds or recognizes the stimulus; and
- Priming can install new thoughts and behaviors, or make old patterns and behaviors more readily accessible, and therefore more likely to be utilized than older, less available, material.

EXERCISES

1. Look at the seven classes of priming above. Choose any four. For each chosen class of prime, write down a list of nine overtly positive priming words in context of your own work (for example, 12 words that prime for *comfort* or *relax* or *heal*).
2. Take a close look at your working environment or office. Look at every picture, object, icon, etc. How many are actually sending priming signals? Are they positive or negative primes?
3. Now go back to your lists from 1 above. How can you make these into, subtle *covert* primes that can be used in your own office or consulting room?
4. Go online and search for images representing the themes of your positive priming words. These can be used in a digital photo-frame placed obliquely to your patient, but within his peripheral vision. Set the images to change about once every three seconds.

6

Structure, Process and Change: the building blocks of experience

Reality leaves a lot to the imagination.—Attributed to ***John Lennon***

Exactly what constitutes the nature of 'reality' and the 'meaning' of life has preoccupied scientists, philosophers, and spiritual thinkers for much of our time on the planet. And even though you are unlikely to be consciously aware of the questions that inform almost every moment of your life, they are there, directing your emotions, needs, moods, desires, and behaviors: '*What is happening to me?*' '*Why do I feel this way?*' '*What does it mean?*' '*What should I do?*'

At virtually every turn, and, often unconsciously, we ask questions and make decisions about our world and our place in it as we navigate through the complexity of daily living, based on the assumption that we understand, or can understand, what's really 'going on'.

For much of the time, this way of managing the world serves our needs. We eat, sleep, have sex, look to people and things we hope will give us something we call 'happiness'. To many of us, the challenge seems to be to control the unruly, unpredictable, unreliable elements of life, thinking that somehow, some day, we'll make it all fit. Sometimes it will seem to work; more often, it won't.

Disappointment sets in, and we start all over again, trying to rearrange the pieces of an ever-changing puzzle. If it doesn't, then we turn to an 'expert' in the particular part of our malfunctioning body-mind in the hope that she can help.

One of our problems as a species is that we use our superior ability to think, but seldom think about the way in which we think. Even less do we suspect that how we think directly affects our experience, happy or unhappy, functional or dysfunctional, sick or well.

This should not be confused either with New Age 'positive thinking' or the hunting down and challenging of Cognitive Behavioral Therapy's 'negative thinking patterns'. We are talking about the structure and process of thinking, believing and knowing—more epistemology and less psychology; more *how* and less *why*.

In order fully to understand what mainstream NLP means when it refers to 'the structure of subjective experience', try the following exercise:

Recall a pleasant experience from your past—perhaps a holiday, or a reunion with a loved one. Make sure it is a specific experience or event.

Now, ask yourself how you were thinking about the memory, how you remember what you were doing, and how you felt. Most people answer vaguely at first, 'I just remember it was good'; 'We had a good time'; 'I was feeling great'.

Now, return to the memory and answer the following questions: How strongly can you re-create your good feelings by recalling the memory? Scale it from 1 (a little) to 10 (as if you were there right now).

Do you remember the experience as a picture? If so:

- Is it in color or black and white?
- Is it moving or still?
- Is it near or far away?
- Are you observing it as if on a screen, or through your own eyes?

Are there any sounds to the memory? If so, are they:

- Loud or soft?
- Words or music?
- Internal self-talk?

What feelings or sensations are involved, if any?

- Where are they located in your body?

- Are they still or moving?
- Do they feel warm or cool?

What other qualities do you notice? Think of all your senses: visual, auditory, kinesthetic (feeling), gustatory (taste), and olfactory (smell). Make a note of all these distinctions.

The experiment above demonstrates the following:

1. your memory was created out of sensory-rich information (that is, you needed to activate, albeit internally, your senses of sight, hearing, feeling, and touch, and, perhaps taste and smell. We call these **sensory modalities**);
2. by acting 'as if' you were there, you re-experienced some degree of feeling or emotion that corresponded with the feelings or emotions you experienced during the original scenario. This is what we call 'state'—the sum total of the psychophysiological changes that take place when you remember, imagine, or experience a particular memory, behavior, or event;
3. your senses had certain qualities: color, size, movement, degree of involvement, volume, temperature, etc (we call these **sub-modalities**, because they are subsidiary qualities of your sensory modalities); and
4. you favored one sense over the others (we call this your **sensory preference**).

Additionally, even though you might have experienced strong feelings or emotions when recalling this experience, you also somehow 'knew' that you were 'here', remembering, and not actually back 'there'.

A simple remembered incident from your past turns out to have a host of qualities that permits you to sort information, code it, and store it in a 'filing system' that allows you to distinguish one event from another, place it on an internal 'time line', and invest it with a unique emotional 'charge'.

Now, try something else.

Imagine someone raking their fingernails down a blackboard (supposing you're old enough to remember blackboards). What is your response?

Or, pretend you have a lemon in your hand. Feel the weight of it and the texture of the skin. See the color of the peel and the flesh in your mind's eye. Hear the sound of the knife as you slice into it, and smell the pungent oil of the skin. Now bite into one half, and swill the juice around your mouth before swallowing it. Notice its sharpness, how it reacts with your taste buds and the enamel of your teeth.

If you did this vividly enough, you either winced at the sound of nails on the blackboard, or found your salivary glands going into overdrive. There is no real blackboard, no lemon. Just the power of your imagination; a part of your brain that is unable to distinguish between what is real and what is imaginary; a cascade of neurochemicals and a physical response.

The fact that people can activate physiological responses merely by imagining or remembering events will, as we will explain, serve an important function in the provision of healthcare (and contribute greatly to our own mental and physical health). By understanding more about how a patient 'sets up' and maintains his particular dysfunction, you will become more strategically positioned to develop practical interventions to empower him to move more systematically in the direction of self-regulation, health, and wellbeing.

One of the fundamental messages of NLP is: *we act on our **representation** of the world, rather than on the world itself.*

The original (and prescient) NLP model of cognition suggested that information gathered from the external world is filtered through our preferred sensory modalities, and then through the constraints of our neurology and our social and cultural conditioning. This contributes to the creation of the internal model of 'reality' by which we function. The degree to which data are filtered dictates how expanded or constrained the model—and, therefore, ***our*** experience—is.

Over recent years, we have gained a fuller idea of how the organs of perception work, thanks to developments in neuroscience, and the abiding curiosity of those scientists who keep inquiring into the mysteries of the 'black box' of consciousness.

Surprisingly, perhaps, perception (along with our ability to predict and plan) emerges from a cortical skin comprised of stacks of cells, each only six neurons deep. These stacks, known as **cortical columns**, are packed together and function in a complex, bi-directional relationship with each other. Each of your senses relies on cortical columns packed into different areas of the brain (vision in the **occipital lobe** at the back of the cortex; visualization in the central prefrontal area; hearing on either side of the **temporal lobe**; kinesthetics in the **parietal lobe**).

Whenever you experience something new, most powerfully as a child, information floods in from the brainstem, fountains up through the cortical stacks, creating the informational phenomenon known as 'bottom-up' processing. When unaffected by previous experience, this 'pure' consciousness is unlikely to be experienced by older children and adults, unless they practice some of the techniques of mindful awareness referred to elsewhere in this book (see Appendix A, pages 357 to 360).

As time passes and your databank of experience grows, this inflow of experience becomes subject to modification. As suggested by Bandler and Grinder, who referred to 'neurological constraints' (stored experiences, beliefs, cultural rules and injunctions, values, etc),[121] information already held in the nervous system flows *downwards* ('top-down' processing). The collision of these two creates a synthesis of new and old—a kaleidoscope of experience and impressions. The way in which this synthesis resolves itself gives rise to what we have already referred to as 'state'. State, in turn, directly impacts affect and behavior.

States are sometimes referred to as 'neural networks', 'neural clusters', or 'neural pathways'. More colorful descriptions, such as 'engrams', 'parts', and 'sub-personalities'[122] are also sometimes applied, influenced, perhaps, by the way these behaviors often appear to function beyond the direct, conscious control of the host.

It has been suggested that states develop out of the brain's tendency to simplify tasks, especially motor skills, but also behaviors, responses, and the feelings that arise out of these.

We all have states to facilitate many different ways of being in the world. When you enter your place of business, you also activate a specific 'working state'. When you arrive home and are greeted by the kids, you step into your 'domestic state'. Your states allow you to have various ways of being-in-the-world (strategies): for playing sports; dialing a cold call; making love; and eating in a restaurant. You probably also have states for worrying about the mortgage; fearing a tax audit; obsessing about an argument with your partner or spouse; and hanging out with your friends.

We usually define state as 'the sum total of the psychophysiological changes that take place when you remember, imagine, or experience a particular memory, behavior or event', or, 'the integrated sum of mental, physical, and emotional conditions from which the subject is acting'.

Even more significant, though, are two qualities of states:

1. Many of them function independently of other feelings and behaviors (we speak about them having defined 'boundary conditions');
2. Once activated, the feelings, emotions, and/or behaviors coded into that particular state will tend to 'run', unless the pattern is somehow interrupted or replaced.

'Reality', then, is a construct of our neurology, in much the same way as 'vision' is an interpretation by the brain, rather than a literal reflection of the external world. It follows, therefore, that at best the map can only *approximate* the world or 'territory' it represents, not least because the territory is too complex to render in exact detail, and our maps, made up as they are from selective data uniquely filtered through personal sensory bias, *differ* to some extent or other from those of the people around us.

However, when we create an internal representation of the 'outside' world, we seldom question the accuracy or validity of that representation, or notice the differences between the maps of the people we meet.

Alfred Korzybski, the founder of the field of General Semantics, made the now-famous observation, 'The map is not the territory', and attributed what he called 'un-sanity' to the fact that we often fail to distinguish between the two.[123]

Acquiring access to the patient's map to ascertain how her representation limits his world is one of the first skills the effective practitioner should acquire. The patient is unlikely to have conscious access to her internal processing, but information nevertheless 'leaks' in a number of ways, both verbal and non-verbal.

To gain insight into the patient's situation, we need to identify her sensory preferences, how she codes the 'meaning' of her experience, and how she creates and maintains negative feelings and repetitive behaviors. With that information in hand, it becomes relatively easy to interrupt and change her experience by changing the structure that supports it.

The information that follows is generalized, and it is important to remember that some people may display idiosyncratic patterns. Observe carefully before making assumptions.

Decoding the patient's inner experience

The speaker may reveal his or her sensory preference (or the pattern of the current experience) in one or other of the following ways:

1. eye moments ('eye accessing cues') may be related to how information is stored in the brain and to innervation of the eye by four cranial nerves;
2. choice of words, also known as 'sensory predicates';
3. position and movement of the body; and
4. tone, rate, and pitch of speech.

Eye movements

The classic NLP model suggests that most right-handed people look to the left when remembering events, and to the right when creating new images (**Figure 6.1**).

Visual processing is suggested when the subject looks upwards, to the left, right, or directly ahead, the vision slightly defocused.

Auditory access is indicated when the eyes are in the midline, more or less in line with the ears. The head is often tilted to one side, or it may be turned so that the listener's dominant ear is nearest the speaker.

Self-talk (also known as 'auditory digital') is often indicated when the speaker looks down and to his left.

Internal kinesthetics (feelings/emotions) may be present when the subject looks down and to the right. It should be noted that olfactory and gustatory processing are usually included within the kinesthetic categorization.

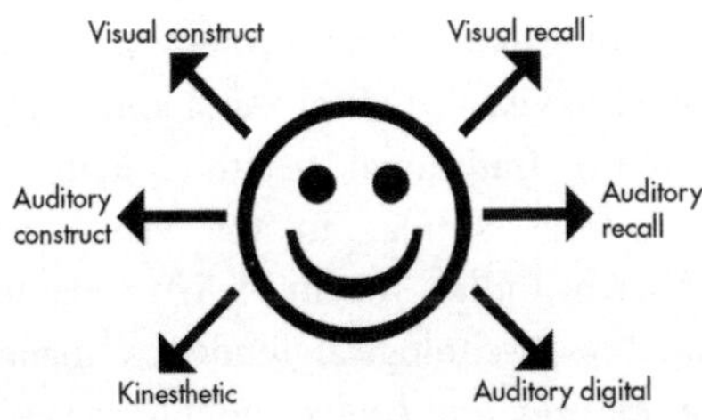

Figure 6.1 Eye accessing cues of a right-handed person. (© Dr Richard Bandler. Reproduced by permission.)

Sensory predicates

Many words and phrases indicate a preference for one or other sensory modalities—for example:

Visual: 'It looks clear to me'; 'I get the picture'; 'We need to focus on this'; 'It's too much in my face'.

Auditory: 'I hear what you're saying'; 'That sounds good to me'; 'I can't hear myself think'.

Kinesthetic: 'I really feel for you'; 'You need to get a grip on yourself'; 'Everything feels as if it's getting on top of me'.

Posture and movement

Visual: Sitting and standing erect, with the head up. Gestures are high, often as if 'sketching' in important details. Tight muscle tonus.

Auditory: Neither upward reaching nor slumped. Gestures are slower and more measured.

Kinesthetic: Often slumped, as if dragged down. Muscle tonus is slack. Gestures are slow and asymmetrical.

Speech

Visual: The pitch is often higher than average, and the rate of speech rapid-fire. There is considerable variation in tone.

Auditory: Speech is somewhat slower, pitched in the mid-range and with less variation.

Kinesthetic: Speech is slow and measured, often lacking color or animation.

Some commentators have even suggested a correlation between physical build and sensory preference. The categories of the now largely discarded physical typology—ectomorph, mesomorph, and endomorph—are said to correspond to visual, auditory, and kinesthetic preferences.

Interestingly, many traditional health systems include physical-emotional categorizations similar to the visual-auditory-kinesthetic distinctions. The ancient Indian system of Ayurveda, for example, refers to *prakruti*, innate bio-psychological tendency, made up of different combinations of *pitta*, *vata*, and *kapha*, roughly corresponding to visual, auditory, and kinesthetic.

Sub-modalities: shades of meaning

But how can we be sure that something we remember actually happened? By what mechanism do we distinguish differences in the time, quality, intensity, and meaning of an experience?

Evolution has equipped us not only with senses by which we 'sample' the external world and make internal representations of what we see, hear, feel, smell, and taste, but each organ of perception also has specialized receptors that allow us to make distinctions that further drive the making of meaning.

The auditory input channel, for example, permits the reception of not only packets of data, but also qualities such as the direction from which a sound comes, the pitch and tonality of a voice, rhythm, direction, and a myriad of other qualities.

Visually, we are equipped to detect color, movement, patterns, and relationships between items within our visual field, distance, etc. Our kinesthetic senses permit physical touch, organ awareness, and inner 'feelings', each of which in turn may be subdivided into an almost infinite array of subtleties. Likewise, smell and taste have qualities dependent on the receptors inside our mouths and nasal passages.

Our internal representations, therefore, are assembled not simply out of varying arrays of modalities, but each modality is 'tagged' by one or more characteristics that keep it distinct from its associated modalities (**Figure 6.2**). Given the almost limitless combinations that five modalities and their attendant sub-modalities possess, we have a powerful methodology for storing and accessing information in a relatively organized way.

Visual	*Auditory*	*Kinesthetic*
Associated/dissociated	Tonality	Location
Size	Volume	Movement (direction)
Location	Inside/outside head	Pressure/weight
Distance	Location	Extension (start- and end-points)
Color/black and white	Pitch	Temperature
Vivid/pastel	Tempo	Duration
2D/3D	Continuous/interrupted	Intensity
Single/multiple images	Clear/diffuse	Shape
Flat or tilted	etc.	etc.
Transitions smooth/jumpy		
etc.		

Figure 6.2 Some common sub-modality distinctions

Changing the map

It follows that if sub-modality coding is part of how the perception-to-meaning transformation really works, changing the sub-modalities of an experience should, of necessity, change the meaning of that experience.

Recall the pleasant memory from the previous exercise and re-enter it as fully as possible. See in your mind's eye what you saw then, hear what you heard, notice the feelings you felt. Recall any smells and tastes that might have been present. Refer to how you scored the intensity of the remembered experience.

Now slowly push the image away from you, or step back from it, so that you are seeing it as if from a distance.

Continue increasing the distance between you and the image. If you recalled the original image through your own eyes, pull back until you see yourself in the scene as if on a screen or in a photograph. Drain out any color. Let the details diminish, as the image moves further from you.

Rescale the emotional intensity and compare it with the first time you calibrated it.

The majority of people who do this experiment find that feelings of pleasure are substantially diminished. Experiment by changing other sub-modalities. If you favor auditory or kinesthetic modalities over the visual, you might have to experiment with changing or turning down any sounds or sensations within the experience to notice an effect. You may also have observed that changing just one sub-modality triggered a domino effect on the others. This is what is known as the 'driver' sub-modality—the single shift that alters the entire Gestalt.

As a general rule, large, bright, close, and colorful images usually intensify feelings, whereas smaller, distant, less distinct, and colorless imagery reduces emotional impact. Association (seeing through the subject's eyes) commonly amplifies responses, while dissociation (seeing the self as if in a picture or movie) decreases them.

Remember to restore the original sub-modalities to your experience before moving on.

Eliciting sub-modalities

Quite simply, ask. Ask, 'How do you do that?'; 'What happens when you think of that?'; 'Where in your body is your (symptom)? If it had a color (shape, size, weight, etc), what would it be?'. Take your time, and guard against being drawn back into 'content'. You are eliciting the structure of the experience, its component building blocks, not its 'story'.

Applying sub-modality change in practice

Simple issues can be resolved with sub-modality changes, literally within a few minutes. Since each person's unique coding system is the basis of his sense of reality, work systematically and ecologically, changing one sub-modality at a time, putting it back if no change takes place before moving on to the next. Ideally, you will find the one sub-modality that triggers a system-wide change.

> ***Case history:*** *The patient, a 66-year-old retired painter and decorator, had a six-month history of mounting anxiety. He was having difficulty sleeping and asked for sleeping tablets. He said he had found life difficult since retiring. He had to look after his wife, his house, and his health, and worried about his ability to cope. A few weeks before the consultation, his roof had begun to leak, and he said his anxiety was stopping him doing anything to fix it—and this, in turn, was further exacerbating his anxiety.*
>
> *After carefully pacing the patient in order to lower his anxiety, the practitioner asked him to describe his 'anxiety' in terms of its location, size, color, etc.*
>
> *The patient said it was in his abdomen, 'black', and spherical, 'like a ball'. He rated his level of discomfort at 7, with 10 being the worst anxiety possible. The practitioner and patient then began changing the qualities of the ball, pushing it further back, changing the color, size, etc. After a few minutes, he found to his great surprise that his rating had dropped to 3. The practitioner ended the consultation by asking him to practice this 'relaxation technique' of changing the sub-modalities of his anxiety whenever necessary.*
>
> *The patient returned two weeks later saying he didn't understand exactly what had happened, but 'for some reason' he felt much calmer and more relaxed, no longer wanted sleeping tablets, and was planning to sort out his leaking roof.*

The initial consultation, the practitioner report, took no more than 10 minutes, including history-taking and outcome-planning. Notice in the above example that at no time did the practitioner offer advice or argumentation to challenge the patient's world-view. Rather than suggest he change his self-defeating self-talk, she moved to another level: that of the *structure* of the patient's *model*, which she then helped him change.

Especially where more complex problems are concerned, bear in mind that how the patient describes his problem differs substantially from how the problem actually functions. This follows from the way in which we, both consciously and unconsciously, edit information in order to reduce it to more manageable proportions.

George Miller calculated that we are only able consciously to process between five and seven 'bits' of information at a time.[124] More than that and details tend to be lost to both short- and long-term memory.

However, what is left out or transformed in the process of creating our models of the world is as important as what is left in. The transformation of direct, subjective experience (Deep Structure) into what is communicated (Surface Structure) is governed by three processes: deletion, distortion, and generalization:

- Deletion is the filtering of data to reduce it to levels we can handle. This, in part, explains why patients forget between 40% and 80% of medical information provided by healthcare practitioners within minutes of leaving the consultation.[125]
- Distortion is the inevitable consequence of selection. Jumping to conclusions, 'catasrophizing', 'remembering' something that wasn't actually said, are all examples of distortion.
- Generalization is an inbuilt human skill that allows us to predict events from what has gone before. However, when only one or two elements of an experience become generalized to 'all' similar events, problems can ensue. Post-Traumatic Stress Disorder (PTSD) is a generalized response to traumatic events such as childhood abuse or car accidents.

NLP's Meta Model (see *The Structure of Magic*, http://www.amazon.com/s/ref=nb_sb_noss?url=search-alias%3Daps&field-keywords=The+Structure+of+Magic) defines several distinctions within each category and provides specific tools by which deletions, distortions, and generalizations can be challenged. It is, however, useful, when gathering information, to favor questions starting with *how, where, when, with whom, how often*, etc, all of which provide grounded, fact-based data, rather than asking 'why?', which often elicits speculation, justification, and defensive behavior. We expand on the art of gathering quality data in a later chapter.

EXERCISES

Building skill sets

Work with just one component at a time; take a day or two for each. This eliminates confusion. Practice consistently in the beginning to identify, rather than act on, what you observe.

1. Listen for sensory predicates, identifying the subject's preferred mode. (Be aware that many patients may present kinesthetically, simply because they are experiencing somatic distress; their preferred modality may, in fact, be different.)
2. Watch for eye accessing cues. Calibrate eye position with the emotional content of the subject's account.
3. Elicit sub-modality distinctions of the problem states.
4. Experiment with changing them and note the effect.

Note: To avoid 'performance anxiety' with your subject and to inoculate against 'failure', use phrases such as: 'Just before we begin, let's try a little experiment', or 'I just need to find something out.' When coaching sub-modality changes, it often helps to use examples and analogies to explain the process. Referring to the controls of a TV set or sound system is one way of doing this.

7

Taming the Runaway Brain: three thinking tools

> *Between stimulus and response, there is a space. In that space lies our power to choose our response, and in our response lies growth and freedom.*—**Viktor Frankl**

Thinking is something we all do naturally, but not necessarily well. The process happens so quickly, naturally, and so far beneath our ordinary, day-to-day awareness that it seldom presents itself for scrutiny.

The human brain—the most extraordinary tool in the universe, the only one we know of that has the ability to rewire itself according to how we use it—is left largely to its own devices. 'Thinking about thinking' is something we are generally quite happy to hand over to other people to contemplate: the philosophers, neuroscientists, and psychotics.

Thinking 'just is', and for the most part we are quite content to leave it that way. Astonishingly, given the number of bad decisions our species has chalked up, education has proved of little help. We have been taught *what* to think, but *not* how to think.

Our species' ability to error-correct has not improved significantly as a result. On the other hand, thinking skillfully—that is, with system and purpose, not to be confused with formal logic—allows us to consider information we might not even have noticed before; extract order and meaning out of apparent chaos; generate theories and hypotheses; and create solutions we can then test.

The complex chronic conditions currently overwhelming the health services are deeply in need of a new reasoning approach. They are baffling, we agree. But they appear baffling not because of their intrinsic nature, but because of the way we have been looking at them.

The old folk story, attributed to Mullah Nasruddin, about five blind men, each trying to describe an elephant by feeling just one part of its body, is an apt analogy. The elephant is, variously, like a snake, a tree, a huge palm leaf, according to whichever part each man feels. Any attempt to synthesize a whole from the parts is doomed to failure, no matter how eloquently each is able to sense and describe the part he is touching.

Most of us find the story amusing because it is so patently irrational. And yet research often follows the same thinking process—that, somehow, if the object is divided into sufficiently small parts, understanding of the 'whole' will follow.

Of course, this approach has served us well in certain areas in the past. We now know a lot about how a germ can cause a particular infection, and which gene can cause a specific deformity. Our knowledge about how people become sick is vast. But, as a result, our single-minded commitment to the twin beliefs of reductionism and causality tells us virtually nothing about how some people never get sick, and others get well.

This occurs largely because of the way in which we have chosen to think about a particular problem. Another Nasruddin story perfectly illustrates this approach.

A man happened upon his friend one night on his hands and knees beneath the only streetlight in the immediate area.

'What are you doing?' he asked his friend.

The man glanced up then back down at the earth he was sifting between his fingers. 'I lost my keys,' he said. 'I've been searching for more than an hour and I still haven't found them.'

His friend was anxious to help. 'Where did you lose them?' he asked, getting down on his knees beside the seeker.

The man pointed somewhere deep in the shadows .'Over there,' he replied.

Perplexed, his friend asked, 'Then why are you looking over here?'

The man looked at him, then spoke slowly as if to an idiot. 'There's more light over here, of course,' he said.

The instant we decide to confine our attention to a specific area of inquiry, a particular set of events—the text of a story—we exclude information that may, in fact, explain the context in which that function or process occurs. To paraphrase Sir William Osler, we look at the disease the patient has, without looking at the patient who has the disease. *We are baffled at the condition we encounter because we are trying to apply a familiar and limited map to unfamiliar territory.*

On being comfortable with not-knowing

Of course, scientists are not alone in thinking this way. Ambiguity is, for most of us, an uncomfortable experience. The compulsion to avoid the discomfort of 'not-knowing' is so strong that often we will accept, without reflection, an explanation—either our own or one provided for us by some authority—that resolves our internal dissonance. This is where a thinking strategy known as 'cognitive bias' comes in. People (and health professionals are not immune) are inclined to adopt one or more ways of resolving cognitive dissonance, each involving deletion, distortion, or generalization of data…at the cost of accuracy and precision.

And yet the ability to tolerate ambiguity, at least for a time, is an essential step towards widening our perspective. Just for the moment, we need to suspend our beliefs and biases in the knowledge that this way only will permit new information to flow in. In order to break out of this particular box, we need to understand how easily our beliefs and perceptions are influenced by an ongoing interaction between the way in which our minds naturally work and the effect that unchallenged linguistic distortions (using language mindlessly) can have on our beliefs.

Consider the phrase 'medically unexplained', one of the descriptors used almost synonymously with 'functional', 'somatoform', 'psychosomatic', or 'psychogenic' disorders. On the face of it, these words, like the ubiquitous 'idiopathic', simply mean that *our current medical knowledge is not able to account for the condition under consideration.*

They do not mean—as is so often assumed by default—that the condition is imaginary or intended to deceive or manipulate. Although most practitioners will deny drawing these conclusions, it happens more frequently than we would like—especially when the health professional is under pressure.

Here are three examples of phrases we have encountered in physicians' letters of referral for patients suffering from what is usually called 'myofascial' or 'fibromyalgic' pain syndromes:

> *'Physical basis for the pain has been conclusively ruled out by all tests…A psychiatric assessment has diagnosed somatoform pain disorder.'*

> *'I suspect the patient has a hidden agenda, since I have determined that there is nothing physically wrong with him.'*

> *'The patient's over-reaction during examination leads me to believe his problem is either hypochondriasis or malingering.'*

Our argument here is not with whether the patient was or was not 'making it up', but with the cognitive mechanism employed by the attending physician in reaching his conclusion. The reasoning is as follows: *All real pain has a physical cause. Therefore, if no physical cause is found, the pain cannot be real.*

This reasoning process, known as syllogistic, is perfectly logical—but only within its own limited framework. If the propositions are correct, then the conclusion is correct. If the propositions are questionable, as in the example above, we—and the patient—are in trouble. The flaws in the reasoning include the facts that only pain with a physical cause is 'real' and that there is no physical cause, simply because one has not been identified.

The speed with which many people draw conclusions and make decisions tends to trick them into believing they are 'right'. If questioned, they insist (and feel) that they have selected this response from a range of possibilities, all duly subjected to full assessment.

A number of researchers, including Benjamin Libet[126] and Daniel Wegner,[127] have demonstrated that a series of complicated mental and physical processes takes place some considerable time before you 'choose' to act in a particular way. Libet and Wegner found there was a gap of somewhere between a third and a half of a second before conscious awareness crept in. A later study, published in the journal *Nature Neuroscience*, suggested the outcome of a decision could be encoded in the brain activity of the prefrontal and parietal cortex by as much as 10 seconds before it entered conscious awareness.[128]

Conscious thought, therefore, *follows* a psychophysiological decision to act, rather than the other way around.

This 'illusion' is so compelling that people tend to defend vigorously their intention to act, even where intentionality can be disproved.

One thing we can be sure of: the mind does not rigorously question the sense or logic of each chunk of information it receives.

The sheer amount of data available to our senses would be overwhelming if we had to weigh up each incoming bit. The brain copes by streamlining. Information is chunked and processed according to general patterns; it responds to situations that resemble previous situations it has encountered, calling on the same feelings and responses as before. Top-down processing collides with bottom-up processing.

Inevitably, as it acquires more 'similar' experiences, these patterns coalesce into biases, mindsets, and, if the owner of the brain fails to remain alert, stereotypes.

A number of other factors can dissuade us from freeing up our thinking and reasoning processes. Four of these are as follows:

1. **Fear**. The fear of making the 'wrong' decision is a major concern within the health professions, and not only because of the risks to the patient's health and wellbeing. Litigation is increasing, forcing practitioners into an increasingly more defensive position. This results in an overdependence on referrals to specialists, multiple tests and opinions, invasive scans and surgery, and over-medication.
2. **Pressure**. As stress mounts, the tendency to revert to familiar coping patterns also increases. Complex and manifold problems encountered in unfavorable circumstances are likely to trigger limbic arousal. Constraints of time increase pressure. And so does a sense that the practitioner does not have the resources to help the person seeking his knowledge and expertise.

3. **Peer acceptance.** Doing something differently from your peers or superiors is a risky business. Or at least it feels risky. If you depart from the 'norm', you will tend to be concerned that someone will challenge you and, by doing so, 'prove' that your approach is inferior or wrong. Despite many organizations' claim that they encourage 'proactivity' and 'individuality', disturbing the status quo is often penalized, implicitly, if not directly.
4. **External demands.** An essentially market-driven model of health delivery as exists in the United States is rapidly being imposed in the United Kingdom and elsewhere in the world. This depends on external measures of 'effectiveness': audits, targets, and guidelines, established, at least partly, on the basis of cost-effectiveness. Meeting targets, then, can easily become an easier option than meeting patient needs.

Any of these constraints can trigger cognitive bias in the unwary health professional. And cognitive bias comes in many elusive forms. Some of these include:

Anchoring bias. Locking on to salient features in a patient's initial presentation too early in the diagnostic process and failing to adjust in light of later information.

Availability bias. Judging things as being more likely if they readily come to mind; for example, a recent experience with a disease may increase the likelihood of it being diagnosed.

Confirmation bias. Looking for evidence to support a diagnosis rather than looking for evidence that might rebut it.

Diagnosis momentum. Allowing a diagnosis label that has been attached to a patient, even if only as a possibility, to gather steam so that other possibilities are wrongly excluded.

Overconfidence bias. Believing we know more than we do, and acting on incomplete information, intuitions, and hunches.

Premature closure. Accepting a diagnosis before it has been fully verified.

Search-satisfying bias. Calling off a search once something is found.[129]

Beyond bias

There are many highly effective means of developing rational thinking processes, but we believe the three tools we outline below are among the most easily understood and applied. The underlying intention of these is to make distinctions between fact and belief, to reduce errors that occur when we confuse one with the other, and to begin to explore some of the mechanisms that set up and maintain the patient's problem. One side-effect of exploring these thinking tools is becoming increasingly mindful of the space, however small, between stimulus and response. As therapist and holocaust-survivor Viktor Frankl observed, in that space lies growth and freedom.

Thinking Tool 1: The Fact-Evaluation Spectrum

Irrefutable 'facts'—especially if you're a quantum physicist or a politician—are pretty hard to come by. Much of what most people regard as 'true' or 'objective' depends on evaluating the evidence on which they choose to place their attention.

Psychologists, such as Edmund Bolles, now recognize that 'paying attention' requires us actively to choose information from a confused buzz of sensations and details to which we then ascribe 'meaning'.[130] This is what we call 'evaluation'.

But, the process of evaluation includes two other mental actions. In creating 'meaning' out of whatever you place your attention on, you also *exclude* certain information from what is available, and you *supplement* what is in front of you with what has gone before.

Far from functioning as objective beings, systematically uncovering absolute truth, even the most scientific humans are architects and builders constructing meaning according to blueprints, some of which they inherit with their jobs, most of which exist and function well below their conscious awareness.

The labels that are then selected to apply to that which has been attended to are quick to develop a life of their own. As we have discussed above, the word becomes the 'thing', and it is easy to forget that someone (yourself, or a 'significant other') created that part of your cognitive map by a process of evaluation. It is now 'true'.

The Fact-Evaluation Spectrum is a tool designed to help you develop the ability to distinguish between verifiable data (fact) and belief, speculation, judgment, opinion, evaluation, etc. In doing this, we reduce our tendency towards premature cognitive closure (making your mind up before all the evidence has been acquired), and acting 'as if' the individual in front of you is physically, psychologically, socially, and spiritually identical to everyone else who matches some or all of the criteria of a particular class or 'condition'.

We do not pretend to know what an incontrovertible fact is (we're not priests or politicians); the guidelines in this section are intended more to caution against mindlessly applying beliefs, judgments, inferences, opinions, etc, as 'true' simply because we believe, or have been told, that they are true.

Belief is a major trap in clear thinking. It is important to understand that a belief differs from a fact, however dearly held. The distinction needs to be made. People often argue as to whether a belief is 'true' or 'false', whereas it might be more productive simply to decide whether it is 'useful' or not. (Inevitably, the issue of religious belief is raised here. Our response is simply this: if your religious beliefs support the health and wellbeing of yourself and others, they are 'useful'. If not, they are not.)

Many of the descriptions we use in day-to-day practice may help us communicate to fellow professionals with some degree of consensuality; however, we need also to be cautious as to how they can (often unconsciously) inform and influence our beliefs and responses.

'Functional', the description of a very large class of complex chronic conditions without specific cause, is such a word. And the word itself often stands in the way of understanding and assisting the patient to restructure his experience.

Definitions vary from source to source, but only slightly. Ideally, a functional disorder is one in which no evidence of organic damage or disturbance may be found, but which nevertheless affects the patient's physical and emotional wellbeing. However, increasingly, the word is taken to suggest the presence of 'psychiatric' elements (see the *Oxford Concise Medical Dictionary*, as an example). Sadly, the belief (that if the cause of a condition cannot be established it can't be 'real') permeates everyday medical care. To the patient, there is a strong element of blaming and shaming, which, given our earlier investigation of the impact of stress on health, is hardly likely to help.

In a bid to minimize this kind of toxic labeling, our first 'thinking tool', therefore, is based on learning to recognize and distinguish between facts and evaluations (inferences, assumptions, judgments, and opinions). Simply put, 'fact', as we use the word from now on, refers to sensory-based information—that is whatever you (or the patient) can see, hear, touch, taste, and smell. As far as possible, these data should be free of value-judgment or interpretation.They should not be evaluated. A group of independent bystanders would, in the main, agree with your observations.

Examples of facts:

The man is sitting, slumped in his chair, head down, looking at the floor.
The woman sits with her arms wrapped around her body.
The child doesn't make eye contact when he says he didn't take the cookie.

Most observers would agree with these descriptions.

Examples of beliefs:

The man is depressed (whereas he might simply be absorbed by his problem or pain).
The woman is insecure or defensive (whereas she might be cold, or sensitive about her 'muffin top').
The child is lying (whereas he might be afraid he will be wrongly blamed yet again).

These are all evaluations we may believe to be true, but have no way of verifying without further information.

Especially where patients' subjective (internal) experience is concerned, we seek to elicit sensory-specific, factual information. By this, we mean how the patient experiences his condition (what he sees, hears, feels, smells, and tastes), rather than the inferences he makes from that experience.

For example:

Patient: '*I feel very depressed. It's just awful. I feel really terrible.*' (All the information here is inferential. The patient responds 'as if' this is the 'true' nature of his experience.)

Practitioner: *'How do you know? What specifically happens that lets you know this?'*

Patient: *'I wake up every morning with a gray cloud over my head and it's just like…Oh, you're never going to get any better, and it's like a lead weight on my chest…'*

This kind of information is separated out from inferences, judgments, and beliefs. It describes the process of his experience using sensory-based information.

Patient: '…*I wake up every morning with a gray cloud*' (visual) *'over my head and it's just like…Oh, you're never going to get any better'* (auditory), *'and it's like a lead weight on my chest'* (kinesthetic)…

As we report at various points in this book, sensory-based, factual information gives us something specific to work with. We can begin to change the experience by changing how the patient structures the experience, rather than being caught up in the 'contents' or story of the experience itself.

Thinking Tool 2: The Structural Differential

In the years following World War 1, Alfred Korzybski, a Polish nobleman and polymath, was puzzled how a species, already so advanced, could have plunged so deeply into chaos. With remarkable prescience, he formulated his ideas of the relationship of language with neurological function into a field he called General Semantics. (General Semantics should not be confused with semantics. The latter is concerned with the 'meaning' of words. Korzybski intended General Semantics to focus primarily on the process of 'abstraction' and its effect on thinking.)

Language, he said, emerged as a 'higher-order' abstraction from certain neurological 'events'. Put another way, 'something' happens in the subject's neurology, a perturbation or **Event**, which exists formlessly and silently. This is also known as 'process'.

The subject then becomes aware of some 'difference' occurring. Korzybski called this the **Object**, since it had characteristics (sub-modalities), but, like the **Event**, no words have yet been attached to it. Both **Event** and **Object** are on a 'silent' or pre-linguistic level.

The subject's **Description** follows his experience. For the first time, words are involved and, of necessity, the words can only partially represent the experience itself. Then, based on the subject's description, comes Inference 1—an *evaluation* about what this 'means'. Following that is an inference about the first inference—Inference 2 , followed by an inference about that inference, Inference 3, and so on, potentially to infinity (or, as Korzybski put it, 'etc').

The language used to describe and infer from the silent level of subjective experience may be regarded as 'story' or 'content'. Since each level can feed back to the level(s) above it, **Inferences** can affect the original **Event**, regulating it either upwards or downwards, changing the subject's experience of the **Object**. Thus 'story' is required to establish and maintain ongoing subjective experience, making it better or worse. Or, to put it another way, without story, structure cannot be easily maintained.

Korzybski represented this with a three-dimensional model of what he called the Structural Differential. **Figure 7.1** is a two-dimensional representation of the process as applied to the medical or psychiatric investigation.

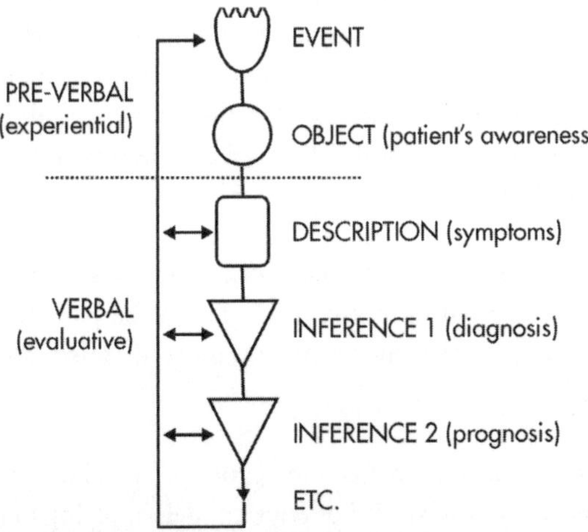

Figure 7.1 The Structural Differential as applied to the medical investigation. Note that everything that is verbalized is evaluative, not 'factual' (Adapted with permission of the Institute of General Semantics.)

In practice, we can use the Structural Differential to map a patient's experience in the following way:

> Some disturbance occurs within the patient's neurology that affects complex homeostasis, and compromises allostasis (for the sake of illustration, let's say he suffers confusion and anxiety when he tries to understand written information). We may never know everything about what causes the disturbance or how it occurs (Event level). Broadly speaking, the Event level is the territory of neuroscience, and its companion fields of psychopharmacology and psychoneuroimmunology (PNI).
>
> The patient becomes aware of a 'problem' (Object level), and then goes on to try to describe it (Descriptive level). Based on the description, the 'expert' creates the first Inference (Inference 1), also known as 'diagnosis'; the patient has 'dyslexia'.
>
> Further Inferences follow, both from the patient and from those around him (Inference 2, Inference 3, etc). These might include: 'He has a learning disability'; 'I am stupid because I have a disability'; 'His feelings about having a disability are making him anxious'; 'He needs treatment for his anxiety about his feelings about having a disability'... etc. Diagnoses of 'co-morbidity' (two or more co-existing medical conditions or disease processes that are additional to an initial diagnosis) often add to the problems at this point, all related to inferential thinking.
>
> Any, or all, of these Inferences can loop back and intensify the experience of 'confusion' that first alerted the patient to an Event. Thus, he may become more anxious, more 'disabled', and even more confused.

Differences in treatments and schools of psychology develop when various theorists observe and develop models applying to different levels of Inference. One might try to curb the anxiety with medication, another might try to alter the subject's 'negative self-talk', yet another might try to retrain the way he moves his eyes when he reads.

From this, it can easily be seen that all diagnoses are Inferences based on abstracted information, and all Inferences (including prognoses and treatment modalities) depend on the quality of the Inferences that precede it. Therefore, the diagnosis (Inference) is not the disease (Event), but only the currently accepted label for a collection of descriptions (symptoms). And these (the Inferences) will change. Indeed, they are changing all the time.

The fact that medical scientists and many physicians accept so readily the 'evidence' presented to them (sometimes by spurious organizations with clearly evident self-interests) has much to do with human beings' hard-wired tendency to seek patterns out of the chaotic data that make up 'reality'. This drive often leads people to detect patterns where 'noise' might predominate. Think for a moment of the face of Jesus manifesting on a badly toasted tortilla, or rising damp on a basement wall. Once 'detected', a pattern is difficult to ignore, even though it might exist entirely in the eyes of the beholder.

In this way, it can be claimed that medical science creates and cures diseases by the inferences it makes and the patterns the ruling authorities decide are 'true'.

Let's look at some examples, starting with the diagnosis of diabetes:

> The World Health Organization's diagnostic criteria for diabetes were defined in the late 1970s, then revised four more times until 1989.
>
> Then in 2011 WHO issued further guidelines for diagnosis using new units entirely and recommended an HbA1c level of 6.5% (48 mmol/mol) as the cut-off for diagnosis of diabetes. The HbA1c measurement, having some clear advantages over fasting glucose, can itself be influenced by a variety of common co-morbidities such as anemia, liver or kidney impairment and genetic defects, known as haemoglobinopathies.

However, even allowing for artefacts in the measuring process, this new classification may still be inadequate.

The *British Medical Journal* reported that diagnoses could be erroneous in up to 15% of cases and suggested additional classifications of diabetes. Classifications of diabetes should now include Genetic Diabetes (such as MODY or Maturity Onset Diabetes of the Young), Secondary

Diabetes, Non-Diabetic Hyperglycemia, and even Unclassified Diabetes (insufficient information to fit one of the other categories). This is in addition to the traditional Type I and II diagnoses.[131]

Meanwhile, in practice, this diagnostic dithering over labeling has had adverse consequences for our patients. For example, over the years, many patients had been told they had normal blood glucose when in fact they were actually diabetic whilst many patients with MODY had been erroneously treated with insulin.

Since the first edition of this book, and possibly to avoid further diagnostic errors, medical authorities in the West have introduced a new condition called 'pre-diabetes'. This is a gray area between normal blood sugar and diabetic levels—in other words, some, but not all, of the diagnostic criteria for diabetes have been identified.[132]

But, is it a disease? Decide for yourself.

Some other examples:

> The diagnostic descriptions of 'acute coronary syndrome', 'social phobia', and 'restless legs' did not exist as separate entities with those labels until relatively recently...with the very active participation of the pharmaceutical companies, all happy to provide medication for new 'conditions'.

> A transient ischemic attack (TIA) is diagnosed if symptoms last less than 24 hours. If the symptoms last 24 hours and one minute it becomes a 'stroke'. The disease process is the same.

Many diseases are notoriously difficult for clinicians to assign diagnostic labels to—and yet this labeling process remains a cornerstone of current orthodox medical practice. As suggested above, when prime cause cannot be established, the most proximal cause is often selected, or a new condition may be created. But the further away from the Event and Object levels that the Inferences move, the greater the potential for confusion.

Also, confusing levels of abstraction with each other (for example, treating an *inference* as an explanation, or even a cause) can lead to the pathologizing of body-mind events that may fall within the range of 'normal' experience and encourages excessive medical and surgical intervention, yet can leave both patient and practitioner still at a loss as to how to relieve the suffering. (We note here that many of the 'symptoms' experienced by a patient diagnosed with transient ischemic attack are identical to those experienced by people in deep meditation or undergoing 'religious experiences'. In one culture this is a highly desirable occurrence, in another a suitable cause for alarm.)

Reference to the Structural Differential allows the practitioner to identify Inferences at various levels of abstraction (both his own and those of the patient), and to plan his response accordingly. It is an especially valuable tool to eliminate confusion caused by interpreting an Inference about the problem as a cause.

Thinking Tool 3: Function Analysis

In the corporate world, function analysis is designed to measure the cost and benefit of introducing a new product or system against the cost and benefit of keeping the old. Whether or not we are consciously aware of it, we apply function analysis to almost every new decision we make, from buying a new sound system to which medication might be best for a particular patient.

Problems arise when function analysis has been conducted 'intuitively' or derives from criteria we have inherited and accepted, without examination, from others.

In the Medical NLP model of whole-person healthcare, we aim to recognize and respond to the psychosocial components of complex chronic conditions and to accord them the same significance as biomechanical signs and symptoms. We want to understand context (the landscape in which the problem occurs) as much as text (the details of the problem itself). We seek answers to questions such as: 'What is the value, need, or purpose of the old condition/behavior to the patient?'; 'How can those values, needs or purposes be met by another behavior or response that is more useful or appropriate?'; 'What are the costs of making a change balanced against the costs of staying the way he is—and, is he prepared to meet those costs?'

And, by 'cost', of course, we mean the price paid or value expressed in emotional, social, spiritual, and behavioral terms. Is it worth it to the patient to make the change? Function analysis helps us move to a higher order of investigation—looking for patterns that may explain the condition's resistance to treatment.

Supposing we are considering the possibility that a patient feels deficient in social support and connectedness. In applying function analysis to the presenting condition, we will be considering if and how the condition is related to that specific emotional shortfall.

For example:

> ***Case history:*** *A single, middle-aged woman developed multiple chemical sensitivities after her neighbor sprayed his garden (and, inadvertently, hers) with an illegal toxic herbicide. She confronted him and reported that he was rude and unrepentant. The allergic response developed soon after the confrontation and spread rapidly to include a wide range of allergens, including house paint, cigarette smoke, perfume and aftershave, and exhaust fumes. (Note: This is 'text'.)*
>
> *In conversation, it emerged that the woman felt lonely and uncared for. She spoke several times about her father, whom she considered cold and uncaring; she became agitated and apparently angry when talking about him. (We noticed that her breathing became raspy and constricted and her eyes watered whenever the subject came up, typical of an allergic response.) The only time he showed any consideration for her was when she was confined to her bed with an 'attack', even though she suspected he thought she was malingering. (This is 'context'. It also reflects the process of abstraction and evaluation taking place inside her model of the world.)*
>
> *She also reported being immensely angry at her neighbor, and had abandoned conventional treatment, explaining that both her neighbor and doctors in general were 'paternalistic' and uninterested in the welfare of others... 'just like my father'.*

At that point, the practitioner's focus shifted to: (1) the possible purpose or intention of her symptoms, (2) whether these needs were being met, and (3) whether it would be possible to find ways of meeting these needs in ways that would make 'being sick' no longer necessary.

From the information elicited, the practitioner constructed several hypotheses for later testing. These included the possibility that she needed: to expand her social connectedness (in this case, by reactivating supportive friendships she had allowed to lapse); to resolve or come to terms with her anger towards her father; to explore whether her neighbor's indifferent attitude was functioning as a subliminal reminder of her father's emotional unavailability; and that she needed to be ill to get the love and attention she needed, etc.

(Interestingly, when we sent her out, after ensuring there was no risk of anaphylactic shock, into a place where people were smoking, with the instruction to 'make the symptom appear', nothing happened. That was the first step in her beginning to understand that she was not completely at the mercy of her condition.)

Our intention was not to impose these theories on the patient, but to seek an 'entry point' in the behavioral loop, set up initially as a protective mechanism, with the intention of helping her to change. At best, we make cautious suggestions. More often, though, the patient notices patterns and connections himself. This is therapeutic gold. But, as with all other cases, change would not have been possible for this patient unless her unmet needs were addressed and the entire 'system' in which she functioned was effectively balanced. Please note that *at no time did we suggest (or even consider) that her responses were 'not real'; they were.* Nor was there any attempt to 'explore' her relationship with her father, or reactivate past pain and disappointment.

The purpose of function analysis, then, is to acquire 'higher-order' information (about how something happens). With this and the other principles and tools already discussed, the Engagement phase of the consultation can begin.

EXERCISES

1. We recommend that you practice the three thinking tools so they can operate in the background of your experience. They are not intended to dominate your attention. As you become more familiar with the processes, you will find it progressively easier to apply them naturally and conversationally.

The Fact-Evaluation Spectrum
Establish whether statements (including your own) are factual or evaluative. Make a mental note whenever a fact checks out as well grounded and sensory-specific. Likewise, notice how easily evaluation creeps in. Test for these by asking questions such as, 'How do you/I know?', 'What is the (sensory) evidence?'

The Structural Differential
Practice locating statements along the Structural Differential. How much, if any, of the patient's description is in fact evaluative? Are the Inferences you detect first-level evaluations, or are they evaluations of the evaluation(s) before it?

Function Analysis
As you listen to the patient, keep in mind the higher order questions, such as, 'What purpose could this symptom/ behavior serve?', 'How does it work?', etc.

2. Review one or more decisions you made in the past and which you now regret. As you do so, notice what diverted your attention from the 'space' to which Viktor Frankl refers. Write down a few thoughts about how things could have worked out differently and better had you become aware of the space in time to avoid a knee-jerk response. (This is not an invitation to beat yourself up over what you 'should have' or 'would have' done. We are simply suggesting you become aware that the space existed—and that it exists at almost any point where you choose to pause and just notice 'what is' rather than 'what should be'.)

Phase 1: Engagement

8

The Rules of Engagement: managing first impressions

Early impressions are hard to eradicate from the mind. When once wool has been dyed purple, who can restore it to its previous whiteness?— ***Saint Jérôme***

The first 30 seconds can be critical to the success or failure of any consultation. Research and experience lead us to the incontrovertible conclusion that people make up their minds almost instantaneously. Reasoning comes later—and that may be too late.

The instant your patient lays eyes on you, he has already begun to form an opinion, assembled unconsciously and at near-light speed, from the way you are dressed, your posture, facial expression, eye contact, and body movements. Within the first few words you speak, the impression is all but fixed.

The phenomenon, extensively studied by psychologists as 'thin slicing'[133] and introduced to the general public by science and psychology writer Malcolm Gladwell in his highly readable book, *Blink*, is familiar to everyone in both social and professional settings. How many times have you taken an instant liking to someone you met at a party? Within minutes, you felt as if you'd known them 'forever'. How many times have you 'just known' something was wrong with the person on the other end of a telephone conversation, even though nothing specific was said?

Aside from the spoken word, people leak information at every turn.

This includes eye movements; facial expression; physiology; gestures; tics and mannerisms; vocal qualities; breathing patterns; changes in skin color and muscle tone. Most of this is absorbed below the threshold of consciousness, but it *is absorbed.* And, once absorbed, it acquires meaning through some of the processes we will discuss below.

The speed with which information is transmitted and received is staggering. Paul Ekman has identified micro-expressions of emotions, such as anger, fear, disgust, happiness, and sadness, lasting as little as 1/500th of a second and shared by cultures throughout the world.[134]

Harvard University's Nalini Ambady and fellow experimental psychologist Robert Rosenthal have demonstrated that 30-second snatches of soundless videos of lectures are all observers needed accurately to predict the qualities of teaching as measured over an entire semester.[135]

The key to concordance and adherence

Awareness that these processes are at work and understanding how to engage with patients at the most productive level can give rise to a set of skills that allows the practitioner to achieve maximum engagement with the patient. This, in turn, improves both concordance between patient and practitioner and adherence to treatment plans, while avoiding, as far as possible, accidental and damaging disconnects.

Lack of warmth and friendliness has been found to be one of the most significant variables adversely affecting patient satisfaction and concordance. Many busy practitioners underestimate how much their attention shifts from the patient to other concerns (computer screens, notes, calls, etc), and overestimate the time they give to listening, eliciting unexpressed concerns, and giving information.[136]

In order to get the feeling for this, imagine for a moment that you are a patient visiting a doctor you have never met before. As you enter the examination room, she is tapping at the keyboard on her desk, eyes fixed on the screen. Without looking up from your electronic records, she says,

'What's the problem?'

'Well, doctor, I have this headache and it's worrying me because—'

'When did it start?' The doctor pauses, fingers hovering above the keyboard, still not looking up.

'About three weeks ago, but—'

'Whereabouts in your head is it?'

'Well, it's actually more a kind of pressure at the back. I'm worried about—'

'Is the pain sharp or dull?'

'Um—like I said, it's more a kind of...pressure, but I think it's—'

And, so it goes.

For you, as the patient, a number of things are happening, aside from your symptoms and any frustration, confusion or irritation you may be feeling at the repeated interruptions.

The first is a 'gut feeling' that something is not right. At this stage (and, had you been alert enough, you might unconsciously have noticed it the instant the physician failed to look at you when you entered his space), you will not have attached any words to the experience. In Korzybski's model, it occurs at the Object level—a kinesthetic internal experience that has qualities, such as heat, weight, movement, and intensity. It is highly unlikely that it will feel good.

In NLP terminology, this is an 'internal kinesthetic'. Neuroscientist Antonio Damasio calls it a 'somatic marker', and he believes that it is a learned response that serves as an automated alarm, a psychophysical signal communicating either 'Danger!' or 'Go for it!'[137]

Somatic markers are 'paired' experiences, he adds. In other words, we learned to feel one way if Dad never praised us for our accomplishments, or another way if Mom gave us a particularly sunny smile every time she saw us. As we navigate through life, we link various experiences, or 'states', into groups or chains according to the characteristics they share. Each of these is experienced as a distinctive kinesthetic or somatic marker. And each of these markers, in turn, may be triggered at any later stage by a word, a look, a tone of voice—any stimulus, in fact, that is a broad pattern-match to the one that set up the original response.

The stimulus may occur unexpectedly, and at any time, long after the original experience has been forgotten. Only later (often much later, and sometimes in front of a lawyer) does cognition kick in and we try to explain the reasons for feeling the way we did. 'She just didn't seem to care'; 'She was too busy to listen'; 'I tried to tell her my sister had died but she kept cutting me off'. (Some lawyers are extremely skilled at helping clients 'translate' these somatic markers into the language of litigation—so be warned.)[138]

This automated stimulus-response is known in NLP as an 'anchor', and it is impossible to know how many have been set up over the years. It follows, then, that we need to do whatever we can in order to minimize adverse responses in the people we hope to help. Entirely avoiding responses that bubble up from the patient's hidden past may be an impossible task. However, the *probability* of a mutually rewarding consultation is significantly increased if three propositions are borne in mind:

1. Patients expect 'carers' to show that they actually care, by their warmth, interest and focused attention;
2. Helping patients *feel* better is an important factor in helping them *get* better; and
3. Patients tend to be reluctant to act punitively against practitioners they like, even when a professional error has occurred.[139]

Our contention—and the balance of research that we present in this book—is that a major part of effective consultation is a mutually respectful emotional and working relationship between patient and practitioner, and that, once set up, is maintained and measured through the medium of communication. What follows from this point on, then, is a collection of principles and techniques modeled from particularly effective communicators, reinforced by research projects, and verified by patients satisfied with the healthcare they have received.

We have also gleaned useful nuggets from less orthodox sources, including: information technology; Game Theory; Contingency Planning; successful business consultants; effective salespeople; presenters; observations made by us or our colleagues; personal experience; and, common (Korzybski would say 'un-common') sense.

Together, these form the basis of the Engagement phase of the three-part Medical NLP Consultation Process. Integrating them into your normal consultation style takes little or no extra time and increases your sense of control in potentially problematical or challenging situations.

Your appearance

Appearance is a significant factor in creating good first impressions. Although the results of studies on physician attire are inconclusive regarding the white coat versus no white coat debate, communication experts agree that patients expect health professionals to be well dressed and smartly groomed. The consensus is well-fitting suits, plain shirts and ties for men, neat suits or jacket and skirts for women. Both sexes should avoid overly strident patterns or colors, excessive jewelry, and unpolished shoes. Many patients react particularly adversely to extravagant hair styles or overly trendy cuts.

Your voice

Most of us take the voices we were 'born with' for granted—until we hear ourselves for the first time in a recording. Even that is often not enough to prod us into taking charge of one of our most fundamental tools of communication. Well, consider this: within less than a minute, your voice can reveal your height, weight, build, gender,[140] age, occupation,[141] and even your sexual orientation,[142] sight unseen.

As sociologist Anne Karpf comments in her book, *The Human Voice,* we are doing something 'terrifyingly intimate' every time we speak, even if all we're doing is to read out a list of rules and regulation about waste disposal.[143] Such a powerful tool needs to be cared for and protected if it is to do its job effectively.

If you are unsatisfied with the quality of your speech and are unable to correct it by applying some of the suggestions below, we urge you to consult a qualified professional to improve your presentation and to prevent damage to your vocal chords. Vocal coach and therapist Janet Edwards identifies two factors particularly damaging to the voice: inadequate breathing and dehydration.

'If you don't breathe into your abdomen, your voice has no support and lacks power,' she says. 'This is also a great drain on energy.' She also suggests a minimum of two to three pints of water ('not soft drinks, tea, or coffee') sipped over a day to ensure adequate hydration.

Another recommendation often given to professionals who use their voices over sustained periods is to locate their unique 'key'. Broadly speaking, key refers to the most comfortable series of notes you can produce while still retaining a wide range of 'highs' and 'lows'. By identifying the key of your speaking voice—which changes from day to day according to energy levels, the amount of talking you do, your physical and emotional state at the time—you can inject variation into your speech and sustain interest while avoiding strain.

Setting your key

We suggest one of the following ways to 'set' your key before starting any sustained period of speaking. The first is to sing (probably best when no-one else is around to witness your efforts) the lowest note you can produce. Then, sing five notes up the scale ('soh' on the doh-re-mi scale). This is the mid-point of your range, giving you flexibility to move up and down while still retaining a 'natural' sound.

If you prefer not to sing, or are not familiar with the notes of the musical scale, take a deep breath, imagine you are sitting down after a long and tiring period on your feet, and make that 'comfort sound' we all know so well—*hunh*! The *hunh* sound is the mid-point of your current vocal range.

Vocal qualities of excellent communicators

Communicating with purpose requires an understanding of how the 'shape' and rhythm of language can affect the listener as much as the words that are used.

As a general rule, only questions should inflect *upwards* (the voice going up at the end of the sentence), whereas neutral statements tend to be *uninflected*, and commands, orders or important information are all *downwardly inflected* (the voice going down at the end of the sentence).

Some nationalities (Australian and Welsh in particular) have a tendency to inflect upwards whether or not a question is being asked. Women in the West sometimes follow the same pattern in the belief that it is a friendlier, more empathetic approach. However, this may sometimes be interpreted as a lack of certainty.

Credible or approachable

Effective communicators and presenters tend to share two qualities—credibility and approachability—both of which have distinctive vocal patterns (see **Figure 8.1**). It is important to distinguish between the two styles, and to know when to apply them.

Approachability (often associated with 'friendliness' and 'likeability') is an aid to gaining rapport, gathering information, and encouraging disclosure. It is marked by variability in pitch, tone, and rate of speech (what Edwards calls 'color'). The voice is animated, rising and falling naturally. Laughing and joking (if appropriate) and moving or gesturing while talking are also permissible in the approachable phase.

Setting your 'key', as mentioned above, helps facilitate the vocal flexibility that characterizes approachability.

Approachability alone, however, may be counter-productive when important information or instructions need to be given. Patients may like an approachable practitioner, but will not necessarily accept his advice as authoritative. This is where 'credibility' will improve concordance and adherence.

Credibility (being authoritative but not overbearing) serves analogically to 'mark out' the importance of a statement from the general 'noise' of conversational exchanges. This alerts the patient, consciously and unconsciously, to pay particular attention to what is being said, while also helping to increase memory and adherence.

Credibility and authority are dependent not on volume, but on vocal style. When striving to be credible, your voice should be less varied, and your movements and gestures more restrained. Information and instructions are delivered with a downward inflection at the end of a sentence. Eye contact should be steady throughout the statement, without being intimidating.

	Purpose	*Tone*	*Pitch*	*Eye contact*	*Physical movement*
Approachable	Rapport Concordance Information	Variable	Variable	Variable	Some
Credible	Instructions Advice Adherence	Monotone	Drop at end of sentence	Fixed	Restrained

Figure 8.1 The vocal patterns of approachability and credibility

Accounting for gender differences

Both men and women may initially find it challenging to allow their voices to move up or down into registers they do not normally use. This is a common response, but one that usually disappears with practice.

It is also important to note that in British and American cultures, the 'meaning' of head-nodding can differ between the sexes. To generalize, men tend to nod when they agree with a statement, while women often nod to show they are listening. There is potential for confusion in both personal and professional settings ('But the doctor thought it was okay for me to keep drinking'; 'But you agreed when I said I wanted to play golf on Saturday instead of visiting your mother'). We suggest, therefore, that, as far as possible, both male and female practitioners inhibit nodding and affirmative phrases unless they intend to confirm or reinforce a statement or opinion.

Using the first 30 seconds

In a time-starved working world, you can carve out 30 vital seconds simply by getting up and going to fetch your patient (supposing that he or she is ambulatory, and that you are, too).

During the walk back to your office, you can lock in two essential requirements for effective communication: rapport and concordance. Much is made of 'rapport' in communication courses and NLP texts and trainings, and the usual means of accomplishing it is 'mirroring'—reflecting the subject's physical postures and movements. This kind of phase-locked 'dance' can be seen anywhere two people are in close accord. Watch out in restaurants and public places for those couples who unconsciously reflect each other's moves: one picks up a drink, the other follows; one sits forward and folds his or her arms, the other follows.

We have some reservations about this single-technique approach to rapport-building. First, it takes considerable practice to lock in to another person, and the risk of detection is always present. Second, it takes time to achieve that level of mirroring, and, time, as we have agreed, is in short supply. Third, our suspicion is that 'phase-locking' can be the *result*, rather than the cause, of two people gaining rapport. And, fourth, according to psychologist James Pennebaker, author of *The Secret Life of Pronouns*, this kind of mirroring may mean nothing other than the people concerned are focusing on each other, not necessarily that they are in accord.[144]

The following method is easy and almost instantaneous, and has proved successful with hundreds of practitioners incorporating it into the 'meet-and-greet' phase of the consultation. Four steps, performed almost simultaneously, are involved.

Achieving rapid rapport

1. Smile—a full-face, not a 'social', smile. Get into the habit of smiling with your eyes as well as your mouth. This so-called 'Duchenne smile', named after Guillaume Duchenne, a 19th-century student of the physiology of facial expressions, involves contraction of both the *zygomatic* major muscle (which raises the corners of the mouth) and the *orbicularis oculi* muscle, which raises the cheeks and forms crow's feet around the eyes.
2. Look directly into the patient's eyes, mentally noting her eye color. In contrast to the quick glance skating across the subject's face, this creates the effect of being fully 'looked at' and 'seen'.
3. Silently project a 'message' of goodwill or well-wishing towards the patient. If you are good at mental imagery, you can create an internal representation of the patient looking healthy, happy, and satisfied. The effect of this is subtly to alter your facial expression to suggest interest, involvement, and positive concern.
4. If, culturally and/or physically appropriate, shake hands. Frank

> Bernieri, chair of the psychology department at Oregon State University and an expert in non-verbal communication, believes a good handshake is 'critically important' to first impressions. Strength is unimportant, he says, but 'web-to-web' contact and alignment of the hands is. Make sure the web of skin between your thumb and forefinger engages the web between the thumb and forefinger of the person whose hand you are shaking.

Handshakes should be avoided if:

- you know or suspect cultural differences: when in doubt, don't;
- the patient is very frail or in pain; the reasons for this are self-evident; or
- the patient is markedly distressed. The risk of linking a psychophysiological state to a touch (kinesthetic anchoring) is ever-present, and it is sensible to avoid the risk of associating your touch to another's distress, especially as you may have to conduct an examination later.

Other caveats include the following: do not present your hand with the back facing upwards (signaling dominance) or downwards (signaling submission) and do not touch the patient's forearm, upper arm, or shoulder with your free hand while shaking hands at first encounter. This is sometimes interpreted as patronizing or manipulative if occurring in the opening stage of a meeting.

Achieving concordance

The following four-part approach is derived from the field of social psychology and the work of Milton Erickson, whose expertise in gaining concordance with his patients was unparalleled. Erickson's language patterns, known in NLP as the Milton Model, were elegant, persuasive, and respectful of his subject's needs. Since his medium was hypnosis, and 'hypnotizability' may be equated with a willingness to follow instructions, his methods were also designed systematically to predispose the subject towards a cooperative mindset.

Yes-sets and negative frames

Erickson knew from long experience that the more agreement he could extract from the patient, the more acquiescent the patient would become. Truisms—statements that cannot be denied—were his vehicle of preference. The process of asking questions that can only be answered affirmatively are known as yes-sets, and three seems to be the magic number. Yes-sets are bundled as conversation or 'small talk'—for example:

> *'So you managed to get an appointment today?'* (Yes)
> *'Good. And, you found your way here okay?'* (Yes)
> *'It looks like it's still raining outside…'* (Yes)

Note: Effective yes-sets should be incontrovertible. Avoid statements that can potentially be denied. 'It's raining' cannot be denied (assuming there's a window nearby), whereas 'It's a nice day, isn't it?' can be—especially if the patient is feeling depressed. Also, take care when using names as a yes-set ('You're Mrs Peterson, aren't you?') unless you're *absolutely* sure you have the correct details at hand.

At this point, some subjects may unconsciously feel they have been too agreeable, so we depotentiate with another linguistic device called a 'negative frame'. This is a language pattern that prompts a negative response while still maintaining agreement. For example:

> *'Well, let's go right through because we wouldn't want to keep you waiting any longer, would we?' (No—meaning, 'I agree'.)*

Some languages, such as French, Russian, and Afrikaans, employ negatives in pairs. Unlike in English, they are still regarded as negative. So, if adapting these techniques to such a language, the pattern can still be used.

> *A joke. A rather pompous professor of linguistics told his class, 'In English, a double negative forms a positive. In some languages, a double negative is still a negative. However, there is no language in which a double positive can form a negative.'*
>
> *A bored voice piped up from the back of the room, 'Yeah, right.'*

The formula:

The formula for the yes-sets and negative frames is as follows:

1. Truism + 2. Truism + 3. Truism + Negative frame

A negative frame is, in turn, constructed as follows: begin with something that is desirable ('go right through'), add the word 'because', and follow this with something that is not wanted and is negatively expressed (such as 'we don't want to wait any longer'), then add the rhetorical tag-line: 'do we?', or 'would we?'.

Desired action + 'because' + undesired (negated) action + rhetorical tag

Reasoned response

The word 'because' acts as a powerful releaser of decision or action—often regardless of what that decision or action might be.

Harvard social psychologist Ellen Langer once conspired with her university librarian to shut down all but one photocopying machine. As a long line formed, Langer sent in one group of confederates to go to the head of the queue and ask permission to use the machine, giving no explanation. Around 60% of students allowed the confederates to go ahead of them.

A second group of confederates asked to use the machine, giving explanations such as, 'I'm late for class.' The percentage given permission jumped to 94.

Then Langer had a brilliant idea. She had another group go to the head of the queue and make bogus requests to use the machine, explaining, '... because I want to make some copies'. Contrary to all expectations, the requests went largely unchallenged. Almost nobody said, 'Of course you do. We're all here to make copies, so wait your turn.' The success rate dropped only one percentage point.[145]

This, along with a number of subsequent studies, gives rise to the (slightly discomforting) realization that many of us respond to linguistic patterns almost as readily as to the content or meaning of certain statements and requests...so long as there's a reason. Any reason.

What this suggests is that our cognitive functions are often in 'park' mode. As mentioned in the previous chapter on cognitive bias, people respond to the 'shape' of things rather more than what the things mean. In contrast to algorithmic thinking (the application of predetermined 'rules' to arrive at conclusions), this form of processing is 'heuristic'.

For our purposes, heuristics may be thought of as mental 'tools' we use in order to conserve brain power, or as 'shortcuts' that aim to get more thinking done with minimum effort. Although the shortcomings of heuristic thinking are evident from the examples given above, heuristics themselves, as we will suggest later, can also be valuable tools *if consciously and contextually applied as a means to an end.*

Our hope, then, by presenting some of the evidence surrounding the issues of first impressions and decision-making, is to sensitize you to the fact that more—much more—is happening than simply inviting your patient to sit down.

The overall object of the Engagement phase of the Medical NLP Consultation Process is to increase a productive sense of 'connectedness' with the patient, and to reduce, as far as possible, the risk of avoidable mishaps and misunderstandings. The starting point of a safe, productive and mutually satisfying first contact is the congruence of the practitioner—that is, an alignment of attitude, intention, communication style, and behavior. And, it's best to bear in mind that, while you are assessing the patient, the patient is assessing you. Diagnosis, for better or worse, is a two-way street.

EXERCISES

1. Yes-sets are key skills to master in this section. Review the four-part structure, and then create sets of your own. The challenge is to make them naturally conversational, but still based on truisms. Test these for effectiveness.
2. Read aloud any three paragraphs from the chapter above. At the end of each sentence, practice inflecting **downwards**. You may record this for learning purposes if you wish.
3. Rehearse giving lifestyle advice to a patient:
   i. with an 'approachable' delivery only;

ii. with a 'credible' delivery only;
iii. with an appropriate combination of the two.

4. Practice the 'rapid rapport' method with the next 20 people you meet.

Phase 2: Alignment

9

The Uninterrupted Story: beyond the 18th second

Listen to your patient, for he will give you the diagnosis.— ***Sir William Osler***

The patient who arrives in the consultation room or hospital bed comes with more than just a collection of symptoms. He has a history, beliefs, fears, theories, and frustrations. He has choices and resources, and the means to help resolve his problems, even though these are as yet unrecognized and unapplied.

He also functions—together with his problems—within a unique and complex set of relationships with the others in his group. In short, he has a pathography, a 'story' about his illness.

Pathographies, a term invented by the 19th-century German neurologist, Paul Julius Möbius, have themes that 'explain' illness (such as 'divine will', 'expiation of sins', 'spiritual journey', 'challenge to survive and flourish', etc). They also have characters, story arcs, climaxes, and endings. A more contemporary discussion of themes can be found in Anne Hunsaker Hawkins's comprehensive study, *Reconstructing Illness.*[146]

This is seldom good news to medical practitioners, pressured as they may be by targets, algorithms, and guidelines. Patients' stories are relegated to the lowest point on the list of viable 'evidence', just below the practitioner's intuition, experience, and insight. The 'theme' of the illness is even less likely to be regarded as relevant, despite the fact that storytelling and resolution, as we will demonstrate later, may be a powerful, non-invasive tool for psychological, and even physical, change.

So, when the patient complains of being treated 'like a number', he has inadvertently put his finger on the problem. In its bid to demystify the complexity of illness and standardize treatment, the growing reliance on statistical analysis, specialist referrals, and technology-based diagnosis can also serve to degrade and depersonalize the intricacies of human experience.

Regrettably, this is the way medicine is still largely taught in many Western countries. Standardized diagnostic criteria, on which both medicine and psychiatry increasingly depend, are created to assist the practitioner in reaching sound conclusions, upon which effective treatment can be based. These linear details (what Robert Ornstein originally called 'text'[147]) are seldom enough to describe or understand the experience of chronic 'functional' disorders. As French philosopher Henri Bergson observed, no matter how many hundreds of buckets of seawater we analyze, we will probably never understand the tides.

Differing agendas

One of the biggest stumbling blocks in practitioner-patient relations arises from the fact that each party has a different agenda. The patient is anxious to present what he or she regards as a 'complete' picture of the problem; the physician, meanwhile, is extracting information with a diagnostic or prognostic value, according to the current medical model.

Australian professor of surgery Miles Little points out that when a clinician 'takes' a medical history, he assumes certain 'editorial functions', determined by linguistic conventions that may be entirely alien to the patient. This process turns the patient's 'story' into text, thus removing it from the patient's lived experience.[148]

In fact, the problem may run even deeper. Doctors (and a very large percentage of other health professionals) function according to a set of beliefs and procedures established during long and expensive training. As far back as 1973, Michael Balint commented on some doctors' use of selective attention to aspects of the patient's narrative in order to direct it into territory more accessible to them (the doctors).

Western diagnostic methods are essentially 'hermeneutic' (that is, they rely on the systematic analysis of text at the expense of context). The doctor's role is to narrow down the textual evidence into the most likely diagnosis, and then to deliver a prognosis, and, it is hoped, an effective treatment. The appeal of translating from story, rich in detail and scope, to simple, linear text is self-evident, and it takes considerable skill, insight, and self-discipline to hold back from this.

In an undifferentiated patient population, text is not enough. People do not live, think, become sick, or die according to a set of logical propositions. They are much more creative than that. Their experience, physical and emotional, is made up of complex relationships, both internal and external, that give their present condition meaning—Ornstein's 'context'.[149] And the place to start with decoding the intricacies and interrelationships within chronic 'functional' disorders is with the uninterrupted story.

Text needs to be understood in context. (Note we are not encouraging the patient to become 'stuck' in his story. The practitioner's intention is to understand the themes, patterns, and emotional forces driving the patient's condition.)

Concerns persist that the garrulous patient will consume what little time is available to him and the other patients on the busy practitioner's list. But this is not as big a risk as it might first appear. Most doctors and medical students know of the 1984 Beckman-Frankel study reporting that the average practitioner interrupted the patient just 18 seconds after he had begun to talk.[150] Later studies show very little improvement. 'If I didn't interrupt', doctors tell us, 'I'd never finish one consultation, let alone my whole caseload for the day.'

In reality, research also showed that patients given the freedom to talk seldom speak for more than 50 seconds. The longest narration recorded was 150 seconds, and the longer stories were later found to have been entirely clinically significant.[151]

Just for a moment, imagine that you are sitting watching a movie with a friend. After just 18 seconds, he whispers, 'What's happening now?' Quite apart from the irritation you are likely to feel, how much of the plot-line could you be expected to know after less than half a minute?

We will discuss the control of the practitioner's time in a later chapter (including how to keep the consultation on track). Time, like physical energy, needs to be spent, but it needs to be spent wisely, with purpose and design, in order to have the investment yield returns. And, in all effective time-management systems, time well spent is, in the longer run, time saved. If the patient's need to be heard is not met in this consultation, he will be back.

The purpose of stories

Stories are essentially the way in which we attempt to organize our experience and extract meaning out of a collection of apparently random events. By allowing the patient to talk, you gain insight into the forces that drive his unique narrative (the same kind of situations, characters, challenges, conflicts, and tensions that you were looking forward to unfolding before you when you were so rudely interrupted by your movie-going companion).

Story helps you understand how your patient's map of the world no longer serves to help him navigate through the bewildering territory in which he finds himself. The greater our ability to detect themes, patterns, and relationships within items of information that we might otherwise have disregarded as 'irrelevant', the easier it becomes to help the patient update his model of 'reality' and move forward.

An example:

Carlotta was referred with 'acute anxiety disorder'. She reported suffering from 'a fear of dying', interrupted sleep, and inexplicable bouts of crying. She recalled being frightened by some representation of death she saw on television when she was a child.

'My mother said, "Don't worry about it. Look how old your grandma is and she doesn't worry about dying."'

Not long after that, her grandmother died, and Carlotta's fear of dying reasserted itself with a vengeance. This fear affected her work (which she loved), her relationships with family and friends (who were frustrated at the illogicality of her fears), and her sleep patterns. A doctor prescribed her sleeping pills and an anti-depressant, but her concerns remained unchanged. She noticed that the symptoms worsened when she became more stressed.

She said, 'I asked all my friends, and they said they didn't ever think about dying. I can't understand why it doesn't affect them.'

Her story: 'I'm going to die, and knowing that takes all pleasure out of life. I'm alone, because nobody else sees and feels things the way I do.'

The practitioner listened to her story without interrupting, then, when she paused, gently observed, 'Whether your friends realize it or not, being afraid of dying is what keeps us alive. If you didn't have that fear, you wouldn't bother to look both ways when you cross the road, or avoid using your electric hair-dryer in the bath.'

Carlotta paused, thought about the remark, then said, 'But, it doesn't seem to bother other people…'

The practitioner quickly agreed. 'So, the real problem isn't being afraid of dying,' he said. 'That's a very protective thought, is it not? It stops you doing anything risky. The real problem is that it's like a parent who's too protective. It's too insistent. So...if it was still there to keep you safe where necessary, would you agree that the real issue is to turn down the message so it doesn't dominate your intention so much of your time?'

Carlotta agreed—and her story could then undergo a quick re-write. Instead of being the victim of forces out of her control, they were reframed as 'communications' from her protective self. She had mentioned having dogs, so, in order to depotentiate the bonded disconnection (the more she tried to not have the anxiety, the more anxious she became), the practitioner added, 'These thoughts are a little like your puppies. If they want your attention and you keep pushing them away...'

Carlotta laughed and finished the sentence, '…they keep climbing all over me and sit on me until I give them what they want.'

The practitioner smiled. 'So, obviously, rather than trying to reject something that's trying to help you, even if it's a bit over-protective, we need to teach it not to be so out of control, wouldn't you say? Just like your dogs need to be properly trained in order to make everyone much happier all round?'

The new story was now in place. The fear of death was trying to keep her safe. The real problem was that it was too uncontrolled—just like a boisterous puppy, full of good intentions, but needing to be properly trained. Since stress made things worse (as it did with dogs), it was obvious that the real issue was learning how to manage and deal with stress...an entirely different, and much more manageable, scenario than before. Once that was in place, Carlotta could rehearse her coping behavior until it became her default response.

In itself, storytelling has another important function—it facilitates the subject's innate ability to self-regulate.

As human beings, we all seem to be compelled to turn the random occurrences of our lives into story. In fact, so deeply entrenched is this tendency, it is likely that we cannot *not* remember and recount our history in narrative form—that is, with a beginning, middle, and an end. Go back, if you can, to an old diary and notice, regardless of how detailed each day's entries might have been, the effect is still episodic. Your own recollection of that period, however, will be presented to your conscious mind as a fluid and fluent story.

The question arises: why should people have this apparently hardwired propensity towards storytelling?

University of Texas psychologist James W. Pennebaker has conducted extensive research into this question, and has come to some intriguing conclusions relating directly to human health and wellbeing.

The drive to meaning

Pennebaker concludes that the act of constructing stories is an innate human drive to help individuals to remember and organize their experiences, but also to create meaning, thus acquiring a sense of predictability and control. The reader will recall from an earlier chapter that predictability and control are two needs particularly important to human health and wellbeing. Once an experience, however traumatic, is given structure and meaning, Pennebaker suggests, the emotional fall-out from that experience becomes more manageable.[152]

Emotional distress is the core reason most, if not all, sufferers from complex, chronic conditions seek help. The ability to disclose and organize the source (or perceived source) of the distress has unequivocally been demonstrated to improve the individual's functionality in a number of domains. These benefits include improvement of immune function (including T-helper cell growth[153] and antibody response to the Epstein-Barr virus[154] and to hepatitis B vaccinations[155]); reduced subjective experience of pain and use of medication; mood regulation; weight management; and even higher grades in college exams. Additionally, the effect is encountered across many cultures, suggesting grounds for universal application of the approach.[156]

At this point, some readers might notice an apparent contradiction between our advocacy of the value of narrative and our rejection of those counseling methods that require the patient to return repeatedly to the traumatizing experience and a discussion of his or her resultant feelings in an endless and potentially damaging recursive loop.

To clarify: the purpose of patient storytelling should not be to wallow in historic suffering, but to help create or restore meaning and resolution to an experience that may be causing problems in the present tense.

Pennebaker and his colleagues found that, while simply narrating a story had measurably beneficial effects, it was possible also to identify the linguistic patterns that most benefited the narrator.

For this, he and several colleagues spent several years developing a computer program called Linguistic Enquiry and Word Count (LIWC) that analyzed participants' journals with a view to identifying the emotional and cognitive style dimensions of the language used.

The emotion category included positive-emotion words such as 'happy' and 'laugh' and negative-emotion emotion words—for example, 'sad', 'angry'.

The researchers created two categories of cognitive words, causal and insight. Causal words and phrases include 'because', 'the reason for', 'as a result of' etc., reflecting the narrators' tendency to link causes for the emotions they were currently experiencing. Insight words reflect the degree to which the subject can become aware of the specific cognitive processes associated with thinking. These include words such as 'realize', 'understand', 'recognize', etc.

Pennebaker and his colleagues crunched scores of essays, to come to the indisputable conclusion that the more the narrator used positive-emotion words, the more his or her health improved.

However, when they analyzed the use of negative-emotion words, they came to a surprizing conclusion: that those who used very many negative words and those who used very few were most likely to have continuing health problems, while those who fell between the two extremes showed greater improvement.[157] This, they decided, suggested that those who used very few negative words coped by repressing their feelings, while those who used many negative-emotion words were likely to be classic neurotic personalities. This is typical of people who reflect on the negative feelings without coming to any useful conclusion.

On the other hand, those people who used a large percentage of positive-emotion words, along with some negative-emotion words, appeared to be recognizing problems along with a sense of optimism that these could be resolved.

Developing attention

Tuning into all this requires a kind of dual attention on the part of the practitioner. Not only should his attention be open to the patient's currently held meaning of the condition ('I saw on the Internet that it's genetic/incurable/only in remission'), as well as his or her emotional-cognitive style, but also to syntactic flaws. By this, we mean, where the structure of the story deviates from 'well-formedness'—that is, does it lack a well-defined, achievable goal or outcome (a guiding reason)?; are there clearly defined steps or events that would lead to this outcome, and are these events arranged in a sensible order?[158,159]

Almost certainly a narrative will be in place, but it will deviate from a preferred structure. The story will relate to how bad the patient feels, and (as yet) not to how well he or she wishes to be. The details may be unclear; the order is in disarray, and the outcome uncertain. But, equally, it may be elegant in its narrative clarity, the only problem being it reinforces the inevitability of dysfunction and distress. Some patients—as many practitioners will agree—will argue strongly to stay sick or stuck, simply because they don't (again, as yet) have a story featuring healing and health.

While Pennebaker's experiments have focused on writing, several studies, comparing the written journal with one spoken into a recorder, show comparable effects. It seems that it is the telling of the story that is important, rather than the medium through which it is told.[160,161]

At this point, accept this reassurance now. We are not asking you to abandon the logical, left-brain reasoning that is the cornerstone of accurate differential diagnosis. Rather, we are offering an adjunctive approach—a way of gaining, managing, and applying knowledge that supplements, and can dramatically enhance, your understanding of the patient's experience.

So the first recommendation is that you relax. Relax while reading this, and relax with the patient in front of you. Remind yourself of the advice given to anxious students by Sir William Osler more than 100 years ago: 'Listen to your patient, for he will give you the diagnosis.' Just for the moment, put aside the need to 'know' what is happening. Your formal training and experience will automatically deal with text. You are listening for context, for meaning and effect, and it is the patient, not the practitioner, who is the expert on this.

Also, as we will discuss in the following chapter, 'listening', in this model, is much more than the non-directive 'active listening' of the Rogerian client-centered approach ('uh-huh', 'okay', 'I see'), or the sympathetic head-tilt of the psychodynamic counselor ('…and, how does that make you feel?'). You are accumulating raw data from a number of sources, verbal and non-verbal, in order to form hypotheses that will later be tested. You are deliberately activating all your sensory receptors, with as little internal judgment and commentary as possible. Out of this, structure, process, and meaning emerge.

EXERCISES

Skill-Set One

1. Spend 15 minutes a day for three days writing, preferably by hand, about your current, thoughts, feelings, behaviors, and problems (and anything else that comes to mind). Rate your current physical/mental state on a scale of one to 10, one being 'not very good' and 10 being 'excellent'. There are few rules to follow—except that, once you start, you cannot stop. Write continuously. Don't stop to think about what you will write, or edit what you have already written. If you can't think of anything to write, write about that until the mental log-jam clears. Do not re-read what you have written until the end of the three days.
2. When you have completed the three days, re-read your journal entries and highlight the text in four different colors, one each for:

- positive-emotion words;
- negative-emotion words;
- insight words and phrase;
- causal words and phrases.

Now check:

- whether positive-emotion or negative-emotion words dominate your text;
- how many insight/causal words occur;
- whether or not the number of positive-emotion and insight/causal words and phrases increases, decreases, or stays the same.

3. Finally, review your physical/mental state and re-rate it from one to 10, noticing what has changed.

Skill-Set Two

1. Think back to your most recent clinical session, if necessary look through your notes or appointment schedules. For any three of these, identify any themes contained within their stories.
2. Now consider a recent less-than-satisfactory clinical encounter with a client/patient:
   a. Approximately how long did he speak before you interrupted?
   b. Did you attempt to ascertain the meaning they had ascribed to their particular situation?
3. Repeat Step 2 above for the next three less-than-ideal clinical encounters you come across. Keep a note for later review.

10

The Clinical Questioning Matrix: eliciting quality data

The scientist is not a person who gives the right answers, he's one who asks the right questions.—***Claude Lévi-Strauss***

Acquiring quality information in any interview or consultation depends largely on the quality of the questions we ask. As we observed in the previous chapter, the process of 'paying attention' simultaneously involves taking in and excluding data. Quite simply, we tend to look for, and find, mainly the information we expect.

This tendency is a cognitive bias known as the 'familiarity heuristic', a mental shortcut, derived from the 'availability heuristic'. This pattern was identified by psychologists Amos Tversky and Daniel Kahneman in the early 1970s,[162] and declares simply: *the more easily something comes to mind and the more familiar it is, the more likely we are to accept it as true.*

To reduce over-dependence on heuristics, and to facilitate an exchange of quality (that is, useful) information, we strongly recommend that the practitioner hold three organizing principles in mind:

1. Reduce the patient's anxiety. This is a priority. All patients in distress suffer allostatic load to some degree or other; unless some neurological coherence is restored, they are unlikely to be able to organize their thoughts, communicate the real issues that concern them, and even accurately hear and remember what you say.

Therefore:

- Pace and lead the patient, by matching either his rate of speech or his breathing (supposing he does not suffer from a breathing disorder); then gradually slow down;
- Acknowledge the patient's discomfort, but avoid telling him to 'calm down'. Lead by example. As Richard Bandler says, 'If you want people to enter a particular state, go there first';
- Pacing also involves matching the patient's representation of a problem. The following extract is from a video recording of a doctor's consultation with an elderly patient. Note the mismatches in the doctor's responses.

Patient: *'I've had this…uncomfortable…this feeling for some time now,'* (gestures towards abdomen).
Doctor: *'What kind of pain is it? Sharp or dull?'*
Patient: *'No, not exactly…not a pain. More a kind of sensation…'*
Doctor: *'When did it start to hurt?'*
Patient: *'Well, not really hurting. Sort of…About three and a half years ago.'* (The patient had earlier mentioned being suddenly widowed three and a half years before, a fact not picked up on by the doctor.)
Doctor: *'Do you have pain all the time?'*
Patient: *'It's more—more pressure, I'd say. It's like I'm…holding too much inside.'* (Looks down and right, left, and back again, indication of an internal kinesthetic accompanied by self-talk, or auditory digital.)
Doctor: *'Pain can be caused by a number of things. What I'm going to do is to send you for some tests.'* (The doctor's attention shifts to organizing referral of the patient.) *'We'll see what's causing it then…'*

2. Listen and watch for structure and process.
   - People organize their behaviors and responses into sequences called strategies (see Appendix D, pages 367 to 369). These sequences have to be repeated in order to result in the same outcome. Strategies may have to be elicited since they function out of conscious awareness. Note especially any two-

point loops (that is, any strategy that does not end when it has served its purpose). This is how the patient becomes 'stuck'.

- Notice repeating patterns of behavior, gestures, or phrases. Patients will often mark out their problem with a particular gesture. This is useful information; rather than recapping the problem, the practitioner can often simply mirror the gesture (in the patient's subjective space, not his own) to recall the entire process. Adopt a curious attitude. Patients will often leave 'clues' as to the real problem for the practitioner to pick up.

3. Explore the context in which the patient and his problem function. Maintaining or resolving a problem may adversely affect the system in which the patient exists, and this needs to be resolved if treatment is to continue successfully. For example:

Case history: *The patient, said to be 'mildly learning disabled', had suffered a serious fall and was unable to walk without constant support. The practitioner noted that her father, who had become her primary caregiver, supervised her every move, including ensuring she was seated 'safely' on the chair before leaving the room.*

The approach, which involved building the girl's confidence and using some of the techniques outlined elsewhere (see Appendix B, pages 361 to 362) in this book, was hugely successful. She was able to jump in and out of her chair, and stand on one leg, and was clearly excited at her renewed abilities.

Since the father had given up his job to look after his daughter, the practitioner was still concerned about how such a change might affect the father's function and self-image as primary caretaker. He said to the girl, 'Your Dad has been looking after you and keeping you safe for a long time because he loves you so much. Now that you're doing so well, how are we going to make sure he doesn't feel you don't need him any more?'

The girl recognized the potential problem immediately, and, after some discussion, decided she would make an effort to involve him fully in all her decisions, including her plans to return to college.

When her father returned to pick her up, the girl excitedly jumped out of her chair, stood on one leg and waved her arms around. Apparently without noticing the change, the father said, 'Don't do that, you'll hurt yourself,' and gently pushed her back in the chair. The daughter shot a conspiratorial smile in the direction of the practitioner, and said with extraordinary wisdom, 'You're right. We'll need to practice together.'

The importance of attention

Too often today, the practitioner's attention is divided between the patient and the computer screen. Far from streamlining the consultation process, digital note-taking has opened a new level of risk in healthcare.

Aside from the unspoken message communicated to the patient ('I'm busy; get on with it. Just give me the facts'), recent research indicates that multi-tasking reduces, rather than improves, the quality of information gathered, instructions imparted, and conclusions reached.

Professor Nick Chater of Britain's Warwick Business School has demonstrated that people are capable of two simple and well-practiced actions at the same time, such as driving and talking. However, when called on to consider a new task or process new information, they stop what they were doing in order to consider their action.[163]

The human brain is designed to deal with only one conscious task at a time. In some cases, it is possible to learn to speed up processing, but we remain vulnerable to what psychologists call 'attentional blink' (a momentary drop-out in the ability to take action) and 'response selection bottleneck' (quite literally, a competition between conflicting actions that leads to delay and even temporary cognitive paralysis).

These phenomena can occur so fleetingly that we are not consciously aware of them, but important data can be obscured.

Contrary to popular belief, women are no better at multi-tasking than men. Professor Chater's research has revealed no significant differences between the sexes when called on to handle more than one activity. Male or female, people are simply not as good at multi-tasking as they like to think.[164]

To minimize this risk, we suggest separating out computer-based tasks from interaction with the patient. In order to avoid loss of rapport, ensure you give the patient 'orientating statements', such as: 'I'm afraid I need to get this information down. But, as soon as I have, we can settle down and have a chat about things…'

Hemispheric lateralization

In many ways, 'whole-person' consultation is also a 'whole-brain' activity. We need to allow input of data we are inclined (for reasons discussed in later) to disregard, and—rather more challenging—we also need to understand and outwit what cognitive neuroscientist Michael Gazzaniga has dubbed the 'spin doctor' in our heads.[165]

Almost everyone who witnessed the business boom of the 1980s got to hear about 'right-brain thinking'. Split-brain experiments had long suggested that the two hemispheres of the brain were specialized: left brain logical, right brain creative. It was a seductive idea, but not an entirely accurate one. We know now that we use both sides of our brains for much of the time. Few, if any, functions are located in only one hemisphere.

However, we also know that each side is uniquely specialized to carry out certain tasks. With the caveat in mind that what follows is generalized, four important distinctions are outlined below:

1. **The brain and body are cross-lateralized.** The left hemisphere controls the right side of the body, and the right hemisphere controls the left side of the body. Medical NLP regards this as important for a number of reasons. These include the role of homolateralization (one-sided dominance) in certain so-called 'learning disabilities', such as dyslexia, as well as childhood behavioral problems, depression, strokes, and even immune function.[166] Incorporating re-lateralization exercises and activities has shown encouraging results with our patients and those of other Medical NLP practitioners who are developing approaches along these lines (see Appendix B, pages 361 to 362).
2. **The hemispheres process differently.** The left hemisphere processes data sequentially. Sounds, symbols, and sequential behavior are all predominantly under the control of the left hemisphere. This is what we mean when we speak of 'text'. The right hemisphere processes data simultaneously. It sees and extracts meaning out of many different elements. It notices relationships. This is what we mean by 'context'. The right brain perceives the picture, the left brain provides the words.
3. **The hemispheres 'make sense' of experience differently.** The

right hemisphere wordlessly 'experiences'. The left hemisphere evaluates, explains, justifies, and defends. Gazzaniga also calls the left hemisphere 'the interpreter', and writes amusingly in *The Mind's Past* about its tendency to work overtime to 'spin' explanations out of experiences—sometimes with bizarre results. (This is characteristic of what in hypnosis is called 'trance logic'; the subject's 'explanation' for carrying out a post-hypnotic command may make perfect sense to him, but is a patent concoction to bystanders who have not been hypnotized.) Note, too, that as we move down Korzybski's Structural Differential (see Chapter 7, pages 92 to 97), we call increasingly on left-brain processing, to the exclusion of the right's.

4. **The hemispheres separate and combine information**. When working together optimally, the hemispheres synthesize data to provide holistic 'meaning'. While the left hemisphere registers the individual features of an approaching friend, the right 'recognizes' his face. One hemisphere hears notes, the other combines them into melody; one side can read words, the other recognizes the emotional tone of the words, the prosody, etc. It follows from the above that the quality of the meaning we extract from our neuronal processes should increase when both hemispheres are engaged, each contributing its own particular skills. Physical damage can adversely affect this—as, regrettably, can education. For various reasons, Western teaching—especially in the sciences—favors the logical, linear, sequential mode of left-brain processing, and mistrusts the rather more exuberant, untrammeled, creative activities of the right. The kind of syllogistic reasoning we mentioned earlier is exclusively the province of the left hemisphere. Evidence-based medicine is an exclusively left-brain invention. Its objective (that is, measurable, reproducible) 'evidence' is valued over the subjective, emotional 'experience' of the right. We are encouraged to believe that only by refining 'factual' data enough can we eventually arrive at 'truth'.

The differential diagnosis

The differential diagnosis—essentially an evaluative exercise that aims to arrive at a diagnosis by a process of elimination—is a cornerstone of Western medicine and a primarily left-brain activity. Valuable as it proves in many areas, it does not always rise to the challenge of certain complex, chronic conditions. Information derived from this kind of thinking alone may be valued, but is not necessarily always accurate. Research has shown that overdependence can lead to a 'high control style' on the part of the practitioner, increased patient dissatisfaction, an overly narrow approach to hypothesis-generation, a premature focus on medical explanations, and inaccuracies in diagnosis.[167]

Where deductive reasoning does not provide us with the results we are looking for, we need to engage another of our highly developed, but largely overlooked, human capabilities, one which does not reside in the left side of our skulls. We need to cross the bundle of nerves, the *corpus callosum*, that bridges left and right, and listen to the melody of the patient's experience, rather than just studying the notes.

The 'open' practitioner

Adopt what Zen writers call 'beginner's mind'. Raw data unfiltered by preconception are valuable data. The practitioner should become comfortable with periods of 'not knowing' what the problem is or how to approach it. As the consultation progresses, information will accumulate, patterns and distinctions emerge, and responses begin to suggest themselves.

It is important to manage one's own sense of pressure when listening to the patient's response to open questions. The patient may need time to find his way through the tangle of his own feelings and symptoms. And while time may be at a premium, quality information will lead to more effective approaches and conclusive results.

The 'open' practitioner not only engages the patient, but also gently encourages further disclosures, with questions such as, 'What else is it like?'; 'How would you describe…?'; 'Exactly how does this happen?' and, if the patient seems stuck for words, 'Just so I understand—if I were having this problem that you've been having, what would I be thinking, feeling, doing…how would I be talking to myself?' etc. In order to elicit a strategy, you may find it useful to ask, 'What happens just before that… and before that…?' until you can identify the first step in the sequence (see Appendix D, pages 367 to 369).

Open and closed questions

Most medical and communication training programs refer to the differences between open (contextual) and closed (textual) questions. Open questions usually elicit stories, anecdotes, metaphors, and subjective, analogical responses. Closed questions tend to lead to yes/no, digital replies.

The method most usually taught is to begin with open questions, and move gradually down to closed questions. Known as 'coning' or 'funneling', this approach, moving from the general to the specific, is widely believed to provide all the data needed to translate the patient's story into the data needed to make an accurate diagnosis. At best, it progressively strips the patient's experience of subjectivity in favor of recognizable signs and symptoms. However, busy practitioners often revert to predominantly closed questions, unaware of the different functions and rich potential of each when skillfully applied. And, when patients are confronted with closed questions, communication and the relationship can suffer.[168]

Furthermore, information relevant to making an accurate diagnosis may not surface if the patient is prevented by excessive closed questioning from responding more fully.[169]

Our broad distinction between the two different classes of question is simply this: open questions seek information (including meaning, beliefs, emerging patterns and impact on the patient's world, or system), whereas closed questions are intended to gain agreement or confirmation (see **Figure 10.1**). To put it another way, open and closed questions engage the right- and left-brain functions respectively of both patient and practitioner, resulting in a richer and more productive sharing of information.

Excluding one in favor of the other, or confusing the purpose of each, will result in data that are difficult to manage, risking overwhelming the practitioner and causing frustration for the patient.

Open questions	*Closed questions*
Result in:	*Result in:*
Analogue information	Digital responses (yes/no)
Process	Content
Internal locus of control (proactive)	External locus of control (reactive)
Consideration	Decision/agreement
Subjective meaning	Objective response
'Being listened to'	'Revolving door syndrome'
Association	Dissociation
Metaphor and symbol	Literal description
Emotional content	Physical content
Deep Structure	**Surface Structure**
(What is really meant)	(What is said)
are preceded by …	*are preceded by …*
Who?	It…?
What?	Does it…?
Where?	Can you…?
When?	Have you…?
Why? (Use with caution)	Are you…?

Prompting questions (aimed at extracting further information)
Such as …?
What else…?
What's it like …?
Do you have any idea (who/what/where/when/why) …?
And…?

Figure 10.1 The proprietary Medical NLP Clinical Questioning Matrix

Open questions

While open and closed questions may be interspersed, we prefer to begin with open questions. These invite information rather than demand it. The history is *received* rather than taken. Although the practitioner is the expert on the mechanisms of illness, the patient is respected and acknowledged as the expert in how *her* condition manifests itself in her body and life. Open questions encourage the patient to adopt an active, rather than submissive, role, and invite her into a mutual, adult relationship with the practitioner.

Open questions usually begin with words such as: Who? What? Where? When? How? and, sometimes, Why? We tend to be cautious of 'why' questions for two reasons: they elicit speculation, and can seem authoritarian ('Why haven't you been taking your medication?').

The information gathered from open questions often involves 'story' and metaphorical and analogical language ('It's like a hot knife in my back'). The answers to open questions often provide an enriching insight into the context within which the patient and his problem function.

Closed questions

Closed questions help sharpen focus on specific details, as well as eliciting agreement or confirmation (the yes-set introduced earlier being an example of the effective use of closed questions). If over-employed, however, they can dramatically reduce rapport and patient satisfaction.[170]

This class of question usually begins with phrases such as, 'Is it…?'; 'Has it…?'; 'Can you…?'; 'Have you…?'; 'Are you ...?'; etc. The 'any' questions are also closed ('Any pain?'; 'Any problem sleeping?'). Closed questions tend to elicit digital (yes/no) responses.

The practitioner should not only aim to become proficient at discriminating between open and closed questions, but also at converting one form to the other 'on the fly' (see the exercises at the end of this chapter).

Starting to question

The first question sets the tone for the remainder of the consultation. 'What's the problem?' is common, but may be regarded as too abrupt.

'How can I help you?' is better, but may place the practitioner 'one-up' on the patient. Our questions of preference are, 'What brings you here today?' and 'What would you like to talk about today?'

To help the patient express herself more fully, especially where the problem that concerns her has not yet been voiced, we suggest you respond to her initial statement with gentle probing. 'Is there anything else you'd like to talk about?' and, 'If we can sort this out today, will that help with everything that's been worrying you?' are typical questions that both accept the possibility that the patient has several concerns, and ensure that the practitioner will not be blind-sided by a succession of new concerns just as he is about to close the consultation (see Chapter 23 for more suggestions on this subject).

Establishing boundary conditions

The problem, however pervasive it seems, is limited, either physically (being localized in the body) or in time. It has an 'edge' or a boundary to it. It also had a beginning, middle (now) and, we trust, an end. We will address the issue of physically perceived location of the symptom in later chapters, but where and when the problem began needs to be established early, as do any events or situations surrounding it (the context).

Consider questions such as, 'What was happening in your life around the time, or just before, this began?'; 'How is this problem for you now?'; 'Who else is affected by this and how?'; and 'What will your life be like when the problem you've been having is resolved?' Any of these will help establish where the problem begins and ends.

The patient's opinion

Inviting the patient's opinion about his problem requires delicacy and discretion so as not to surrender your role as a trained professional. However, patients often have insights of which they are unaware until asked. We suggest a gentle inquiry along the lines of, 'We sometimes find that patients have ideas about their own situation. In case I've missed something important, do you have any inkling or hunch about what's been happening?'

The importance of emotional cues

Do not allow signs of heightened emotion to go unacknowledged. These might include agitation, reddening eyes, a downcast or darting gaze, changes in breathing rate or skin coloration, or a breaking voice. Equally, do not presume to 'know' what these minimal cues mean. Physical distress alone accounts for only a quarter of the reasons patients seek help from health professionals, even when the presenting complaint is somatic.[171] Use a gentle remark such as, 'I notice you seem to have some emotion right now. Would you like to talk about it?' Accept the patient's decision, whether or not she decides to open up.

If the patient loses direction

If it is clear that the patient is departing radically from his concerns (and this happens less frequently than many practitioners fear), you can gently bring him back on track with a remark such as, 'I think that's probably important and we'll remember that so we can come back to it. But can I just clarify…(and return to the main thread of the consultation).'

If the patient has a 'shopping list'

Patients sometimes bring a number of concerns to the same consultation. We disapprove of the notices appearing on the doors of some centers saying something like: 'Appointments: 10 minutes each. Only one problem per appointment.' Two options exist: the first (which we will expand on in a later chapter) is to look for a shared theme—for example, excessive stress. The other is simply to say to the patient, 'There are a number of things here. I'd like us to deal with the one that's most important to you. Which would you like that to be?'

A key question for follow-up visit(s)

In follow-up visits, 'What have you noticed that's different or better?' will orientate the patient towards solution and resolution. Failure to do that will direct the patient to access what has not yet improved, or what is 'not there' (for example, absence of pain). Our intention is to guide the patient towards noticing change, however small, and building on that. Around 60% of patients presented with a solution-oriented question that presupposes change have been shown to report a positive result, whereas, if the question inquires about their problem state, 67% report little or no change.[172] Sometimes, patients will respond, '*Oh, I've been up and down…*' Briefly inquire about the 'downs', then elicit the 'ups' in full, sensory detail…and anchor the response (see Chapter 11, pages 145 to 157).

EXERCISES

A. Identify whether the following questions are open or closed:

1. Is it a sharp/dull/aching, etc. pain?
2. Can you move your arm easily?
3. What have you tried so far?
4. How would you describe your relationships at work?
5. Are you feeling stressed?
6. What else can you tell me about it?
7. What is the (symptom) like?
8. Where do you feel it?
9. What do you mean by (patient's description)?
10. Any problems at home?

B. Convert the following open or closed questions into their opposite form:

1. Do you understand these instructions?
2. Have you had this a long time?
3. What brings you here today?
4. How well do you sleep?
5. Is the pain worse when you move?
6. Is the depression very bad?

7. How is your appetite?
8. Which side is the pain on?
9. Do the anxiety attacks come often?
10. Any worries about your family?

C. Question three patients (or willing friends) about a problem or concern, and annotate their strategy as described in Appendix D. Pay particular attention to any two-point loops in their strategies.
Strategy 1:
Annotation:
Two-point loop? Y/N
Strategy 2:
Annotation:
Two-point loop? Y/N
Strategy 3:
Annotation:
Two-point loop? Y/N

Phase 3: Reorientation

11

Accessing Patient Resources: the potential for change

*The world as we have created it is a process of our thinking. It cannot be changed without changing our thinking.—**Albert Einstein***

One of the presuppositions of NLP, and a guiding principle of the work of Milton Erickson, is that all patients have the resources needed to produce change.

To some, this may seem overly optimistic, especially where both patient and practitioner feel baffled and helpless when confronted with a particularly complex and chronic condition. To those patients and physicians who genuinely feel they have 'tried everything', the statement may even seem platitudinous or blaming.

In Medical NLP, we modify the statement slightly. We suggest that both patient and practitioner have resources that have not yet been investigated or applied, and *of which they may not yet be aware.*

Problem-based medicine tends to regard illness as the result of a deficit. A patient regarded as deficient in some way or other requires 'fixing'. The role of practitioner and patient then becomes one of the active and informed acting on the passive and uninformed.

The patient's resources

Among the resources that patients bring into treatment may be included:

- the desire to achieve a healed state (or else they would not have sought help);
- the evolutionary drive of all living entities to strive for allostasis at every point in their lives until the moment of death;
- successful changes and healings they have accomplished in the past; and
- the ability, under guidance, to envisage an existence in which allostasis is restored.

Several factors may, however, initially stand in the way of identifying resources. It may be (and often is) that the patient has not yet fully engaged with one or all of the resources mentioned above. Secondary gain (psychology's assertion that people sometimes stay sick to achieve some hidden benefit) may often be used to explain a patient's 'resistance' to treatment, thereby aborting further investigation.

Many patients (and, we would say, many practitioners) have not even considered the presenting condition as a symptom of the body-mind system's attempt to regulate itself, albeit unsuccessfully. Also, the patient's problem-state of mind may preclude recollecting 'successful' or 'happy' times in the past, or imagining improvements in the future, simply because, at this stage, it seems too risky.

Some 'patient-centered' approaches suggest that only a 'non-directive' approach is ethically acceptable, and that interventions that take place outside the patient's conscious knowledge are unacceptable. We disagree. We have no problem in regarding the patient's request for help as a mandate to proceed *in his interests*. The fact that he might be better served when some parts of the intervention take place covertly is, in our opinion, unavoidable.

The *outcome* (and this part of the treatment *must* be negotiated with the patient's full consent) informs everything else we do.

Identifying, accessing and stabilizing resources

Resourcing, then, is accomplished by three processes: behavioral shaping (or response shaping); informative feedback; and the NLP core skill of anchoring. Since effective anchoring is a technique critical to all successful

NLP interventions, and one that is particularly important to resourcing, we recommend that some time is spent in mastering it.

Successful resourcing requires a creative balance between an overt uncovering of patient strengths and more oblique methods bringing together as yet unacknowledged positive experiences, abilities, and behaviors. It is important to pace the patient's experience appropriately. Focusing too soon or too directly on what is *not* wrong will damage rapport and engagement and be perceived simply as a dismissive things-are-not-as-bad-as-you-think attitude.

The power of anchoring

Anchors are often explained in terms of classical conditioning as a stimulus that elicits a particular response.

Russian psychologist Ivan Pavlov's experiments at the turn of the last century demonstrated how a specific tone, sounded when a group of dogs were given food, could eventually trigger salivation, even when food was not present. The experiment, together with a series conducted later by B. F. Skinner, much of it with pigeons, excited some psychologists. They envisaged being able to correct human behavioral 'errors' with little effort, and even less concern for how the 'black box' of the human brain functioned.

It was a belief that led to many spurious and inhumane 'treatments' and child-rearing models. The fact that we are deeply patterned—and patternable—organisms is undeniable. We respond automatically to many stimuli (think of hearing a song that automatically recalls emotions belonging to the distant past). But we are also much more than that. Unlike a dog or a pigeon, we have the capacity to reflect on our behavior; to act (when we know how) on our patterning; and even to use it for our own self-regulation and personal evolution.

Anchors, then, are a means to an end. As stimuli that predictably evoke specific psychophysiological states, they may be incorporated as tools to facilitate the integration and effective functioning of a wide range of other psychophysiological capabilities.

An anchor may be set up accidentally or deliberately. It may result from several repetitions or a single, traumatizing incident (as with some phobias). Heightened emotion, such fear or grief, makes us more susceptible. Anchors can occur singly or in sequences. Triggers may occur in any of the senses: sight, sound, touch, smell, or taste. The more senses involved in creating both stimulus and response, the more intense the 'internal' experience is likely to be.

Most importantly, anchors are irrelevant until they are triggered, or 'fired'.

Anchors, not pathology

Until we are aware of how they are established and how they function, most anchors are set up and triggered outside our conscious awareness. Many responses, otherwise thought of as pathological, may, in fact, be seen as caused by negative anchoring.

Take, for example, the following:

> ***Case history:*** *The patient complained of developing a 'social phobia' when meeting new people. The practitioner noted that the condition had surfaced some weeks after the sudden and tragic death of the patient's mother, and had progressively worsened since then.*
>
> *Interestingly, he described the symptoms of his 'phobia', not as 'anxiety', as might be expected, but as 'sadness' and 'despair'. During the consultation, the practitioner anchored the 'sad' feeling and asked him to 'follow the feeling back' to when he had first experienced it. The patient recalled with considerable emotion the funeral of his mother at which he was battling to contain his grief, while meeting and shaking hands with scores of mourners.*
>
> *When the patient had recovered his composure, the practitioner asked permission to 'test something'. He reached out, shook hands with the patient, and the patient instantly collapsed back into the sad and despairing state he had felt at the funeral. Immediately, he recognized that his 'phobic' response was not caused by meeting new people, but was triggered by the physical act of shaking hands: an anchor that had been set up at a time of heightened emotion.*

Anchors, as we will demonstrate later, not only explain aspects of many chronic conditions, but can be effectively 'installed' to therapeutic effect. Anchors may be intrapersonal (self-anchoring) as well as interpersonal (operating between people). The triggers may be real and external (a handshake, the sound of fingernails raking down a blackboard), or entirely imaginal—that is, the response may be triggered simply by thinking of a particular event (pause and think for a moment of sucking a segment of lemon). Anxiety disorders often involve a physical response to the memory, or future imagining, of a sensitizing event that is long past.

Setting anchors

The most commonly applied therapeutic anchor is kinesthetic. But although it is significantly easier to link a physical touch with an emotional or physical response, it may not always be appropriate to touch a patient.

However, when touch is permissible, such as in taking a pulse or palpating, we suggest that you *tense* the muscles of your hand and fingers as you touch the patient, *then relax them*. This subliminally cues the patient himself to relax (see behavioral shaping, below), as well as anchoring relaxation to your touch.

Auditory anchors might include a specific word or phrase, a sound or a tone. We advise practitioners to set up a specific phrase (such as the Ericksonian favorite, 'That's right…') as early as possible in the consultation each time he notices a positive response from the patient.

Visual anchors could be set by nodding, smiling, or making a specific gesture. Olfactory and gustatory anchors are less likely to be deliberately used in consultation. However, we need to be aware that the smells associated with hospitals and clinics may set up negative anchors in some patients.

We have found that we can help some patients minimize nausea while undergoing chemotherapy by addressing the issue of smell and sensation as anchoring.

Conditions of anchoring

In order for anchors to be effective, the following conditions must be met.

Anchors link a specific trigger to a specific response. Therefore:

1. Remember, or create, a desired state. Heighten the state by marking the sensory detail as rich as possible. Make it big, bright, and appealing. If anchoring overtly, agree on a name to avoid confusing it with any other states.
2. The anchor needs to be precisely timed, set just as the state begins to 'peak'. Make sure that it is released a moment before the state begins to subside. The intention is to stabilize the most intense stage of the experience, not to capture its dissipation.
3. The trigger must be unique. An anchor that can be accidentally 'fired', by a casual touch or ambient sound, will rapidly lose effectiveness. Use more than one sense to create the trigger, if possible (for example—a tense-to-relaxed touch, together with the words, 'That's right…').
4. The process must be tested for effectiveness. Don't trust to chance.
5. The process must be repeatable. If it is to be used therapeutically at a later date, an anchor needs to be durable enough to be fired when needed.

Later, we will discuss the setting and application of anchors more specifically, but, at this point, we would like to explain why we have spent so much time on the engagement phase of the consultation.

The practitioner as 'meta-anchor'

Clinical outcomes may be demonstrably enhanced by positive expectation and belief (including that of the practitioner).[173,174,175] Some studies even suggest that strong belief and positive attitude can measurably affect the patient's cellular function.[176] While this research is regarded with skepticism in more orthodox circles, there is no doubt in many patients' mind that certain practitioners have the ability, somehow, to make them 'just feel better'.

Whether or not the connection between practitioner attitude and patient response is ever widely accepted, we believe a practitioner who exhibits strong congruence, optimism, and engagement may function, at least in part, as a 'meta-anchor'. His state, if strong and coherent enough, may, in fact, collapse the patient's state in whole or in part—that is, he becomes the doctor-drug to which Michael Balint refers.[177]

Pitfalls to avoid

Given our susceptibility to anchoring, the practitioner should avoid accidentally setting up negative anchors or reinforcing unwanted behavior. Practitioners are often encouraged to practice 'active listening' by regularly acknowledging the patient's disclosures by nodding, sounds such as 'uh-huh', and encouraging statements like, 'Okay' and 'I see'.

These should be used with caution, and carefully timed. Nodding, smiling, and other gestures of acknowledgement made at the precise point where the patient is expressing his pain or distress may well anchor in the response we are striving to modify. (As we discuss elsewhere (see page 367), active listening tends to encourage the patient to speak more than he intends, simply because the practitioner's non-specific verbal responses are frequently interpreted as a prompt for more information). Difficult as it might be in the beginning, it is important to remain fully engaged, but neutral, at these times, reserving comments and other acknowledgements to be used in ways we will discuss later in this chapter.

> ***Case history:*** *One of the authors was commissioned by a large London hospital to help chaplains of all denominations who were reported to be suffering from burnout. When interviewed, they all agreed they felt exhausted and debilitated by their perceived inability to help the many patients they encountered who were suffering from chronic, painful, and often terminal illnesses.*
>
> *As is our usual procedure, the job began with a period of observation—and the following was noted. Patients often appeared to be fairly relaxed and in good spirits, chatting, reading, or watching television. When the chaplain appeared, he would sit down with a concerned and serious expression on his face, lean in towards the patient and inquire along the lines of, 'So, how are you feeling today?' The sonorous words and body language of the chaplain clearly signalled that he expected the patient to report negatively—which is exactly what happened. The patient visibly*

slumped, his expression becoming inwardly turned and reflective, then he would reply in some variation of, 'Not so good today…'. Patient and chaplain each appeared to be 'performing' the way the other expected them to.

To the observer, it seemed clear that the chaplains had become anchored to the perceived suffering of the patients, who in turn responded to the chaplains' over-serious and concerned demeanor.

The chaplains were taken aside, and the principle of anchoring explained to them and rehearsed (somewhat reluctantly at first) in adopting a more upbeat and positively expectant manner. After a couple of days, the tone of the meetings changed noticeably. The chaplains became more 'human', teasing and joking with their charges, and the patients responded with visible pleasure at the chaplains' visits. Later, the chaplains reported feeling more relaxed, energized, and optimistic about their work.

Anchors and strategies

When you experimented with the third part of the exercise at the end of the previous chapter (and, if you haven't, we suggest you return and do so now), you might have noticed that each part of a subject's strategy depended on the part that immediately preceded it.

Without that part (or any other), the strategy cannot run as a sequence. In terms of the conditioning process, a specific stimulus leads to a predictable response (S > R). The important thing to note here is that the response, in turn, functions as a stimulus to the next S-R unit, and so on, until the strategy has run its course. This is known as a 'chain'. Anchoring, as we will now see, becomes the building block of the principles and techniques designed to identify, access, and stabilize the patient's resources. (For more on strategies, see Appendix D, pages 367 to 369.)

Behavioral shaping

All conditions have limits or boundary conditions. There are times, or places in the body, where they are not experienced. The patient has a repertoire (as yet unrecognized) of behaviors that divert him from his suffering. No experience—however much the subject may protest to the contrary—can be maintained at the same level all the time. The human nervous system is not structured in a way that permits this to occur.

However, since the patient may feel overwhelmed by a problem and be incapable of finding his way past it, the purpose of shaping is gently and respectfully to guide him towards a greater awareness and activation of his capabilities, and to help him develop a more proactive and self-efficacious attitude.

To this end, we are interested in: exceptions to the problem state (times when the problem does not occur); the ability to shift and maintain attention to experiences outside the problem state; past successes and achievements; reducing the problem's size and impact by attending to its components, rather than the whole (splitting); and accessing and developing solutions and solution-states (also referred to as desired states).

The patient will already have some, if not all, of these resources. But it is almost certain that he will not be aware of them. As long as he is associated into the problem, his (unsuccessful) struggle will be to dissociate—and 'dissociation', in his terms, will be to engage in the frustrating attempt to not-have the symptom.

By trying not to have the problem, he has inadvertently placed himself in the paradoxical bind we call a 'bonded disconnection'. The more he struggles to disconnect, the more closely bonded he becomes.

Shaping is not in itself a therapeutic technique. As with elements of the earlier stages of the consultation (including engagement; lowering systemic overload; priming; respecting and listening to the patient's story; and applying the Clinical Questioning Matrix), the purpose is to orientate the patient in the direction of improvement, healing, and health.

By incorporating elements presupposing the capacity to change, you are assisting him to expand his incomplete or deficient map. In doing this, you also help him to change the qualitative feel of his experience.[178]

It is important to gauge your patient's response, and to move at a pace that is comfortable for him. To move from his problem-state to a desired state may be perceived, consciously or unconsciously, as an unbridgeable gap. The processes outlined in this chapter are intended to prepare him to 'receive' the elements of change.

Thus, the practitioner's role here is twofold: to help the patient successfully dissociate so he can more easily perceive his situation within a *wider* context (the rest of his life), without collapsing back into it, and, simultaneously, to begin to notice some of the resources mentioned above.

Stacking anchors

Initially, the practitioner's role will be to collect and build on the elements he elicits indirectly and conversationally. The process of 'stacking' anchors is his instrument of choice. Stacking is accomplished by setting multiple anchors in the same location, using the same trigger. The intention is to build a 'mega-state' by adding together the qualities of each component.

For example, a stacked anchor may be built out of qualities such as optimism, curiosity, humor, and adventurousness. Once you have created a stacked anchor, test for a response. First, change conversational direction momentarily ('By the way, how did you get here today?'). This is known as 'breaking state'. Pause, then re-fire the anchor using exactly the same trigger, watching to ensure that the patient re-enters the target state. If he does, the consultation continues. If not, return to the elicitation and anchoring stage of the process.

Do not assume that an anchor has been set simply because you have gone through the steps. Always test it before proceeding.

Feedback

The British astrophysicist, Sir Fred Hoyle, once calculated that a blind man trying to solve the Rubik's cube by trial and error at a rate of one random move a second would take 1.35 trillion years, or, around 300 times the supposed age of the earth.[179] However, if he received feedback in the form of yes/no guidance from an experienced cubist, it would take him less than 90 seconds.

In today's politically correct atmosphere, students are often warned against 'telling' people what to do. This uncompromising approach is regrettable, especially as the patient arrives in your office or greets you in his hospital bed with the presupposition that you have knowledge by which he can benefit.

We agree the autocratic orders delivered by some egocentric practitioners have a detrimental effect (and may get you sued). However, with rapport and deep engagement, and simple good manners, giving effective feedback to the patient enables an efficient transfer of your knowledge to his resource-bank.

In giving informative feedback, you have three verbal options:

- right-wrong (R-W);
- no response-wrong (N-W); and
- no response-right (N-R).

Without doubt, telling people what they are doing wrong has a negative effect. As any good schoolteacher knows, the learner can easily become demoralized and passive when progress is measured by failure.

Research indicates that reinforcing 'correct' responses is considerably better—but by far the best results are obtained by consistent and appropriate guidance as to right and wrong maneuvers.[180]

The following technique achieves this conversationally without patronizing overtones.

The 'And...But' pattern

The practitioner can deliver feedback while continuing to shape the patient's responses and behaviors, weaving them in with the And...But Pattern.

As we've mentioned before, 'but' is an example of a 'turning' or 'inclusive' word that reduces the impact of the statement immediately before it, or dictates which part of the sentence should be considered and which can be ignored. 'And' is a conjunction that connects thoughts, clauses, and sentences sequentially into a single whole.

For example:

Patient: *'It's just so difficult to lose weight...'*
Practitioner: *'I know it's been a challenge* [pace], ***but*** [directs away: **W**] *you have to admit you have lost some weight,* ***and*** [connects: **R**] *that deserves some credit, doesn't it?'*

Patient: *'That's true* [practitioner may choose to anchor here]...*but I'm always hungry.'*
Practitioner: *'**But*** [directs away: **W**] *that only means you're not yet eating the right kind of foods, **and*** [connects: **R**] *some good foods are better and fill you up more, wouldn't you say?'*
Patient: *'Well, I could do better, I suppose. I'm not very good at this.'*
Practitioner: *'**But*** [directs away: **W**], *you've already lost quite a lot of weight. You're already doing pretty well* [pace]. ***And*** [connects: **R**], *if you do a little advance planning, it will be much easier. **But*** [directs away: **W**], *of course, that means thinking ahead a bit.'*
Patient: *'I guess I could do a bigger shop on Saturdays...'*
Practitioner: *'Good thinking* [pace]. ***And*** [connects: **R**] *then you can enjoy the rest of the week without having to run out to the supermarket...'*

Conducted elegantly, the process may be seen as a gentle, good-natured game. However, the practitioner is urged to avoid at all costs what is known as a symmetrical argument, which arises when he responds to the patient's 'Yes, but...' with a counter-argument. If the patient's argument is met by a counter-argument, be sure he will follow that with a counter-counter-argument, and so on, until the practitioner surrenders. This is known colloquially as 'being yes-butted', and it's a frustrating and fruitless experience.

Your options are to use the patient's responses to reshape meaning and direction before that happens...and to avoid the 'bait' when it's dangled in front of you.

EXERCISES

1. Anchoring is the core skill of effective NLP. We urge practitioners to become as proficient as possible in the technique, not just to link positive states to external triggers, but because, as we will illustrate in subsequent chapters, anchoring is a fundamental principle involved in virtually all Medical NLP techniques—including ones you develop yourself.
    - Begin by practicing self-anchoring. The process involves

accessing and amplifying a strong desired state, and then linking it to a specific physical trigger (e.g. touching finger to thumb, or pressing on a knuckle). Break state, test and repeat, until you can re-enter the state at will. Give some consideration to the quality of the state. Identify the sub-modalities involved, and then intensify them.

- Extend your skills to creating kinesthetic anchors with others. Guide and amplify your partner's state, then anchor it. Break state, test and repeat, until your partner can re-enter the state at will. Pay special attention to your subject's minimal cues (changes in color, breathing rate, posture, etc) so you can also begin to learn to 'read' state changes in your patients.
- Extend your anchoring to the auditory and visual channels. We have made some suggestions for non-kinesthetic anchoring above. Another aid is to visualize a transparent screen between you and your subject and place your gestural anchors precisely in place each time you set and fire them. Should you shift the position of your body in relation to the screen, you must ensure that you stretch or bend your arm precisely to position the anchor in the same place.

2. **Feedback** and the **And…But Pattern** are best practiced in stages. Simple feedback might initially involve a simple, 'That's right' accompanied by an affirmative nod of the head where you are reinforcing a desired behavior or response, and a slight head-shake when you wish to divert the subject away from a position he has taken. Ensure that you immediately follow the 'negative' response with a more resourceful alternative. Adding 'and' or 'but' to the process should follow naturally as you become more comfortable with delivering feedback in a way that remains respectful of the patient's world-view.

12

The Symptom as Solution: when the body speaks

Wisdom is with you always, overseeing your body, even though you may not recognize the fact. Do something against your body and this wisdom will eventually admonish you—***Jalāl ad-Dīn Muhammad Rūmī***[181]

You may already have experienced this. You're in a café in a country where nobody speaks your language. You have an overwhelming desire for a coffee and the waiter is standing by to take your order. If you're lucky, you can get by with the universal language of gestures (miming sipping from a cup, pointing at the Lavazza machine).

But supposing your needs are a bit more complex. You want half-caffeinated, half-decaf. Skimmed milk, topped up with hot water, but extra foam. And, since you're watching your weight, you want to know if he'll bring you some artificial sweetener.

Suddenly, it's not so easy. On an unequal battle-ground, neither side can win. You may even 'kiss your teeth' and throw your head back in exasperation, but if this happens to be in a country where that gesture means 'yes', he rushes off to bring you something you don't want. Or, if your waiter is African or West Indian, where 'teeth-kissing' is a supreme insult, you may get a lot more than a sugar substitute for your pains.

This is the position the patient suffering from a complex, chronic 'functional' disorder finds herself in. At some level, she knows a lot about her dis-ease, but words just seem to widen the gap of understanding.

Now, put yourself in the waiter's shoes. He's confronted by a gesticulating, increasingly angry or frustrated customer, whose mimed gestures are becoming increasingly bizarre ('What on earth does a little square shape drawn in the air followed by several pats on the midriff have to do with coffee? Oh, good—he's said, "Yes". At last…').

This is the position the practitioner finds herself in when she tries to sort through the avalanche of signs, symptoms, and complaints the patient is sending in her direction. In a world where logical, linear, sequential, digital data are considered superior to feelings, imagery, relationships, and subjective experience, it's no wonder that the practitioner and the patient in our analogy will attempt to generate even more words in the hopes that some consensual 'explanation' will emerge. It's no surprise that the person who holds most power in the relationship will jump at a piece of information (the head-toss and teeth-kissing) that seems to make sense, *in terms of her own map*, and run with it. But, as this happens, both parties slide further down the greased pole of the Structural Differential, away from the patient's experience and into the abyss of ever-increasing inference and abstraction.

There is another way, and this is what this book is about.

But, first, a case history:

Case history: *A woman in her mid-30s had returned to the doctor's practice after the latest, unsuccessful, investigation into a painful allergy that had been making her life miserable for the previous three years. Because it usually occurred at night, marked by large, inflamed wheals, suspicion fell on possible allergens, such as dust mites, laundry detergents, and synthetic fibers. However, extensive tests had failed to identify the cause, and the patient despaired that her problem would ever be resolved. Depressed, anxious, and suffering from sleep deprivation, she described how her condition was destroying her relationship; she felt 'cut off' from her partner, who was becoming increasingly frustrated with her reluctance to have sex. 'It's as though we're living in different worlds and we're separated by a wall we just can't get through,' she remarked bitterly. As always, we suggest practitioners go back to basics when a problem seems overwhelmingly complex. This is similar to what therapist Sheldon Kopp calls going 'back to one'[182]—temporarily abandoning theories and assumptions, and returning to the baseline of the Medical*

NLP consultation: gathering sensory-based information.

Pursuing a conventional investigative approach had, so far, proved fruitless, so the practitioner decided to re-enter her 'beginner's mind' state. Hoping, at least, to be able to restore a more optimistic direction in which they could both work, she asked the patient, 'When the problem is finally resolved, what will you be able to do that you haven't been able to do so far? What will be different and better about your life now?' (These are standard, presuppositional, solution-oriented questions characteristic of Medical NLP. They are usually applied early in the first consultation, but the practitioner should feel free to check back at any point to see if the patient's outcomes have clarified or changed.)

To the practitioner's surprise (and, she admits, to her dismay), the patient began to weep. Sensing that the woman needed to dissipate her grief and despair, she resisted the urge to comfort her, remained engaged and present, and did what many health professionals find particularly difficult to do in their busy and pressured world...absolutely nothing.

After a while, the woman raised her head, dabbed at her still streaming eyes and said indistinctly, 'I want a baby. My life is empty without a child.'

'And, have you talked about this with your partner? What does he think?'

The woman drew a long, shuddering breath, and then let it out. 'He wants one too—very much...but, I don't think it's possible.'

On reflection, the practitioner admitted that she responded according to what she believed the woman was saying, rather than to what was actually meant. She said, 'You might have to approach it differently, especially if making love is painful, but I don't see any reason why you shouldn't be able to have a baby.'

The patient paused, then leaned forward and spoke softly, but emphatically. 'You don't understand. It's not that. It's that I know he's not the right one. I want a baby, and he's willing to have one, too, but I don't want it with him. I've never admitted that to anyone, not even myself. The idea of having a baby with someone I don't love makes my skin crawl.'

It took a moment or two, the practitioner later admitted, 'but, then it was as if all the lights went on'. Some gentle questioning fleshed out the picture. The 'allergic response' occurred only at night, and only when she was with her partner. She hadn't noticed it before (and nor had any of the specialists she had consulted), but on the few occasions she'd been away from home on a work assignment and sleeping on her own, the symptoms hadn't appeared.

'What do you think that means?' the practitioner asked. The woman smiled faintly. 'That it's all in my head? That's what the other doctors think. I can see that from the way they talk to me.'

'Of course it's in your head,' the practitioner said. 'But, it's also very much in your body. It can't be in one and not the other.' The remark seemed to resonate with the patient, so the practitioner continued. She explained that the function of the immune system was essentially protective. Its role was to distinguish between 'me' and 'not me', and to defend against anything it perceived as threatening the boundary between the two. 'It's just a guess,' she added, 'but could it be that your immune system knew something you hadn't really thought out clearly for yourself. What do you think?'

The patient's words tumbled out. She had known 'at some level' that the relationship had to end. She realized she was being unfair to her partner by not telling him that she didn't love him. She thought she had to be open with him. She was nervous about his response, she said, but added, without a touch of irony, that she needed to 'grow a thicker skin'.

The premise that unresolved emotional issues can be expressed as physical symptoms is almost as old as the practice of medicine itself. But, the search for the 'deeper meaning' of 'psychosomatic' disorders has traditionally been long, arduous, and often unrewarding. This is further complicated by the abundance of theory-driven schools and models of therapy, each of which competes for supremacy over the others.

Our proposal, then, is that the process of helping the patient to restore both physical and emotional balance can be substantially quicker and easier when we learn to defer less to dogma and more to the expertise and communication style of the undisputed expert in the problem at hand: the patient who is presenting it.

When permitted to speak freely, the patient usually presents a narrative rich in detail and meaning. But, unlike the logical, linear signs and symptoms that traditionally govern clinical investigation, meaning emerges in a form of description that is usually overlooked. This is densely packed with words, phrases, imagery, actions, and behaviors that represent (present again) the problem state in a more dynamic form.

More than mere linguistic and behavioral artifices, these 'stand for' a much more complex inner landscape. This is what linguists refer to as metaphor.

The significance of metaphor

Traditionally, a metaphor is a figure of speech which, normally used of one class of object, action, etc, is extended to another. In everyday conversation, and, especially in consultations, metaphors are everywhere—so much so that we rarely notice them.

If we return to our analogy at the start of the chapter, we can point to a number of examples: the health professional as 'waiter', the patient as 'customer'; their communication problems as a battle' fought on an 'uneven battleground' where there could be no 'winners'.

Then there are the non-verbal metaphors: the little square packet of sweetener 'drawn' in the air, the patting of an expanding waistline, representing, 'I'm watching my weight', the 'kissing' of the teeth and the 'tossing' of the head.

Similarly, imagery used by the patient whose case history is presented above includes various forms of walls and barriers that, nonetheless, create 'emptiness'. She craves something to fill the emptiness, but 'part' of her is repulsed by the idea of that happening with someone she does not love. Failing to speak out about and resolve this inner conflict, her immune system takes over the job. In evolutionary adaptive terms, we might even propose that it is preventing her from reproducing with an unsuitable mate. Her skin, literally, 'crawls' to prevent that happening.

Metaphor in whole-person healing

The metaphoric content of communication cannot be ignored if we truly mean to practice 'whole-person' healthcare. In either screening metaphors out or dismissing them as verbal flourishes that have nothing to do with 'fact', we lose information that could considerably increase our understanding. We choose text over context, facts over story, left brain over right. We drain off the lifeblood of subjective experience, and then blame the corpse for its lack of co-operation.

The truth is: *we cannot communicate without metaphor*. It is not merely the way in which we add color, depth, and poetry to bald facts, but it is how we organize and make sense out of our experience, express the inexpressible, and seek resolution when our complex homeostasis becomes dangerously upset. Above all, *the symptom itself can function as a metaphor*—and, as such, can help practitioner and patient uncover the structure, origin and meaning of the presenting problem, and therefore arrive significantly more quickly and easily at resolution.

The origins of metaphor

Elsewhere in this book (see pages 77 to 81) we look at the component parts—the 'building blocks'—of subjective experience. The sensory modalities and their distinctive qualities, the sub-modalities, are to our sense of 'reality' what bricks and mortar are to a building. But what gives meaning and purpose to the building is metaphor.

If the building is a house, is it also a 'home', or perhaps a 'sanctuary' for you and your family, or perhaps a 'showpiece' that places you in a particular position in your society? Size and shape may expand the possibilities for its use, but the *concept* driving its design and construction dictates how we will relate to it.

Linguist George Lakoff and philosopher Mark Johnson believe that our language and thinking are both metaphoric in nature.[183] Additionally, they suggest that both our verbal and non-verbal actions are metaphorically structured. We cannot accurately describe our inner world in linear sequential terms, simply because our experience of that unique landscape *precedes* its arrangement into the grammar of communication. And we cannot act without in some way expressing the greater complexity of that inner world.

Some cognitive linguists believe that our primary metaphors are unconsciously acquired in our early years, largely by associating experiential domains (say, the closeness of your mother's embrace with enjoying 'close' friendships in later life).[184]

Metaphoric constructs, each with its own neural network, both trigger and shape our physical and emotional responses in hundreds of different two-way interactions. The fact that they usually function below the level of conscious awareness is significant. The neural circuits that allow us to operate on both literal and figurative levels leave their traces indirectly—through certain words, phrases, actions (such as distinctive gestures), and, as we have already said, the appearance and development of symptoms themselves.

Metaphor in NLP and Medical NLP

Traditionally, NLP uses practitioner-generated metaphors adjunctively with other techniques. These are usually isomorphic—that is, stories or anecdotes that follow the structure of the problem but with a suggested solution appended. Derived from the work of Milton Erickson, who had a vast repertoire of therapeutic stories, they are intended to bypass conscious awareness to be embedded in and acted upon by the patient's unconscious mind.

Practitioners trained in Medical NLP use metaphors in this manner wherever relevant; telling a story about 'someone else' who solved a similar problem can be immensely encouraging to a patient. However, our focus in this chapter is on another class of metaphor—that spontaneously generated by the patient.

Patient-generated metaphors

The metaphors that emerge spontaneously in the patient's story and during information-gathering fall into two distinct categories: linguistic metaphors, and the symptom itself.

The felt sense

Although from our earlier discussion about sub-modalities, it is easy to understand that metaphors derive from the way we use our sensory modalities, all problem-based metaphors have at their core a kinesthetic, or 'felt sense'. This is almost a truism; all patients seek help because, in one way or another, they 'feel bad'. In Korzybski's model, there is an awareness of some neurological disturbance at the Object level. It is this felt sense which disturbs them and from which they seek respite. However, unlike conventional medicine that may seek reduction or elimination of the felt sense, Medical NLP regards it as an entry-point to the silent, flowing level of the Event. Integrating transformational approaches into the regular consultation process requires that the practitioner works at 'tuning' his senses to listen for and observe the patient's metaphoric communication.

Linguistic metaphors

Some years ago, Western medicine recognized and paid attention to what was then called 'organ language'. Phrases such as 'pain in the neck' and 'heart-broken' were given equal weight along with objective signs and symptoms in arriving at diagnoses.

Today, we (the authors) prefer the term 'somatic language', which should not be confused with what physicians often refer to as 'somatization'. Somatic language comprises figures of speech, used unconsciously, but semantically related to the physical and/or psychological problem presented by the patient. When practitioners begin to pay attention to this phenomenon, they are often astonished by the layers of meaning present in the patient's speech.

Here are just a few examples of somatic language phrases encountered in our own consultations:

> *'My boss makes me so hot under the collar. I'm scared one day I'm just going to blow my top'* (from a man with high blood pressure).

> *'I've had enough. I've had a gut-full of things'* (from a patient diagnosed with irritable bowel syndrome).

> *'I'm always there for other people, but they don't give me the support I need'* (from a woman whose rheumatoid arthritis reduced her to walking—when she could walk—with sticks).

> *'I know I should leave my husband, but each time I think about it I get cold feet'* (from a woman diagnosed with Raynaud's disease, a condition 'of unknown cause' marked by highly reactive arteries of the fingers or toes, painful spasms and unduly cold hands and feet).

> *'People always expect me to mother them, but nobody ever asks about*

what I want' (from a woman faced with a diagnosis of breast cancer and the prospect of a mastectomy).

'*I feel as though I'm going to drive off a cliff*' (from a car salesman with agitated depression).

'*My father always told me to keep my head down and not draw attention to myself*' (from a golf pro who developed the 'yips'—a term used by golfers to describe a nervous response that causes them to lose form—each time he came near to winning a championship).

It should be emphasized that patients never consciously use true somatic language. The words and phrases occur without any discernible awareness or irony. We caution against drawing them to the patient's attention lest we abort the unconsciously driven communication process, or embarrass him with his 'Freudian slip'. Equally, guard against jumping to conclusions. Without supporting evidence, it would be presumptuous and potentially damaging to attribute a specific meaning where meaning may not exist.

Using patient-generated somatic language

Patients will often report feeling 'really listened to' when the practitioner simply matches the somatic language used. But utilizing it therapeutically requires exploring and expanding the imagery to include the potential for solutions. Sometimes a simple reframing of the patient's metaphor is sufficient. Here is the practitioner's response to the golfer who had lost his form:

'*Well, "keeping your head down" when you swing is a good thing, isn't it? So, your Dad gave you some good advice there.*' (This is said lightly, and the patient gets the joke.) '*But, we know he wanted the best for you, so what else could he have intended by telling you not to draw attention to yourself?*' (Here the father's positive intention is presupposed; contrary to some psychoanalytical theories, we believe very few parents deliberately set out to make their children miserable.)

Patient: *'…Maybe not to take risks in case I failed? Perhaps, in his way he was trying to keep me from getting hurt…'*

'Maybe. And, you mentioned earlier that he'd never had the experience of really achieving anything important in his own life. Did I understand that correctly?' (The patient agrees.) *'So, I wonder how that will change for him when he experiences real success through his son's achievements.'*

This reframing simultaneously suggests that the patient will return to form and that his achievements will serve both him and his father. The conversation continues in this direction with some further tips about managing stress, etc, as a win-win solution for everyone, and is negotiated without recourse to, or even any suggestion of, antidepressants or betablockers to deal with the golfer's nerves.

The symptom as metaphor

Taken as a whole, the patient's story, including his language patterns, provides the practitioner with tools further to explore the condition.

All of the above presupposes a kind of 'enfoldment' of all the characteristics of the problem—including its history and biology—into the symptom. Attempts to 'unfold' the complex nature of this complex state have, thus far in Western medicine, been essentially linear, left-brained, logical and, clearly, incomplete. By alternating this essentially left-brain approach with the creative, right-brain, relationship-detecting talents of your cognitive processing abilities, a 'bigger picture' will begin to appear.

The questions to bear in mind when reviewing the totality of the condition as presented are:

1. How does it work?
2. What are its origins?
3. What need is it trying to meet?
4. What other (healthier, more resourceful) behavior or response would satisfy that need?

How the problem works

How the condition 'works' is discussed at some length elsewhere in this book (see Chapter 6, pages 69 to 81 and Appendix D, pages 367 to 369). The way the patient structures his experience—his preferred sensory modalities, sub-modalities, and the sequences involved (strategies)—may be elicited (chunking down) directly by questioning, or indirectly by noting eye accessing cues and sensory predicates. Be sure to calibrate and test to ensure that your observations match the patient's internal experience.

Origin, purpose, and intention

Medical NLP is less concerned with 'causes' than with solutions. Nevertheless, understanding how the problem was established (or is perceived to have been established) and its purpose or intention can provide a useful starting point for restructuring the experience. Our intention in establishing a symptom's origin is not to dwell unnecessarily on a stressful experience, but to understand how the patient set up his response to the experience.

Here is an important Medical NLP presupposition: it is not what happened in the past (injury, etc) that is the problem but how the individual is responding in the present to what happened in the past.

Here are some useful guiding presuppositions:

1. At some time in the past, the patient's ability to respond and adjust effectively (restore allostasis) was compromised, either by a single sensitizing experience, or by a series of unrelieved stresses;
2. The autonomic arousal presently experienced by the patient results from both the 'imprint' of the original stressor(s) and his ongoing failure to resolve the problem. He has failed to fight or flee. Now he is 'frozen';
3. At the time, the patient, consciously or unconsciously, may have drawn certain generalized conclusions about his situation: e.g. 'If I'm sick, my parents will look after me rather than fight with each other'; 'All men [or women] are untrustworthy'; 'If I get fat then my stepfather won't want to touch me again', etc. The symptom, therefore, functions protectively. It is striving

to prevent the patient re-experiencing the original sensitizing experience by diverting him to some response or behavior that is (unconsciously) perceived as preferable. (In this way, rather than being regarded as an exogenous and inexplicable force creating disease, the symptom is reframed as a disturbing, but nonetheless positively intentioned, aspect of our own internal system of checks and balances.)

Detecting origins

The origins—real or perceived—of the problem may be simply detected by a process known as 'Affect bridging' (explained in full in a later chapter).

Once the origins of a problem have been identified, we may need to explore its purpose or intention and the sequence of actions involved in its execution. One process for achieving is the NLP principle of 'chunking'.

Establishing purpose or intention

Chunking is a term borrowed from computer programming. It refers to how we group and organize 'bits' of information. The technique linguistically shifts a subject's consciousness, either deeper into the details and sequences of a particular experience (chunking down), or towards a more generalized, experiential 'core' state (chunking up). Chunking down can also be seen as the molecular approach, and chunking up as the molar approach.

'Chunking across' reveals similar examples of the same experience.

Metaphors, similes and analogies are examples of chunking across. We will discuss the therapeutic application of chunking in greater detail in later chapters (notably Chapter 16–pages 223 to 226). For now, though, we can apply chunking to access the purpose or intention of a symptom, and to explore alternative means of satisfying that need.

To do this, simply ask the patient, 'If [the symptom] had a positive intention, what would it want to accomplish for you?' Whatever the patient answers, respond with, 'So, if you had [the reply], what would *that* want for you that's even more positive?' Repeat the question until the patient is unable to access any more levels. The word or phrase she uses will usually be a nominalization, with somewhat abstract or even 'spiritual' connotations.

Examples given during a consultation about excessive drinking are:

'It relaxes me.'
'I'm better able to cope.'
'I feel less of a failure.' (Reframed by the practitioner to, 'I feel more successful.')
'More fulfilled.'
'More at peace.'
'More connected.'

Meeting the need

Solutions are often self-evident, once the origins and purpose have been disclosed. For example, the woman with the mysterious allergy decided to review her relationship with her partner; following through with her decision to leave him was enough to resolve her emotional distress. The 'allergy' was still absent a year later.

The practitioner can also assist the patient by chunking across to explore alternative responses. All questions in this class are variations of *in what healthier and more resourceful way can the purpose or intention of the symptom be met?*

Here are some 'solutions' to a few of the cases mentioned earlier:

- The woman diagnosed with Raynaud's decided her 'cold feet' actually prevented her from rushing headlong into potentially problematic situations. Now, she regards the symptom (when it occurs) as a warning signal for her to look more carefully at whatever she might be intending to do.
- The patient with rheumatoid arthritis realized that her family and friends might not have realized she needed support, but she felt she lacked the confidence to approach the subject. She asked for help on how to ask for help, then laughed when we pointed out what she'd just said. She added, 'I guess I just have to do it!'
- The woman with breast cancer decided to focus her attention on those people who saw her as an equal partner in their friendship, rather than striving to satisfy those who continually made demands on her.

Please remember that the interpretation must be generated by the patient, not by the practitioner.

EXERCISES

1. Start by keeping a metaphor log. Pay attention not only to your patients, but to newscasts, television programs, and conversations with your family and friends. Listen for words and phrases that suggest something is 'like' something else (see our comment at the end of this chapter). Notice when someone doesn't feel 'grounded', or is 'off center', or whether they see life or their work as a 'battle', a 'journey', or a 'bowl of cherries'. How much of a match can you detect between the metaphors they present and the way they lead their lives?
2. Write a mini-saga (no more than 50 words) about patients' symptoms. Start with the words, 'I am X's symptom. I want…'
3. Without necessarily applying an intervention, gently probe for the unspoken, unmet need of a patient's symptom. Use the questions suggested in this chapter, or ask yourself, 'What could this be doing for X? How is it protecting her? From what?'

A final message to our more pedantic readers: yes, we do know the difference between a metaphor and a simile. We simply use the word 'metaphor' as a convenient…well, metaphor.

First the patient, second the patient, third the patient, fourth the patient,

13

A Different Kind of Reason: entering the patient's world

fifth the patient, and then, maybe, comes science. We first do everything for the patient; science can wait, research can wait.—***Bela Schick***[185]

The astute practitioner, confronted with a condition that is not readily identifiable, recognizes that he needs to do something both challenging and rewarding. He needs to enter the patient's world.

This is a reversal of the conventional relationship in which the patient is expected to submit to the superior knowledge and expertise of the practitioner. That dynamic has been shown by studies to be counter-productive. Where the patient feels intimidated by the 'authority' of the medical encounter, he will often not disclose the information necessary to arrive at accurate diagnosis and appropriate treatment. In fact, he may even prefer to reveal sensitive information to a computer, or by filling in a questionnaire—even in the knowledge that his confidentiality may be compromised.[186]

Within the patient's world, the problem-behavior will have a logic that extends beyond the symptoms and their cause. The landscape in which he has lost his way needs to be explored and understood before the problem-behavior can be changed.

This approach is, to borrow George Engel's terminology, 'biopsychosocial'. As the word suggests, it recognizes that the patient's biology is intimately related to, or may even be affected adversely by, his relationships and emotions.[187]

We derive the metaphor of 'entering' the patient's world from the martial arts. Many styles historically evolved out of social and religious conditions that forbade meeting violence with violence. Instead, the nature and direction of the attacker's own energy was captured and redirected in a direction other than its original target. Later, more 'spiritual' forms, such as Aikido, re-cast the attacker as a 'partner', and developed elegant, almost balletic, strategies to avoid injury, either to the attacker or to the defender.

In the Medical NLP model, the practitioner is required to 'enter' the patient's map of the world, without necessarily colluding with its distortions, with the intention of re-orientating him in a more useful and appropriate direction. Just as the skillful martial artist needs knowledge, flexibility, and practice to resolve conflict in a spirit unfamiliar to the rest of society, so the Medical NLP practitioner benefits from three skill-sets not normally encountered in a medical context: **normalization**; **dissociation;** and **utilization**.

Normalization

In essence, normalization means we accept whatever the patient presents to us as 'making sense' *within a certain context*. Ultimately, the practitioner's job is to understand what that context is.

Normalizing the patient's experience can be deeply transformational, not least by removing feelings of shame, blame or being 'beyond help'. Only then can the patient relax his efforts enough to entertain the possibility of change.

As an example, we cite the many patients we see whose tension visibly begins to dissolve when we explain their 'anxiety disorder', or 'post-traumatic stress disorder', as simply a name given to a natural, evolutionary survival mechanism that needs to be modulated or updated.

Dissociation

Thus far, the patient has been striving unsuccessfully to dissociate from the symptom in the belief that this will solve the problem itself. In doing this, he inadvertently establishes a bonded disconnection. Medicating his feelings, or suggesting that he will get better if only he challenges and reforms his 'negative thinking patterns', collude with this belief by failing to recognize and validate the purpose and reality of his pain.

By providing only symptomatic relief, both these approaches leave the structure of the core problem intact, and may even risk weakening the patient by removing the 'challenge' to his system, without facilitating his biological and psychological capacity to adapt and grow.

Change, however, cannot take place from within the problem-state, so the patient needs temporarily to be able to step back from his current response or behavior to view it from a more detached perspective. This can be done overtly, by suggesting he see the response or behavior literally on a screen (with himself in the picture) or, indirectly, using language patterns presupposing temporary detachment—'If we could look at this a different way, a bit like a fly on the wall…', etc. This serves to reduce the patient's anxiety when reviewing the problem, as well as opening opportunities for you both to generate new meanings and responses.

Utilization

Utilization recognizes everything the patient brings to a consultation as raw materials of change. The most obvious of these is, of course, the symptom itself.

Many Medical NLP techniques are created by symptom-solution linkage—that is, by connecting the 'trigger' of the problem-state to a new and more appropriate response. This is highly effective in many conditions otherwise considered intractable—and even more so when the new response more effectively meets an underlying need.

Later chapters expand on this theme, but for immediate application, we offer here several 'indirect' interventions based on utilization.

Paradoxical binds

How often does it happen that you absolutely know that if only someone did what you suggested, he would get the result he wants? In real life, of course, people often don't, or won't, follow what you might regard as excellent advice. This is not necessarily because they are being obstructive, but because the change somehow doesn't seem to 'fit'.

Paradoxical binds are linguistic devices that recursively link action X to the outcome Y by making not doing Y the motivation to do X. Confused? *Well, the more confused you become, the more determined you'll be to understand.*

Try this with a friend:

Have him clasp his hands tightly, palm to palm, and extend both forefingers so they are parallel to each other. Deliver the following instruction exactly and with conviction:

> *Now, notice how your forefingers will automatically come together until they touch. I want you to try your best to resist, but the more you resist, the more you exhaust your ability to resist, until those fingers move together and touch…*

…and simply sit back and watch. After a while, you will notice signs of effort. Your friend will pull the fingers apart, but each time the tendency to move together becomes stronger until he surrenders. Whatever explanation he chooses to give, the result is the same. By binding the response directly to the amount of effort he expends resisting it, the outcome becomes inevitable.

Here are some examples:

> *The more you allow the fever and runny nose to run their course, the more quickly your body will destroy the germs causing your cold.*

> *You say it's difficult to relax, so, instead of trying to relax, become as tense as you can be before you allow yourself to relax.*

> *You don't have to stop worrying. In fact, you may be the kind of person who needs to worry—so, I'd like you to set aside exactly 30 minutes at the same time every day so you can concentrate only on worrying as much as you can until you don't need to worry any more.*

(This latter approach—setting a special time during which the symptom must be indulged—has proved useful as an adjunctive treatment to Obsessive Compulsive Disorder.)

Framing and reframing

'Framing', 'preframing', and 'reframing'—setting up or changing the context in which a particular situation or problem is experienced—is an important skill of Medical NLP.

There is no doubt that our attitudes to certain events alter according to the context in which we experience them. There is also considerable evidence to suggest that the meaning and degree of emotion we attach to our experiences directly affects the performance of our immune system through the mediation of the complex orchestration of our hormone, peptide, and cytokine flow.

The sound of a creaking stair during the day may not even be noticed; in the middle of the night, it can trigger feelings of fear and anxiety. Sustained anxiety may eventually result in a deterioration of both performance and the function of cells and organs. Adrenalin-fuelled experiences create different qualitative experiences according to the context in which they occur—'exciting', where the subject is involved in activity he enjoys, 'stressful' when it is activity he fears or dislikes. Since the biochemical impact of 'excitement' differs from that of 'anxiety', reframing proves a useful tool: *'So, when you notice that you're beginning to become stressed at all the things you have to do, you can start to become excited at the prospect of finding ways to manage your time and energy.'*

Three of the most useful applications of framing follow.

1. Preframing

Since the 'expectations' of patient and physician have been identified as a significant component of successful treatment outcomes, preframing is designed to set up both patient and practitioner for improvement and change.[188,189] In general, preframes involve suggestions and assumptions rather than direct statements. Preframes are therefore also classed as presuppositions.

Avoiding the negative preframe. Clinicians often deliver negative preframes while seeking informed consent. This can increase the patient's anxiety and elicit a 'nocebo' response. For example, an overemphasis on side-effects of medications is known by most practitioners to increase patients' experience of some of those effects. Negative preframes often prompt the patient actively to search for these events; they may even cause the adverse response by the same mechanisms that underlie the placebo response.

Examples of commonly used negative preframes in everyday clinical practice include:

'After the surgery, you may experience some swelling, pain, or tenderness and notice some bruising over the scar site. It will be uncomfortable for some weeks afterwards.'

'The glyceryl trinitrate spray you use under the tongue when you get angina will probably give you a headache.'

'The pain may actually get worse following the injection in your knee.'

'We need to do an exercise ECG, chest X-ray, and blood tests to check whether you have heart disease, or whether you might get a heart attack.'

It is relatively simple to deliver relevant information while at the same time actively seeking to reassure the patient, encourage him to tolerate unavoidable discomfort, and orientate him towards improvement and recovery:

'After the surgery, some people experience tenderness and bruising over the operation site. This is quite natural, and, if it does happen, as you begin to recover the swelling goes down and the bruising and pain usually clear up over the next few days.'

'The glyceryl trinitrate spray used under the tongue can give ***some*** *people'* [presupposing 'but not you'] *'a headache as the angina pain clears and your breathing gets better.'*

'You may notice the pain gets worse after the joint injection before it

begins to get better and your knee becomes more comfortable.'

'We need to do an exercise ECG, chest X-ray, and blood tests to make sure your heart is okay. If anything shows up on the tests we'll be able to give you the best possible treatment to make sure your condition improves.'

An audit by Medical NLP Master Practitioner Dr. Khalid Hasan, consultant anesthesiologist at Britain's Queen Elizabeth Hospital, Birmingham, reveals that preframing patients to recover easily and comfortably significantly reduces bed time, and the need for perioperative medication, including pain-killers and anxiolytics.[190]

2. *Content reframing*

The content reframe specifically seeks to change the meaning the patient has attributed to his experience without directly challenging it. A content reframe is specifically called for when the subject has used one or other of the Meta Model violations known as 'complex equivalence' (X is the same as, or means, Y) or 'cause-and-effect' (X causes Y).

Note: The Meta Model as presented in Bandler and Grinder's *The Structure of Magic* is a revolutionary tool for extracting Deep Structure (the actual meaning of a statement) from the Surface Structure (what is said). We urge practitioners to become fully conversant with all the patterns to clarify their own thinking and reasoning and to increase their effectiveness when working with patients.

Meaning and appropriate action are further constricted where nominalizations (processes represented as events, also known as 'reification') are used. For example:

Statement: *'My anxiety'* (nominalization) *'gets really bad as soon as I get behind the wheel.'*

Content reframe: *'Being anxious'* (process returned to the nominalization) *'whenever you get behind the wheel could also remind you to stay alert and drive carefully'* (the 'meaning' of anxiety is changed).

Reframes should never be delivered without adequate pacing and rapport to avoid seeming dismissive or platitudinous. To give another example:

> *'Being over-anxious* ***can*** *be worrying'* (pace). ***'But'*** (turning word) *'being anxious to just the right degree'* (presupposes 'degree' of anxiety can be adjusted) *'can remind you to stay alert and drive carefully... so let's take a look at how we can be sure that the level is just right'* (preframe).

The following are examples of practitioner-generated statements patients brought into our consultations, followed by the reframes that reassured them during subsequent, probably unnecessary, appointments:

> Statement: *'Your lifestyle and lack of exercise are causing these symptoms and increasing your risk of getting heart disease. You have to change all this.'*
>
> Reframe: *'Your symptoms are messages from your body telling you that now is a good time to start eating more healthily and getting some regular exercise.'*
>
> Statement: *'Colds are caused by a virus. We don't give antibiotics for that.'*
>
> Reframe: *'The mild fever and the stuffy nose are signs that your immune system is fighting off the virus really well. We wouldn't want to do anything that might interfere with your body's natural responses.'*
>
> Statement: *'The growth was cancerous and if left it could have spread and become terminal.'*
>
> Reframe: *'The growth was cancerous, but luckily we've found it early enough to remove it and do everything we can to make sure you remain well in the future.'*

3. Context reframing

As its name suggests, 'context reframing' seeks to normalize or validate responses or behaviors by transferring them to a wider or different context.

One of the earliest presuppositions out of which NLP developed was that *all behavior has value, although sometimes that behavior is better suited to a different situation.* For example, 'anxiety' may be perceived as a 'problem'. 'Being anxious', though, is a natural and protective response to a real or potential threat, and can serve to help us avoid the perceived danger or create contingency plans to deal with it when it comes.

In order to create a context reframe, ask, '*Where else might this response or behavior be useful?*' Context reframes are appropriate when the speaker reasons or explains an experience using a Meta Model violation that involves judgment while deleting information that could justify the judgment. Listen especially for the word 'too', although this might be implicit in the statement. Examples are 'I'm too busy'; 'I'm too anxious'; 'He's demanding'; 'I'm stressed'.

Asking where else this behavior or response might be useful or relevant, we replace the problem frame with one that suggests relevance and change. 'Being busy', for example, may be reframed as useful 'when there are specific tasks to be done' (implying, or stating overtly, that there is also a benefit to relaxing, where appropriate).

Obsessive behavior may often be brought under control where treatment includes providing a context frame in which the behavior would be appropriate (we know of a woman who had a cleaning obsession that she re-directed into setting up a popular and highly profitable celebrity housekeeping service). Patients may even be comforted by context reframes applied to certain organic disorders—the sickle cell anemia trait, for example, may be regarded as 'useful' in an area with a high incidence of malaria, since it confers added resistance to the malarial parasite.

Reframes of all kinds will not 'take' if they are not matched to the situation at hand. Richard Bandler advises the practitioner to use all sensory modalities to replicate the subject's complaint, and then asking himself the questions, 'What else could this response/behavior mean?' and 'In what other situation could this be useful?'[191]

Utilization in practice

The following is a transcript of part of a consultation with a young professional woman referred after being diagnosed as having 'psychotic episodes'.

> ***Case history:*** *The patient reported problems with a former boyfriend who was making her life a misery. According to her version of events, it was a classic case of 'stalking': wherever she went, there he was; silent calls and hang-ups several times a night; suddenly appearing when she least expected it. She would often look out of her bedroom window in the middle of the night and see him standing in the shadows of the trees on the other side of the road. Sometimes he would ride past her, motorcycle helmet covering his face, 'just to let me know he knows where I am at any time and can reach me whenever he wants'.*
>
> *There was just one problem: the ex-lover was in Canada, and she lived on the other side of the world. Moreover, she knew he now lived abroad. But her explanation was 'simple': he had profound psychic powers that allowed him to appear wherever, and in whatever form, he desired.*

Many practitioners we speak to report similar cases: spell-casting, the evil eye, psychic control, 'spirit' manifestation. Some of these are examples of different cultural beliefs and interpretations, others of 'psychiatric' disorder.

Problems of this class occur when the subject fails effectively to resolve conflicts caused by a collision between internal and external 'realities'. Whether we regard these experiences as 'real' or not is irrelevant—and frankly we don't presume to know. However, responsibility for helping sufferers of such conditions, broadly diagnosed in the Western paradigm as 'psychiatric', increasingly falls on primary care physicians.

This pressure, coupled with the widespread, but ill-founded, belief that 'mental illness' is the result of chemical imbalance in the brain, is confusing, and we sympathize with those who resort to psychotropic medications in the hope that the symptoms will come under control. Not only are these problems perceived as complex and deep-seated, but, to the unskilled practitioner, complaints as apparently bizarre as 'remote stalking' can be unnerving.

Our assertion is: they need not be. By focusing on structure and process, we can supplement our existing helping skills without colluding with the patient or directly attacking his beliefs.

This is especially important when consulting with people from cultures in which such beliefs are not exceptional. Many cases of 'disordered thinking', when viewed in the context of the culture in which they occur, turn out to have reasonable explanations. Only relatively recently, for example, has it been recognized that many patients of Caribbean backgrounds diagnosed by British psychiatrists as schizophrenic were in fact suffering from a particularly acute form of stress triggered by racism.[192]

Our approach, then, seeks not to challenge and replace the patient's 'reality' with our own, but to help the patient discover new choices and coping strategies. To accomplish this, we need to look at the symptomatic behavior and ask ourselves two questions: how can this be acting to protect the patient, and how, in his model, could it be explicable or 'true'?

With the patient referred to above, the practitioner's reasoning went in the following way. When people experience the loss of a loved one, they often refuse to accept that the relationship has ended.[193] Even though the loved one has died or left, they seem to see or hear them unexpectedly. Thoughts about the loved one occur frequently and unbidden, and attempts to exclude these thoughts seem to increase their frequency and intensity. They try to cope with their feelings of loss and grief by attempting to separate from them—but, at the same time, they might feel guilty about 'forgetting' the loved one in those moments in which they succeed in thinking about something else.

All these responses are commonly experienced and generally regarded as 'normal'. Now, supposing the subject succeeds to some degree in separating out from the unwanted experiences (that is, she successfully denies responsibility for generating the thoughts and feelings), but the experiences themselves persist. *Her left-brain 'spin doctor' then has to come up with a 'rational' explanation for why it is happening.*

Note: The client's comments are in bold typeface. The practitioner's comments are italicized; explanations of his language and therapeutic patterns are bracketed.

Client: 'He was always trying to change me—make me into something else.'

(The client demonstrates resistance to being changed by an outside element or person. The practitioner notes this; change needs to be within the patient's control.)

'In what way?'

Client: 'To make me a better person. More assertive, he said. To stand up for myself.'

(The practitioner notes the phrases 'a better person' and 'to stand up for myself'.)

'Is that something you'd want for yourself?' (The practitioner tests whether the patient really does want to be in control)

Client: 'Well, yes, but not when someone is putting so much pressure on you all the time.'

(Change needs to be self-directed.)

'So, if you could find a way that you could do that for yourself?'

(The practitioner tests for concordance.)

Client: 'Yes, of course.'

(The practitioner anchors the agreement by nodding and smiling, then seeks gently to prompt into rejecting her own earlier presupposition that the ex-boyfriend was too powerful to resist.)

'That's right. So, when you have this experience of his "powers"...' (said in a slightly disbelieving and contemptuous tone).

Client: (*Grimaces*) **'He thinks he's great, but I think he's actually very weak. That's why he has to use psychic stuff to get at people.'**

'That's right and he's not the strongest wizard in the world? That may

be what he thinks he sees reflected in the mirror but thinking he's great is a kind of shield, a protective barrier, deflecting anything he directs at you, wouldn't you say?'

Client: 'Oh, yes.'

(The practitioner anchors her response, and then begins to employ primes directed at the client protecting herself by 'reflecting' and 'deflecting', rather than by counter-attack. This is an ecological consideration. We seek to provide peaceful resolution to both internal and external conflicts wherever possible.)

'And, if you find you have real powers of your own—they don't even have to be psychic—to deflect his powers, would you use them?'

(The practitioner analog-marks the embedded command, 'you have real powers of your own...to deflect his powers...use them'.)

Client: (Uncertainly) **'Uh...Well, I wouldn't want to hurt him, even now. That's not the kind of person I am...'**

'Oh, I'm not suggesting that for a moment. But if there were a way for you to set things up so that he or anyone else couldn't do anything that wasn't in your best interests, you wouldn't be responsible for what happened to them, would you? I mean, if I throw a ball too hard against the wall and it bounces back and hits me in the ribs, is that the wall's fault?'

(The practitioner paces the patient's concern, and then reframes it to return the responsibility for any actions to the 'originator'. This is reinforced by the ball metaphor. Note, too, the faintly confusing 'hypnotic' language.)

Client: (Laughs) **'That's an idea. Like a shield. It'd need to be really tough.'**

(The patient begins to assemble and solidify information suggested subliminally (at no point do we say, 'do this' or 'do that'; this way, we avoid symmetrical argument and the 'yes-but' response). By processing unconsciously and then formulating a solution, the patient is 'taking ownership' of her own response.)

'It would.'

Client: 'Like a really strong mirror…'

(A practical solution: armor that is strong, but portable.)

'Made out of?'

Client: 'Steel maybe, only light enough not to bother me as I move about…'

(The practitioner anchors the qualities and also presupposes that, by taking the proposed actions, the patient can then safely forget—note the embedded command—about consciously responding to a perceived threat.)

'Steel, light. That's right. So, if you could set that up and kind of forget about it, knowing it would continue protecting you, would that be something worth having? And then you can forget the whole thing?'

Client: 'For sure!'

(Strong concordance.)

'And then the problem you've been having isn't your problem any more, so, when that happens, how would you be feeling and acting differently and better now?'

(Note the temporal shifts in the practitioner's language. The problem is expressed in the past tense and the solution—acting differently and better—is presupposed as already existing in the present: 'now'. The question also prompts the patient into a transderivational search to provide subjective meaning to the 'artfully vague' words 'feel', 'differently' and 'better'. This is intended to increase the patient's adherence.)

Client: 'Great. I could just...live my life and enjoy it.'

'And what's interesting to me is that you would ***be a more assertive person****. Stand up for yourself. In a strange kind of way, he might just have helped you to* ***get something you wanted****—except he was going about it the wrong way, and now you can* ***do it for yourself...****'*

(Embedded commands, in bold type, reframing and 'handing over' responsibility for change to the patient.)

Client: 'Yes.' *(Laughs, nods)*

'So, let's just go through it and make sure it fits. Close your eyes and think about what your shield, your protective mirror, would be like...'

(Begins to coach the patient into adopting her new strategy.)

Creating explanations for irrational events is a characteristic of altered states, and often appears bizarre to the observer. The only explanation this patient had was 'psychic control'. In all other areas of her life, she was, by any assessment, entirely reasonable, rational, and sane. On any other subject, in any other situation, she had a grounded, realistic, and reliable perspective. She was, quite literally, being 'driven crazy' by her inability to come to terms with the rejection.

Thus, in Medical NLP, we move, invited, through the patient's territory, with respect for (but not necessarily collusion with) his world view. The changes we help him make accord with and expand his map of reality. Then, when the patient takes ownership of the change, we withdraw. There is no room for 'therapist's ego'. *First the patient...always.*

EXERCISES

1. Select three symptoms a patient might bring to a consultation (e.g., 'My mind races so much at night I can't get to sleep') and write out ways you can: normalize the experience within the context of the patient's life; find a utilization for it and, reframe it—first by content, then by context.
2. Become alert to narratives and symptoms that suggest 'disordered' thinking. Each time you encounter an example, pretend you are the patient and seek out the possible (not necessarily the actual) logic that would need to make the details 'hold water'. Write down your explanations. Regard everything the patient says as 'true', then ask yourself the questions:
   How could this appear true?
   What could this be true of?

14

Getting to Where You Want to Go: directions, outcomes and goals

*If you don't know where you're going, you might end up some place else.—**Lawrence Peter 'Yogi' Berra***

Imagine turning up at the airport booking desk and asking the clerk for a ticket.

'Where would you like to go?' she asks.

'On holiday,' you reply.

'Yes, I understand...but, where?'

You shrug. *'Just...you know...somewhere that's not here.'*

A look of exasperation flashes across her face, but she quickly regains his composure. *'Well, yes, of course. But, where exactly is not here?'*

You glance at your watch; your holiday time is ticking away. You lean across the desk and speak in measured tones. *'You're a travel agent, aren't you? Well, I want to travel. Give me a ticket, and give it to me now!'*

Logic, common sense and master of the malapropism Yogi Berra tell us that if we don't know where we're going, we're likely to get nowhere fast. Few people would even consider embarking on a long-awaited vacation without spending some considerable time and effort deciding on a destination. And, when we get to where we want to go...what then?

A consultation without established outcomes is analogous to trying to buy a ticket from a travel agent without knowing where you want to go.

Despite the United Kingdom's description of the doctor as a 'health navigator', remarkably little outcome-orientation occurs, either in medical training or in official proclamations regarding health 'delivery'. The word 'outcome' is starting to appear on forms and discharge summaries from various clinics, but this is usually a summary of the end-point of the consultation. And patients and health professionals alike assume that the end-point should be either an absence or a continued 'management' of the condition.

Two factors influence this thinking style: Western society's overall problem-orientation (relationships, work, and health are all considered to progress as a result of removing or solving problems), and our lack of practice in identifying what we do want, in place of the problem we presently have. Test this for yourself.

Think of an ongoing problem or shortfall in your life. Ask yourself what your preferred state would be.

Chances are, you answered either in terms of an *absence* of the problem ('less stress at work'), with a nominalized (reified) goal, or a lack of specificity ('more recognition for my efforts'). Both classes of response reflect a problem- or deficit-oriented thinking style. For several reasons, attempts to rectify the situation without having alternatives to move forwards will almost inevitably lead to further problems.

The most significant of these is that 'success' can only be measured in terms of the problem itself. This shifts our attention back on to the problem or deficit, and runs the risk of reactivating the very psychophysical patterns we are trying to resolve. Equally, if problems (especially behavioral patterns) are removed without replacing them with more resourceful alternatives, new patterns may emerge to fill the 'neuronal gap'. This is especially evident with purely behavioral approaches to Obsessive Compulsive Disorder, in which new obsessions and compulsions often replace the old.

Why plan?

A truly solution-oriented approach combines the resources and expertise of both practitioner and patient and requires thought, planning and application.

We are reminded here of a patient diagnosed as schizophrenic who complained that the more he tried to ignore or challenge his 'voices', as suggested by a cognitive therapist, the more strident and disruptive they became. We suggested that he try to ignore the 'quiet times' between the voices, which he later reported, was 'incredibly difficult'. Anyway, he added, he wasn't going to bother because the voices had 'gone away'.

Although healthcare in the West is said to be 'patient-centered', many patients still expect health professionals to take most of the responsibility for managing their treatment.

Patient-centeredness, as developed out of the University of Western Ontario 'Disease-Illness Model', sought to redress the overwhelmingly 'doctor-centered' approach that preceded it.

Echoing the 'customer is always right' retail model, it encouraged patients to be proactive and involved in important decisions regarding their healthcare.[194]

In practice, though, this 'transformed clinical method' overlooks the fact that the patient is often reluctant to make suggestions. She also may be unaware of what is required of her. The health professional, nevertheless, remains legally liable in the event of misadventure.

Our contention is: this 'patient passivity' occurs mainly because no clear outcomes have been negotiated.

The Medical NLP model contrasts with most existing models currently presented in education and practice. Few make reference to 'outcome', except in terms of adherence to treatment programs, in seeking to understand the reason for the patient's attendance or to answer questions, such as, 'What further help can I receive?' What is singularly lacking in these models are tools for formulating, as a partnership, well-formed, practical, measurable, *continuing* outcomes.

In other words: *How does the patient get, and stay, better?*

Medical NLP seeks to develop directions, outcomes and goals that answer questions central to the patient's wellbeing, such as: *'Can I get better?' 'Will I get better?' 'How can I get better?'* And *'How will I know I'm getting better?'* In sum, we need to answer the question posed earlier in this book: *'What does this person need to live a fuller, happier, and healthier life?'* And then we work in partnership to meet those needs.

The requirements of effective outcomes

In order to negotiate effective outcomes, a number of requirements need to be met. The most important is to distinguish between direction, outcome, and goals.

Direction may be thought of as essentially solution-oriented and continuous. As discussed earlier, we regard the patient as bringing with her previously untapped resources, including the innate biological drive towards allostasis, previous successes, and a desire to be well.

The practitioner needs to keep this in mind to avoid encouraging passivity in the patient. It is important, too, to recognize that, once the general direction towards healing and health has been established, the patient may elect to follow an equally productive path that the practitioner had not foreseen. This should be recognized and respected, even though it might not fit accepted wisdom or belief.

Example of direction: Following a specifically defined healthy lifestyle.

Outcome broadly corresponds with clinical effectiveness. Quite simply, has the treatment been a success *from the patient's point of view?*

Outcome should not be confused with the kind of measurement imposed by medical economists, politicians, or insurance assessors. Patient satisfaction as measured by reduced waiting times is not to be equated with patient satisfaction with the outcome of treatment.

Example of outcome: Enjoying the (specified) benefits of a healthier lifestyle.

Goals, often confused with outcomes and solutions, are measurable markers of progress. This is a business model that is useful to measure incremental change, but, in the absence of overall direction and/or outcome, however, an overemphasis on goals at the expense of direction and outcome can limit the ongoing process of healing and health.

Example of goal: Reducing weight by 1.5 kg a week, exercising three times a week, etc.

For simplicity's sake, we will, from now on, refer to 'outcome' to mean the synthesis of direction, outcome, and goal, unless we specify otherwise.

In the Medical NLP model, the practitioner acts as a guide, teacher, and mentor to the patient, as well as a companion on the healing journey.

Our criteria for well-formed outcomes are not intended to be dogmatically applied, but merely to provide a kind of checklist so the practitioner can help the patient to keep his outcomes within the bounds of possibility or reason.

Obstacles to effective outcome-planning

Effective outcomes require careful thought. The patient (and, it must be admitted, the practitioner) can often inadvertently limit the possibilities for change by committing to ill-defined outcomes:

- **The problem is too narrowly defined** ('Your serotonin levels are low. That's why you're depressed.'). **The problem is too broadly defined** ('If in the past month you have felt down, depressed or hopeless, and have been bothered by having little interest or pleasure in doing things, then you are suffering from depression.'). For some years, this 'two-question test' was favored by Britain's National Institute for Health and Clinical Excellence (NICE) to diagnose depression. Many clinicians feel, quite rightly in our opinion, that this diagnostic tool is inadequate and results in a considerable over-diagnosis of 'depression'. Notice how this kind of limited questioning focuses on text at the expense of context (for example, the loss of a loved one, redundancy, etc). Finding yourself 'going round in circles' is often the result of an overemphasis on 'story' or content.
- **The solution is too narrowly defined** ('You need to take medication to correct the serotonin deficiency.').
- **The solution is too broadly defined** ('You need to get out more. Don't sit around worrying so much.').
- **The outcome is premature.** Although it is important that the patient is introduced to solution-orientation as early as possible in the consultation process, an outcome that is fixed too early will limit options that may emerge during the rest of the consultation process.
- **Favoring a familiar or 'established' approach to the problem, or**

intuitively acting on subjective bias. If an outcome occurs very early on in the consultation, or, comes to mind too easily, it needs to be closely examined.

- **Talking without purpose.** While 'talking it through' may be helpful to some people, especially those who have little social support, it should not be confused with developing solutions.
- **Getting caught up in content at the cost of process.** Remember to be cautious of asking the question 'Why?' The risk of triggering a torrent of speculation is high. Instead, favor answers in to questions asking, How? Where? When? With whom? How often? etc.

Now, go back to the problem you were thinking about a few moments ago, and ask yourself what you'd like instead.

Unless you are familiar with solution-oriented thinking, you might have experienced a kind of mental hiccup.

We seldom think in terms of alternatives to 'not having' the problem state. And yet that question alone is sometimes all that is needed to open the patient up to proactively seeking resolution. (Asked this question on the phone, patients frequently arrive for their appointment with a solution already in mind.)

Return to your problem and begin redefining it positively—that is, in terms of a desired (or solution) state rather than as an absence of the unwanted state.

Restore process to any nominalizations by turning abstract nouns into verbs. Identify which part of the problem is within your control, and focus your attention on exploring that. Thus, 'less stress at work' might become, 'I will remind myself to take time out for a few moments and clear my mind even when I have a lot to do', and 'more recognition for my efforts' might be reframed as, 'I will explore ways to measure my own achievements so that I know when I have done a specific job well'.

The NLP change process is often presented as moving from a present or problem state to a desired state (the solution) through the application of appropriate resources. But even before we introduce those resources (*how* she will change), we need to ensure that the patient knows *where* she is going. She will also need to be able to see for herself *that* change is occurring. Not only does she need an expanded map, but she also benefits from new co-ordinates.

Measuring for change

Details of the problem-state will, of course, have emerged during the information-gathering stage of the consultation. Since part of our intention is to have the patient share responsibility for his healing and health, it is important that a system of measurement is in place, and that *the measurement is relevant to the patient*, rather than to the therapist or 'expert'.

Quantifying the patient's level of comfort

The simplest of these scaling devices is what in Medical NLP is known as the Subjective Measurement of Comfort Scale (SMCS). Unlike existing scales designed to measure the severity of a condition (often regarded as an 'objective' guideline to arrive at a diagnosis), the SMCS was designed to provide the patient with a means of focusing on progress, rather than on pain.

Before any intervention begins (as early as the closing stages of the questioning phase of the consultation) ask the patient the following:

'If your problem could be measured on a scale from one to 10, with one being most comfortable and 10 the least comfortable it's ever been, where would you put it right now?'

The wording is important. Notice especially that 'pain' and 'discomfort' are excluded. We are measuring *comfort.* Be sure the patient understands this, or self-measurement will be slewed. Second, we do not give the patient the option of a zero point. This is to avoid a return to the pursuit of a state of no-symptom; we presuppose in the wording that there is enough comfort to make 1 a desirable goal, even though some of the problem is still present. This is intended to encourage coping behavior.

Third, prompting the patient to reframe her condition in this slightly disorientating way (locating the degree of comfort rather than discomfort) begins the process of dissociation, a prerequisite of effective transformation. She starts to 'look at', rather than 'be in', her experience.

Make a note of the patient's SMCS level, and suggest the following,

'So, when the level moves down from (whatever number is selected) to anything less, you'll know you're making progress, isn't that so?'

The process of eliciting outcomes can begin as soon as the SMCS measurement has been completed.

Eliciting outcomes

Although the patient's outcome is important, the practitioner may need to help her edit it for well-formedness. Start by asking the following questions, or variations thereof:

'After you've been able to find a way past the problem you've been having, what will be different or better?' 'What will you be doing differently?' 'How will you be thinking about yourself?' 'What will other people notice about you?' etc.

Structure your questions to elicit responses expressed in all sensory modalities.

In order to experience ourselves and our world differently, we need to see, hear, feel (and sometimes smell and taste) things differently.

Prompt, if necessary, to fill in any gaps.

Note: At this stage, the patient might say simply, 'I don't know…'

Since she has probably never before been asked what she wants instead of what she does not want, she may simply not understand the question. In which case, clarify it (we find explaining that 'the brain needs a direction to go in order to make changes' often helps). Another possibility is that the patient is worried about saying 'the wrong thing', or is suffering from simple performance anxiety. In any event, do not back off. Simply utilize the patient's response and proceed as follows:

'Of course you won't know exactly what will be different and better yet. At this stage, we're just imagining how it could be better. Just make it up…'

Or, jump-start the process by using a variation of the Magic Wand Question popularized by brief therapists:

'If tonight, while you're sleeping, someone waved a magic wand and you woke in the morning to find your problem had been resolved, how would things be better?'[195]

Once the patient has expressed an outcome in all sensory modalities, check that the following criteria are met:

- **Positive, specific and active.** As already mentioned, an outcome should be formulated in terms of what is wanted, not what is not wanted; or, in the case of behaviors, a desired direction in which to move. The outcome should be detailed, without becoming overwhelming. Ensure that it is stated in the present tense. The practitioner can assist in this process by exploring the patient's own model of health, as opposed to her model of disease. Patients with chronic or 'functional' conditions (as well as the professionals they consult) often focus on the latter, thereby depriving both parties of viable, salutogenic alternatives.

- **Realistic and achievable.** This can be challenging to some health professionals. This is especially true where their patient's condition has been declared 'incurable' or 'terminal'.

Our contention is that to install or reinforce the belief that a patient's condition is 'hopeless' could, in itself, be injurious. We simply do not know with absolute certainty that a given outcome will be the same for every patient, every time.

However, we might need to adjust the outcome where instantaneous results are not achievable, or the patient has clearly unrealistic expectations.

- **Process-orientated.** What does the patient need to do as a first step towards change? What specific actions and behaviors does she need to follow in order to maintain progress? It is especially useful here to restore all nominalizations to their verb (action) forms—even if you need to 'invent' new words to fill the need. Adding the suffix '-ing' is one way to accomplish this. 'Cancer*ing*' suggests a greater possibility for change than the noun 'cancer'. Restoring process suggests the condition is something that the patient (or the patient's body) is 'doing', rather than something he 'has', or that has her. It presupposes the possibility of change.
- **Within the patient's control.** As far as possible, especially where behavioral changes are required, the locus of control should rest pre-dominantly with the patient. It is especially important that any outcome dependent on someone else's behavior or response ('I'll feel better when my children stop fighting') is re-negotiated. We often find it necessary to point out to the patient that, although we have no power to change other people, we are able to control our responses to them.

- **Positive intentions preserved.** The purpose or intention of a condition should be thoroughly explored (see the chapter, *The Symptom as Solution: when the body speaks*), and these should be preserved or met by the new response or behavior. Occasionally, the need may be fairly straightforward. For example, one benefit of a state of elevated anxiety, low mood, and poor motivation may simply be to allow the person to get some rest from the stress of overwork.
- **Deleted information restored.** Missing information should be followed up or explored. Common responses include deletions such as, 'They've tried everything and nothing helps.' Consider who 'they' are, what specifically they have tried, whether absolutely nothing has helped, or whether something might have helped, even if just a little.
- **Presuppositions explored.** Consider the statement, 'I've tried absolutely everything and it's just getting worse.' The presupposition in 'tried everything' is that there is indeed nothing at all left to try. The patient's complaining tone may indeed conceal the fear that his condition could end in disability or even death. Exploring presuppositions helps reveal undeclared reasons for seeking consultation.
- **Ecological.** Outcomes should be tested for ecology to ensure they will have no negative impact on areas other than the specific context in which change is required. This includes the effect on immediate family members, associates, and work, as well as in areas such as entitlement to state benefits, housing, access to carers, etc. For example, a patient with a past history of epilepsy who has been fit-free for 10 years may wish to stop all anti-convulsant medication. However, he also needs to consider the risk, however small, of losing his driving license, which may, in turn, affect his employment.
- **Time-related.** Certain interventions benefit from a specified time frame—for example, periodic targets for each stage of weight loss, number of minutes spent exercising, etc. Defining times and specifying 'chunks' keeps outcomes well grounded and measurable.

Trouble-shooting outcome-planning

The importance of having well-formed outcomes cannot be overestimated. The following suggestions are offered to overcome any problems you might encounter.

Performance anxiety. The phrase, 'Just before we begin…' is a useful conversational device to depotentiate your patient's fear about not doing things 'right'. Others that can take the pressure off include, 'I just need a little information, first…' and 'Let's try a little experiment…'

Speculation versus certainty. Patients may be disinclined to commit themselves to an opinion with any certainty. You can circumvent this by inviting speculation. Ask questions such as, 'If you did know [X], what would that be like?' or, 'If you were to take a guess, what would that be…?'

Identifying obstructions to progress. 'If you could think of one thing that stops you from [Y], what would that be?' Any answer to this question can offer additional information useful in developing strategies and intervention. For example, 'I'm afraid of falling' (as opposed to 'I can't walk properly') can direct treatment to resolving fear, rather than focusing entirely on any physiological problems related to walking.

Acclimatizing to the new outcome

Once a well-formed outcome has been successfully negotiated, the patient will need to acclimatize to the changes involved. The purpose is to create a new neural network to facilitate transition from the problem state. (In certain circumstances, clarifying outcomes alone may precipitate change, even though the process is not intended to be transformational in itself.)

Apply the following process to your own redefined outcome:

1. Run through an entire day in your imagination from a dissociated perspective, watching yourself from the moment of waking to going to sleep at night, with the new outcome in place. Do this vividly, engaging all sensory modalities except the kinesthetic. 'Edit' the scenario, if necessary, to correct any problems or deficiencies.
2. When the scenario has been optimized, associate into the scene,

ensuring that you see, hear *and* now feel all aspects of the new behavior or response 'as if' it were actually happening now.

3. Repeat this several times until you find the process running comfortably and easily.
4. This method, important in effective change work, is further explored in the chapter on Repatterning and Future-Pacing.

EXERCISES

1. Write out an outcome of your own, and then refer to the conditions of well-formedness referred to above. Rewrite any sections that need editing.
2. Review any lifestyle plans you may offer to patients to ensure they meet all the conditions of well-formedness.
3. Listen carefully to plans expressed by patients, friends or family and (mentally) test for well-formedness. If there are any violations, suggest (respectfully) how these might be corrected.

15

Thinking in Time: temporal language, permanent change

Time, place, and space are illusions, having no existence save in the mind of man which must set limits and bounds in order to understand.— ***Robert E. Howard***[196]

Think about the last meal you had. Did you enjoy it? Did you linger over each mouthful in full appreciation? Or perhaps it was a sandwich, grabbed at your desk?

Now, think of the meal you ate before the last one. And, the one before that…And, here's the question:

'*How do you tell the difference between your last meal and the ones before?*'

Take a minute to think about this. Compare the two memories. Notice the distinctions between the two. Check the sub-modalities, first of one, then of the other—then together. Here's a guess. The two representations are in different positions in your internal field. One is probably smaller and less distinct than the other. One may even be still, like a slide or photograph, the other moving, like a movie or video.

Now, to challenge yourself, think ahead to your next meal. Decide what you'd like to be eating, where you'll be, who your dining companions will be. More differences.

And, whatever they are, there *are* differences. If there were none, you would have no way of making the kinds of distinction that allow you to separate your life into the categories we call past, present, and future. Without those distinctions, your internal and external life would descend into chaos. Quite literally, you would not know whether you were coming or going.

On a day-to-day basis, most of us have a kind of consensual agreement about 'time'. We agree that everything before today happened in the 'past'. Where we are now (roughly) is the 'present'. Later today, tomorrow, and everything after that are in the 'future'.

We also agree, more or less, when we are 'on time', or not. But after that, things start to become somewhat less clear. Some of us have 'time on our side'; others are always 'running out of time'. We try to get our kids to calm down during exams, reassuring them that they have 'plenty of time' in which to answer the questions. On the other hand, we tell each other how there 'just don't seem to be enough hours in the day', or how that patient who wanted to talk about his family concerns was 'wasting' too much of our precious time. And of course, as we get older, time starts to 'go by' more quickly each year.

Time seems to be something that 'happens to' us—and it happens very differently, according to the situation we are in at the time.

Remember, for example, how slowly time passes when you are standing at a bus stop on a rainy day without an umbrella, or how quickly it whizzes by when you are having fun. Equally important is the distinctive way in which each of us codes time and its passage. This determines not only whether we seem to have enough or too little, but whether the past or the future directs our subjective experience more than the present moment.

Most of us run into trouble over the issue of time because we fail to notice that it is a nominalized word, suggesting a commodity, rather than a process. Time, we are saying, is not a 'thing'.

We have subjective ways of measuring movement from one place or event to another; we have clocks and watches and an awareness of the cycles of day and night and the seasons. But the 'passage' of time—as Albert Einstein upset the scientific world by demonstrating—does not exist in the way we think it does.[197]

The framework of time

Happily, when things are going smoothly, we can continue along our daily lives without too much concern about the 'reality' of time. But when they are not, we can benefit ourselves and our patients by recognizing that, as physicist Sir James Jeans puts it, the 'framework' of time in which we place our experience is personal to individuals or small groups.[198]

The 'personal framework' of time, as experienced by the patient, is the focus of this chapter. Should you repeat the experiment at the start of the chapter with a friend or colleague, you will almost certainly find that the way in which he distinguishes between his last meal and the one before that differs in some degree from your own.

Patients experience and respond to their chronic condition in a number of different ways: in terms of the anxiety it produces; the extent of the effect it has on their lives; the meaning attributed to the condition; the implications for the quality of their future existence, etc. And one of the most prevailing influences concerns time—how long the condition has existed, the duration of an 'attack', when they can anticipate some respite or, in the case of conditions said to be 'terminal', how long they have 'got'.

In fact, enormous semantic confusion surrounds our sense of time. Einstein and the New Physics showed us that all knowledge about 'reality' begins and ends with experience. Experience, in turn, is dependent on our senses. Certainty begins to dissolve before our eyes (and our ears and feelings) when we start to recognize that how, where, and when we apply our attention can affect that quality of our experience. Quite literally, then, we are 'making time'.

The 'meaning' of time

Our attitude to the passage of time is a quality of our relationship with both our internal processes and the world outside. As mentioned above, the experience of waiting for a bus in the rain is likely to be not only 'dragged out', but also unpleasant.

'Type A' people are characterized by an exaggerated sense of urgency. Both their internal 'sense' of the passage of time and their behavior appear restless and 'driven'.[199] Conversely, athletes, artists, musicians, meditators, and martial artists are among a group of people who regularly experience something widely known as 'flow'—a highly pleasurable, timeless state in which activity seems to happen without effort or intention.[200]

The subjective experience of time is a black hole in medical science. Aside from the number of days a patient will occupy a hospital bed, or how long the patient himself will have to endure his pain, time simply does not enter the clinical picture. This is a major omission. How we perceive time can kill or cure.

The birth of time as we know it

Not that far back in our collective history, our attitude to time was different. We lived according to natural cycles—the rising and setting of the sun, the changing of the seasons. Fine measurement was a crude affair. We have used dripping water, trickling sand, knots on a string and marks on a burning taper. But these units of measurement were arbitrary. An hour or a minute or a second simply did not exist as such. Most of us got up as soon as the sun rose and went to bed when it set, until two inventions changed all that. And, in changing the way we marked the unfolding of events, we changed the very fabric of our lives.

Dutch scientist Christiaan Huygens's pendulum clock brought sequential, rather than cyclical, time to our immediate attention.[201]

This was followed by the invention of the electric light, and, suddenly, we were no longer bound by the rhythms of nature—so work, usually for the poorer classes, could extend deep into the night. And while the material benefits were far-reaching (for those who 'controlled' time and the means of buying it from others), for most of us the separation from nature was profound.

Problems with linear time

As a chronocentric (centered on time) society, we have lost our sensitivity to the cycles in nature and to those of our own bodies. We eat, drink, make love, have children, sleep, wake, work, and retire according to the linear measurement of time, instead of when we are hungry, thirsty, horny, paternal, tired, feel rested, or are ready to slow down. Most of us live and die in the thrall of linear time without ever realizing that it does not really exist.

Everything we do (in our Western culture) is based on multiples of something arbitrarily called a 'second'—in fact, nothing more than 9,192,631,770 cycles of the frequency associated with the shift between two energy levels of the isotope caesium 133.[202] This is the nearest we can get to a 'thing' called Time.

Here's a little experiment about how the myth of linear time runs your life:

Using a watch or clock with a second hand, close your eyes as it points to the 12 o'clock mark. Now, mentally review what you have to do today—then open your eyes when you 'feel' one minute has past.

Supposing you didn't cheat by counting off the seconds, how accurate was your estimation? Was your guess less or more than one minute? If it was markedly less than a minute, you are likely to feel tense, 'rushed', as if 'there is never enough time'. If it was markedly more, you are likely to be feeling calm, relaxed, laid back—or bored—with the experiment.

Now...what was your emotional response when you interpreted your particular estimate?

Interestingly, most people are vaguely unsettled by either response: the first because of their underlying sense of hurry, the second because, somehow, they are 'wasting' time.

The toxicity of time

So profoundly influential is the experience of linear time on the health and wellbeing of both patient and practitioner that we have felt compelled to create a word—'chronopathic'—to describe the disorders in which the perception and experience of time play a significant part.

To that, we have added 'hyperchronic' (the sense of time passing too quickly) and 'hypochronic' (time dragging) to describe the experiences and responses of those suffering from chronopathic disorders. At the top of all the surveys of doctor dissatisfaction we have reviewed from both the United Kingdom and the United States is lack of time. At the top of all the surveys of patient dissatisfaction we have reviewed from both countries is...lack of time.

It is saddening that the very interaction intended as a healing encounter should be marked by one of the disorders it should be seeking to resolve. In earlier chapters, we discussed stress and allostatic load as underlying factors in all chronic conditions. Here, we contend that the subjective perception of time can be one of the most important contributors to allostatic load.

The 'toxic' effects of time-perception are not entirely restricted to feeling its lack. The 'passage' of time is experienced in different ways, each with its own impact on the individual. But the most prevalent, and arguably the greatest, risk factor is the feeling of having too much to do with too little time in which to do it. Hyperchronicity is virtually unrecognized as pathological in Western medicine, except perhaps as an element in the catch-all diagnosis of 'stress'.

Medicine's response to this is limited: take time off and reduce your commitments…or, take the pills.

Time-poor patients, once described as suffering from 'hurry sickness', are vulnerable to a wide range of illnesses. These include abnormal heart rate and blood pressure; elevation of blood hormones, including adrenalin, insulin, norepinephrine, and hydrocortisone; increased gastric acid and insulin production; breathing disorders; sweating; and musculoskeletal pain.

Patients suffering from hyperchronicity are particularly susceptible to cardiovascular disease, type II diabetes and metabolic syndrome.

As may be expected, hyperchronicity affects high achievers driven by goals, deadlines and targets—all characteristics of what economists call 'turbo-capitalism'. A short time ago, this was considered to be essentially a male response, but an increasing number of women are reported to be presenting with similar life and work patterns—and the consequences thereof.

To our knowledge, only one country in the world has officially recognized the consequences of time poverty and turbo-capitalism on the individual. Japanese researchers have made a positive connection between a model known as 'lean production', purported to improve economic productivity, and sudden death from cardiovascular and cerebrovascular disease. These types of death, known as karoshi (**Figure 15.1**), are said to be caused by increased workload, shift work, and abnormal demands on the worker's time.

過労死

Figure 15.1 Karoshi, or death by overwork

But 'too little time' is also a health factor for patients lower on the socioeconomic scale, especially unemployed single mothers. Hurry sickness is not simply the price you pay for being rich.

Time and chronic disorders

The patient's felt sense of time will usually differ from his experience of its duration. The felt sense is often one of constriction. As we have said elsewhere (see pages 175, 243, 265 and 322), feelings of discomfort are usually constricted, localized and intense. Duration—in chronic disorders—is expanded; the problem seems to stretch endlessly across 'space'.

Time distortion is a characteristic of altered states, and illness is, by definition, a state that differs from the patient's default 'normal' state.

Depending on the condition, the degree of discomfort is related to the degree of attention being paid to both felt sense and duration, and to how and where on the continuum of his personal model of time the patient places the 'cause' of the problem.

The former (focusing on the problem) is a well-known amplifier of the experience of pain. Conversely, when our attention is diverted (for example, while playing a sport we enjoy), we may not even notice an injury when it occurs.

The second form of coding—in which the patient places the cause of his problem in his 'past' or 'future'—is always a factor in conditions such as depressive or anxiety disorders. 'Panic attacks' recur wherever the patient, consciously or unconsciously, runs an internal representation of an event happening sometime in the future. Reactive depression is always a response to an event (real or imaginary) in the past.

Likewise, post-traumatic stress disorder and phobias are present-time responses to earlier, sensitizing events. However, as Viktor Frankl pointed out, since two people experiencing the same 'objective' experience may have entirely different reactions and interpretations, it is evident that it is less what happened in the past that causes present-time problems, but the way in which we are responding to it. The past (or the future) is experienced 'as if' it is happening now—and our physiology responds 'as if' it is real.

A number of other conditions can affect our experience of the passage of time, including age (a sense of time ranges from undifferentiated at birth, through various phases until around the age of 16, when the 'existence' of linear time is established); socioeconomic status (an extended sense of time is more prevalent among middle-class children); and even body temperature. Certain drugs, both prescription and recreational, ranging from thyroxine and caffeine, through cocaine to cannabis and amphetamines, directly affect the experience of time.

Time, healing and health

Paradoxically, the experience of time changes when we learn to pay attention to specific symptoms or sensations 'as they are', in the present moment, without judgment or expectation (awareness at Alfred Korzybski's more fluid, wordless *Object* level). The 'felt sense' of time expands, while duration contracts.

It is our belief that many systems—such as some forms of meditation; yoga; T'ai chi; hypnosis; certain breathing techniques; reorganizing the patient's model of time (see below) and some of the Medical NLP techniques we will discuss further in later chapters and Appendix A (pages 357 to 360)—affect therapeutic change by reversing the constricted sense of time, and activating the mechanism that counter-balances the fight-or-flight response. This 'relaxation response', as it has been named by Herbert Benson, seems to transcend linear time.[203]

NLP and the time line

One of NLP's many major contributions to applied psychology is the observation that, just as people have individual sensory preferences, they also have unique ways of coding their experience of time. As the example at the start of the chapter showed, we make and store distinctions between experiences that occurred in the past, are occurring in the present, and may occur in the future.

We also organize these experiences sequentially, characteristic of our culture's tendency to represent events spatially. That is, when we think of the meal we ate two days ago, it will tend to be placed in our internal landscape 'as if' it occupies an actual position different from where we placed the meal we had yesterday. This has become known as a 'time line'—a personal construct or 'map' of experiences in time–space.

Most NLP books and courses have a fairly lengthy method of 'connecting' similar experiences in order to reveal each person's construct.

We consider the following method easier for most people to understand and to use in some of the ways we will discuss later. Here is the kind of suggestion we offer to patients:

> *'Imagine your life, from birth until now, represented by a road, a pathway or a stream, with the earliest part—the time of your birth—furthest away, and the most recent part, the present, nearest to you.*
>
> *'There's no right or wrong way to do this, so just point to let me know where in your imagination that road or path or stream appears to begin.'* (The patient points.) *'Thank you. Now, where is the present?'*
>
> (The patient indicates the present.) *'Thank you. Now…if the future were also a road or path or stream, how would that run?'* (The patient points.) *'Thank you.'*

We consider it important to add the following as part of the set-up for later change work:

> *'Of course, this is not a real thing. It's just the way the brain makes a map of how we use time. But sometimes the brain tends to act as if the map is real. And if it isn't detailed enough, or in the wrong place, or doesn't suit our purposes, we might need to change it. Does that make sense?'* (Make sure you have the patient's understanding and agreement before proceeding.)

Note: Before we proceed, we suggest you elicit your own time line for future use.

Time line variations

Almost as many different permutations of time lines exist as there are people. Some may place the past behind them, others to one side. Yet other people perceive the past in front of them, or encircling them, or as extremely short or even non-existent. Likewise, the future may be curved, sloping, wide, narrow, short, or long. Two points should be borne in mind here:

1. The patient's organization of his time line has subjective relevance (even though it may be outside his conscious awareness).
2. Whatever other characteristics might be revealed, he will be either associated into his time line (it seems to pass through his body) or dissociated from it (the time line passes from past to future separated by a distance from his body).

Cultural variations

Some writers suggest that different cultures have distinctive ways of coding time, and experiences show that this may be true—up to a point. Certainly, many people claim to detect (and sometimes suffer at the hands of) cultural time-keeping that differs significantly from their own. But, in practice, our own experience has been that where health problems exist, we can proceed using the same approach with patients from other cultures as we do within our own.

The time line as a diagnostic tool

In Medical NLP, the first application of the time line is as a diagnostic tool. **Figure 15.2** shows some observations made by ourselves and other practitioners. The patterns are just some of the many possibilities you may encounter. In using the time-coding diagnostically:

1. Accept it as if it were a 'real thing', and ask yourself what effect this could have. (For example, if the past—particularly a traumatic

past—were running continuously as a kind of internal movie in front of a subject, he would almost certainly be considerably disabled by the subliminal memories, or would 'keep running into' the same kind of experience.)

2. Always check with the patient. As an example, we suggest asking, 'Now, if time were really running past without touching you, how much would you feel in control over your life? How would it be to step back into your own life?'

Figure 15.2 will help the practitioner to use time constructs as a diagnostic tool.

Please note: You should still calibrate to the speaker and test whether his subjective experience matches that suggested by the way he arranges his time line. See Glossary: 'Calibration'.

The language of time

The patient's linguistic patterns

Pay special attention to the patient's temporal language. Note phrases such as, 'I'm always putting things off' (suggesting that the patient's goals are not physically positioned on or in his representation of the future); 'Time is passing me by' (suggesting dissociation); 'I can't see a way forward' (the future is literally obscured); 'I can't stay on track' (direction needs clarification); 'I'm always short of time' (a truncated future); etc.

These will provide you with clues as to how to proceed once the patient's time line has been reorganized.

The practitioner's linguistic patterns

Since people process verbs differently from tense to tense (distinctions between different time frames being necessary in order to extract meaning from the communication), the Medical NLP practitioner uses temporal language to support a recoding of the patient's perception of his problem. A general rule is as follows:

1. *Draw resources from the future* ('When you have found you are feeling better...');

Orientation	*Effect*
1. The time line is markedly separate from the patient's body	Time is "passing me by"; "things are out of reach"; "no control" over events
2. The past is directly in front of the patient	Extremely common in behavioural patterns that keep repeating; where the patient is adversely affected by, or reminded of, the past (including abuse and other traumatic experiences), or keeps "making the same mistake"
3. The future is behind the patient	Characterized by disorganization; inability to plan; feelings of 'hopelessness'; literally 'no future' or confusion, when asked about anything beyond the present time
4. Extremely short or non-existent future	Often encountered in patients with a diagnosis, or fear, of terminal disease
5. Both the past and the future are in front of the patient	Sometimes associated with confusion between the past and future.
6. The time line runs from left to right in front of the patient	A frequently encountered arrangement (possibly related to hemispheric organisation and reading Western languages from left to right). Good for planning and organisation, but sometimes associated with a sense of detachment
7. The past or future is steeply inclined	The past or future has been or will be a tough climb
8. The time line encircles the patient	Often accompanied by feelings of being 'trapped' and 'running to stay in the same place'
9. The past is directly behind the patient's head	Amnesia; inability to 'look back' at the past; failure to 'learn from past mistakes'

Figure 15.2 Time line observations

2. *Place the problem in the past* ('…and the problem you've been having has been sorted out…'); and
3. *Anchor the solution-state in the present* ('…what specifically do you find is different and better…now?').

Note: Use the past continuous tense ('the problem you were having') rather than the past tense ('the problem you had') to avoid mis-matching the patient and losing engagement.

Reorganizing the time line

We have two purposes in reorganizing the time line when it seems to be dysfunctionally arranged—to provide a new, subjectively more appropriate, or useful, frame for the patient's experience, and to access resources and make changes at different perceived times in the patient's life.

Sometimes a simple reordering is enough to produce generative change—for example, moving the past behind the patient, and opening up the future in front of him. We may speculate that 'experiencing' the past as 'behind' him changes his processing mode from a 'present, all-pervasive' problem to 'something that happened and is now over'.

A strong element of creativity and experimentation is necessary on the part of the practitioner, especially where complex and unusual configurations are encountered. We recall one patient (a fellow practitioner suffering from 'burn-out') who visualized her future time line 'like a huge funnel, sloping down towards me, with massive amounts of "stuff" pouring down at me like an avalanche'. She described feeling 'absolutely engulfed by everything'. No surprise there, then.

Rearrangement required several steps—including reversing the flow of tasks yet to be tackled so they moved away from, and not towards, her—and considerable experimentation before she began to regain a sense of control.

Changes are always made with the consent and co-operation of the patient. 'Let's try something…' is a more respectful and productive approach than, 'Do this!' Some patients experience a strong kinesthetic when rearranging a time line; if this fails to settle down, rearrange it until it feels comfortable. An individual's time line should be presented as neither right nor wrong, but simply as useful or not useful.

Among the many possibilities available, we regard the arrangement shown in **Figure 15.3** as the most compatible with both remedial and generative change.

Tips for reorganizing the time line

All instructions may be prefaced by suggestions such as, 'I want you to imagine you can actually take hold of the very start of your time line and begin to swing it around…', etc. Add the reassurance, 'All your experiences, learnings and memories will stay in their proper sequence, as we…' etc.

1. Reassociate the time line into the patient (if dissociated), metaphorically placing him back 'in' his own life (have him pull the time line towards him until it 'clicks into place');
2. Have the patient swing the beginning of the past around until it runs diagonally towards either his left or right shoulder. A useful suggestion is, '*You know how those people who somehow just bounce back from problems always say, "Just put it behind you and move on"? Well, this is your chance to put it behind you—but, if you need to look back at the past, it's there…*';
3. Arrange the future running directly out in front of him, encouraging him to extend it out 'over the horizon'. This suggests a long life with lots of time still ahead;
4. Have the patient widen out the future time line ('*So you have lots of room to put all your options, choices, opportunities*', etc); then,
5. Throw the entire future time line into bright sunlight ('*People sometimes talk about having "a bright future". Make it as bright as that…*').

The final step in this process is to place the internal representation the patient made of his direction, outcome, or goal on the future time line, 'just a few steps in front of where you are now'. Suggest, 'This is the direction in which you want to move. Make sure it's bright and compelling—something that really pulls you into it—and, we'll come back to it a little later.'

Now, summarize for the patient:

> *'So, what you've done here is to put everything that's happened behind you in the past so you can start to let it go. Of course, you can look back at it, if you need to, but it won't be distracting you'* ('in your face'; 'on top of you'; or any other metaphorical description the patient has given about his problem-state) *'any more. And it's good to know that whatever has happened has already happened and is over with, and where you are now is in the present, with a very long, wide and bright future pulling you into it...isn't it?'*

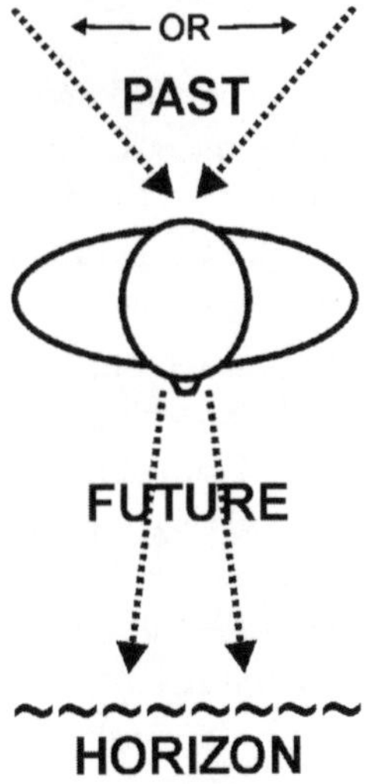

Figure 15.3 Time line arrangement (seen from above). The past time line now runs diagonally from behind towards the patient's head, either from the left or the right (depending on his preference), while the future is directly in front, opening up and extending over his imaginary horizon.

The purpose of eliciting and reorganizing the patient's time line may be regarded as expanding his internal map of reality. Even if we choose to regard this simply as a metaphor, the presupposition that problem states began—and, can potentially conclude—in the 'past', and that a 'different' future can be envisaged, is a more hopeful model than the fear-ridden one with which he has been operating: that the problem is present tense, all-pervasive, and likely to extend indefinitely into the future.

EXERCISES

1. Elicit your own time line and re-orientate it as suggested in **Figure 15.3** above. Notice how it feels.
2. Create a well-formed outcome and place it on your time line, a little in front of you. Ensure that it is richly detailed in all sensory modalities. The outcome should be a dynamic representation of you functioning in the situation it represents.
3. Explore how your life would be different were you to be strongly drawn into this outcome. Use all your senses to create a full representation.
4. List all the resources you have and all those you would need in order to turn this outcome into your personal reality.
5. Now, see yourself stepping into the future, taking on all its qualities and moving on, watching how your life plays out as you disappear over the distant horizon.
6. See the future you reappearing, floating up above the horizon and back, bringing with you all the experiences you have gained from your time-travel adventure. Have the future you drop down inside you as you are now, allowing all the knowledge, experiences and learnings to integrate with you for your use, starting…now.

16

Medical NLP Algorithms for Change: steps to transformation

When we are no longer able to change a situation, we are challenged to change ourselves.—***Viktor E. Frankl***[204]

If you've come this far and are prepared to entertain the possibility that people have internal maps of reality that are different from your own, congratulations.

If you've come this far and feel it is possible to recognize that your own map may be neither better nor worse—just different—and are prepared to co-create a new cartography, you have broken through one of the most impermeable barriers we know. This is the one that separates 'right us' from 'wrong them', the attitude that drives the delusion of superiority characteristic of the worst excesses of scientism, religion, and politics. Once breached, this shift has the potential to change ourselves and the world around us in ways almost beyond comprehension.

For, as a species, we create maps, and then ally ourselves with those whose maps correspond most closely to our own. Logic has little to do with it.[205] Our willingness to act for those who comply, and to ostracize or punish those who do not, often depends on power granted by some external 'authority', whether it is those who pay us, who control the statistics, prescribe the drugs, or promise us eternal life.

Our intention in this book is not to overturn a 'paradigm', discard scientific method, or introduce yet another 'alternative' medicine. It is to suggest that we learn to relate to, and work with, the uniqueness of the individual in front of us, in terms of her model, and not just to impose our own. Contrary to some opinion, we do recommend following scientific method. We urge practitioners to work systematically: gathering data, forming a testable hypothesis, testing, and then altering it, if necessary. The difference is that we apply it to each person who consults us rather than relying exclusively on the theology of statistical 'proof'.

In this chapter, we will introduce several algorithms (step-wise approaches) for change. These are not to be confused with recipes or prescriptions. They are intended to provide a framework within which you can explore more creative, big-picture, whole brain approaches. If we are careful to avoid premature cognitive commitment, Medical NLP's synthesis of algorithmic and heuristic thinking (nothing more than using 'both sides' of the brain, text and context) can lead to creative and effective outcomes that match the patient's unique needs. This can only come from exploring and respecting the patient's map.

Even some neuro-linguistic programmers advocate or claim 'acuity' when, in practice, they are prescriptively imposing techniques on to their subjects with little consideration for, or understanding of, the subjects' uniqueness.

The ability to think heuristically and algorithmically, to be mindful of rules but not bound by them, is similar to what Ellen Langer has called 'mindfulness'.[206] In incorporating this approach into your practice, we anticipate that you will find newer and, we hope, even better ways of becoming 'the difference that makes a difference'.

In this chapter, we will broaden our understanding and application of several core principles of NLP in order to integrate them into Medical NLP's three major algorithms for change.

1. The power of association and dissociation

The word 'dissociation'—like all nominalizations—is apt to cause problems. To many psychiatrists, it is a symptom of an often severe personality disorder, a breakdown of another nominalization, the 'ego boundary'.

To hypnotherapists, it describes the characteristic trance phenomenon of 'watching the self' thinking or carrying out suggestions.

To practitioners of NLP, it is a deliberately induced state of 'stepping out' of an experience or memory and observing oneself from a bystander's point of view (Perceptual Position 3), usually resulting in a reduction in the intensity of an experience. We have noted earlier that the patient's attempt to 'separate from', to not-have, her problem serves to keep in place a self-perpetuating causal loop.

Negation can be represented linguistically, but not to our essentially non-linguistic right cortex.

The more we try to not-have a symptom, thought, or experience, the more the symptom or behavior persists (whatever you do right at this moment, don't think of the color blue). Since the patient's attempt at dissociation is unsuccessful, he is tacitly seeking the practitioner's collusion in exorcizing her negative kinesthetics.

Much biomedicine is organized in precisely this way: to attempt to remove, chemically or surgically, the 'bad' experience. The belief that medicine can—and should—somehow provide freedom from the ups and downs of life is pervasive.

Increasingly, disappointments, losses, frustrations, and challenges present themselves for medical solutions, fuelled by the promises of 'cures' and 'breakthroughs' by the media and the pharmaceutical industry. This medicalization of everyday living has given rise to what Frank Furedi has dubbed the 'therapy culture', which routinely defines people facing challenges as 'vulnerable', 'at risk', 'emotionally scarred', or 'damaged'.[207]

The purpose of incorporating the principles and techniques presented in this book into the consultation process is not to 'fix' or 'cure' those who are faced with non-acute and non-organic problems. Instead, we seek to help them develop new skills to cope and grow from their experience.

The cliché that draws a distinction between temporarily helping a starving man by giving him a fish, or permanently resourcing him by teaching him how to fish, is apposite here. The word 'doctor' derives from the Latin verb *docere*, to teach. Teachers educate, and 'education', in turn, originally meant 'to lead out'. Ideally, the process of 'healing', should, at least in part, involve helping the patient to access, develop, and draw out her own resources in order to be able to respond to those challenges, physical and emotional, that are unique in her world.

Elsewhere in this book (see pages 218 to 220), we have pointed out that Medical NLP aims for 'successful' dissociation *as a prerequisite of any substantive change work*, rather than as an end in itself. In order for the patient to be able to recode or re-experience her condition, she needs to be guided into an observer-state, effectively removed from her condition, but nonetheless allowing it to be present, temporarily free of the constraints of past or future concerns. This is where, with the guidance of the practitioner, the structure of her problem can be reorganized. After that, she may be re-associated into the more desirable state.

The first Medical NLP algorithm for change, therefore, is:

Dissociate—Restructure—Reassociate

This means simply that the patient 'steps out' of her problem, the change is effected 'over there', and the changed state, with all its sensory experience, is brought back 'into her body'. Many 'bespoke' techniques can be created using this algorithm.

2. *Anchoring revisited*

Anchoring, you will recall, involves linking a trigger (visual, auditory, and/or kinesthetic) with a specific response. Thus far, we have used it to stabilize certain resources, largely to help the patient develop a health- and solution-oriented attitude to her situation. We are assuming you have practiced setting and firing anchors with both patients and yourself. Anchors, however, have much wider applications—and, indeed, are central to many, if not all, successful Medical NLP techniques.

Simple anchors

Imagine the possibilities for healing that open up when you simply connect the start (or some aspect) of a problem-state with a more resourceful response. Richard Bandler has described anchoring the sensation of an ambulatory blood-pressure harness monitor against an anxious patient's chest to feelings of deep calm and relaxation (thus turning a 'reminder' of the problem into its 'cure'), and linking the smell and sight of roses with feelings of massive pleasure to short-circuit an allergic response.[208]

First create a powerful resource-state by stacking anchors. Then identify the start of the problem-state (or a moment before, if possible) and link this trigger to the resource-state. Repeat until the new sequence replaces the old. If you teach the patient to develop, set, and fire anchors, you will substantially help her deal with her specific problem, as well as providing her with a strategy that will increase her overall sense of self-efficacy.

> ***Case history:*** *A student who reported becoming anxious when giving presentations as part of her college course sought help after being diagnosed with 'anxiety' and being offered either cognitive behavioral therapy or medication. From our point of view, this was a classic case of a diagnosis made on the basis of text to the exclusion of context. It emerged that she became anxious at college, and not in front of other groups, suggesting long-term therapy or medication was excessive. Instead, a state of calm confidence was elicited and anchored. She became rapidly adept at firing her anchor and later reported that giving presentations had ceased to be a problem.*

(Coincidentally, we have actually seen a training video for new doctors with exactly this scenario. The diagnosis and suggested treatment were the same as for the patient referred to above. At no point did the trainers suggest that doctors should ask whether the problem existed in any context other than college. Therefore, the generic diagnosis of 'anxiety' was made. This is an example of the 'representative heuristic'—and the consequences thereof.)

Collapsing anchors

Similar affective states may be stacked to create complex, intense anchors. Dissimilar anchors will 'collapse', resulting in a neutral state, or one that favors the more powerful of the two. This process can be used to 'extinguish' unwanted responses caused by a wide range of stimuli.

1. Start by creating a strong, 'positive', stacked anchor. Do this systematically. Elicit past, strongly positive, experiences, associate

the patient into each, and anchor on the same place. Test thoroughly for effectiveness. We highly recommend including 'the ability to cope' as a component of the stack. Change state.

2. Elicit the unwanted response and anchor it *on a different place on the body*. Test and change state.
3. Fire both anchors simultaneously and observe the patient's response. Usually, he will display signs of confusion or disorientation. Hold the anchors until these minimal cues subside. Release the negative anchor *first*, and then the positive anchor.
4. Change state and test the patient's response to the original negative stimulus.

Case history: *The patient presented with anxiety and disturbed sleep, complaining that the problem had started when she moved to an apartment near a railway line. Although she said the sound of passing trains was 'not too bad', she found herself lying awake, becoming increasingly agitated, expecting one to come past.*

A strong, positive anchor of calm and relaxation was set. The negative response was anchored, and then both anchors were collapsed. The patient was given the task of 'willing' trains to come along for exactly three days, and was told not to go to sleep on each of those nights until five trains had passed. She reported on her second consultation that she had 'failed' to complete the task since she kept falling asleep before the second or third train. (This intervention combined collapsed anchors with 'prescribing the symptom', a paradoxical technique developed by Milton Erickson.)

Since almost all Medical NLP techniques involve collapsing anchors (this is explained further in *Re-patterning and Future-pacing*), either directly or indirectly, the second algorithm for change is:

Establish a Positive Anchor—Identify Negative Anchor(s)—Design a Technique around Collapsing Anchors

3. Chunking

The third core skill involves chunking up for both purpose/intention and down for process or procedure (strategy). Both states, present and desired, need to be chunked in each direction in order to apply this algorithm. By doing so, and, with appropriate framing, the practitioner simultaneously assists the patient to meet the positive intention of her problem and to develop a more appropriate strategy to achieve her desired state (see *Structure, Process and Change*).

Chunking up for purpose and intention

The example is of a patient who seeks help for 'drinking too much'. Traditionally, a practitioner might ask when, how much and even why the patient drinks. Two questions we regard as potentially useful are, *When did you start?* and *What caused you to start?* Take note of the answers, since these questions place the origins of the problem behavior within the patient's model of time (see earlier chapter on time and its effects on pathology).

Ensure that the patient understands the concept of positive intention. It is often enough to include this during the normalization stage of the consultation. Most patients respond with relief when we explain that symptoms and behaviors function protectively, and often 'want something more for you, including getting you to pay attention to some need that may not yet have been met'.

We can add the suggestion that, if the need is ignored, symptoms or behaviors sometimes change or become more intense. This both normalizes changes in the frequency or intensity of symptoms, and presupposes that the patient can take more responsibility for her own wellbeing.

Chunking up for positive intention involves a series of questions, all of which are variations of, 'What does drinking do for you?' The answer given ('It helps me relax'; 'It gives me confidence'; etc) is acknowledged, and then chunked again. 'And, when you have [the patient's reply], what else does that give you that's even more positive?'

The patient's response ('It makes it easier for me to cope', etc) is acknowledged, and the chunking continues.

'And, when you have [the patient's last reply], what else does that give you that's even more positive?'

When the patient arrives at her core value, she will most likely express it as a nominalization, often with transcendent or spiritual overtones: *peace, fulfillment, comfort,* etc. Almost inevitably, the core value will represent a protective intention. *This must always be respected and the need met by whatever intervention you choose to apply.*

The practitioner then asks the patient to recall or create an example of her core value, guiding her into a sensory-rich experience. Anchor the core value.

Chunking down for sequence or strategy

With the core value of the positive intention elicited and anchored, the practitioner begins to chunk in the opposite direction, in order to establish the sequence (strategy) the patient has been using in order to start and maintain her behavior. As explained in Appendix D (see pages 367 to 369), strategies are most easily elicited by first observing the patient's description of the behavior, noting especially the respective sequences of eye accessing cues and sensory modalities used.

Prompt with variations of these questions: '*What's the very last thing that happens before you* [the response or behavior]*?*' '*And what happens then?*' '*And what happens next?*' etc. Continue until the entire strategy has been elicited.

Since a strong neural network already supports the strategy of the problem-state, the new strategy should be adapted to fit the existing sequence as closely as possible. For example, should the patient's problem strategy involve, say, A > K > V > K, it may be easier to design a new A > K > V > K strategy that results in a positive, rather than a negative, outcome.

For example (using an actual transcript):

Patient: '*After work, I think: "You deserve to relax; you've worked hard." And then I remember what it feels like to be completely free of all my worries, and I see it like being like a space where no-one else can get at me; the drink is like a barrier all around me. The problem is I know this way is harming me…*'

Practitioner: '*So, when you realize you need to take time out to relax because you've worked so hard and can take some time out in another* *way that's healthier, which allows you to see yourself in a space where, just for the time being, nobody else can get to you, would you be interested in experimenting with it?'* (This opens the way to exploring and testing alternative strategic routines: yoga, meditation, listening to music, etc.)

However, ensure that any two-point loops (see Appendix D, pages 367 to 369) are taken into consideration, and, if necessary, resolved. Of course, a two-point loop may be a useful inclusion in a positive strategy. Richard Bandler's 'the more…the more' pattern ('The more you start to worry about [X], the more you remember you have the resources to cope') is an example of a linguistically installed positive two-point loop reinforcing a patient-centered locus of control.

Mapping across

With both the core value and the strategy of the problem-state identified, the objective now is to map both across to a desired state (**Figure 16.1**). The intention is to collapse two meta-anchors—the problem-state (PS) and the desired state (DS). For that reason, the desired state must be detailed, desirable and very clearly identifiable to the patient before attempting the transition.

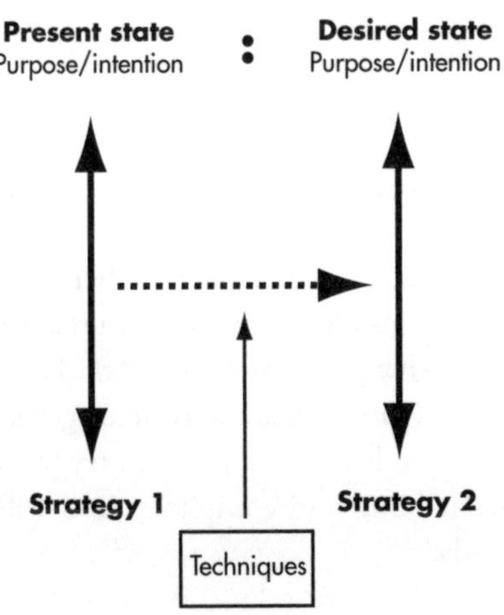

Figure 16.1 Mapping from problem-state (PS) to desired state (DS)

Chunking, especially when identifying strategies, should be meticulous and detailed. It provides large amounts of information that can drive effective change. The third Medical NLP algorithm for change, therefore, is:

Chunk for Purpose/Intention (subjective and experiential), as well as for Strategy/Procedure (objective and sequential).
Chunk across for similar examples of the feeling, response or behavior.

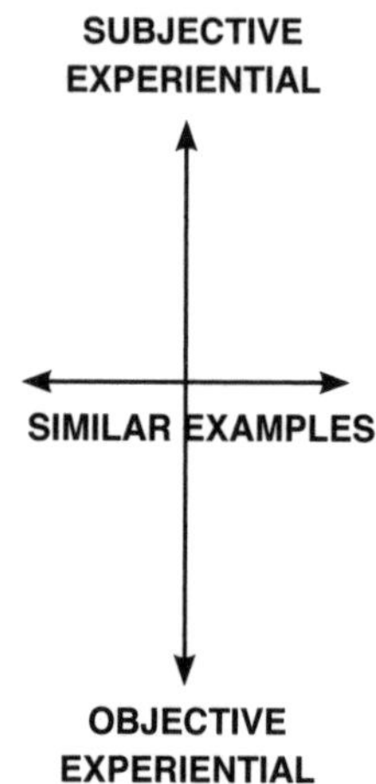

Figure 16.2 Chunking

The patient's perspective

Not only is the patient the expert on how her condition manifests in her experience, but she also has intuitive resources regarding how well a proposed alternative to her problem-state will fit. This is where you should be particularly alert to her responses to your suggestions. To avoid failure and loss of confidence, it is important not to try to impose overt change without her understanding and complicity, and without fully meeting hitherto unmet needs.

Transition: creating acceptance

Once the purpose or intention of a problem has been established, it is often easiest to invite the patient's opinion on how to proceed.

Social psychologists (and salespeople) are aware that people's commitment is often greater to their own opinions and decisions than to those suggested by others. (There are, however, exceptions to this 'rule'. Older patients and those particularly submissive to the practitioner's 'authority' may readily agree to your suggestions. We strongly recommend that you ensure the patient is fully congruent, whether he is making her own suggestions, or responding to yours.)

Questions that may facilitate patient concordance include:

> '*Now we understand your symptom* [X] *has really been wanting to protect you, how can we find a way that that protectiveness* [X] *can instead help you achieve your new outcome* [Y]?'

> '*If you could have* [positive intention Y] *without having to have* [symptom X], *how interested would you be in doing that?*'

> '*We know we need to do something differently if we want a different result. If we can find a different way to do things so that you had more of* [negotiated outcome Z], *would that be something you would want?*'

Once you are confident that you have the patient's full agreement, test for any suggestions or solutions that might spontaneously emerge:

> '*That's good. Now, just before we begin* [allaying performance anxiety], *if you could think of a way to do things differently, what would that be?*'

Surprisingly, patients often volunteer a new way of doing things.

Recent research reveals that many people have access to more accurate information about their health status than the average doctor—their own insight and intuition.

The answers to the simple questions, 'How do you rate your own health?' and 'Do you have any thoughts or opinions about your situation?', for example, are more accurate predictors of health and longevity than the most comprehensive tests and medical records.[209]

If the patient presents an insight or intuition, consider it a gift, and proceed immediately to exploring the suggestion for well-formedness. If it is semantically well formed and is likely to meet the elicited positive intention, proceed immediately to installing it as a strategy.

Installing a strategy

New strategies can be installed in several different ways. These include:

1. **Anchoring.** Elicit the steps in sequence. Anchor each in a different place on the body (the knuckles of one hand may be easiest and least invasive). Fire them repeatedly in sequence until the new strategy runs automatically when the trigger event or feeling is invoked.
2. **Role playing.** This involves practical rehearsal, with the practitioner taking the part of any 'significant other' in the patient's scenario.
3. **Mental rehearsal.** We explore this in greater detail later in the section, *Repatterning and Future-pacing.*
4. **Linguistically.** The 'language of influence'—informal hypnosis—is the subject of the following section, *Hypnosis in Healing and Health: the language of influence.*

All four of these approaches may be employed during the same session. We encourage this approach, known as layering, using several appropriate techniques to ensure strong, new behaviors and responses.

Other approaches to consider

The Swish Pattern in essence collapses one anchor, the problem state (PS), with a stronger, more desirable state (DS), so that the latter extinguishes the former, or creates a 'neutral' state. Effective Swish Patterns require:

1. a desired state that features at least two, preferably three, sub-

modalities (one digital and two analog seem to work best);

2. movement from an associated state to a dissociated state (where ongoing behavioral changes, such as healthier eating habits, are intended), or from associated to associated (where a fixed state, such as 'being a non-smoker', is the objective); and
3. repetition—the Swish should be repeated until the patient cannot easily recover the PS. The patient should open her eyes between repetitions to break state, and always start the next round with the PS, until the PS has been de-activated and the trigger automatically activates the new neuronal pathway to the desired state.

The 'classic' Swish Pattern involves setting up the DS as a small, dark square in the bottom right-hand corner of the patient's visual representation of the PS, and then rapidly expanding the DS while shrinking the PS, accompanied by a '*sw-i-i-sh*' sound from the practitioner to add an auditory component.

Other variations include:

- putting the DS far out on the patient's horizon line with the PS in whatever position it naturally occupies, and then rapidly reversing the positions of the two states; and
- concealing the DS behind the PS, and then opening up a window in the center of the PS and rapidly expanding it so the desired state pops through.

Note: Although the Swish Pattern as outlined above relies on strong visual qualities, both auditory and kinesthetic Swishes can be designed, following the same principles. Where a kinesthetic lead is followed, remember the rule that negative feelings are experienced as contracted and localized, whereas positive feelings are expansive.

EXERCISES

Association, dissociation and the Swish

1. Experiment with association and dissociation to become familiar with your own responses. When dissociated from an undesired experience or memory, how would you prefer it to be?
2. Construct the appropriate desired state using all sensory modalities.
3. Chunk both the PS and the DS to establish purpose or intention as well as strategy for each. Explore how you could satisfy the positive intention of the PS with a strategy that is more appropriate than that of the PS.
4. Practice anchoring, role-playing, and mental rehearsal to install the new strategy, and test each one for effectiveness.
5. Practice the Swish Pattern until you have at least three different ways of doing it.

Monitoring levels of wellbeing

1. Make a habit of scanning your body with the following question in mind: 'How are my patterns of sleep, energy, appetite, general activity now, compared with last week (or month ago)?' If any of these are markedly worse, take whatever steps are necessary to explore further. (This exercise is not intended to foster hypochondria, but, rather, to help you attune to fluctuations in your health and wellbeing that only you can detect, and which may prove significant.)
2. Ask similar questions of your patients in order to measure their levels of health, wellbeing and *ikigai*.

17

Hypnosis in Healing and Health: the language of influence

*With mere words, healthy subjects can be made ill, and ill subjects can be made healthy.—**Abbé Faria***

Hypnosis is a process that nobody really understands, but about which everyone has an opinion. Despite the fact that it has a 200-year history as a valuable tool in the practice of Western medicine, many health professionals still regard it with suspicion and fear.

The real problem, of course, is the word. As another nominalization, 'hypnosis' suggests some-'thing' that is implanted inside the patient to operate independently of his 'will'.

This has prompted the most recent researchers to turn to neural scanning in order to find out where it lives and what it looks like when it's at home.

Predictably, changes in brain function have been found, most notably in the brainstem, *thalamus* and *anterior cingulate*, suggesting, in part at least, that it can be observed as affecting the level of executive functioning of the brain. However, none of these studies[210] explains how such a wide range of effects can take place under hypnosis, although they do agree that certain changes are characteristic of the state.

For example, diminished peripheral awareness and increased focal attention are common, as is suspension of the experience of linear space and time. One theory is that a 'dislocation' between the *somatosensory* cortex and the higher brain centers, somehow, gives the nervous system permission to create or ignore certain subjective experiences.

Of course, neural activity does not occur in isolation. It is contextual, and our experience is that the phenomenon we call hypnosis, in fact:

1. is less rare and exotic than often thought;
2. occurs naturally and spontaneously as part of a continuum of consciousness, rather than a discrete condition;
3. developed as an evolutionary response to certain conditions; and
4. emerges as the function of a relationship of one kind or another.

Because we feel that at least part of the reservations of the medical profession result from the word itself and the image projected by the popular media, we will more frequently use the terms 'trance', 'trance state', 'unconscious response', 'other-than-conscious processing', and 'altered state' as synonyms, depending on the context.

Characteristics of trance

The trance state exhibits three important characteristics: focus, abstraction, and association/dissociation.

Focus, as we have said, involves a reduction of peripheral data. Rather than scanning the internal or external environment, the subject deletes any information not consciously or unconsciously perceived as relevant to the issue at hand, whatever that happens to be.

Abstraction refers to the process of withdrawing from the external environment, moving progressively inward at the expense of competing data from the 'outside'.

Dissociation occurs when the subject disidentifies with his physical and psychological boundaries, uncritically becoming merged (associated) with the experience contained within the boundary conditions of the current trance state.

A state in which the subject has little or no overt contact with the external world is known in NLP as 'down-time' trance.

Trance states are accompanied by various degrees of suggestibility, from the gentle exhortations of the hypnotist to 'relax and let go', to the phenomenon of post-hypnotic suggestion, the apparently automatic behavior carried out after the subject emerges from the trance in which the suggestion has been implanted. We are not claiming that 'suggestibility' exists as some 'thing' inside the subject. Rather, as we will discuss further below, it is a function of certain classes of relationship.

Signs of developing trance

It is comparatively easy to observe specific changes related to developing trance in the subject's physiology, especially when the practitioner's vision is wide and relaxed. The most common markers include:

- defocused or fixed gaze;
- flattening of the facial muscles;
- reduced muscle tonus;
- altered breathing rate;
- changing blink rate; and
- slower, sometimes slurred, speech.

These minimal cues may emerge spontaneously as the subject becomes increasingly absorbed in his internal world, or in response to the practitioners suggestions. 'Suggestions', in turn, may be direct or indirect (see *Inducing and amplifying trance* later in this chapter—page 242).

Everyday trance states

Trance can develop spontaneously. We are all deeply familiar with the process of becoming completely absorbed in a book or film, or of arriving at a destination without any conscious awareness of having driven there through busy traffic.

When that happens, we might not immediately realize that someone has spoken to us, or have been aware of the passage of time. Where film, drama, and well-crafted literature are involved, we enter a curious state of dual awareness: part of us is immersed in the challenges and emotions of the protagonists as if they were happening to us, while at the same time we are well aware that we are reading a novel or clutching the DVD remote control.

These state changes are accompanied by natural trance phenomena, such as analgesia (forgetting a headache while engaged in an interesting conversation); amnesia (forgetting to carry out a task agreed while involved in another absorbing experience), and negative hallucination (experiencing something as 'absent', even when it is in plain sight of others).

The continuum of consciousness

The spectrum of consciousness extends from conditions in which conscious cognitive processing is significantly reduced, to heightened states of awareness, usually associated with 'peak' or 'religious experiences'.

From the 'blackness' of the former to the heightened sensory virtual reality of the latter, an almost infinite range of possibilities exists. We drift in and out of a rich variety of altered states without noticing. Familiarity is what prevents us from noticing the shifts that come with changes in our sensory input; social demands; biological rhythms, and emotional fluctuations.

Our 'default consciousness' is considered ordinary to us simply because no 'unordinary' quality comes into our awareness. We do not regard it as a trance state, even though our attention encompasses only what presents itself as 'important' at that particular moment. Our foci of attention are reduced, but still serve our immediate needs. When we simply 'are', we are in our most habitual altered state.

Thus, 'everyday' trances are unlikely to cause problems; indeed, if we define trance as involving focus, abstraction, and association, we may well have created a number of varying trance states appropriate to the different roles we are required to play during each day. However, when trance hijacks our freedom to involve ourselves in experiences other than those contained within itself, problems arise. Our default consciousness fades, along with our ability fully to function within it, as we become increasingly absorbed in the characteristics of the problem-trance.

The function of trance

Trance experience has been a favored pursuit of our species since the beginning of time. From the altered awareness induced by driving tribal drums and the ingestion of sacred organic substances, to the 'buzz' of contemporary club music and recreational drugs, humans have been inexorably drawn towards heightening or changing their experience of 'reality'. But what predisposes us to state-alteration in the first place?

One theory is that trance evolved as a protective mechanism for where physical fight or flight failed. The cascade of endorphins that accompanies both the 'freeze' and the trance state, so the theory goes, reduces (somewhat) the experience of being torn limb from limb.

Many of the markers of trance occur in human beings in times of extreme crisis, including a loss of physical sensation and extreme distortion of the subjective sense of time. Some researchers believe that Multiple Personality Disorder (MPD), characterized by several different and discrete 'personalities', is the product of trauma-induced trance-formation.

Certainly, 'deep' trance, with its rigidity of limbs, slow, shallow breathing, and absence of reaction to external stimuli, has, on the surface, much in common with the 'playing possum' response observed throughout the natural world. These behavior patterns also seem to have much in common with unwanted feelings, responses, and behaviors that patients often claim 'just happen', no matter how illogical they seem or how much they want to suppress them.

Another shared characteristic is that of trance logic, the tendency to 'explain' the symptom in terms that may seem utterly absurd to the observer. This parallels Michael Gazzaniga's 'spin doctor' or 'interpreter', suggesting that the experience of trance occurs wordlessly in the right cortex, while the left struggles to make sense of the behavior.

A further argument to support the 'protective mechanism' theory emerges from studies of childhood trauma, some cases of which are believed to create states dissociated from the hostile environment and associated into a 'safe' fantasy world or alternative 'identity'.

According to some neurobiologists—who call these trances 'imprints'—such experiences are 'fixed' in our neurophysiological structure by chemical washes, presumably creating a kind of template of situations to be avoided in the future. Several factors appear to be instrumental in creating and amplifying trance, including: heightened emotion; repetition; a sense of reduced control; and sustained allostatic load.

Our contention, in advancing this model, is that many 'functional' disorders share key characteristics with trance, and that part of the Medical NLP practitioner's role is to disassemble the problem trance, while creating more resourceful responses based on widened, rather than constricted, perception and cognitive processing.

Relational trances

Trance itself is a product of relationship—whether it is the relationship between hypnotist and subject, subject and object of absorption (a movie or book), or the patient and his problem.

Bonded disconnection is a particularly insidious trance-deepener. The more focus, absorption, and association are applied to attempting to 'not-have' the problem, the more deeply entrenched it is likely to become. As Korzybski pointed out, the quality of the inferences made about the experience can feed back to higher levels to deepen allostatic load.[211] This inevitably occurs when the problem is framed as 'other' than 'ourselves'.

Attempts to make changes at this level of separation are unlikely to be successful.

We know from experience that adopting the 'one-up' role of advisor or coach has minimal impact on the structure and process of complex 'functional' problems—and recommend that you avoid this, unless absolutely necessary (such as instructing the patient how to take his medication). Avoid too, the trap of entering into a symmetrical argument with the patient in the hope that your superior logic will prevail. Symmetrical arguments, you may remember, are usually characterized by a series of 'yes-but' answers to all your well-meaning suggestions.

This latter approach runs counter to the *Ko Mei* principles of Medical NLP and risks placing the practitioner as 'other' to the patient, thereby reducing his ability to influence.

Effective influence is, by nature, en-*trancing*. The etymological origin of the word 'trance' is the present participle of the Latin verb *transire*, to 'go' or 'cross over'. The sheer number of English words deriving from this compound verb (*transit, transition, transitory, transfer*, etc) reflects the multi-ordinality of the word 'trance' itself.

We may think of 'going into trance' variously as crossing over the boundaries of conscious and unconscious, external and internal, left hemisphere and right hemisphere, body and mind.

We might also consider the 'effectiveness' of trance as a mutually agreed breaching of the boundaries between 'you' and 'me'. In trance, the boundary conditions between patient and practitioner become increasingly permeable, so that 'your' thoughts may merge seamlessly with 'mine', your 'suggestions' become my 'decisions'.

Needless to say, it is especially important to be ethical and respectful as these distinctions are breached.

The family trance

Patients and their problems do not exist separately from the system in which they live, and the most immediate system we should consider is the family. It is fairly self-evident that one member's chronic illness may disrupt the lives of siblings, parents, or children. This, in turn, can worsen the patient's condition, particularly if there exists an atmosphere—real or imagined—of resentment or blame.

Two other issues need to be examined to facilitate healing and health:

1. The role that the patient or the patient's problem plays in the family dynamics and the effect recovery might have on the system as a whole;
2. The practitioner should explore any 'gains' the condition may bring, either to the patient or to his primary caregiver(s).

In chunking for positive intentions ('What does this condition do for you or your family that wouldn't happen if you were well?'), it may emerge that the symptom acts to prompt other family members to provide the nurturing the patient desires.

Such a strategy, albeit an unconscious one, may be effective, but at a price—for example, a depletion of the family's energy, patience, and financial reserves. Equally, the caregivers may be meeting their own needs for significance and meaning within the relationship; they are 'needed', and therefore important.

Another possibility—most frequently encountered in children who present with behavioral disorders or problems such as bed-wetting and soiling—is that the condition acts to distract the parents, or other members of the family, from problems perceived as potentially more threatening to the patient's safety than the condition itself. Some patients, adults included, appear somehow to have the capacity to create or maintain an otherwise distressing condition for some perceived 'greater good'.

> ***Case history:*** *The patient, a 34-year-old married man with two children, presented with 'work-related stress'. Although he had one of the worst cases of weeping eczema the practitioner had ever seen, he initially made no mention of his skin condition.*
>
> *When the practitioner referred to it, the patient shrugged and said that even though his condition had not responded to treatment, it was 'under control'. He explained that his widowed mother came to his home every day to clean and dress the eruptions. He admitted that his relationship with her was conflicted and that he resented her 'fussing', but felt he could not ask his mother to stop caring for him because 'I'm the only person she's got left in her life and she needs to feel needed.'*
>
> *Some months later, the patient called, in considerable distress, saying his mother had died unexpectedly of a cerebral hemorrhage. When the patient arrived for his appointment, the practitioner was stunned. The patient's skin appeared new and pink and without blemish. When the practitioner had the opportunity to ask about any treatment he had received, the patient seemed slightly embarrassed. He said, 'It's the strangest thing. I was unbelievably shocked and guilty when I heard about my mother's death. I felt somehow I hadn't done enough for her. But, within a few hours, the itching stopped, and a few days later I noticed that the eczema was drying up. It disappeared in less than a week. Do you think the two things had any connection?'*

The possibility that the patient's problem was caused, or at least, maintained, by a need to provide his mother with a 'purpose' in life cannot easily be dismissed. However, rather than implying that some gain or benefit may be causing or maintaining any problem, which we regard as presumptuous and disrespectful, it is preferable to open the subject of family dynamics in the following manner:

'Now, because this problem has been going on for some time, the roles of all the people around you will change when you start to get better. Even though they may have been upset that you have been ill, there could be the chance that in some way they will feel they are not needed or appreciated any more. How would you suggest you could make them still feel important even as you're getting better?'

The intention here is to encourage the patient to begin to alter his role as a passive recipient of care to an active agent of his own recovery, while ensuring that the system within which he lives regains balance. When we asked one little girl the question suggested above, she smiled in delight and responded immediately, 'I'll ask my Daddy to help me with my homework—even if sometimes I know the answers.'

Conflicting trances

Conflicting responses and behaviors are commonly encountered in many 'functional' disorders. These are usually signaled by linguistic markers, such as, 'On the one hand I…and on the other…' or 'Part of me wants [X], but another part wants…'

If conflicting trances are seen to have been set up at different stages in the subject's development, each with the positive intention of meeting a specific need, deconstruction and integration are both practical and effective. We will discuss approaches to resolving conflicting trances in the chapter, *Patterning and Future-Pacing*, but, for the moment, we advise practitioners to begin to approach each state as discrete and functioning in some way (at some time in the patient's life) as a protective mechanism, even though they are presently experienced as functioning in opposition to each other.

Chunking to core values and positive intentions often allows us to resolve conflict.

> ***Case history:*** *The patient, a new father who had been diagnosed with Obsessive Compulsive Disorder, reported that 'one part' of him wanted to be a good, responsible, and normal parent, whereas 'the other part'*

was convinced that if he did not carry out certain rituals, his family would die. His obsessive behavior, though, was causing problems with his wife and, he believed, was also affecting his baby son.

After the practitioner helped the patient to reduce the level and automaticity of his sympathetic arousal, they arrived at the understanding that both 'parts' wanted safety and security for him and his family, but were pursuing it in mutually destructive ways. Together, the patient and practitioner worked to resolve the conflict (see Re-patterning and Future-Pacing, pages 293 to 314), and the patient returned home to 'see what happens'.

On his second consultation, some weeks later, the patient reported that his obsessive behavior had 'just gone away'—except for one ritual he needed to discuss. He said he felt compelled each night to kiss his fingers four times and place them gently on his sleeping son's cheek.

The practitioner asked whether he felt that this ritual helped him and his wife to sleep better at night. The patient said, 'I'm pretty sure it does'. The practitioner then suggested that the ritual might even help his baby sleep well and grow up secure in his father's love and protection, and the problem was permanently laid to rest. (Incidentally, this approach is also a neat example of a reframe of the meaning of the 'problem'.)

Two other forms of interpersonal trance may be encountered. These are what we call the 'couple trance' and the 'cultural trance'.

Where problems in relating are concerned, the couple trance may often be found to exist as a self-reinforcing loop, in which certain actions of one person trigger a response in the other, which, in turn, sets off another round—and, so it continues.[212] In designing interventions, the practitioner should take this two-point loop into consideration.

Cultural trance refers to the unquestioned acceptance of the rules and injunctions of one's cultural or religious group, and the conflicts that this might cause. Problems often occur simply because the 'rules' imparted by the group are 'self-sealing'—that is, they discourage new information or interpretations that might challenge the belief. The practitioner should be particularly careful not directly to challenge the belief-system, nor attempt to impose his own world-view.

Case history: *The patient, a young man who was about to be married, presented with erectile dysfunction. Although he was due to get married,* *he was shocked while changing after a work-out at his local gym to 'catch himself' looking at the bodies of other men. Coming from a deeply conservative and religious family, he 'just knew' this was 'wrong' and that he deserved to be punished.*

He spontaneously shifted into a significantly altered state when asked to pay attention to the memory of the experience of looking at other men—'to simply watch yourself and notice what happens'. This is controlled dissociation, a valuable approach to disassembling trance states.

Anxious not to pre-judge whether or not the patient had homosexual inclinations, the practitioner then invited him to 'go inside and ask' what 'other meanings' this behavior might have (the presupposition here was that there might be meanings other than the one that was limiting him).

The man remained silent for some minutes, and then emerged from his state of absorption, visibly relaxed and smiling. He confided that he had never seen another man's naked body and wanted to see how he 'shaped up' by comparison. Apparently, he had decided that he had shaped up well enough, and called back several months later to report that he was happily married and sexually fully functional again.

'Undoing' trance

It may seem paradoxical that we can induce trance to 'undo' trance, until we recognize and accept that neuronal networks have the potential to reorganize themselves when their boundary conditions are breached and new information is introduced and accepted.

Psychiatrist Dr. Susan Vaughan believes that effective change-by-communication directly alters neuronal networks,[213] while Nobel prizewinner Eric Kandel, one of the world's leading experts in neuroplasticity, suggests that information (words) may even alter the way our genes express themselves via a rearrangement of the connections between the nerve cells of our brains.[214]

As the subject dissociates from external triggers and reduces the flow of data competing for his attention, he relaxes and moves further away from higher-order levels of verbal abstraction and deeper into the non-verbal levels of Object and Event experience. Put more simply, he 'does' less, and 'is' more.

By becoming a relaxed, permissive observer of his own internal functions, he effectively removes the two strongest bulwarks of trance: physiological tension and semantic evaluation. Without either words to tell his story or a pattern of muscle tension to help maintain the state, the boundary conditions of a specific trance can begin to disassemble.

We contend that moving closer to the silent, purely experiential level is a necessary precursor to restructuring experience; we are still surprised how often patients spontaneously self-regulate when they master this ability simply to 'let go and let it be'.

As we explain in the exercise section at the end of this chapter, this is a valuable skill specific to Medical NLP and with many useful applications. Patients who understand and master this process have a powerful tool to support them in dealing with bouts of chronic pain, depression, anxiety, compulsive behavior, etc. Arthur J. Deikman notes that the ability to shift attentional awareness into what he calls the observing self 'reduces the intensity of affect, of obsessive thinking, and of automatic response patterns, thus providing the opportunity for modification and control, for increased mastery'.[215]

Inducing and amplifying trance

One of the misconceptions that still dominate is that people cannot be hypnotized 'against their will'. While it may be true that, when the subject is fully aware that the hypnotist is 'trying to put me under', he will be able to counteract suggestions to relax and focus, it is nevertheless entirely possible to facilitate the development of trance without ever using words such as 'hypnosis', 'trance', and 'relax'. As we have stated elsewhere (see page 251), states are contagious; we seem to be equipped with a tendency to entrain one to another. 'Suggesting' that the patient enter an altered state therefore can be accomplished by entraining.

This is a skill elevated to high art by Richard Bandler. 'If you want someone to relax, or go into any other state,' he says, 'go there first.' However, we should add that, while the ability to enter a trance state in which you can still function in full conscious awareness—called 'up-time' trance—is an extremely useful and energy-preserving state, it does require practice.

We have observed more than one student trying to hypnotize a colleague only to succumb himself.

You may lead the patient into an altered state by:

- slowing and pacing both your breathing and your word-groups to match the patient's out-breath (measurement of heart rate variability [HRV] shows us that the sympathetic nervous system is activated on the in-breath, and the parasympathetic nervous system on the out-breath. We are therefore 'chaining' together a succession of 'mini-breaks' to create one contiguous state of relaxation and inwardly turning attention);
- reinforcing each sign of developing trance by gently acknowledging it with a nod, an encouraging smile, or a repeated phrase, such as, 'That's right';
- following a series of linked factual statements (truisms) with a recommendation or suggestion that directs the subject towards trance—for example, 'So, you've had the tests and we've looked at the results and seen they are negative' (all verifiably true) 'and so now you can relax and I'll show you how you can learn to reduce stress more effectively…'

As trance develops, it may be wise to reassure the patient that it's 'okay to close your eyes for a few moments to relax if that feels more comfortable. I'll let you know when it's time to come back into the room.'

The fallacy of the 'deep' trance

The representation of trance as a hole into which we fall, sink, drop, or float—the 'deeper' the better, if we wish to 'fix' a particularly recalcitrant condition—may be a useful metaphor to use with patients. However, 'levels' of trance are artificial measures created in research laboratories and bear little relation to real-world transformational work.

The assumption that a 'deep' trance is a prerequisite of major shifts in perception and capability is misplaced. Deep, somnambulistic trance often leaves the subject slow and unresponsive, while a state barely perceptively different from the subject's default consciousness is often enough to permit effective work to be carried out. A certain level of skill and sensory acuity is required by practitioners to recognize the developing trance state and to exploit it effectively.

The practitioner's role

In many ways, our role as practitioners is to help 'de-hypnotize' the patient who is in the grip of bonded disconnection, by changing his relationship to his problem.

Even in the face of strong 'resistance', this may be accomplished in any number of ways. We have already given several examples of this, including the tried-and-tested, 'When you have (accomplished the desired state), what would be different and better?' Another example might be to ask the patient simply, 'Why *should* you change?', or, even, 'Why *shouldn't* you change?' The purpose of overcoming 'resistance' is always to satisfy patient needs and never to dominate or control.

However, we do, on occasion, use these questions gently to provoke the patient to argue for change, rather than—as is often the case—to present every argument for why he has to stay the same (the 'yes-but' symmetrical argument referred to above). Do not be surprised if he seems disoriented when you change tack this way. Paul Watzlawick suggests that this kind of shift in logical typing undermines the patient's 'game', which is entirely based on the (often unconscious) presupposition that the practitioner's role is to *make* him change.[216]

A number of possibilities to create bespoke approaches quite naturally occur when we understand that, while structure and process can be changed and outcomes designed, these have the greatest potential for success when we have helped the patient to change his relationship with his problem—and, possibly with others in his familial or cultural environment.

Trance, NLP and concordance

Very little distinction can be made between trance and NLP processes and techniques. By definition, when the subject turns inwardly to focus on certain processes and procedures, he may be said to be 'in trance'.

Equally, concordance and adherence—two qualities necessary to effective treatment outcomes—may be thought of as a form of trance. Andre Weitzenhoffer, a researcher and prolific writer on the subject of hypnosis, often remarked that spontaneous responses to suggestions in the waking state were indistinguishable from those elicited by hypnosis. Few practitioners will have considered trance as a significant factor in good clinical practice. We suggest they do.

EXERCISES

Non-evaluative self-observation

You will undoubtedly recognize this pattern from earlier discussions in this book:
from external, verifiable 'reality' into a more internal state of absorption.

1. Make three factual statements followed by one statement inferring comfort, relaxation, etc. (For example: 'You are sitting back in the chair, your feet on the ground, your hands in your lap, and you can allow yourself to relax, just a little more…')
2. Follow this by two factual statements and two inferential statements. Follow this, in turn, by one factual statement and three inferential statements. From this point on, all statements can be overtly 'hypnotic'. Pace the statements to the subject's breathing, ensuring that phrases match the out-going breath.

Note: This pattern can be used to practice self-hypnosis. Factual statements may be sights, sounds, or sensations in and around you. When you wish to end the trance, simply tell the subject (or, yourself) slowly and comfortably to come back into the room, wide awake.

1. Scan your body internally for any pain or tension. If you have a specific 'negative' emotion or worry that dominates your attention, notice how and where it manifests itself as a kinesthetic.

2. Give the kinesthetic permission to be there as it is and, in your imagination, step back, out of your body, and simply observe what is happening purely as a physical experience.
3. Describe out loud (if possible) the characteristics (sub-modalities) of the experience, being careful to avoid semantic evaluations, such as 'painful', 'worrying', 'awful', etc.
4. Stay aware of changes as they occur, and describe them (again in purely physical terms), as the experience resolves itself. Patients must be guided through this process, possibly several times, so they fully understand it and can have the confidence to apply it on their own.

Note: We often use this to depotentiate the response to a specific problem, and then follow it with the appropriate intervention (see following chapters).

Creating trance-inducing language patterns

By definition, 'induction' means 'inwardly turning'. In creating trance-inducing statements, we reverse the inference-to-fact process discussed earlier. This progressively leads the subject (or oneself) into more focussed levels of awareness in which suggestibility and change may be the natural consequence.

18

Coherence, Chaos and Octopus Traps: the presenting past

> *Look into the future and you see worry, look into the past and you see regret, look into the present and you shall find the purpose of life.—* ***Anonymous***

Mary G survived a challenging upbringing, a world war, early widowhood, and cancer. Then, at the age of 72, two days after Christmas, she was admitted to hospital and died within hours from a condition of which there had been no warning signs.

Her daughter, Helen, said later, 'I still feel incredibly guilty. When I was sorting out my mother's things, I found a letter in her purse that I had written her several weeks before, telling her that we were moving away and couldn't say at this stage when we would be able to see her again.

'I didn't mean to suggest that we'd never see her again; just that we didn't yet know how things would work out. My mother had always been fiercely independent, so I didn't think for a moment there would be any problem. I just thought we would be able to sort things out at some later date. But, somehow, I feel, especially from the way the letter had been folded and unfolded, that she had thought she might never see my husband and me and her grandchildren again.

'I can't help thinking she died of a broken heart.'

As fanciful as this might seem, Mary's daughter may be right.

If Mary G had been living in Japan at the time, the diagnosis might have been *Takotsubo*, or 'Octopus Trap Cardiomyopathy'. As it was, her death was ascribed to 'congestive heart failure'.

Octopus Trap Cardiomyopathy is a condition that gets its name from the hallmark bulging out of the apex of the heart. To Japanese researchers, this resembled the shape of the *Takotsubo*, or octopus trap.[217] The condition, though quite rare, affects mostly postmenopausal women who are under some form of exceptional mental stress. Grief, anger, and resentment are often factors in the victim's mental condition. The early studies suggested that a significant disturbance of the central nervous system discharges abnormal amounts of catecholamines, predominantly norepinephrine, which results in chest pain, myocardial stunning, and sometimes fatal arrhythmia.

The 'broken heart syndrome'

Meanwhile, Western researchers are starting to refer to 'broken heart syndrome', a metaphorical description beloved of romantic writers and resonating with most people. Sadness and loss are often accompanied by feelings of pain and constriction in the chest, even if heart failure doesn't ensue.

An early pioneer in the association between emotional and physical pain, Colin Murray Parkes, 30 years ago published a comprehensive study demonstrating the phenomenon was more than a literary device. He showed that many people who failed to adjust to the loss of a loved one became susceptible to a wide range of illnesses, with heart disease heading the list.

Since then, the Mayo Clinic's Dr Chet Rihal has studied the 'broken heart syndrome', and confirms a strong link between emotional loss and cardiac problems. Among other findings, he notes roughly 10% of people who survive a heart attack after the loss of a loved one are likely to have another attack within a short period of time.[218] However, by far the majority of people coping with grief and loneliness survive without serious problems. Genetics and general health undoubtedly are factors in their ability to restore allostasis, while social connectedness, which we explore elsewhere (see pages 35 to 36), is another significant factor.

Despite overwhelming evidence that people absorb, filter, and adapt to a perfect storm of data that assaults them every moment of every day,

Western medicine remains vague about the mechanisms that sometimes make stress toxic, and even life-threatening. Even though most researchers and practitioners of all specialties accept the corrosive effect of 'stress', the treatment modalities are patchy—suppress negative feelings, usually by pharmacological means, or remove the presumed source of stress.

We believe the inconsistent, and often ineffective, approach to the stress 'epidemic' results from a failure to distinguish between challenge (which is experienced and responded to with enthusiasm and self-efficacy) and what a study by Cornell University's Center for Advanced Human Resources calls 'hindrances', events which leave individuals feeling overwhelmed, ineffective, and ill.[219] Far from helping the victim recover, some studies have even shown that, rather than improve conditions, removal of all perceived hindrances causes the subject's health and wellbeing to deteriorate even further.

As we've said many times, the default ruling therapeutic response is to try and block the *effects* of the imbalance (the racing heart, the churning stomach), by the use of drugs, and even, in rare cases, by sympathectomy (the severing of key nerves transmitting sensations to the brain). The alternative is some form of 'talking therapy'—counselling, Cognitive Behavioral Therapy, and so on.

By and large, stress-related conditions are regarded as a product of the mind. Indeed, people suffering intense emotions often consider themselves somehow lacking in mental or moral strength. In reality—and, of vital importance—*emotions originate in the body, not in the mind.*

This is so important to the core values and approaches of Medical NLP that we will repeat it: ***Emotions originate in the body, not in the mind.***

Anyone who has ever experienced anger, loss, grief, joy, bliss, or any other powerful emotion, understands this intuitively. Hearts race or ache, stomachs knot and churn, throats choke up. Despite all attempts to ignore them, the symptoms persist until either time or circumstances (or, sometimes death) put them to rest.

Until recently, the involvement of heart and gut in emotional crisis was regarded as incidental—a side-effect of an overload of stress hormones—and little more. Now, in certain more enlightened research establishments at least, the inner 'wisdom' of both heart and digestive tract are starting to be recognized.

Both systems are now known to have many thousands of brain-like neurons which function by perceiving fluctuations in the environment and adapting their behavior accordingly. They are even known to log their responses to make later behaviors faster and more flexible. In short, they are capable of creating memories.[220,221]

Most pharmacological research has focused on the brain and the substances it produces. Drug companies continue to seek the 'magic bullet' that will alter brain function and bring about positive changes in mood and behavior.

However, aside from their semi-autonomous neuronal function, the heart and gut—effectively 'mini brains'—produce a range of neuro-chemicals of their own, including adrenaline (for sudden spurts of energy), atrial natriuretic factor, or ANF, to regulate blood pressure, and serotonin (the mood-regulating neuro-transmitter), more than 90% of which is produced in the gut. The heart even manufactures its own supply of oxcytocin, the so-called 'love peptide', which floods the body when people fall in love, bond with infants, or stroke their cats.

The most startling point about all this is that both heart and gut 'talk' to the brain and vice versa. There is even some evidence that either system can perceive problems and react accordingly before conscious awareness dawns.

The effects seem to be trans-cultural; societies across the world intuitively accept the heart and gut areas as central to their models (and their experience) of psycho-physical-spiritual stability. In the West, people have many idioms that point to a somatic origin: 'following the heart' (desire), 'knowing in my heart of hearts' (certainty), 'gut feelings' (intuition), and 'not having the stomach for it' (cowardice or fear), to highlight just a few.

And, in the area of personal and spiritual development, many conventions, such as the Vedic and Sufi traditions, have given rise to various heart-centered exercises and meditations which are strikingly similar to the clinically effective patterns and processes described later in this chapter.

The wandering nerve

On reflection, though, it should come as no surprise that the brain, heart, and digestive system are all involved in the fight-or-flight response. The vagus nerve, the largest in the body, meanders from the brainstem to the heart and down into the abdomen. It not only regulates the parasympathetic nervous system, thus damping down our runaway emotions, but it also communicates directly to the immune system through the neurochemical, acetylcholine. Without the action of the vagus nerve, the human heart would race at around 115 beats per minute, instead of the more usual 72 or so.[222] When it is activated, it is often accompanied by a warm, spreading, liquid feeling in the area of the heart.

Dr. Stephen Porges, of the Department of Psychiatry and the Director of the Brain-Body Center in the College of Medicine at the University of Illinois at Chicago, regards the vagus nerve as central to the development of mammals as socially engaged creatures. A key player in 'neuroception'—the ability of neural circuits to distinguish whether situations or people are safe, dangerous, or life threatening—the vagus nerve is deeply involved in the phenomena of empathy and entrainment (which we discuss in Chapter 3; see pages 29 to 33).[223,224]

Porges believes that, as the pathways responsible for heart-regulation moved from the *dorsal motor nucleus* of the vagus in reptiles to the *nucleus ambiguus* in mammals, a 'face–heart connection' evolved. This gave rise to an engagement system that would enable social interactions to regulate the visceral (internal feelings or somatic markers) state.[225] This, Porges adds, is why a baby coos at a caregiver but cries at a stranger, or why a small child is attracted by a parent's embrace, but regards a stranger's hug as an assault.[226]

According to Porges's theory, faulty neuroception may lie at the root of several psychiatric disorders, including autism, schizophrenia, anxiety disorders, depression, and Reactive Attachment Disorder. Imbalance in the vagal response means a risk of system-wide dysfunction, or even collapse, it would seem. On the other hand, early research suggests that vagus nerve stimulation (VNS), using electrical impulses, may prove useful in treating a wide range of conditions, from intractable depression, migraine, and anxiety disorders,[227] through fibromyalgia[228] and epilepsy, to various auto-immune diseases, including rheumatoid arthritis.[229]

The dangers of over-stimulation

As always, balance is everything. Over-stimulation of the vagus nerve can cause a drop in blood-pressure, dizziness, and fainting. The light-headedness that often follows violent vomiting, or straining to pass a particularly solid bowel-movement, is caused by over-stimulation of this nerve, a response otherwise known as *vasovagal syncope.*[230]

Deliberate over-stimulation of the vagus nerve, known as the *Valsalva Maneuver*, is sometimes employed to calm a racing heartbeat, or to lift a heavy weight. The Valsalva Maneuver involves taking a deep breath and holding it while closing the glottis (the vocal folds of the throat) to trap the breath and pushing the belly outward.

Gentle rubbing on the eyeballs or drinking or splashing the face with extremely cold water can also stimulate the vagus nerve.

It is important to note that the Valsalva Maneuver and the eyeball-rubbing techniques should not be practiced without medical supervision. Although allostatic overload is a dominant factor in most modern physical and psychological ills, some people may be at risk if their parasympathetic system is fired up too much or too quickly.

Fortunately, however, the vagus nerve can be stimulated in less invasive ways. In fact, influencing the vagal response may be at the heart (ambiguity intended) of many traditional approaches to health, including yoga, *t'ai chi*, and, especially, various breathing techniques, such as India's ancient *pranayama* and China's *qigong*.

Dr. Mark Liponis, who has studied a wide range of breathing patterns, suggests that certain exercises, especially those involving abdominal breathing, may stimulate the vagus nerve, sending acetylcholine cascading through the body, triggering the relaxation response, and damping down inflammation.[231]

The natural instinct of most human beings is to move away from uncomfortable experiences, both internal and external. The widespread use of psychotropic drugs, including the ubiquitous selective serotonin re-uptake inhibitors (SSRIs) prescribed in their billions for anxiety and depression, is an attempt to facilitate this. Self-medication—including off-prescription drugs, alcohol, sex, and food—is a common response to the discomfort of an under-performing vagus nerve. However, attempting to suppress uncomfortable feelings may be more damaging to cardiovascular and other tissue health than the emotions themselves.

People who do not express emotions, including those who suffer *alexithymia*, a sub-clinical inability to identify and describe subjective emotions, have been shown to suffer both altered immune responses and an increase in the inflammatory markers, high sensitivity C-reactive protein (hs-CRP) and Interleukin-6 (IL-6).[232]

In pointing out the above, we emphasize that we are not endorsing the now-discredited pseudo-therapy of pillow-thumping to discharge 'repressed anger'. Rather, and, as we will demonstrate, we have found that learning to be mindful of, align with, and resolve, the physical manifestation of strong emotion is what helps restore flow and functionality, not 'letting it all out'.

Overwhelming emotions almost always have their origins in past experience. The pattern-matching capabilities of the human brain work swiftly, often beyond conscious awareness, and sometimes to debilitating effect. The fact that events already experienced should resurface and find new footholds in the present should be regarded as phenomenological invitations to heal, rather than a punishment from the past.

In effect, this is a clear shift away from a predominantly mind-based healing approach, to one in which the body—more specifically the viscera—not only functions to 'communicate' a systemic imbalance, but also to suggest a route through which auto-regulation might take place.

But how will we know what works?

Most new systems are greeted in the mainstream with suspicion, and, probably, with some reason. It is generally believed that no universally accepted 'objective' measurement of the effectiveness of any treatment purporting to 'fix' stress (or any other psychological) disorders actually exists, therefore anything without an acceptable evidence-base tends to be rejected out of hand.

However, as we mentioned in an earlier chapter, a system for measuring the *down-regulation* of a person's autonomic nervous system (ANS) that is often described as gold-standard, placebo-free, and evidence-based already exists.

A window on the autonomic nervous system

Predominantly used by cardiologists to measure fetal cardiac distress, Heart Rate Variability (HRV) is regarded as a 'window' on the functioning of the ANS. General health and wellbeing of the subject is high when both arms of the ANS, the sympathetic and para-sympathetic systems, are functioning in harmony. If they are not, dysfunction and possibly even death may be imminent.

What makes this truly paradigm-shifting is the fact that the technology mentioned a few paragraphs back can also not only measure the effectiveness of any treatment, but also help individuals learn how to access and function in optimal states at will.

In simple terms, heart rate variability (HRV) is the measure of the intervals between heartbeats. These intervals need to be infinitesimally variable in order to respond to changes in the individual's environment, both internal and external. Depressed HRV (also known as low coherence) is associated with under-functioning of the system; elevated HRV (high coherence) signals optimal functioning.

Despite its universal acceptance as a reliable indicator of incipient heart failure, little attention has been paid to using HRV technology to measure up-regulation of the nervous system—otherwise known as 'coherence'. Coherence is not, as is often assumed, a deeply relaxed, 'down-time' state. Coherence has its own distinctive characteristics that stand apart from the more usually accepted three states of consciousness, waking, sleeping, and dreaming.

As humans, we tend to experience emotions sequentially—surprise followed by excitement followed by happiness followed by nostalgia, for example. However, people exhibiting high coherence, in which heart, brain, and autonomic nervous system are functioning in synchrony, describe a state of deep comfort and relaxation running *in parallel* with high focus and attentiveness. Various meditative traditions refer to this integrated state as 'mindfulness' (Buddhism) or 'restful alertness' (Transcendental Meditation). As one subject reported while demonstrating high coherence, 'I feel very sharp and dynamic in my dealings with the outside world, but inside I'm extremely calm and quiet.'

Coherence not only refers to increased synchronisation between the two branches of the autonomic nervous system, but also to a shift toward heightened parasympathetic activity, increased heart-brain synchronisation, improved arterial flexibility, and entrainment between diverse physiological oscillatory systems.[233] Some of the markers of coherent functioning include a sense of emotional and physical wellbeing, behavioral flexibility, and improved cognitive performance. Regular experience of coherence has been demonstrated in a number of studies to facilitate the body-mind's ability to self-regulate.

In the West, the measurement of coherence as a marker of health and wellbeing is largely disregarded. As one consultant cardiologist explained, 'We simply don't have a drug or a procedure that can improve coherence. We know a lot about the breakdown of health and we can measure that quite accurately. But we don't have a model of health that corresponds to the concept of improving coherence, so it isn't really even on medicine's radar.'

Once again, it's a different picture in Japan.

Ikigai, health and longevity

Ikigai is a Japanese word with no English equivalent. In English, it is often translated as 'subjective wellbeing'. However, Japanese researchers have associated *ikigai* with a number of qualities, including a sense of meaning and purpose and a joyful or welcoming attitude to life. High *ikigai* is associated with health and longevity; low *ikigai* with disease and reduced life expectancy.

A seminal longitudinal study conducted in 1994 and recently published surveyed tens of thousands of Japanese between the ages of 40 and 79. Embedded within a large number of questions was one that simply asked, 'Do you have *ikigai* in your life?'[234]

Over the following seven years, researchers monitored the subjects, taking into consideration various accepted risk factors, known as 'confounds', including age, gender, body-weight, smoking, alcohol consumption, diet, stress levels, and history of disease. When the data were analyzed, *ikigai* emerged as a highly accurate predictor of who would still be alive at the end of the study. Simply put, nearly 95% of those who reported having a sense of meaning in their lives were still alive after seven years, compared with 83% of those who had reported no meaning in their lives.

All this considered, we look forward to the study that correlates *ikigai* with high coherence—and which demonstrates to the full satisfaction of the Western scientific world that health and wellbeing, as well as the techniques and treatments designed to promote them, are as measurable as dysfunction and disease.

For those practitioners who do not have access to the technology to measure HRV (and it is becoming increasingly available to even lay practitioners), a simple and fairly accurate marker of an individual's state of coherence lies in his breathing pattern.

Mainstream medicine pays little attention to breathing, except where respiratory tract or cardiac disorders are suspected. In these cases, investigation is restricted to respiratory rate, dyspnea (difficulty in breathing), tachypnea (unusually rapid breathing), blood oxygen saturation, the sound of breathing (for example, wheezing or vesicular), and recession (caused by abnormalities of the muscles of the chest wall).

The Medical NLP practitioner, on the other hand, is encouraged to be alert to:

- rapid breathing;
- upper chest breathing;
- sighing;
- sniffling;
- yawning;
- irregular breathing;
- audible breathing during rest;
- apnea (suspension of breathing);
- unusual or effortful breathing; and, especially,
- breathing through the mouth.

All these behaviors result in over-breathing which forces carbon dioxide from the lungs, stripping it from blood, tissue, and cells. This, in turn, prevents oxygen from being released from the hemoglobin into tissues and organs, a phenomenon first identified in the early 20th century and known as the Bohr Effect.[235]

A number of research projects now suggest that reduced carbon dioxide levels can cause excessive cortical excitability, resulting in anxiety,[236] depression, and a wide range of physical and psychological disorders.

The 'Fat File Syndrome'

According to cardiologist Claude Lum, hyperventilation may give rise to a collection of 'bizarre and often apparently unrelated' symptoms which may affect any part of the body, any organ or system.[237] Lum coined the phrase 'fat file syndrome' to describe what we in Medical NLP refer to as the 'revolving door syndrome', where patients keep returning, or move from practitioner to practitioner, amassing an impressive array of chronic symptoms, none of which responds to conventional treatment.

It follows, then, that helping patients shift the pattern of breathing away from hyperventilation will not only be beneficial to overall health, but, since a modified breathing pattern can reduce cortical excitement, will also increase receptiveness to any advice or treatment that follows. Simply put, a relatively simple shift in the breathing pattern is the quickest, most effective, and most easily measured way of improving coherence. Experiencing, or even remembering, events that evoke feelings of love, gratitude, or other positive emotion, can also have a measurable effect.

Many breathing exercises exist which purport to have beneficial value, but the easiest to learn focuses on a simple relationship between the in- and out-breaths. Put simply, the in-breath increases sympathetic functioning of the nervous system (which is an argument against encouraging anxious people to 'take a deep breath'), while the out-breath activates the parasympathetic response. A slightly prolonged out-breath, then, triggers a sense of calm alertness, conducive to attentive listening, improved understanding, and greater adherence to new instructions and advice. Both in-breath and out-breath should be through the nostrils.

Even a brief period of this kind of mindful attention on the heart-beat and breathing pattern can have a far-reaching and beneficial effect on the subject's wellbeing.

Biological feedback

Our personal experience has been extremely encouraging. Patients who are taught to become mindful of their heart rate and breathing pattern and to use both as a kind of biological feedback process have reported marked improvement in a wide range of conditions, including anxiety, depression, high blood pressure, irritable bowel syndrome, chronic pain, and chronic obstructive pulmonary disorder (COPD).

Before-and-after HRV readings seem to support the theory that the improvement in health and wellbeing is mirrored by an increase in coherence.

For those readers interested in following current research in cardiac coherence and health, we suggest you visit the website of the HeartMath Institute in Boulder Creek, California.[238] The institute is a leader in current research on stress, emotions, 'heart intelligence', and other diverse areas related to human physiology and performance, including heart-brain interactions and cardiac coherence. It offers a number of approaches to improving health and wellbeing. A version of the basic HeartMath technique follows:

As you breathe in and out, imagine that the air moves through the chest wall, so that it is the heart, rather than the lungs, that expands and contracts.

After a few moments of 'heart breathing', recall a strongly positive emotion, like love or gratitude.

Continue the exercise for five minutes or so.

Our recommendation is that the following program, which is slightly more complex and involves using the individual's own heartbeat as a biological feedback device, be adopted by practitioners as well as their patients. As we discuss elsewhere in this book (see Chapter 3, pages 29 to 33), emotions are contagious[239]—and, therefore, our assertion is that coherence is, too.

EXERCISES

Exercise 1

1. Place the palm of your left hand on the center of your chest. Comfortably curl the fingers of your right hand around your left wrist and find your radial pulse just beneath your thumb.
2. Sit quietly for a few moments, simply being mindful of the rising and falling of your chest beneath your palm. Stay neural and detached as you do this. Do not take deep breaths. Simply

allow your breathing to settle into its own natural rhythm.

3. After 20 or 30 seconds, slightly lengthen your out-breath without altering the in-breath. Find the maximum exhalation you can comfortably make. Your count may be something like 3 in, 5 out, or 4 in, 7 out...whatever seems most comfortable to you. The important thing is to maintain a small in-breath and a longer out-breath for the duration of the exercise.
4. Now alter your rhythm (still short in, longer out) to match your pulse rate. In effect, you are using your own heartbeat as a biofeedback mechanism.
5. While maintaining the steady rhythm, led by the beating of your heart, recall some person or event that evokes a strongly positive emotion of peace, love, or gratitude. If thinking about an individual, our advice is to choose carefully. Ensure it is someone who is without 'baggage', and for whom you can have unconditionally positive feelings, without expecting a response. Since few adult relationships are truly unconditional, we suggest choosing a child or a beloved pet. In neither of these cases do we expect 'pay-back' for our love.
6. Relax into the feeling, while maintaining the ratio of small in-breath to longer out-breath for a few minutes. If your mind wanders, simply return to the practice when your awareness returns.

You can adopt this exercise as a daily meditation, say 15 minutes twice a day (the optimal time, we find), or you can simply practice a few breaths at any time you feel the need to 're-connect' or ground yourself...or, better yet, both.

You can also do this 'on the fly', without interrupting whatever you're doing to sit down and close your eyes. Simply put your attention where the palm of your hand was resting, then follow the instructions above, from 2 onwards. Those practitioners familiar with the core NLP technique of anchoring (discussed elsewhere in this book—see pages 147 to 152) may experiment with anchoring this subjective experience of coherence, remembering that the effect will be deepened with regular practice.

Since the effect seems to spill over into the rest of your life from some time after even a few minutes of this practice, we also suggest you do it several times a day, whether you feel stressed or not. In time, this becomes a pre-emptive strike against autonomic overload.

The next technique should be used wherever any strong emotion, such as anxiety, fear, anger, and even jealousy, threatens to engulf the individual. The Medical NLP model, which subscribes strongly to the belief that bodily feelings are somatic markers of cortical dynamics (another way of saying when you become mindful of the physical expression of your emotions, you are opening a doorway into the workings of the brain), has developed several simple techniques to resolve relatively complex 'psychological' experiences.

Exercise 2

1. As soon as you become aware of the emotion, scan your body. Notice where the emotion expresses itself. It will usually concentrate somewhere along the mid-line down the body, where innervation is most dense.
2. Simply mindfully observe the physical expression of your emotion. Breathe mindfully, small breath in, longer breath out. Avoid judgments and inferences, such as 'painful', 'awful', 'scary', and even labels, such as 'anxiety' or 'anger'. Simply observe, openly and objectively and with a sense of curiosity. Remember, these 'somatic markers', or symptoms, are communications that something in the body-mind system is off-kilter. They are not there to hurt or punish you.
3. Pay attention to their physical characteristics—size, shape, temperature, coloration, or any other qualities—without attempting to change or remove them. Give them full permission to move or change in whatever way occurs spontaneously.

4. Notice particularly how the sensation moves and where it is blocked. You will almost certainly find that you have tensed up to prevent the feeling from moving. For example, anxiety is often experienced as a sensation fountaining upward from the stomach into the throat where most sufferers tense up, fearing irrationally that it will cause them some terrible harm.
5. Give any blocked sensation permission to complete its movement. This often requires courage, but it is particularly important. Relax around the sensation and let it move of its own accord. When resistance is removed, the sensation always accelerates into feelings of greater comfort, if not of complete resolution.
6. Continue as long as is comfortable. Do not fall into the trap of trying to use this technique to block the emotion. That will only set up further tension and discomfort. If you need to pause the process for any reason, simply make a mental 'bookmark' to come back to the point where you left off, and resume the process as soon as you can.

The importance of practice

This is a skill, and requires practice. A key prerequisite is an easy, non-judgmental detachment from the experience. We suspect a substantial cause of pain derives from people's tendency to verbalize their subjective experience as a way of desensitizing themselves against the neurological perturbation. However, as an examination of the Structural Differential reveals, this process of 'naming and framing' is usually catastrophic. The inferences, both verbal and visual, feed back into the higher levels of experience, increasing physical and emotional worsening of the experience at every pass.

The first time you are successful at simply allowing a somatic 'event' simply to be, without any attempt to control it, you will almost certainly be struck by the effectiveness of such a simple process. Change can occur spontaneously and quickly and in the right direction. The body-mind system has an inner 'wisdom' that always moves towards auto-regulation, given the right circumstances. We are facilitating a natural process, not 'making it happen'.

Also, be aware that change can be experienced in many different ways. The symptom may simply fade away. Or, it may occur less frequently. Or, your nervous system may simply 'forget' how to do it. Or, it may transform into another feeling or sensation. It may even intensify, until it goes over a threshold, rather like an over-inflated balloon bursting.

In all these events, and any others than might occur, simply stay open and curious, allow whatever happens to happen in its own way, following the symptom whatever it might be doing, and be prepared to surprise and delight yourself when change occurs, spontaneously and without effort.

*Optimal experience is something that we make happen.—**Mihaly***

19

From 'Functional' to Functioning: restructuring dysfunctional states

Csikszentmihalyi[240]

Patients suffering from chronic and 'functional' disorders are stuck—literally and metaphorically. The experience of being trapped by a body and mind that no longer perform naturally or follow orders can be overwhelmingly debilitating.

With many of the conditions eluding diagnosis and effective treatment, the frustration experienced by the patient often infects the practitioner, with demoralizing results.

Subjective 'stuckness' is easily demonstrated. If the sub-modalities of either patient or practitioner are examined, we will almost certainly see that they lack movement: stills or snapshots, rather than movies, full of color and movement. Their representations of the problem lack process and action. Their sensory representations are restricted, or loop continuously in a self-maintaining cycle of failure. The successful resolution of a problem will always be accompanied by a shift from 'still' to 'moving'.

Healing, whether or not it involves a 'cure', is a return to optimal experience, or 'flow'.

We are often asked by hopeful newcomers to Medical NLP for 'the' cure for depression (or anxiety, chronic pain, post-traumatic stress disorder, etc). Our reply is always, 'It depends on the patient.' The pre-supposition that the prescriptive approach of Western medicine can be applied to all patients suffering from superficially similar disorders misses the essential point. Medical NLP holds that the patient who has the condition is the key to relieving the condition that has the patient.

Therefore, even though in this chapter we review the underlying structure and process of three components commonly encountered in complex, chronic conditions—depression, anxiety, and pain—these are not intended to be applied prescriptively.

Rather, we urge you to remember always to return to basics—structure, process, purpose, and intention—and then to develop approaches out of the principles and techniques outlined earlier in this book. In the following chapter, we will present a number of patterns that can be used as templates for further interventions. Avoid being too constrained by formal diagnoses. Although all clinical guidelines categorize conditions and make specific recommendations, these are *evaluative* statements and cannot accurately reflect the fullness of the patient's experience.

Do not confuse text with context, the patient with his symptom, the diagnosis with the disease itself. Therefore, the headings we give to the following sections are intended as general, not definitive, descriptors.

Note: Since we regard allostatic load as an underlying cause or component of all 'functional' disorders, we suggest encouraging patients to adopt a regular program designed to evoke the Relaxation Response, the psychophysiological counter-balance to the fight-or-flight response (see Appendix A, pages 357 to 360). The Relaxation Response has been demonstrated to have a regulatory effect on many disorders classed as 'functional' or 'somatoform', possibly by restoring hemispheric balance.[241,242,243] The simple technique outlined in the Appendix also introduces the essence of 'mindfulness meditation', the practice now being embraced by Western medicine, without an unnecessarily long learning curve.

Depression and the myth of chemical imbalance

If you've ever sought help from the mainstream medical profession for depression (or, for that matter, schizophrenia, attentional deficit, or bipolar disorders, social phobia, and, even, restless legs), the chances are you would have been offered a psychoactive drug, as first-line treatment.

Equally likely is the fact that you were probably told by your doctor or psychiatrist, or may already have read or heard somewhere, that your problem was a 'chemical imbalance' in the brain.

The shift in the approach to mental illness over the past two or three decades has been profound. Where once social and family were considered to be the likeliest causes of emotional disturbance, now it is a failure of your neurochemicals to order themselves correctly.

It's a seductive theory, and one which both doctors and patients have embraced. First, it gives permission to administer medication, the treatment they know best; second, it removes from the patient and her family any suggestion of responsibility or blame.

As we see it, there are two serious problems with this approach: how can a patient suffering chronic disturbances of any kind be treated in isolation from the context in which she exists—and, how can anyone claim the existence of a 'chemically unbalanced brain', when there is absolutely no evidence as to what a 'chemically balanced' brain might be?

Furthermore, there is

- *no evidence* to support the theory of chemical imbalance;
- *no evidence* in the form of a condition-specific diagnostic test for anymental illness;[244]
- *no evidence* that many drugs, such as the SSRI anti-depressants, perform markedly better than placebo.[245]

In fact, even David Kupfer, overseer of the *Diagnostic and Statistical Manual of Mental Disorders (DSM) Fifth Edition*, the American Psychiatric Association's diagnostic and prescriptive 'bible', admits in the press release of the publication's latest edition, 'We've been telling patients for several decades that we are waiting for biomarkers. We're still waiting.'

This astonishing admission does nothing to rein in the taxonomic enthusiasm of *DSM-5*'s contributors, who have created even more 'psychiatric disorders', all 'treatable' with medication. These range from 'disruptive mood dysregulation disorder' (severe and frequent temper tantrums); 'binge-eating disorder' (over-eating 12 times in three months); 'oppositional defiant disorder' (children who won't listen to their parents); and 'hoarding disorder' (difficulty in discarding possessions regardless of value).[246]

But, rather than finding themselves united by a global description of drug-treatable mental illnesses, some psychiatrists on both sides of the Atlantic have challenged the validity of the 100-page volume and what one source calls its 'diagnostic hyper-inflation'.

Even more dramatically, the Division of Clinical Psychology of Britain's distinguished Psychological Society met publication of *DSM-5* by calling for the abandonment of all psychiatric diagnosis and the development, in its stead, of alternatives which do not use the language of 'illness' or 'disorder'.

Diagnoses such as schizophrenia, bipolar disorder, personality disorder, attention deficit hyperactivity disorder, conduct disorders, etc, are of 'limited reliability and questionable validity'.[247] Instead of assuming a physiological basis for mental illness—as yet unproven—they point to socio-economic factors as being far more accurate predictors of emotional distress.

The theory of biochemical imbalance remains so well entrenched that it has seldom been questioned. The response of the pharmaceutical industry has been to launch thousands of psychotropic drugs costing billions of dollars in the 'war' against mental disease. The promise continues to be an effortless chemical 'tweak' and an end to behavioral problems and mental suffering. However, in the case of many mental illnesses, the outlook remains bleak. In fact, the long-term condition of some sufferers, notably schizophrenics, has actually worsened since the early- to mid-20th century, when treatments ranged from camphor injections; electro-convulsive therapy; deliberate infection with malaria; to insulin-induced comas; ice-water showers; and lobotomy.[248]

Astonishingly, according to two major studies by the World Health Organization, if you suffered a psychotic episode in a poor country, such as India or Nigeria, you'd probably be more or less back to normal in a couple of years, whereas if you were unfortunate enough to be a citizen of one of the developed countries, you would, in all likelihood, end up chronically ill. Meta-analyzes of the outcome literature reveals that clinical and social outcomes are significantly better for patients in 'Third World' countries than for those being treated in the West.[249,250] Explanations for this apparent anomaly include greater familial and social integration in these two countries, and, paradoxically, little or no medication.

These findings, reviewed in detail in Robert Whitaker's highly readable (and disturbing) book, *Mad in America: Bad Science, Bad Medicine, and the Enduring Mistreatment of the Mentally Ill*,[251] have been greeted with almost as much disparagement and anger from some psychiatrists as did Robert Rosenhan's iconoclastic '*thud*' report.[252] And, yet, both the theory and the problems it causes persist.

Moods (and probably the levels of certain neurochemicals, including serotonin) may doubtless be affected by certain activities and triggers, such as exercise, sunlight, and sex. However, some people might regard it is cavalier, not to say dangerous, to administer profoundly mind-altering drugs based on the assumption that two or three neurochemicals, out of the 100 or more that have been identified, are out of whack.

Resistance to change

Resistance to changing tack in the way certain drugs, antidepressants in particular, are prescribed is high. So entrenched is it, that even doctors in general practice are allowed to prescribe highly psycho-active drugs—sometimes on the flimsiest of diagnostic criteria. Even though research suggesting most of the leading SSRIs are of little use to anyone—except, possibly, people with extremely severe depression, as has been widely publicized—prescriptions, at the time of writing, continue to be issued at a rate of nearly 200-million a year in the United States,[253] and nearly 40-million in the UK.[254]

Understandably, pharmaceutical companies embrace the chemical imbalance theory with enthusiasm. Almost all the major brands suggest in their publicity material that chemical imbalance in the brain 'may' be the cause of depression.

Also, while certain drugs may have a place as a response to acute mental problems, the model of chemical imbalance has been extended across the board to cover the widest possible range of conditions, from major psychotic incidents and florid hallucinatory experiences to the break-up of a teenager's relationship, or worry about incipient changes in the work-place. As we've remarked elsewhere (see page 219), life experiences that would have been considered normal a few years ago are becoming pathologized, with scant proof that pharmacological intervention is in the subject's real interests. Aside from the risk of side-effects, including habituation and addiction, our concern is that such a response does little to improve the patient's ability to respond appropriately to life's vagaries.

The theory of chemical imbalance affecting the 'normal' functioning of the nervous system has a lot in common with that which underlay the Victorian concept of 'neurasthenia', a term first coined by psychiatrist George Beard in 1869. This diagnosis, describing a nebulous condition marked by mental and physical fatigue, listlessness, and medically unexplained aches and pains, dominated medical thinking for more than a century.

The term was dropped from *DSM* in 1969...but the concept is neither dead nor buried.

Diseases related to neurochemical imbalance were unknown in Japan. However, as soon as Western pharmaceutical companies invented and imported the concept of nerves and electrical nerve-impulse into the country, using the analogy of trolley-buses derailed from their power sources (something to which the Japanese could relate), the country began to suffer from a near-epidemic of what became known locally as *shinkeisuijaku* (**Figure 19.1**).

神経衰弱

Figure 19.1 Shinkeisuijaku

Given the high-achieving, time-poor, and over-crowded world in which many millions of Japanese live and work, it was readily accepted as an 'explanation' of the country's widespread but inchoate sense of anxiety and stress—what we would call 'allostatic load'.

Some observers, including cultural analyst Junko Kitanaka, see the introduction and acceptance of *shinkeisuijaku* as the first psychological 'disease' of the common man, and the first instance of large-scale medicalization of everyday distress in Japan. It also serves as a particularly graphic example of how the ruling WEIRD (Western, Educated, Industrialized, Rich, and Democratic) paradigm is being deliberately extended far beyond its source. This is what writer and commentator Ethan Watters eloquently calls 'the globalization of the Western mind'.[255]

The pharmaceutical industry's infomercials are no more scientific when preaching to domestic audiences. For example, one slick advertising video for Zoloft® (sertraline), one of America's top-selling brands, suggests that feeling sad, lonely, or that 'things' don't feel the way they used to, is 'depression', a condition that 'may' be caused by a failure to produce enough serotonin, and which requires medication.

No life-event is mentioned as a possible cause of depression; no suggestion is made that behavioral and dietary change may help. Your friends and family are irrelevant. The fact that your mother, or a beloved pet, might have died, doesn't rate a mention. Instead, a highly simplified animation shows how the drug turns a sparse trickle of serotonin into a positive flood of feel-good chemicals leaping across the nerve-endings in the brain, resulting in an almost immediate existence of sunshine, clear skies, flowers, and birds.[256]

So how can a dictum as shaky as the chemical imbalance explanation continue to survive in the face of such scientific challenge?

Eliott Valenstein, author of a meticulously researched and well argued book on the subject, *Blaming the Brain*, views it starkly. 'A fallacious theory,' he says, 'is regarded as preferable to admitting ignorance.'

Valenstein traces the medical profession's commitment back to the 1950s when the accidental discovery of some mood-altering drugs opened the door to the belief that psychopharmacology would mean an end to mental illness. The result has been worldwide reliance on drugs to treat depression, and massive profits for the pharmaceutical companies involved.[257]

Many doctors still argue that patients report positive results after using SSRIs. We have no way at the moment of establishing how much of this is a placebo response and how much has to do with the fact that the patient is able to experience some 'difference', even though it may not be the happiness or wellbeing implied by the drug companies' marketing copy.

Dr. Joanna Moncrieff of University College in London believes this is the explanation for how psychotropic drugs used to treat 'psychiatric conditions' really affect people with depression and other emotional 'disorders'. She argues that the effects reported by patients may result from the drugs' psychoactive qualities—in much the same way as alcohol, cannabis, and cocaine can alter the user's mood. Some drugs dampen down thoughts and emotions; others create a pleasant soporific effect. The fact that patients are put into an altered mental and physical state does not mean that the drugs have effectively treated their condition, she says, but may simply have suppressed or masked their feelings. Or, the patient may simply feel 'different'.

None of this is intended to suggest that there is no role for medication in certain cases of depression, particularly when acute. But we agree with Dr. Moncrieff, who urges her colleagues to give patients true 'informed consent' by telling them that the prescribed drug may simply make them feel different and could suppress thoughts and feelings. We suspect that many people would reject such drugs, while some, particularly those who have been severely distressed over a period of time, may welcome these effects as preferable, at least for a time.[258]

For the most part, though, we prefer patients who consult us because they are feeling low to explore some of the suggestions in this book, as well as to try exercise (where possible), diet, and the support and love of family and friends. From experience, we know that depression is caused or deepened among people who: lose structure to their days; eat badly; don't get any exercise, and avoid social contact.

These alternative 'treatments' are not as strange as they might at first sound. Britain's Mental Health Foundation lists a number of benefits of exercise for sufferers of depression, including:

- reduced stress and mental exhaustion;
- increased energy;
- improved sleep patterns;
- a sense of achievement;
- focus in life and motivation;
- reduced anger or frustration;
- improved appetite; and
- a better social life, with more fun.[259]

Furthermore, side-effects (supposing the exercise regime is geared to the individual's capabilities and needs) are non-existent.

Few, if any, drugs can make these claims in good conscience.

Diet has been associated with mood fluctuations, as well as several mental diseases and behavioral problems—including attention-deficit hyperactivity disorder (ADHD), autism, and even schizophrenia.[260] Some studies suggest that a diet high in B vitamins, omega-3 oils, and plenty of vegetables—the so-called Mediterranean diet—may be useful in helping to control depression.[261]

There is no doubt that considerable damage has been done to both the patient's capacity for self-efficacy and the healer's 'art' by the current belief that depression is exclusively a biochemical disorder. As we have mentioned elsewhere (see page 120), where diagnostic criteria exclude the events and experiences surrounding the offending condition, and seek only to tackle the symptom itself, the patient is deprived of important healing resources. The 'brain flaw' explanation is not only the source of even greater problems, including stigmatization, reduced proactivity, and, in some cases, chemical dependence, but it creates an extraordinary new and unsettling phenomenon—experience stripped of meaning.

If anything makes humans human, it's our experience and the meaning we attach to it. To act as if our life experiences are irrelevant and our problems reducible to a malfunction as perfunctory as a leaky valve or derailed trolley bus, is to drag us even more deeply into the mechanistic, reductionist mire which can create more problems than it solves.

Process, as we repeat many times, needs to be restored to the experience and description of depression, as well as of many, if not all, of the complex, chronic conditions that prompted us to write this book. Since English has no verb to describe the process of 'depress-ing', we urge you always to remember that it is not a 'thing', but a behavior or response.

The structure of depression

Patients suffering from feelings of depression often:

- are orientated to the past, rather than the present or future;
- adopt a specific, 'downcast' physiology;
- think 'globally' (that is, are unaware of exceptions to their experience);
- worsen their condition by trying to dissociate (and failing);
- are running a two-point loop (Ki- > Ad- > Ki- > Ad- >, etc—see Appendix D, pages 367 to 369, for further information); and
- have static, dark, depressing sub-modalities.

Developing interventions

Consider:

- adjusting the time line;
- changing physiology;
- dissociating (coach into an observer position);
- eliciting exceptions to their problem-state (anchor);
- negotiating a well-formed outcome (anchor);
- helping to create an exit point (imagining moving to a 'different' future) to the auditory-digital-kinesthetic loop; and
- conditioning and reinforcing new behavior (more information on re-patterning and 'future-pacing' in later chapters).

We also suggest that the practitioner explores and addresses the following:

- lifestyle issues;
- daily structure;
- diet and exercise; and
- social support.

Not only do these problems surface when a patient becomes depressed, but serious disruption of any or all of them may actually trigger a depressive response.

Anxiety

Anxiety should always be regarded (and reframed) as a protective response that is either overactive or de-contextualized. Anxious patients are usually trapped in:

- a two-point loop that runs from past (sensitizing experience) to future (visions of the event recurring), ignoring present 'reality';
- the continued experience of an associated, physiological response to representation (re-presentation) of the feared event;

- overwhelming sub-modalities of feared event;
- diminished and constricted sub-modalities of coping abilities.

Developing interventions

Consider:

- time line change (place the sensitizing incident, trauma, etc in the past);
- dissociating and orientating to present experience (coach into an observer state and observe physiology from a 'safe distance');
- allowing spontaneous sub-modality changes to promote psychophysical dissipation;
- 'edit' sub-modalities;
- condition and reinforce new behavior (re-patterning and future-pacing).

Note: Post-traumatic stress disorder has a similar structure to anxiety disorders and panic attacks. It may be approached as suggested above.

We emphasize the need to incorporate coping strategies into all outcomes, rather than simply 'blowing out' the behavior. This not only inoculates against the problem regenerating, but also increases the patient's sense of self-efficacy.

Case history: *Duncan presented with chronic neck pain, anxiety, and retrograde amnesia (inability to recall events immediately preceding a trauma) following a car crash at an intersection late at night. A motorist Duncan failed to see shot a red light and smashed into the side of Duncan's car.*

Of all his symptoms, the inability to remember what happened seemed to bother Duncan most. He said, 'It's like part of my life has been taken away from me. The harder I try, the more confused I become.'

Retrograde amnesia is usually self-limiting (that is, memory returns without further treatment after a while), but since Duncan was becoming increasingly distressed at his lack of improvement, he sought further help from one of the authors. He believed knowing what had happened would help him recover more quickly from the injuries he had received.

The practitioner began by identifying the last thing Duncan remembered before the accident, and the first things he recalled after the event. He invited Duncan to lay these events out like a movie clip with a blank stretch that corresponded with his amnesia.

Then, step by step, Duncan added new frames in response to the questions, 'What is the most likely thing to have happened immediately after the last thing you remember?', and, 'What is the most likely thing to have happened immediately before the frame in which your memory returned?'

Painstakingly, Duncan and the practitioner reconstructed the events according to both what seemed probable, and what Duncan had been told by witnesses. Throughout, he was reassured by the practitioner that, since he had survived the crash, any protective need for the amnesia was no longer necessary. Likewise, if he uncovered some purpose or learning he could derive from the experience, it was likely the effect of the trauma could be reduced.

Suddenly, it was as if his brain realized what was required of it, and the remaining frames of his 'movie' filled in spontaneously. After examining the sequence closely, Duncan was convinced that it represented a true memory of his experience.

Also, he said, he realized that he couldn't rely on green lights when he was driving, but needed to stay alert for other motorists who were not obeying the traffic signals.

At that point, finer details from his memory started flooding back and Duncan felt he could relax and put all his attention on healing his body.

Pain

Pain is one of the greatest, most enduring, mysteries of medical science and the human condition. While the most common medical description is 'an unpleasant sensory and emotional experience associated with actual or potential tissue damage', chronic pain, as experienced by millions of sufferers, continues to resist the most advanced pharmacological and remedial treatment available.[262] It is also one of the most widely reported reasons for primary care attendance. According to a World Health

Organization 15-country study, pain is the main reason for 22% of patients seeking medical assistance.[263]

Chronic pain can affect all areas of a patient's life. A report in the *In Practice* journal series outlined the problem. 'Chronic pain detrimentally affects all aspects of physical health, not only those directly related to the underlying cause. It is associated with significant disability, unemployment and loss of other physical roles. These produce social and financial problems, which include reduced earning capacity, family disharmony and isolation.'[264]

Other psychological consequences include reduced self-esteem, anxiety, and sleep disturbance. Recent research has suggested a higher mortality rate, particularly from cancer, among people with widespread pain.[265]

Running parallel to the challenge faced by the victim of chronic pain is the fact that the medical care system is severely taxed by the demands placed on it. As the *In Practice* report adds, 'It stimulates a huge number of prescriptions, investigations and referrals, causes frustration in its resistance to treatment, and leaves patients and doctors with low expectations of successful outcomes.'

The categorization of pain continues to challenge the medical profession. Some sub-groups of 'medically unexplained' pain include:

- pain without injury (for example, tension headache and trigeminal neuralgia—studies show few discernible indicators of injury or abnormality);
- pain 'disproportionate' to the severity of the injury (for example, the passing of a kidney stone); and
- pain after the healing of an injury (for example, whiplash, phantom limb syndrome).[266,267]

Victims in any of these three categories are often frustrated and depressed by the failure of the medical profession to diagnose and treat what is to them a very real and distressing problem. Counseling or psychiatric intervention improves the situation for few people. The inference, that their pain is not 'real', may not be verbalized by the attending clinician, but it is often sensed by the patient.

What makes pain different?

The failure of most cognitive approaches to medically unexplained pain may derive from the failure to recognize how it differs from other affective disorders.

Emotions such as fear, lust, rage, and attachment may all be responsive to rational challenge, as with the cognitive behavioral therapies, since each of them has both an identifiable affect center in the brain and an easily identifiable external 'cause'. People fear something specific that has happened or might happen, or desire something or someone relatively easily identifiable. A subject-object (internal-external) relationship exists, and that relationship is the focus of treatment.

However, no affect center for chronic, medically unexplained pain has been identified, and a specific, easily identifiable, external 'cause' is usually absent. Therefore, no subject-object relationship exists, and the pain 'just is'.[268]

Treatment that suggests the patient's problem is the way he is thinking about the pain, rather than the pain itself, is, understandably, a frequent cause of added distress. The pain is real. Medical NLP approaches the problem somewhat differently. Before proceeding with any intervention, it is necessary to elicit a *representation* of the pain at the Object level, and then externalize it so there can be a relationship with which to work.

Revealing the glyph

At various points in the book, we have suggested using questions such as 'What's it like?', 'What else is it like?', and 'How does it happen?' in order to elicit the structure and process of an experience. We are looking for sensory-based descriptions (size, shape, color, movement, etc), rather than evaluative statements such as 'awful', 'terrible', 'bad', etc.

The patient will often report his experience as a three-dimensional object—for example, 'a sharp knife', 'a hot red ball', 'a bright burning ribbon, like a magnesium strip'. In Medical NLP, such a representation is called a 'glyph' (from 'hieroglyph', meaning a carved object that represents more than itself), and, for therapeutic purposes, it is treated as 'real'.

This creates a subject-object relationship that the practitioner now seeks to restructure by exploring sub-modality changes, especially those involving the restoration of movement. We offer several ways to work with the glyph later in the book (see pages 284 to 291).

Patients suffering from chronic pain are often:

- in high limbic arousal;
- disorientated in time (past experience and future anxieties compounding present experience);
- trapped in bonded disconnection (intensifying their experience by trying to not-have it);
- generalizing their experience (convinced that one or more episodes denotes the inevitability of further 'attacks');
- unaware of the visual and auditory components of their experience; and
- inattentive towards exceptions to, or changes in, their experience (deletion).

Developing interventions

Useful approaches include:

- establishing a regular program to invoke the relaxation response (see Appendix A, pages 357 to 360);
- reorganizing the time line to separate out clearly past, present and future pain (Milton Erickson, who experienced a lifetime of chronic pain, based many of his interventions on reducing the subjective experience by marking out 'past' and 'future' as existing separately from 'now', thereby suggesting that the patient had only 'present pain' to contend with.);
- resolving or depotentiating the cause (if a single event) or history (using Visual-Kinesthetic Dissociation, etc (see Chapter 20, pages 300 to 302);
- dissociating (moving to a 'safe place' and observing the 'self ' from a distance is a commonly applied 'hypnotic' technique in pain control, especially involving acute or episodic bouts, such as dental surgery or childbirth);

- observing and dissipating (coaching into an observer state and observing physiology from a 'safe distance', allowing spontaneous sub-modality changes to promote psychophysical dissipation).

Case study: *Sean, a 28-year-old man, whose foot had been blown off by a landmine 25 years before, presented with low back and leg pain having had lumbar surgery six years previously. Drug and physical therapies had failed. He was insistent that the explosion was not in any way a problem, and that he was simply seeking to find relief from his chronic pain, which he rated as 7 on the Subjective Measure of Comfort Scale (SMCS).*

While he was talking, the practitioner paced and led him into a more relaxed state before briefly introducing him to a technique to activate the Relaxation Response (see Appendix A, pages 357 to 360). When describing the pain, he used metaphors, such as a 'pestle' being pushed into and moved up and down the lumbar scar.

He experienced the pain as 'burning, red pressure'. The practitioner invited him to transfer the image to a PC monitor. The patient exhibited considerable V r and V c eye-movement behind closed lids (characteristic of vivid visualization) and then reported that he had been successful. The monitor—an old green and black model—was situated in his lower, left visual field.

He repeated the process, but this time created a more desirable state. He chose 'the best screen available', large and flat, on which he projected himself as healthy, active and pain-free, using vibrant colors. He reported a feeling of comfort spreading through his body.

Under the guidance of the practitioner, Sean repeatedly 'swished' from the small, dark screen to the larger one, until he could no longer easily recover the trigger image. He reported that his level of pain had reduced to 3 on the SMC Scale. The practitioner continued the consultation using a variety of embedded suggestions of comfort and coping abilities to help the patient build a model of future experience and behavior.

At the second consultation, two weeks later, Sean reported that the effect had faded and that his own attempts to practice the Swish Pattern had failed. The practitioner responded by suggesting that trying to overcome pain might increase its intensity, and coached the patient into sitting back, dissociating, and 'simply observing'.

The kinesthetic spontaneously began to expand and move, and changed color to 'flame' (a sub-modality shift to visual). The flame moved up Sean's body and back, finally separating out and moving away, to become a source of warmth 'like the sun'. He finished the consultation in a smiling, relaxed state, engaged and interested in the process. He was keen to continue practicing these methods at home, if required.

Cross-lateralization

Anecdotal evidence suggesting a strong relationship between hemispheric lateralization and a wide range of chronic disorders is gaining increasing support from researchers in various fields. Simply put, homolateralized brain activity (abnormally favoring one hemisphere over another) has been implicated in conditions as wide-ranging as dyslexia, certain 'learning disorders', obsessive compulsive disorder, depression, medically unexplained pain, anxiety, psychosis, and even immunological disorders.[269]

For this reason, we often use 'whole-brain' exercises adjunctively with other interventions. Since the body-brain system operates bidirectionally (brain function influencing body-function and vice versa) and is cross-lateralized (each hemisphere directing and being directed by the opposite side of the body), it follows that interventions that reduce homolateralization and increase whole-brain activity deserve attention.

A number of Medical NLP approaches have been developed and/or adapted from this premise. These include breathing, meditative and physical techniques and are further discussed in Appendix B (pages 361 to 362).

Also, see Appendix C, pages 363 to 365, for the Medical NLP algorithm for managing pain.

EXERCISES

Glyphing

1. Glyphing—use the glyph question ('What's it like?') with every client in your next client session. Make a note of any glyph responses you elicit.
2. When that occurs ask the second glyph question ('So, what's happening now?')
3. The third glyph question, the transformative enquiry ('What needs to happen for it to be with you differently?') suggests an intervention. Avoid authoritarian, directive approaches. Simply say, 'So, let's find out what happens when you let that [the answer to Question 3] happen…'

20

Working with the Glyph: the shape of the unconscious mind

*All that we are is the result of what we have thought. The mind is everything. What we think we become.—**Gautama Buddha***

Some years ago, one of the authors (GT) was privileged to witness a South American shaman working with a number of people who were suffering from various afflictions, ranging from physical pain to what many Westerners would regard as psychotic episodes. The performance was electrifying.

Healthcare systems evolving out of non-Western cultures are often dismissed as 'traditional' or 'folk' medicine. The implication here is that they somehow fall short of a superior system developed by a Western, educated, industrialized, rich, and democratic scientific elite (see pages xii, 3, and 268).

However, many of these approaches are of interest in the continuing development of Medical NLP. Our observation has been that some of the methods used are at least as effective as their Western counterparts—albeit most often within the culture in which they are practiced.

This allows supporters of the statistically driven randomized control test approach to file the phenomenon away as a simple example of the placebo effect. A powerful belief in a specific treatment, they say, can yield a positive clinical outcome, even with a protocol that has been shown 'scientifically' not to work.

This, we believe to be true. And, it emerges from two recent studies, so do more primary care physicians than might be expected. A national study conducted in the US showed that more than half (56%) of a random sample of family physicians knowingly prescribe placebos in the form of antibiotics and other substances, both active and inert,[270] while a stunning 97% of their counterparts in the United Kingdom admitted to using placebos at some point or other in their practices.[271] The important point is simply...they know it (or rather, 'something') works.

In other cultures, belief—or the 'meaning' of the treatment—is often regarded as an integral part of treatment, a phenomenon now supported by developments in PET scanning. While many areas of the brain are activated by the application of a placebo, some, including the *anterior cingulate cortex*, *dorsolateral prefrontal cortex* and *basal ganglia*, are related to interpretation of threat and the initiation of a physical response, such as the production of opioid, or pain relieving, chemicals.

Traditional practitioners, known variously as *shamans, curanderos,* root doctors, native healers, medicine men (or women), *kahunas*, or *sangomas*, seem fully aware of this hardwired response, and a considerable part of treatment appears to involve achieving 'buy-in' (otherwise known as compliance, or concordance) and a thorough 'explanation' of how the disorder has arisen, and how it will be resolved.

In the case of the shaman referred to above, and as is common with many similar 'schools' of traditional medicine, most diseases are attributed to the victim having been cursed, usually by a disenfranchised employee or resentful family member.

The translator explained that conditions for diagnosis and treatment had to be precise: the shaman wore garb and face- and body-decoration dictated in every detail by centuries of tradition; chants to prepare both patient and practitioner were equally precise.

The patient presently consulting the shaman had been unable to move his shoulder more than a few centimeters in any direction without palpable agony. All other treatments thus far had proved ineffective against the pain.

A cursory examination by a Western eye would have diagnosed some form of bursitis, probably subacromial—an extremely painful inflammation and swelling of the fluid-filled sacs that act as cushioning between the rotator cuff and the part of the shoulder blade known as the acromion. Victims of bursitis often find the simplest movement, such as combing the hair, little short of agonizing.

According to the translator, however, the patient had been cursed by a jealous brother-in-law, who had secured the services of another, less scrupulous, shaman in order to deliver, quite literally, a body-blow to the victim. The means of the psychic attack, it emerged, was an invisible knife that had become lodged alongside the shoulder blade. Details of the weapon were quite specific—double-edged, steel-bladed, about eight inches long, and of modern, rather than traditional, design. The shaman and the patient seemed in perfect accord about the means, motive, and opportunity for the attack.

After some preparatory chanting, the shaman began pushing and pulling at the patient's shoulder blade, twisting and dragging as if to remove a physical blade embedded in the joint. Suddenly, he bent and clamped his lips on the patient's flesh, then fell back with a triumphant grunt. He fell to his knees, spat theatrically and even managed to throw up a thin, green trickle of bile.

It was necessary, the translator explained patiently, for the shaman to vomit up the offending blade, or he would inherit the patient's unhappy condition.

Then, with no real sign of surprise, the patient rubbed his shoulder, shifted his position cautiously, then swung his arm in increasingly energetic circles, clearly absolutely free of any discomfort.

In Medical NLP terminology, the double-bladed knife would be described as a 'glyph'.

Glyph work is an important tool of Medical NLP. It is simple, effective, and, often, quite remarkable in its effectiveness. If we steer the patient away from linear description and value-judgments (Inferences) towards a purely felt sense (non-evaluative self-observation), the symptom may be experienced as a three-dimensional 'form', which in Medical NLP we call a glyph (see previous chapter).

The patient may not believe he has been cursed by a family member (although we have encountered just this complaint on more than one occasion), but a pain may nevertheless be experienced as, and described as a physical 'thing'— 'like a wire, burning very hot, white, like phosphorous', to quote one example given us. Anxiety may be 'like a dark, cold hole' in the stomach. Pain is often experienced as red or black. Sometimes it appears as a symbol or even a figure.

> ***Case history:*** *A young doctor who read the first edition of this book asked the question, 'What's it like?' of a patient suffering from fibromyalgia. The patient instantly replied, 'It's an angel.'*
> *'I have to say I was excited and delighted,' the doctor recalls. 'An angel seemed to me to be a really appropriate representation of what fibromyalgia often "does" for people.'*
> *'The solution seemed pretty obvious to me, so I said to her, "Well, angels have wings—so why not ask your angel to fly away?"'*
> *To his surprise, the woman vehemently rejected the suggestion. She went away and, after that, dealt with other doctors in the practice (although it was reported back that she was 'doing well').*
> *The doctor recounted the story at one of our seminars, and asked, 'What happened there? Why did she respond the way she did?'*

This is an extremely useful example of two issues relevant to glyph work and Medical NLP:

1. The glyph is exclusive to the individual. It has form, substance, and meaning that relates to her subjective experience only.

And, possibly even more important to remember…

2. There is a difference between helping the patient and curing the disease. The former respects the patient's internal experience; the latter attempts to superimpose an externally applied solution to 'fix' the problem.

The first half of the doctor's intervention succeeded in eliciting a form to the patient's pain. The figure of an angel suggested protection, so it's a fair assumption that when he tried to urge it to fly away, the patient dug in her heels.

Here's the lesson. *Never* try to take away a glyph, symptom, or behavioral response without establishing and recognizing its significance, and then ensuring its 'positive intention' is met.

A more appropriate question might have been, 'How can your angel be with you in a way that's different, and brings you the help you need?'

Almost always, patients asked this kind of question have no trouble in coming up with creative solutions. The glyph corresponds to the Object level of Korzybski's Structural Differential. Richard Bandler's observation that 'experience' had characteristics (coded in sub-modalities) was, in the opinion of the authors, little short of revolutionary.

Until then (and even now), cognitive therapists attempted to effect change only at the language level, unaware that the Event occurring within the subject's nervous system is perceived with form and substance in the form of a metaphoric shape, before it can be translated into words.

Neurological function at the Object and Event levels appears to be more fluid than that at the level of Inference (largely because the way we speak or think about our experience helps to maintain its structure). The glyph is marked by the following characteristics:

- it has defined characteristics;
- sometimes it is unnecessary to elicit a glyph overtly; the subject, when asked, 'what's it like?' will usually describe it with surprising ease and specificity, as if it exists as a tangible 'object' with existence independent of the subject;
- it is often perceived them as painful and threatening (although not always—see the anecdote about the angel, above);
- all involve a kinesthetic of movement—although the movement is either blocked or looping (no resolution). The patient resists the possibility of movement in order to try to dissociate from the experience. He is often deeply fearful to let the movement complete or continue its path…although, paradoxically, that is exactly what is needed.

Case history: *A psychiatrist colleague, who also practices as a family doctor, was consulted by a Filipina woman in some distress.*
She told him her son had been arrested back in the Philippines on a trumped-up charge, and she was desperately worried that he would not receive the help he needed. At the same time, she complained of a severe pain in her throat, caused, she said, by a fishbone she had swallowed a few days before.
The doctor examined her but could find no sign of any fishbone. Since

she continued to complain, he referred her to an Ear, Nose, and Throat specialist. The specialist was also unable to find any fishbone, and, agreed with the psychiatrist that the woman was probably suffering from globus hystericus, brought on by her anxiety about the fate of her son.

When she was given a diagnosis, she was even more distraught, complaining that doctors in England were incompetent and bemoaning the fact that she would have to return to the Philippines to consult someone who understood her condition.

Some weeks later, she arrived at the psychiatrist's consulting rooms without an appointment. Curious to hear what had happened during her trip back to the Philippines, the psychiatrist invited her in.

She told him that she had managed to find a lawyer to represent her son who was released from custody. At the same time, she consulted a local healer who confirmed that she had, indeed, swallowed a fishbone which was now lodged in her throat. After some maneuvering, and using only his fingers, the healer triumphantly flourished the offending fishbone.

Seeing the psychiatrist's expression of incredulity, the woman removed a Kleenex from her purse, unwrapped it and presented the fishbone that had been 'removed' from her throat. It was, the psychiatrist reported, a skeleton of a small fish, about 5 cm long and perfect from head to tail. Something in the woman's expression told him that she would not tolerate any contradiction, so he decided the best option was to smile, and congratulate her on the satisfactory end to her problems.

Remember: we always proceed as if the glyph is 'real'. Most patients are aware that it is a metaphoric representation of their problem, but, in some cultures, it will be regarded and treated as if it had a physical existence of its own.

Either way, it is lodged in the patient's awareness, and it is our contention that resistance to 'what is' causes as much, if not more, psychic and physical pain than the condition itself. These feelings are always localized. 'Bad' feelings have distinct boundary conditions and are contracted in nature. 'Good' feelings, such as excitement, joy, love, and orgasm, on the other hand, are expansive and unbounded, sometimes transcending the confines of the body.

Working with the glyph

It is sometimes possible to resolve a problem by working with the glyph alone, especially where no particularly traumatizing event is perceived as, or is actually, responsible for the response.

One of the conditions for resolution involves moving out of resistance to the experience. Resistance is painful. Resistance (at this stage) is the only response the patient has at her disposal. Apart from the physical tension required to resist an unwanted internal experience, the kind of Inferences made by the patient and others reviewing her problem have the potential for 'locking' the experience in place, or even making it worse.

It is a prerequisite that the patient acquire the skill for (temporarily) tolerating the symptom, and then learn how effectively to dissociate so that the structure and process can be changed. It cannot be changed if she is actively resisting, or trying unsuccessfully to dissociate from, it.

Resolving the glyph

The glyph may be approached in a number of ways. The following protocol is one of Medical NLP's most effective interventions.

1. Create meaning. Explain or elicit the purpose or intention behind the symptom while reassuring the patient that it is responding excessively or out of context (reframe).
2. Create acceptance. Encourage the patient to accept the experience: 'Just for the moment, allow it to be there. Don't try to change it. Simply let it be the way it is.'
3. Dissociate. 'Now, either take a step back or put it out in front of you so you can observe it, almost as if it's happening to someone else. Just be the observer and watch the way it is.'
4. Elicit physical qualities without judgment or inference. For example, ask, 'What's it like?'; 'What's it doing?'; 'What's happening now?' Ensure that what the patient describes is structural and sensory-based, rather than evaluative or inferential. If she seems stuck, prompt (but do not lead) with gentle questions such as, 'If it had a color, what color would it be?'; 'What shape is it?'; 'Are

the edges hard or soft, distinct or fuzzy?' etc. Test especially for a sense of movement. Movement will usually be stalled or looped.

5. Promote change. Create a spirit of experimentation while you do this. Non-evaluative observation, without direct intervention, is our preference. Give permission for the glyph to change itself, but do not directly try to change it.
6. Encourage the subject to notice how change 'happens' spontaneously when we stop resisting it. Discourage the subject from being similarly interventionist.
7. If the subject seems stuck, prompt gently and with as little direction as possible. For example, ask, 'I wonder what would happen if the color became a bit less intense?'; 'Ask the (ball, knife etc) what needs to happen in order for you to experience it in a more appropriate way', etc.
8. When the patient reports some positive change (allowing the glyph to change always leads to positive, relaxed, expansive feelings), have her reassociate with it, checking that the internal kinesthetic has been positively transformed.
9. Suggest that she allows the feeling to 'expand and flow through every, organ, every muscle, nerve and cell', etc.
10. Then have the patient mentally project herself into the future, noting how her feelings, behaviors, and responses will be different.
11. Repeat until the new response is automated.

'Swishing' the glyph

Glyphs may also be 'swished'. That is, its sub-modalities changed very rapidly to those of a more resourceful state.

1. Have the patient create a more useful and resourceful symbol of her (healthy) state.
2. Push the unwanted glyph into the distance, making sure that all its sub-modalities are turned down, until they disappear. Then bring the new glyph up, very rapidly, into the same space, and with the same qualities, as the glyph the patient has changed.

The glyph as a 'meta technique'

In Chapter 6, we referred to a family doctor who used the glyph, a 'black ball', identified by her patient as a 'relaxation technique' to accomplish significant relief from anxiety and depression. By doing this, the doctor effectively created a 'meta technique' operating at a higher order than the problem itself.

So successful have some readers found the technique that we wish to identify Dr. Arti Maini as its creator, and to describe the underlying process here.

Dr. Maini's patient had a rich pathography, which would have taken considerable time to address, item by item. Undoubtedly, it would have been difficult, if not impossible, to alleviate the patient's emotional distress by discussing and advising him on tackling the external problems that were besetting him. However, he had little trouble in identifying his glyph as black and spherical, 'like a ball'.

Dr. Maini also chose to steer the patient away from the current knee-jerk response of medicating problems that may be simply the vicissitudes of everyday life.

Instead, by allowing the glyph to surface, the complexity of the patient's experience collapsed into a manageable 'thing'. Her approach, framing as a 'relaxation technique' and handing over manipulation of the glyph, effectively restored control over the patient's experience.

The glyph parallels the theories of physicist David Bohm regarding the 'implicate' and 'explicate' aspects of 'reality'. In Bohm's enfolded 'implicate' order, space, time, and sequential details no longer dominate, but all aspects are enfolded into a comprehensive 'whole'.[272]

'This order,' Bohm wrote, 'is not to be understood solely in terms of a regular arrangement of objects (e.g. in rows) or as a regular arrangement of events (e.g. in a series). Rather, a total order is contained in some implicit sense, in each region of space and time.'

The astute reader (we hope) will detect several associations with the glyph and the psychophysical complexity out of which it emerges, as well as text (the sequential details of the patient's and the practitioner's understanding of events) and context, the field in which the patient (and the practitioner) function.

Philosophizing aside, here is a simple protocol to help you create meta techniques of your own:

1. Elicit the glyph by asking questions such as, 'What's it like?', 'What happens in your body when…?', 'How do you know to…?' etc. Do not proceed until you have a clear and fully sensory-based description of the phenomenon. Ensure the glyph has distinct boundary conditions: size, location, defined edge, and so on.
2. Ask the patient to ascertain what changes might alter her experience. Encourage her to experiment.
3. If the patient is stuck, make some tentative suggestions. Would she like to knock, kick, throw, or blow it out of the confines of her body? What would happen if she shot it out into the sun and blew it up? What (imaginary) tools might she need to help her move it out of her space?

Or, and we'd argue that this might be the preferable approach…

What needed to happen for the glyph to continue to exist within her body differently?

EXERCISES

1. Take a few moments to relax, preferably with your eyes closed.
2. Scan your body, from the inside of the top of your head, right down to the tips of your fingers and toes. Notice any anomalies—discomfort, tightness, sensations that differ in some way from the surrounding internal landscape.
3. Ask yourself, 'What is this like?' and pay special attention to the physical attributes of the experience: size, color, location, movement, etc.
4. Now, either:
   a. observe the glyph, with detached interest. Allow it to transform in its own way,

   or,

   b. Experiment by changing the characteristics—pushing it out of your body, blunting sharp edges, deepening or softening colors or textures, etc.
5. Notice how this transforms the experience, over both the short and long term.
6. Create an explicit technique or meditation out of your experience, and test it on an ongoing basis.
7. Do the same with at least six of your patients or clients and track their experiences.

21

Re-patterning and Future-Pacing: making and maintaining change

*It is possible to believe that all the human mind has ever accomplished is but the dream before the awakening.—**H.G. Wells***

More than 30 years ago, the creators and developers of NLP could only speculate how many of the techniques they were using empirically could actually work. How was it possible that some people could free themselves from a long-standing phobia, allergy or trauma—sometimes in a matter of a few minutes?

Up until then, psychological change, we were led to believe, was possible, but only with considerable time and effort. Even today, the 'brief' cognitive therapies require upwards of eight sessions, and success often needs to be boosted with psychotropic drugs. However, research from the frontiers of brain science reveals that the belief that neuronal function can only be affected pharmacologically and/or with considerable psychological effort is questionable.

The key is the capability of the brain called neuroplasticity.

A few decades back, it was widely believed that the brain was a closed, machine-like system, functioning only within the boundaries of its genetic heritage. The neuronal patterns we started out with were the neuronal patterns we died with—give or take the ones we lost along the way to the ravages of time.

But the brain, as we are looking into it in the 21st century, is a very different affair. We know now that it co-creates our 'reality' according to past experiences and present events.

We can recognize how its moods and memories resonate in every cell of our bodies. We are beginning to realize that it mediates the way our bodies store and communicate the emotional assaults we experience.[273] Added to that is an extraordinary ability to invent internal realities that can have as big an impact on our health and wellbeing as an external trauma or a germ or a gene. We have even come to suspect, through the new science of epigenetics, that it helps us hold our DNA in trust for later generations—for, if we drink, or smoke, or stress too much[274] (or, conversely, alter the length of our telomeres by meditating regularly[275]), we may pass the consequences on to our descendants for centuries to come.

Above all—and, this is probably the brain's most extraordinary quality—it is the only organism that we know of anywhere in the universe that has the capacity to evolve itself. By an experience, an act of imagination or learning, people can create a psychophysical reality that is more (or less) capable, resourceful, and healthier than the one they had a day, or a month or a year before.[276]

Repatterning, in the Medical NLP model, may be seen as a protocol that is aimed first at the neurological/experiential stratum, and then at the levels of behavior and its evaluation. This takes place in two main stages: the first, deconstructing and replacing the dysfunctional pattern with a more useful and appropriate response or behavior; and the second, applying conditioning techniques (future-pacing) to accustom the patient, both cognitively and neurologically, to the changes it is hoped she will enjoy in her post-treatment life.

In order to understand better how the techniques we present below are structured, it should be recalled that most Medical NLP techniques rely on:

- dissociation;
- repatterning;
- re-association; and
- collapsing anchors.

Future-pacing and why it works

For many years, 'visualization' and other imaginal techniques were regarded as likely to have minimal effect on real-world functioning. Its popularity among followers of 'New Age' complementary therapies increased suspicion among many mainstream scientists, even though there were indications that it could be an effective supplementary approach to enhancing sports performance.[277]

This is changing and for good reason. It works.

> *Think of the number three for a moment. Imagine it written up on a surface inside your head. As you do that, your visual cortex lights up exactly as if you were seeing the same digit. Now, imagine picking up a heavy barbell and begin to perform a series of curls—the same exercise you might do with free weights at a gym. Hear your personal trainer urging you on. Imagine (without actually moving your body), that your bicep is beginning to tire; lactic acid is burning like hot wires. The weight seems to be getting heavier…*

Experiments show that if you did this regularly enough with full absorption, your muscles would actually get stronger—only 8% less than if you had actually done the exercise.[278]

For some years now, scientists, including V.S. Ramachandran, have used a device called a 'mirror box' to treat problems such as phantom limb pain, reflex sympathetic dystrophy pain (chronic pain persisting long after an injury has healed), and 'learned' pain. The mirror box works by reflecting an image of a healthy limb onto its wasted or absent counterpart.

The illusion 'rewires' the patient's neurology to facilitate improvement or recovery from his physical condition.

A problem encountered with mirror box therapy is that the longer the pain has persisted, the less effective treatment is likely to be. However, Australian scientist G.L. Moseley demonstrated that patients who were taught to simply imagine moving their injured limb reduced or completely eliminated their pain.[279]

Future-pacing—a form of conditioning—then, incorporates the imaginal capabilities of the mind, together with practical application of the new behavior pattern, wherever possible. It is important, when designing an intervention, that the patient's response to both thinking about the problem, as well as his actual real-world experience, is tested (using the SMC Scale, if appropriate).

After intervention and future-pacing, patients should be encouraged to resume their normal (or their new) activities as soon as possible and report back for readjustment or reinforcement, if required. (A useful injunction is, 'I'd like you to go back and notice specifically what's different and better so we can talk about that next time.')

Despite the simplified NLP model of internal processing outlined earlier, we do not mean to suggest that each sense is entirely localized in its own area of the brain.

The work of Harvard Medical School's Alvaro Pascual-Leone has confirmed considerable cortical overlap between senses and has demonstrated that various 'operators' organize sensory data from different sources in order to create experience. These operators are in constant competition to process signals effectively, depending on both the significance and the context of the signal.[280]

Designing a future-pace

Rule 1: Ensure that it is fully represented in all sensory modalities, in as much detail as possible.

Rule 2: It should meet all the requirements of well-formedness. It must also be attractive and relevant to the patient and his model—not that of the practitioner.

Rule 3: A future-pace for an *ongoing* response or behavior (for example, exercising three times a week, or following a specific eating plan) should be *dissociated.* This is thought to prompt the brain to continually move to 'close the gap', facilitating maintenance.

Rule 4: A new state (for example, being a non-smoker) should be represented as *associated*, in order to 'lock in' a discrete condition with clear boundary conditions.

Rule 5: The new state, response, or behavior should be placed on the patient's time line. If necessary, create a means of metaphorically locking it in place.

Rule 6: After the patient has been future-paced, she should be fully reassociated, together with her new pattern(s), using suggestions to 'float back above your future road or pathway, bringing into the present all the experiences, learnings, and resources from your new future, and drop down into your own body so that you can fully own and apply everything you've learned now as you get ready to move on from here into the future…' etc (note the hypnotic language).

Before applying any of the patterns below, ensure that:

1. the patient's time line has been adjusted, with past events (including the problem) 'behind' her, but not hidden; and
2. the agreed outcome/direction is well formed in all sensory modalities and placed on her future time line, a little in front of her.

Note: All interventions are designed to be completed within a single session. Do not attempt to carry a pattern over from one consultation to the next. Interventions should be executed rapidly to ensure pattern recognition by the brain. Repeat until automated.

Remember to apply the Subjective Measure of Comfort Scale before and after each intervention.

The patterns

Re-storying the narrative

Elsewhere in this book (see pages 162 and 163), we report how the act of story-telling helps put the patient's experience into a form that makes sense to her. Writing down or delivering a narrative version of illness—the patient's 'pathography'—is, in itself, a therapeutic act. However, sometimes the practitioner can assist the patient by helping her to re-create her narrative. In this way, and working together, patient and practitioner can arrive at a more resourceful, and, often healthier, conclusion.

This process differs from the well-known Ericksonian technique of isomorphic metaphor. The latter is an entirely practitioner-centered approach, in which a story is created that parallels the problem condition, but with a resolution that suggests a new perspective and behavior to the patient.

Re-storying is, quite literally, a re-writing of history…at least, the history as it is remembered and re-presented by the patient. In order to do this, the patient and practitioner in partnership need to identify the 'theme' of the patient's pathography, and then locate the point in the narrative where the story becomes problematical. The challenge then is to decide on a replacement theme, or a more useful resolution. This is largely an exercise in re-framing, so the practitioner needs to consider whether the content or the context of the patient's experience needs to be changed (see *Framing and Reframing*, in Chapter 13, pages 177 to 180).

Very often, exploring the possible 'positive intention' of the symptom or condition will suggest a way forward.

Case history: *A young woman, extremely ambitious and hard-working, had become hypothyroidal, and sought help to lose weight and regain her energy.*

Her story was one of fear—mainly that she would lose clients and her standard of living if she didn't work the long and tiring hours she believed were necessary. She had stopped all recreational activities, and it had been some years since she had taken a holiday. However, since she had already proved resistant to 'taking it easy' when it had been suggested to her by her primary care physician, the practitioner suggested re-storying her narrative.

He reviewed the patient's written pathography, noting, as he did so, that negative-affect words far outweighed their positive counterparts, suggesting the patient had been unable even to imagine a way out of her impasse.

The practitioner explained the Medical NLP model of the 'well-intentioned disease', then asked her, 'What do you regard as your biggest problem, aside from the thyroid trouble itself?'

Instantly, she said, 'I know I work too hard—but I have to.'

'And, what does hypothyroidism do for you?'

'It slows me down.'

The practitioner said nothing, and simply waited for the patient's

response. It was a few seconds coming, then surprise flooded her face. When other people told her to slow down, she said, she felt immediately resistant. They just didn't understand. 'But, when my body told me in such an eloquent way, I suddenly realized I had to listen,' she said.
The remainder of the re-storying involved exploring meditation, dietary options, regular check-ups, and a simple program of activity designed to create, rather than deplete, energy.

Simple scramble pattern

The scramble pattern may be used alone to change simple behaviors and responses.

It may also be used adjunctively, with other patterns, to disrupt more complex constellations of problems.

The principle is simply to interrupt a sequence by repeatedly 'scrambling' its component parts. A scrambled pattern should always be replaced with an alternative response to reduce the possibility of relapse.

Identify and number four or five distinct steps in the patient's process. For example: (1) 'I notice people watching me'; (2) 'I begin to breathe erratically'; (3) 'I feel my cheeks becoming warm'; (4) 'I think, "I know they've noticed what's happening"'; (5) 'I start to blush.'

Starting with the original sequence, coach the patient into experiencing each step, using its number as a cue.

Begin to call out the numbers in different orders, increasing the speed as you go.

After six to eight cycles, stop and test.

If the unwanted response is not extinguished, repeat, ensuring that the patient is fully associated into each step as you call out its number.

Full sensory scramble

1. Have the patient associate into and hold the negative kinesthetic as strongly as possible.
2. Using a pen or your finger, have the patient follow with her eyes (without moving her head) through all eye-accessing positions in rapid succession. Ensure she tries to maintain the kinesthetic at its highest level throughout.

3. Increase the speed, and randomize the movements.
4. Continue for 60–90 seconds, change state, and then test.
5. Repeat, if necessary, until the negative kinesthetic has been substantially reduced.
6. Future-pace.

Visual-kinesthetic dissociation (fast phobia cure)

Visual-kinesthetic dissociation is the earliest, and one of the most commonly applied, techniques developed by the founders of NLP. It can be used to treat simple phobias, including 'social phobia', fear of public speaking, etc. It can also be incorporated in more complex protocols, as shown below. This version incorporates a final step (essentially a future-pace).

Note: Where the patient may have an extreme response to accessing thoughts about the trigger event or object, it is important to ensure she is 'double-dissociated' (that is, she is watching herself watching her dissociated self carrying out the procedure, rather than watching the procedure herself).

1. Instruct her to 'step out of, or float up from, your body, so you are watching yourself from a safe distance, watching the events. You don't have to watch the events yourself.' Ensure the patient is fully relaxed, and anchor the state in case you need to bring her back into a calm and more resourceful state.
2. Have the patient imagine sitting in a movie theater, with a small, white screen placed in front of her and a little above eye level. On the screen is a small, still, monochrome picture of a moment or two before the sensitizing event that led to her phobic response (Safe Place 1).
3. Instruct her to imagine creating a movie containing 'all the experiences, responses and feelings you have had about this problem'. Reassure her that the movie, when it is run, will be small, distant and in black-and-white, and when it is complete, the screen will 'white out' (Safe Place 2).
4. Have her float out of his body and up, into a position from which she can both observe herself and control the running of her movie.
5. Instruct her to switch on the projector and run the sequence

from Safe Place 1 to Safe Place 2 very rapidly, allowing the screen to white out when it is finished.

6. Have her float down into her body and then step up into the white screen at the end of her movie.
7. Turn on all the colors and sounds, and have her rewind the movie, experiencing events and sounds, associated, in reverse order until she emerges in Safe Place 1.
8. Have her return to her seat and repeat steps 3 through 7, from three to five times, before testing. Notice that the final step is always run through from end to beginning (Safe Place 2 to Safe Place 1).
9. Keep testing, and when the phobic response has been substantially reduced (to a 1 or a 2 on the SMC scale), you can begin the second part of the intervention.

Future-pace as follows:

1. Sitting back in her seat, the patient expands the screen until it extends to the edges of her peripheral visual field.
2. Have her create a full-color, richly detailed movie of her coping resourcefully in the situation that previously triggered the phobic response. Suggest she incorporates a soundtrack comprising music that she finds particularly uplifting.
3. When she is satisfied with the movie and its soundtrack, have her run it (dissociated) from beginning to end, two or three times, each time starting at the beginning.
4. Then, she can step into the movie (associated) and run it 'as if' she were actually experiencing this reality now. With her permission, you may also hold the safety anchor you set at the beginning of the intervention.
5. Suggest she takes a few moments to run the resource movie several times, making sure she always starts at the beginning, until she is satisfied that everything she sees, hears, and, now, feels will support her in coping positively from now on. Reinforce with presuppositions and embedded commands to take on this new pattern as a permanent response.

V-K Dissociation is a powerful and useful technique. However, we caution against its indiscriminate application. Sometimes phobias serve an important purpose and disruption, without taking ecology into consideration, could be detrimental to the subject, as the example below illustrates.

> ***Case history:*** *The subject, a leading consultant pediatrician with a disabling fear of spiders, volunteered for treatment on one of our training courses. He believed his fear arose from waking up on two occasions to find large spiders on his pillow when he was a child in Africa.*
> *However, when the trainer probed further, the subject recalled a further incident in which his baby sister was bitten by a spider and went into anaphylactic shock. He became markedly distressed at recalling his fear at being so powerless to help his sister. Even though he was only five years old at the time, he felt guilt at not having been able to 'do something' for his sister (who, happily, survived).*
> *The trainer asked how that experience might have served a positive purpose in his later life, and the subject promptly replied, 'Now I can cure anaphylactic shock in babies.' This suggested his childhood feelings of helplessness had contributed to his choosing to be a doctor.*
> *Mindful that a simple 'blow-out' of the phobia might impact the subject's career, the trainer abandoned his plan to demonstrate the V-K Dissociation Pattern, and elected instead to apply a different intervention to resolve traumatic events, described below, in order to preserve all ecological considerations, while still resolving the disabling fear of spiders.*

The advanced Medical NLP swish pattern

The version of the swish pattern outlined below is unique to Medical NLP and has the added value of automatically placing the problem-state (PS) on to the patient's past time line.

1. Check that the PS is in the position it naturally occurs in, in the patient's internal representation.
2. Place the desired-state (DS) directly behind her.
3. Simultaneously, send the PS around her on to her past time line,

while bringing the DS directly through her body into the position previously occupied by the PS. As this happens encourage her to create a strong kinesthetic of the DS moving through her body (see **Figure 21.1**).

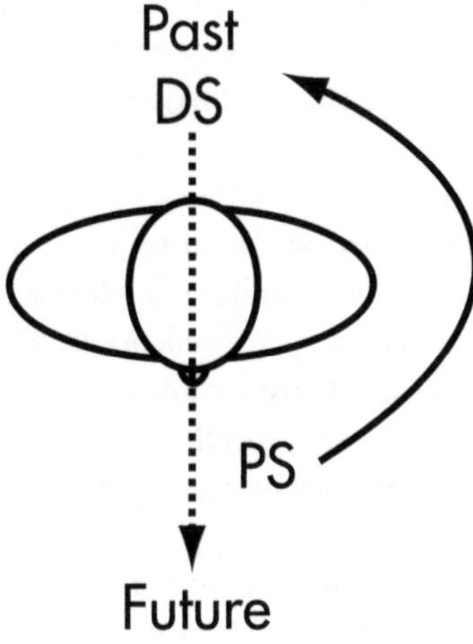

Figure 21.1 The Medical NLP swish pattern

Other variations include:

1. putting the DS far out on the patient's horizon line with the PS in whatever position it naturally occupies, and then rapidly reversing the positions of the two states; and
2. concealing the DS behind the PS, and then opening up a window in the center of the PS and rapidly expanding it so that the DS pops through.

Note: Although the swish pattern as outlined above relies on a visual lead, both auditory and kinesthetic swishes can be designed, following the same principles.

Resolving internal conflict

Internal conflict is often marked linguistically: 'Part of me wants to [X], but another part wants [Y]', or, 'On the one hand I [X], but on the other I [Y]'). Sometimes the patient will 'mark out' different parts, gesturing to one side of his body and then to the other. We suspect this may reflect opposing hemispheric activity. Also, be aware that New Age self-diagnoses such as, 'I always sabotage myself', or 'I have a fear of success/failure' often indicate internal conflict.

1. Explain that the parts are often set up at different times in the patient's life and have therefore developed differing approaches to trying to meet her perceived needs, even though both are motivated by a shared positive intention.
2. Externalize each part, together with all its characteristics (dissociation). This may be accomplished by having the patient extend both hands, palms uppermost, and 'place' one part in each. Suggest, 'Each hand now holds a part with all its beliefs, behaviors and qualities.' Have the patient code the totality of each part with a distinctive color.
3. Chunk each in turn to find shared positive intention (see Chapter 12).
4. Point out that, since both parts have a shared positive intention, they can cooperate in creating a range of possible new responses that will allow the patient to have more appropriate responses.
5. Have her describe the 'positive traits' of each part—for example, one might be 'creative', the other 'reliable'.
6. Ask how each part could benefit by sharing some of the qualities of the other—for example, creativity could be more reliable rather than sporadic, while reliability could be helped to 'loosen up' with a bit of creativity.
7. When the patient has found the 'middle ground', have her fix her attention on the space between her hands and begin to float them together, eventually blending the two colors to represent the new 'third' state. Reassure both parts that the intention is not to eliminate them (they might be needed in a specific context), but to widen their range of responses.

8. Have the patient bring her hands towards her body and imagine the new color and all its qualities flowing into her body and life (re-association). Give lots of hypnotic suggestions presupposing more choices and a wider range of responses.
9. Future-pace new potential responses, and test this by having the patient think of how she could respond to situations that previously caused her problems.

Resolving trauma

Important note: The treatment of serious traumatic events, such as severe physical or sexual abuse, should not be attempted without adequate training. See the *Resources* section for specialized workshop training.

Trauma—often long-forgotten, and including childhood abuse and neglect—is coming under increasing suspicion as a major factor for the later development of a wide range of medically unexplained conditions, including many involving chronic pain.[281] Compelling neurophysiological evidence is emerging that the patient suffering from extreme 'overwhelm' can become locked into a self-perpetuating cycle of psychological arousal, undischarged 'freeze' state and actual physiological changes.

Because of the down-regulation of the frontal cortex, the patient's inability logically to process the 'reality' of the threat profoundly affects his capacity to break out of the condition. One significant effect is that his response to 'time' becomes dislocated. In the words of behavioral neurologist Robert C. Scaer, the sufferer is caught up in past events, unable to relate to present events, and oblivious to the future, except to the perceived threat of pain or annihilation.[282]

The treatment of 'functional' disorders caused, or exacerbated by, trauma (if they are diagnosed) is currently heavily slewed towards symptomatic relief by pharmacological means (blocking the kinesthetic) and/or some form of 'talking cure', often encouraging the patient to challenge or deny the devastating effect of his thoughts and feelings.

Both these approaches, in one way or another, deny the somatic 'reality' of the patient's experience. And, in seeking to have the patient do the same, they not only inadvertently disregard the patient's somatic experience as a 'doorway' to his internal map, but attempt to brick up an opening to integration, healing, and health.

The ability to perceive, find meaning in, and act upon the felt sense has been demonstrated to have powerful clinical application in a wide range of medical conditions, including migraine; vertigo; hypertension; and immune disorders, such as multiple sclerosis, arthritis, and cancer.[283]

The patterns below seek to integrate what we know so far about the patient's relation to time, his ability to reconnect with the frontal cortex, the importance of meaning and metaphor and, above all, the validity of his somatic response.

The affect bridge

Affect bridging is a technique designed to identify events perceived as causal. We do not automatically accept these revelations as 'real', but regard them as part of the patient's model, and therefore potentially useful in restructuring the maladaptive behavior or response.

Note: We advise caution in setting up an affect bridge to avoid associating the patient into a deeply disturbing event. Therefore, our instructions should always include suggestions that she 'go back as your adult self, and observe from a safe place, as if on a television or movie screen'. This minimizes the risk of full abreaction and possible re-traumatization.

1. Have the patient fully experience the somatic response to the problem state and anchor when the experience is at its height.
2. Hold the anchor and instruct the patient to 'follow the feeling back to the first time you felt this way'.
3. Release the anchor as soon as the patient identifies the source and, if necessary, have her dissociate as described in the note above.

***Case study:** The patient, aged 27, had problems eating anything but soft food, such as scrambled eggs and porridge.*
His gag response was anchored and bridged back to a long-forgotten incident in which, as a small child, he had choked and lost consciousness while eating bananas and custard. (This is a simple, clear example of the symptom—gagging—acting as a solution to, or protection from, the patient's underlying problem. See Chapter 12, pages 159 to 172.) The intervention described on the following page was applied.

Changing responses to past experiences

The severity of traumatization is often associated with the subject's perceived loss of control at the time of the trauma. Therefore, this pattern depends on accessing and stacking strong coping resources. Although the number of steps involved may seem daunting at first, there is a logical structure which, when mastered, allows for improvisation and adaptation.

Have the subject identify the traumatic event. Do not immerse yourself or him in unnecessary detail. Reassure him that 'while we can't change what happened, we can change our response to what happened' (this paces the patient's belief or experience about the gravity of the experience, while opening him to hope about his ability to change).

1. Return him to his present, 'more adult', associated self and explore the resources by which the 'past self' would have been able better to cope had he had them at the time of the trauma. Have the subject convert the resources into a symbol—for example, a color or a light.
2. 'Send' the resources back down the past time line to the younger self, and then have the subject move rapidly over the past time line to associate into the body of the younger self in time to receive the resources 'from the future'. Test by asking the subject how he would feel differently or better with these resources. When satisfied, have him 'keep those feelings' and return to his present, adult self.
3. Send the adult self back as an observer to watch and report on how the traumatizing incident would have played out differently when the subject had the means better to cope.
4. If any anger, frustration, fear, etc persists, especially where a significant other was responsible for the trauma, give the subject permission 'in the privacy of your own mind' to say, do or feel whatever was not said, done, or felt at the time. You may observe considerable activity, physical, and emotional, during this phase. Remain engaged and wait until the process is complete. Dissipation of the freeze state may express itself as 'silent abreaction' (usually gentle weeping)—a positive development, calmly to be supported.

5. Have the adult self associate into the scenario and reassure the younger self that he is safe and will survive, overcome, and flourish now.
6. Have the subject step out and associate into his younger self and receive that information he was lacking at the time.
7. The subject then steps back out into his adult self, and re-associates with his newly resourced younger self by drawing him back into his (adult) body.
8. Use hypnotic language. An example: 'Now, with all the resources you have given your younger self, combined with the greater knowledge and experience of your adult self to protect it, rapidly travel back up the past towards the present, allowing your unconscious to transform, recode, and reorganize all your past experiences in the light of these new understandings.' Use multiple injunctions to reinforce the effect.
9. When the subject reaches the present, he stops and watches himself moving into the future. Encourage him to notice and report how his responses, behaviors, and feelings are now in the light of the 'new' past experiences.
10. Have him travel right to the end of the future time line, and then float up and back, and re-associate into his body, integrating all the resources and experiences from both past and future for use from the present moment on.
11. Repeat this several times, floating back to before the traumatic event (with all the positive resources), up the past time line to the present, and then as in step 9, into the future. Anchor in the full-sensory representation of present comfort and optimism and future self-efficacy.
12. Test for responses to past event. If some distress persists, repeat the process or layer work with other principles, such as V-K Dissociation, reframing, collapsing anchors, etc.

Note: This pattern may be used 'content-free'—that is, without explicit knowledge or revelation of the original traumatic event. If the patient shows reluctance, acknowledge his need for privacy, and simply proceed with reference to 'the original situation or event'.

Metaphoric transformation

Metaphoric transformation resembles the previous pattern, with one important exception: the use of patient-generated metaphors and memories to drive change. Do not necessarily expect to 'understand' how the metaphor is relevant to the patient's subjective experience; by definition, it represents something much more extensive and encompassing than its surface appearance.

1. Prepare the patient by explaining the principle of 'unconscious association'; tell him that the unconscious mind makes many connections and will present those which are particularly relevant at this time.
2. Have him fully associate into the kinesthetic of the problem state.
3. Ask him for his earliest memory. We're not asking him to speculate on the 'cause' of his problem, but simply to move back into the very earliest memory he can retrieve.
4. When he does that, suggest his unconscious mind has presented a specific memory as a metaphor (an image, symbol, or other spontaneous representation). This functions either to identify the 'cause' of the problem, or to suggest a solution.
5. Ask, 'If you could, or, if you needed to, how would you prefer to remember this in a way that will help you deal differently and better with the problem you have been having?'
6. Assist the patient in designing a new, more useful memory.
7. Anchor his responses, and then follow steps 9 through 11 as outlined in the previous pattern.

Case history: *The patient, in his early 40s, presented with symptoms of extreme allostatic load, and revealed that he had been 'compulsively' unfaithful to his wife.*
When she found out, their relationship came under extreme strain. He suggested he was drawn to other women as 'a kind of mother substitute', since he had grown up with a punitive mother and no father. His earliest memory was of being trapped inside with his mother, trying desperately to get out to the safety of his grandmother's house. The door was locked. When asked how he would like to change the memory, he said instantly,

'I don't want to leave my mother. I just want to know the door can open.' He made the change to the memory, completed the intervention, and reported experiencing an overwhelming sense of optimism and peace.

The alternative reality pattern

This, esoteric sounding, pattern emerged from an extended conversation with a physicist—who was suffering from a knee injury that had resisted treatment—about the theories of alternative realities and the unreliability of memory.

The former proposes an infinite number of potential realities, only one of which materializes when a specific action is taken, and the latter is based on recent research suggesting that memories are 'reconstructed' each time we access them.[284] The pattern has subsequently proved useful in a wide range of situations, both as a stand-alone intervention and adjunctively with other treatments. When introducing the concept of alternative realities, it may be useful to refer to several popular films, such as *Sliding Doors* and *The Matrix*, which explore the theme.

1. Set up in parallel formation several 'potential' past time lines, including one that incorporates the accident or incident perceived as having caused the problem (**Figure 21.2**).
2. Have the patient float up and over the causal incident and back down on to that time line some considerable distance before the event.
3. Set up a 'switch' (the analogy of the rail switches used to divert trains onto another line is useful) just before the problem event.
4. Select an alternative line that events can switch to instead of following the old route through the problem event and beyond. Elicit as much detail as possible about the chosen alternative reality.
5. Have the patient move rapidly up the old reality, then switch to the new version, and on.
6. Repeat this at least five times, and then test.

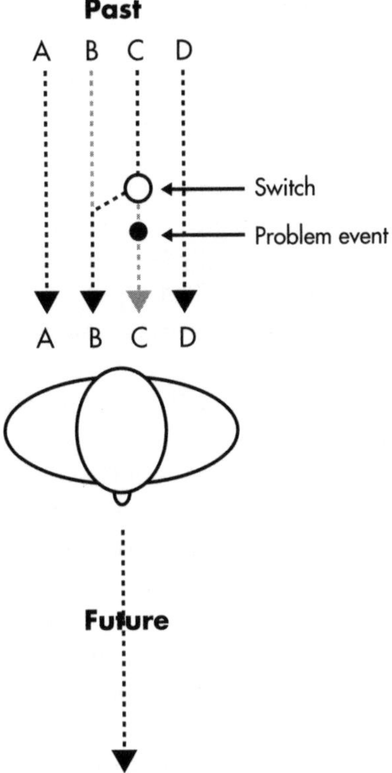

Figure 21.2 The alternative reality pattern (seen from above). Instead of running from C to C and into the future, this pattern diverts the past at the switch, just before the problem event, to the 'alternative reality': C to B.

Dealing with multiple conditions

Patients will sometimes present with several loosely related problems. The practitioner's options are as follows:

Have the patient arrange the problems in order of importance and suggest starting with the most important one, leaving the others for further consultations.

Suggest you both explore all the problems for any underlying or common factors. This process utilizes chunking and reframing.

1. Write a brief description of each problem in its own column.
2. Chunk each in turn for its positive intention. Ensure this is a core issue—that is, that the patient is unable to proceed any further.
3. Find the commonalities that all the problems share.
4. Chunk and/or reframe until a single, shared intention is identified.
5. Select the appropriate intervention and apply.
6. Test to ensure that changes are reflected in each problem area. Ensure that the core change generalizes out into all.
7. Future-pace each outcome individually.
8. Test again to ensure the appropriate changes have been made.

Case history: *The patient was clinically obese, and his knee pain was so intense that he could only walk with sticks. He complained that he was bored, had lost all interest in life, and, while he knew he had to change his diet, was unable to find the motivation to do so. He also felt his wife was becoming increasingly distant, and he worried that she might leave him. Together, the practitioner and the patient agreed that: (1) his eating was seeking to buffer him against his general feelings of malaise; (2) his lack of motivation protected him from failure; and (3) his wife's apparent withdrawal could mean she didn't want to add to his problems, not necessarily that she wished to leave him.*

All three intentions were reframed in positive terms: (1) feeling good; (2) succeeding in his efforts; and (3) re-engaging with his wife. In exploring for commonalities, the practitioner asked, 'When you've become slimmer and fitter [the presupposition here is that he would become slimmer and fitter, not that he might do so], what will you be doing that these problems have prevented you from even considering until now?' (This last question prompted a spontaneous chunking process and the patient identified a commonality he believed all his problems shared.)

The man looked down at the floor and began to cry softly. He said, 'We used to take lovely walks in the countryside. I really want to do that again.'

When the man had dissipated enough distress to allow him to resume, the practitioner redirected the patient towards a plan that would gradually reduce his intake of food and increase his activity.

He was instructed to seek out his wife's help maintaining his lifestyle changes, and planning walks in the country.

The patient started to leave in buoyant mood, excited about 'getting my life back again' and anxious to speak to his wife. When he was at the door, the practitioner called him back—to hand him the sticks he'd forgotten at the side of his chair.

The challenge of 'Yes'

The following pattern, developed and used with considerable success by UK-based general practitioner and surgeon Dr. Naveed Akhtar, gains its effectiveness by eliciting both a sense of playfulness and a commitment to change—both important contributors to putting movement back into a life that appears 'stuck'.

'It seems that some people who are depressed, struggle to make decisions, refuse to socialize, and lack motivation. So I present them with the "Yes Game" as follows,' he says.

'When I'm confident that I have enough rapport with them, I suggest they try this exercise to see for themselves how their mood can change with just a simple shift in mindset.

'All they have to do, I tell them, is to say, "Yes" to every invitation or suggestion they receive during one week. Of course, it has to be appropriate…nothing dangerous or upsetting. All suggestions must be within reason. But, apart from that, they must agree not to turn down anything that is asked of them.

'This means, any time anyone invites them out, to go to a movie, or dinner, or try a new hobby, whatever it may be—they have to say, "Yes"… and follow through on the commitment.'

Our own experience with this pattern is: the better your engagement with the patient, the better the outcome. Plus, it's always worth pointing out to those who agree that they've already said their first, 'Yes'.

Case history: *The husband of a 60-year-old lady died rather suddenly and unexpectedly. For several months, she became very depressed and reclusive. Her job as a primary school teacher started to become affected. She was prescribed anti-depressants and had several counseling sessions but there seemed to be very little improvement in her mood.*

She would visit the GP often, and during one consultation mentioned that several of her friends and family members had asked her to go out with them, but she always refused. She felt guilty for going out when her husband was not around to go out with her.

She was then asked to play the 'Yes Game' as described above. Within a few short weeks, she was going out with friends and work colleagues, had started dancing again and met a nice gentleman with whom she had struck a close friendship. By committing to a set instruction she no longer felt guilty, having 'permission' to enjoy herself, and was able to move forward with her life.

22

Making Something of Your World: small changes, big returns

Even a soul submerged in sleep is hard at work and helps make something of the world.—***Heraclitus of Ephesus***

What could be more dangerous than eating glass, swallowing swords, or snacking on *casu marzu*, a Sardinian rotten cheese riddled with maggots that can launch themselves 15 cm into the air at every bite?

The answer may surprise you. According to *Guinness World Records*, it's...going without sleep.

After high-level consultations, the famous arbiter of the furthest limits of human endeavor decided against including a category for the longest period without sleep. The decision was made on the grounds that going without sleep for extended periods could prove more dangerous than some of the most extreme, life-threatening challenges recorded around the globe, including glass-eating, sword-swallowing, and consuming putrid milk products.

It was a sensible decision. Growing evidence of strong links between sleep disorders and serious health problems highlights the need for health practitioners of all specializations to explore and apply effective treatments for insomnia.

We've known for thousands of years how important a 'good night's sleep' is to health. But it is only relatively recently that researchers have highlighted the dangers of too little, or disrupted, sleep.

In our search for underlying principles of healing and health, and in the belief that relatively small changes can result in large rewards, we have added these thoughts on sleep to this edition of *Magic in Practice*. The aim is to instruct and inform those who might be unaware of the cost of sleeplessness. Also, since we subscribe to Heraclitus's observation that the sleeping mind is still at work below the level of consciousness, we also suggest some simple changes that can optimize sleep and help make something vastly better of the individual's world.

Disrupted sleep patterns, insomnia, and simply 'burning the candle at both ends' can all have calamitous results.

According to a report by the Institute of Medicine of the National Academies, sleep disorders represent an 'under-recognized public health problem', and have been associated with a wide range of health problems, including hypertension, type 2 diabetes, depression, obesity, and even cancer.[285]

It has been estimated that 5- to 7-million people in the United Kingdom, and possibly 10 times as many Americans, may suffer chronic sleep disorders that may directly and negatively affect their health and longevity.

Obesity

Most researchers agree that lifestyle factors, such as over-eating and lack of exercise, are driving the obesity epidemic. However, recent research involving 28,000 children and 15,000 adults suggests that lack of sleep may double the risk of becoming obese.

According to Professor Francesco Cappuccio, of the University of Warwick's Medical School, a 'silent epidemic' of reduced sleep runs parallel to the obesity problem—a trend that has been noted in adults, as well as in children as young as 5 years.[286]

Lack of sleep, he believes, may trigger hormonal changes, including over-production of ghrelin, a known appetite stimulant, and reduction in the hormone, leptin, which suppresses the appetite.

Professor Cappuccio has called for more research into other possible mechanisms linking reduced sleep with increased chronic conditions in affluent societies.

Type 2 diabetes

Independent research at the University of Chicago Medical Centre suggests that suppression of slow-wave sleep in even healthy young adults significantly decreases their ability to regulate blood-sugar levels and increases the risk of type 2 diabetes.[287] Researchers interrupted the restorative sleep stage known as 'slow-wave sleep' of a group of lean, healthy volunteers between the ages of 20 and 31. After only three nights of interrupted sleep, their sensitivity to glucose became significantly reduced.

While their bodies needed more insulin to cope with the same amount of glucose, insulin secretion did not alter to compensate for their reduced tolerance to glucose after only three nights of selective slow-wave sleep suppression. In that short time, the young, healthy subjects became clinically at risk of developing type 2 diabetes.

The University of Chicago researchers estimated this decrease in insulin sensitivity to be comparable to that caused by gaining 44 to 66 kg in bodyweight.[288]

Happily, though, the risk of developing type 2 diabetes can be significantly reduced with just three hours of 'catch-up sleep' a week.

Until now, it has been believed that sleep deprivation could not be redressed by weekend 'lie ins'. Research by Dr. Peter Liu, of Los Angeles Biomedical Research Institute at Harbor-UCLA Medical Center (LA BioMed), has demonstrated that men's insulin sensitivity, or ability to clear blood sugar or glucose from their bloodstream, significantly improved after three nights of catch-up sleep at the weekend.[289]

'We all know we need to get adequate sleep, but that is often impossible because of work demands and busy lifestyles,' says Dr. Liu.

'Our study found extending the hours of sleep can improve the body's use of insulin, thereby reducing the risk of type 2 diabetes in adult men.'

Type 2 diabetes, the seventh leading cause of death in the US, affects nearly 26 million Americans and costs the nation an estimated $174 billion a year.

Metabolic syndrome

Obesity and type 2 diabetes, along with high cholesterol and increased blood pressure, are co-factors of the condition known as 'metabolic syndrome'—also now linked with interrupted or inadequate sleep. One of the biggest studies yet carried out suggests that too little sleep can nearly double the conditions leading to heart disease.

A University of Pittsburgh School of Medicine study of 1,214 adults between the ages of 30 and 54 has demonstrated that both too little and too much sleep can trigger metabolic syndrome. Those who slept between seven and eight hours a night were 45% less likely to suffer these symptoms than those who slept fewer, or considerably more, hours each night.

Professor Martica Hall emphasized that the link with sleep had been established independently of other factors previously associated with metabolic syndrome, including smoking, over-eating, and lack of exercise.

Depression

Excessive, shallow, non-REM sleep may, at least in part, also explain the undisputed link between sleep disorders and depression. Recent studies have noted excessive REM in anxious and depressed patients. But, rather than causing insomnia, depression has been shown to follow periods of chronic sleeplessness. Both younger and older people are affected, and behavioral disorders among juveniles appear to have a direct link with short or interrupted sleep.[290,291,292]

Studies presented at the 19th Annual Meeting of the Associated Professional Sleep Societies (APSS) in Denver, and published in the *Journal of Behavioral Sleep Medicine*, give credence to the theory that insomnia could contribute to, or be a predictor of, depression, and that resultant and prolonged bouts of sadness, hopelessness, and loss of interest in life activities make patients less likely to recover. One study has shown that sufferers of insomnia were more than 10 times more likely to be still depressed after six months, compared with those not suffering from insomnia. The insomniac group was 17 times more likely still to be depressed after a year.

Treatment targeting insomnia is therefore likely to improve the recovery rate from major depression, the researchers conclude.

Cancer

Groundbreaking research at Stanford University Medical Center suggests that melatonin, one of a class of antioxidant compounds produced during sleep, might be implicated in a suspected link between sleeplessness and cancer. When circadian rhythms are disrupted, less melatonin is produced, fewer free-radical compounds are mopped up, and the DNA of the sufferer's cells may become more prone to cancer-causing mutations.

The researchers, led by Dr. David Spiegel, also propose a link between suppressed melatonin production and ovarian and breast cancer. Oestrogen prompts cancerous cells to continue proliferating. Shift workers and others with disrupted sleep patterns may produce less melatonin and more oestrogen.[293]

The second link lies with a hormone called cortisol, which normally reaches peak levels at dawn then declines throughout the day. Cortisol is one of many hormones that help regulate immune system activity, including the activity of a group of immune cells called natural-killer (NK) cells that help the body battle cancer.

One study found that people who are at high risk of breast cancer have a shifted cortisol rhythm, suggesting that people whose cortisol cycle is thrown off by troubled sleep may also be more cancer-prone. In past work, Spiegel and his colleagues found that women with breast cancer whose normal cortisol cycle is disrupted (peaking levels in the afternoon rather than in the early morning) have a lower survival rate. These women also slept poorly.

Spiegel also cites recent findings that night-shift workers have a higher rate of breast cancer than women who sleep normal hours. This is reflected in animal studies. Mice whose circadian rhythms have been interrupted show much more rapid tumor growth than normal mice.

These theories have since received strong support from a study, published in the *British Journal of Cancer*, which suggests that women who get by on less than six hours' sleep have a significantly increased risk of breast cancer.[294]

Dr. Masako Kakizaki, who tracked nearly 24,000 Japanese women over eight years, has called the results 'significant'.

Further analysis of the data revealed that women who slept an average of eight hours every night were 28% less likely to develop tumors.

Although some experts have dismissed the sleep-cancer link, two out of three recent cohort studies of sleep and breast cancer report a significantly decreased risk among long sleepers.[295,296]

Medical NLP approaches to insomnia

Most medication, especially used over the long term, is inclined to produce side-effects. It is important that non-invasive, non-pharmacological interventions should be regarded as a first-line approach to all but the most serious sleep disorders. Here, we offer a few Medical NLP-based options we present to participants on Society of Medical NLP training courses. Although these are not intended as a full representation of the alternatives available, we suggest that readers experiment with the following underlying principles:

1. Reduce anxiety and allostatic load in the insomniac. This is probably the most important contribution a Medical NLP practitioner can make to dealing with sleep disorders.
2. Encourage the patient to tolerate each period of sleeplessness along with its accompanying anxiety, and to adopt a curious, observer stance (3rd Position). By shifting out of resistance to the condition and into the experience of detached 'witnessing', the patient will experience a spontaneous calm which often leads to sleep.
3. Practising the Relaxation Response (see Appendix A, pages 357 to 360) will, over a period of time, almost certainly improve sleep and other dysfunctional patterns. Since continued practice also leads to an increase in energy, ensure the patient does not do the technique too late at night.
4. Explore the conditions of previous times when sleep was deep and restful and elicit sub-modalities. Future pace the subject using these sub-modalities.
5. Rehearse restful sleep as follows:
    1. Dissociate the subject by having her imagine floating out of her body and observing the developing signs of deep sleep.
    2. Elicit these from her (having the subject describe these changes

profoundly alters the present state of consciousness), as well as suggest some she might have missed. Notice whether she follows by showing signs of deepening relaxation, pace, and validate ('that's right…') in order to deepen the state.

iii. Have the subject reassociate into the 'sleepy' state and anchor to something which will inevitably occur at night (such as the head hitting the pillow).

Note: While talking to the patient, the following language patterns are particularly useful: *Presuppositions, Nominalizations* and *Embedded Commands.*

Richard Bandler focuses on internal dialogue when working with insomniacs. Most people who suffer from sleep problems talk to themselves in rapid, agitated tones. He suggests not changing the content of the internal monologue, but rather gradually slowing down the rate of speech, making the internal voice increasingly sleepy, punctuating it with long pauses and yawns.

Finally, the simplest of all techniques, based on the principle of paradoxical intervention, pioneered by Viktor Frankl: Frankl taught his clients to extinguish unwanted behaviors by deliberately practising them. This technique was later adapted and widely applied by Milton Erickson.

Paradoxical sleep exercise

1. Make sure you're comfortable and ready for sleep (your normal sleep clothes, position, bedtime, etc).
2. Close your eyes and deliberately try to stay awake (without opening your eyes) for as long as possible.

Note: This really works!

23

Nine Minutes and Counting: fast-tracking change

> *Nothing is a waste of time if you use the experience wisely.*—***Auguste Rodin***

The most frequent objection we hear from doctors and other front-line health professionals is, 'It's all very well, but I just don't have the time to do all this stuff…' The complaint often comes from physicians in general practice, most of whom are restricted to consultations of nine minutes or less.

This chapter is intended for all busy health professionals who need to optimize their clinical outcomes in the least possible time. It incorporates some of the ideas introduced earlier in this book, as well as some new approaches, all brought together in one place so practitioners may use it as a ready reference until completely familiar and comfortable with the ideas. Remember to retain flexibility—it is the ideas and algorithms behind the methodology that are important rather than the actual wording.

In the UK, healthcare is free, but demands of time and resources limit the number of patients the doctor can see and how much time can be spent with each patient. Physicians in general practice are under constant pressure from government-imposed economic targets to improve their performance; this, inevitably, leads to larger case-loads and shorter times spent with most patients.

In the United States, doctors are paid for every patient they see by insurance and Medicare according to why they see the patient, and what procedures they perform, not by the amount of time they spend with the patient. The 'code for diagnosis or procedure' dictates that they receive fixed sums for specific procedures. If they spend too much time on one procedure, they lose money; if they manage to get the procedure done rapidly, they have more time to do something else, and, therefore, to make more money.

Dissatisfaction among patients is rife on both sides of the Atlantic. A survey by Picis, a Massachusetts-based technology solutions provider for the healthcare industry, has shown that 68% of respondents in the United Kingdom and 63% in the United States feel the quality of healthcare delivered in their respective countries has declined or stagnated over the past 10 years.[297]

While the length of primary care consultations in Britain has increased somewhat over past years, with each patient visit now averaging 9.36 minutes,[298] patients still express dissatisfaction with the length of their appointments. Many patients underestimate the duration of their visit, but still feel they don't have enough time with their doctor.[299,300,301] Both reactions, in our opinion, suggest that the real reason they seek help is not being satisfied.

Our first response to practitioners who feel they don't have enough time to do 'all this stuff', then, is to suggest (gently, we hope) that what they are currently doing in the time available to them simply is not working. We assure them (as if they don't know) that if they fail to meet their patients' needs, the patients will be back again...and again...and again. This is known informally as the 'revolving door syndrome'. As we constantly remind our patients, if you do what you did, you get what you got.

How to maximize the time you've got

So, is it possible to get significant results using Medical NLP principles and techniques when time is at a premium?

Dr. Khalid Hasan, consultant anestheseologist at a leading hospital in Birmingham, England, believes so. Preliminary audits of his results support this belief. His department consistently shows a reduced need for pre- and post-operative medication, easier surgical procedures, fewer complications, less perceived pain, and reduced bed-stays. 'I know this works,' he says.

'If I have five minutes with a patient before she goes to surgery, it's a lot, so I have to make sure the time counts. Obviously, I go in with as much information as I can gather, so I'm as prepared as possible. There is still information I need, and things I have to discuss with the patient. But, while I'm doing that, I'm doing a number of other things as well.

'Most importantly, I prime the patient for comfort and relaxation. I do this with the words I use, the tone of my voice and the rate of my speech. Whenever I see a particularly relaxed state developing, I anchor it, since that will be useful in the operating room when the patient is going under.

'I presuppose the operation will go easily and that her recovery will be comfortable and as pain-free as possible. I also orientate her *beyond* the surgery and the period of recovery to a time when she will be back to normal, as good as, or possibly even better than, before. I do this by asking questions such as, 'So, what's the first thing you'll be doing when you're feeling better...And after that? ...And after that?'

'This nudges the patient's attention away from the hospital environment and in a very positive and resourceful direction—the future. It primes her to expect and to notice things other than fear and discomfort, things such as what will be new and better in her life. Of course, the word "now" suggests feeling better is something that starts in the present, not something she has to wait for in the future.'

The structure of Dr. Hasan's approach is supremely elegant in Medical NLP terms—a graceful fusion of design and practice, and one that can be easily adapted to any consultation with any patient or client. Central to his approach are specific steps to reduce allostatic load; if the patient is in a state of limbic arousal, the chances are that he will fail to take in much of what you say and do. And, quite naturally, when patients don't comprehend, their adherence to behavioral advice or medication regimens is likely to drop.

Elsewhere in this book (see pages 112 to 116 and 227 to 228), we make several suggestions as to how clinicians can improve recall, concordance, and adherence, given that between 40% and 80% of information given to patients by healthcare professionals is forgotten within minutes of it being delivered.[302,303] Reducing the patient's stress levels will almost certainly improve understanding and memory.

This chapter offers several tried and tested tips, tricks and 'hacks' that can help the busy health professional optimize his time.

How to avoid post-consultation stress disorder

You've just spent the last 20 minutes in the ER with a man suffering chest pains.

You're pleased to tell him that all the tests show that there is NOTHING WRONG, that it is NOT CARDIAC PAIN, that the ECG emphatically did NOT SHOW A HEART ATTACK and that there is absolutely NOTHING to WORRY about. But, the more you talk, the less convinced he looks, the more anxious he feels and the longer the consultation takes. Now the other (more urgent) patients are waiting longer and longer, and time pressure slowly starts to build...

A clinician, practicing medicine to the highest standard with the available resources, has just excluded serious or life-threatening disorders. Yet, the patient remains worried, still convinced that he has something wrong. And so there is 'post-consultation stress', even though the patient is well and the clinician has done good work.

Shouldn't he be happy and grateful if you've just told him he did not have a heart attack?

This is a common scenario repeated daily in clinical settings across the Western world. Now let's consider this from a new perspective.

You may remember (see page 219) that the mind cannot process negation (words such as *not, no, don't, can't, mustn't, shouldn't* etc). These exist in language, but not in the way the brain makes sense of the world (see our discussion on pages 54 and 55 about turning and exclusive words).

The classic examples, 'Don't think of a pink elephant', and 'Don't think of the color blue', demonstrate this simple, but profoundly relevant, fact. Brains require images in order to understand. Try and create an image of a man *not* digging a hole, and you might begin to have a little more sympathy for that hard-working lump of grey jelly between your ears. In order to process a negation, you have to create an internal image of the state (a man with a spade and a hole, perhaps) and then find a way to negate it…by which time it may already be too late.

So, now go back six paragraphs to the heartfelt reassurance given the worried chest pain patient and count the number of negations. Astonishingly, many doctors routinely 'reassure' the worried well this way—then are surprised when the patient fails to be reassured.

When you said, 'There's nothing wrong', his brain processed the word 'wrong' first, then attempted to negate it, or to create some other meaning derived from past experiences of 'nothing wrong'. In either case, it's already too late, and the patient has gone into limbic hang-up.

Before he can collect himself, he hears 'not CARDIAC'...'not show a HEART ATTACK'.

That jumpy little nutmeg-sized organ in the brain, the amygdala, hits the panic button. After all it's heard a highly professional, reputable, well-educated, and experienced medical expert (you) sound a succession of warning cries:

'...WRONG...CARDIAC PAIN...ECG...SHOW HEART ATTACK…' and, ***'WORRY ABOUT...'***

In an already busy, not to say chaotic, environment, the patient's cortex (the 'spin doctor' in his brain) has to process these words and derive meanings from all those negatives you've thrown at him. Any wonder then that he's not fully reassured? The less-than-convinced patient is then discharged with the instruction to see his primary care physician to discuss it further (thus adding more pressure to the whole healthcare system).

(Some parents, on the other hand, know all about using negatives. Telling a child, 'Don't run', or 'Don't make a noise' often results in a polar response from the child. Relax. Your kid isn't simply being ornery; it's the way his brain works…).

The solution?

Let's analyze and reframe those negations.

You might say something like this: 'I'm pleased to say that the ECG is completely clear, your heart is healthy and strong, and we can be confident that everything is just as it should be. The discomfort you experienced was almost certainly the result of overwork/indigestion/anxiety, and that's much better news than whatever it was you were afraid of.'

Of course, we encourage you to use your own words. Take some time now, before any emergencies occur, and start to build up a collection of positively oriented words, phrases, and sentences that you can use when the appropriate situation arrives, as it almost certainly will.

You can further hone your skills by reviewing your own past consultations, and by listening to your colleagues, and identifying and correcting any negations that occur.

How to speed up and simplify the consultation

1. Make sure you have as much information about your patient as possible. Assuming his problem is chronic, chances are you will have seen him before, or maybe spoken to him on the telephone. Check his notes, if available, or use whatever other means you have of catching up with your patients' status. Remember, though, to keep 'beginner's mind', regardless of the information you already have.

   Remember the two most important rules of the Medical NLP consultation:

   Rule One—do whatever needs to be done in order to reduce the patient's allostatic load; use your voice, your body language, your priming skills...whatever it takes. Make sure the patient is in a condition to receive whatever intervention you can offer.

   Rule Two—always follow Rule One.
2. Presuppose a successful outcome to this and any other sessions you might have together. Sentences beginning 'when', 'while', 'after', 'as soon as', etc will help you create useful presuppositions. For example, 'When you're up and about again, what will you be doing with your spare time?'

   Remember: when you understand the power of presuppositions, even though you might not notice their effect while you are using them, after you have an opportunity to review your work and as soon as you can, you will almost certainly want to try using such patterns as much as you can.
3. Anchor any and all signs of comfort, optimism, relaxation—anything, in fact, that might prove useful later (as an anesthesiologist, Dr. Hasan is in an ideal position to make use of any anchors he has set when the time comes for him to administer the anesthetic. At the same time, he establishes

himself as an anchor through his voice, actions, demeanor, so that simply coming into his presence will fire the anchor and create an appropriate 'state' for his patient...another example of what Michael Balint meant by 'the doctor as drug'.[304]

4. The final suggestion is: when in doubt, choose one thing to do and do only that. You will learn to 'layer' your work with experience—you will still get exemplary results.

Notice that all this takes somewhat longer to describe than to do. The secret is practice—develop a repertoire of presuppositions and orientating statements, and practice them, as Dr. Hasan and many of our other alumni do, in front of a mirror, until you are completely comfortable with them.

The next objection we get is, 'My patients always hijack the consultation. I can never get them to leave.'

We have met many doctors who admit that they write prescriptions for their patients because they don't know how to terminate the consultation. Patients, too, often wait for a signal that they can go, and a prescription is usually taken to mean the consultation is over. Prescriptions should only be issued if they are genuinely needed—although one of our associates, Dr. Naveed Akhtar, has found that writing down behavioral instructions on a prescription pad not only has the same effect, but also helps increase adherence.

His technique? Simply ask the patient to describe in detail what happens when the unwanted behavior is not present: 'What's it like when you wake up, free of the anxiety/depression/pain?' Then reduce behavior surrounding this 'non-experience' to explicit steps: 'Well, I get up out of bed without dozing, have a shower, meditate, and have breakfast...'; write them down, and charge the patient with carrying out these 'instructions' without fail for at least a week.

However, tricks and techniques to get the patient out of your office shouldn't be necessary if the boundary conditions of the consultation (where it begins, what will be dealt with and how it will end) are set up in advance. We do not mean to suggest practitioners put up those patronizing and alienating notices telling patients to restrict themselves to one problem per consultation. That also won't be necessary.

Ensuring patient satisfaction

Familiarize yourself with Medical NLP's proprietary **I-N-D-I-A** pattern and sprawling, frustrating, and time-wasting consultations will be a thing of the past.

1. Prompt the patient to articulate her requirements by asking questions. For example, **inquire** with genuine interest, 'What brings you here today?', or, 'What would you like to deal with during our time together?' Listen closely, while keeping your awareness wide.
2. **Nudge.** 'Is there anything else?' (You are, quite literally, prompting the patient to share all concerns.)
3. When the patient has finished, **define** the parameters of the session—'So, when we deal with that [use the patient's exact words], will you have what you came here for today?'
4. Then, **inoculate** against second thoughts—'Is that everything? Are you sure there isn't anything else?' Don't be afraid of prompting the patient to come up with further issues. It's better you know about this as early as possible in the consultation. There are three possible directions the consultation can take.
   - Should the patient confirm that there is nothing else, continue with Step 5.
   - Should she mention any other concerns, listen, then repeat Steps 2, 3, and 4. You want to make sure she has completely exhausted her reasons for coming before you proceed.
   - Should she present a 'shopping list'—far more than can be handled in the time available—pace her by nodding and agreeing that she has had a lot to handle, then add, 'Of course, I want to give you the best possible care, so could you tell me which of these issues is the most important, so we can deal with that now, and then perhaps we can make another appointment to deal with the other issues.'
5. When you both **agree** on a single topic, continue with the consultation.

Inquire. Nudge. Define. Inoculate. Agree. These five steps will ensure that you stay on track and can proceed, confident that your time and the consultation will remain under your control to the mutual benefit of you and your patient.

Avoiding the pitfalls of 'active listening'

Contrary to what is usually taught about 'active' and 'patient-centered' listening, saying things like, 'Uh-huh', 'I see', 'Okay', simply to show you're listening, has its downside. As we've said elsewhere in this book (see page 151), this sort of response risks anchoring the patient to negative or painful experiences. And, there's something else. Studies have demonstrated that, far from getting all necessary information, active listening interrupts the flow of thinking, and can actually prompt the patient to introduce new topics and continue talking, even if she's finished telling you about her presenting problem.[305]

How to deal with wandering agendas

All clinicians are familiar with the patient who goes seriously off-track or keeps introducing new topics. Some suggestions that helped others in practice include:

1. Make sure you maintain the rapport you have already established. Pace the patient by nodding and smiling, then hold up your hand, palm facing the patient at about 45 degrees (less aggressive than a full-on flat palm gesture, but nevertheless signaling the need to pause), and say politely and congruently, 'I'm sure that's important, so can we just hold that thought until we get this other issue sorted out?'
2. Make sure you inflect downwards at the end of the sentence; this is really an instruction disguised as a question. Immediately, continue, 'If we still need to, we can come back to that if there's still time during this appointment, or we can make another appointment so we can discuss it more fully.'"

3. Still smiling, lower your hand, and return immediately to the main topic.

How to end the consultation respectfully

Even though most doctors rely on a computer to access patient notes and other information, make sure you also have an official-looking file or folder full of sheets of paper open on your desk in front of you. From time to time, you can jot down a few quick notes, even if you don't normally do that during a consultation.

1. When the time comes to wrap up the consultation, face the patient squarely, smile, and say something like, 'Well, thank you. I hope that helps. You can always call or make another appointment if there's still a problem, or something else you want to discuss [safety netting]. But [turning word], I'm sure you'll find you're feeling better soon…'
2. As you say that, close your folder, signaling the end to the consultation, push your chair back and stand up.
3. Still smiling, guide the patient to the door, your hand behind his back, but not touching his body. Do this gracefully, without hurry or any sense of distraction.

EXERCISES

Of course, we encourage you to use your own words. Take some time now, before any emergencies occur, and start to build up a collection of positively oriented words, phrases and sentences that you can use when the appropriate situation arrives, as it almost certainly will.
Also, practice the patterns above, especially the five-step INDIA model. Repetition creates fluency.

24

Communicating for Life: the way forward

*Effective communication is not what you mean to say, but what the other person understands.—**Medical NLP Presupposition***

This final chapter draws together the Medical NLP consultation process into a coherent whole, discusses ways of increasing patient adherence, and points the way forward. We hope, by incorporating even some of the principles and techniques we have discussed, that you will have the means to equip the patient for future challenges, so that the symptoms that brought him to you in the first place will have served their purpose—to prompt him to reorganize at a higher, more complex, and more effective level of functioning.

The three phases of the Medical NLP consultation process (**Figure 24.1**) below function as a map by which the practitioner can locate his present position and then move to whichever other area may become necessary.

She should not be constrained by the structure; like all sufficiently detailed maps, it should be used as a guide only. Navigating through the landscape in partnership with the patient, and with curiosity, flexibility, and 'attitude', is the crux of the healing journey.

The way forward

The clinical effectiveness of all but a few treatments depends on two factors: how well the patient remembers information and instructions, and how closely he adheres to them. Recall and adherence are automatically improved when practitioners follow some of the principles and techniques referred to elsewhere in this book (for example, providing orientating statements (see page 231), entering and working from within the patient's model (see page 80), and discussing and agreeing treatment programs and well-formed outcomes (see pages 196 to 198)). Further suggestions follow below.

Phase	*Purpose*	*Tools*
1. Engagement	Managing first impressions Rapid engagement Achieving concordance	Instant Engagement Technique Yes-sets + negative framing
2. Alignment	Gathering quality data Entering the patient's world Accessing and stabilizing resources	The Uninterrupted Story Patterns, metaphors and meaning Anchoring Shaping Feedback Priming Preframing, framing and reframing Negociating outcomes Patient-generated metaphors Sub-modalities Glyphs
3. Reorientation	Developing and applying interventions Increasing patient self-efficacy	Medical NLP change algorithms Hypnosis Conditioning and future-pacing

Figure 24.1 The three-part Medical NLP consultation process

Recall

Research consistently shows that the patient forgets between 40% and 80% of medical information provided by healthcare professionals, often within minutes of leaving the consultation. The more details provided, the fewer are remembered.[306] Furthermore, almost half the information given is incorrectly recalled.[307]

Improving recall

The following strategies can help patients remember better for longer.

- Do not exceed the patient's conscious processing chunk size (remember the Law of Seven Plus or Minus Two—see page 80).
- The practitioner's explanatory frameworks must match those of the patient.[308]
- Seek feedback from the patient in his own words. By repeating instructions, patient recall is increased by 30%.[309]
- Present information in a form that matches the patient's sensory preferences, but also offer versions in other modalities. Spoken (auditory) instructions alone are the least effective.[310] Written instructions (visually presented) have been shown to increase recall, but difficulties occur among non-native speakers or those with low education or literacy.[311] Graphics, such as cartoons and pictographs, are a particularly useful adjunctive means of conveying information to patients, increasing both recall and adherence by up to 80%.[312]

Adherence

Fewer than half of all patients follow treatment plans and instructions. Britain's National Audit Office reports that wasted drugs alone could be costing the country up to £100 million a year,[313] whereas in the United States, the cost has been estimated at more than $100 billion.[314]

Adherence is a function of many processes. These include:

- the quality of the relationship (the 'emotional resonance') between practitioner and patient;
- effective communication;
- understanding of, and respect for, the patient's real reason for seeking help (not necessarily immediately evident); and
- semantically well-formed outcomes, with clearly defined steps.

Remember: if *both* practitioner and patient cannot put the requirements into specific, sensory-based (factual) words, they are unlikely to be carried out.

Increasing recall and adherence

One of the important messages of this book is that *patients do not necessarily know **how** to get better*—or, to put it differently, they may lack the solution-oriented neurological pathways necessary for change. Also, it is important that new neural paths need to be activated, preferably several times (conditioning), in order to function.

New pathways and a mechanism to set them in motion may be installed as follows:

1. Divide instructions into several (three to five) distinct steps;
2. Outline each step clearly; then
3. Ask a question that can be answered only after the patient has mentally run through the necessary steps.

Take, for example, balance-assisting exercise instructions given to a patient diagnosed with labyrinthitis (inner ear disturbance):

Step 1: *Take a look at the instruction sheet.*

Step 2: *As you can see, the exercises are simple…(the exercises are then repeated/demonstrated)*

Step 3: *and you need to do them regularly five times a day for the next four weeks so you can start feeling better.*

Question: *Now, when do you think would be the best times of day to do them so you can easily fit them all in?*

After the question has been asked, be sure you allow the patient time to consider his response. If he answers too quickly, back up and have him go through it step by step.

Two important factors to remember

Both recall and adherence are directly affected by two factors: attentional narrowing, and state-dependent learning.

Attentional narrowing occurs when stress and anxiety trigger sympathetic arousal—a common result of carelessly delivered diagnosis, prognosis and treatment options. The central message of a communication ('You have X disease') can severely occlude supporting information, impairing both memory and recall.[315]

State dependency is an equally common phenomenon whereby information acquired in a particular psychosocial/physiological context (environment, mood, degree of sympathetic arousal, etc) can only be fully retrieved when that state is reactivated.

Thus, if the patient's anxiety levels rise during the consultation, she is unlikely to remember instructions and advice in a more relaxed environment at home.[316] It is important, therefore, to remember to *recognize and reduce the patient's allostatic load* ***before*** *you proceed.*

A mongrel approach

We began this book by wondering how it could be that, at this highly advanced stage of human development, our species could find itself so profoundly disabled by such a wide range of physical and emotional disorders that appear to have no medical explanation. One of our suggestions was that scientific inquiry, responsible for so many other extraordinary achievements, continues to approach the human body-mind as an assemblage of almost unconnected parts rather than the deeply complex and highly organized dynamic system it is.

The purpose of *Magic in Practice,* therefore, was to outline a three-part 'whole-person' consultation process that develops and maintains a 'healing relationship' between patient and practitioner, respects the patient as a unique individual, and helps him learn, or re-learn, more resourceful patterns for physical and psychological wellbeing.

In doing this, we acquired a mongrel approach. We foraged in many different fields for fragments we could model and use to create a more coherent picture, not simply of how people become ill, but how they can get better.

We were guided in this by the organizing principles of Neuro-Linguistic Programming, as co-created and developed by Dr. Richard Bandler. We have acquired from his guidance and inspiration the compulsion to be curious, experimental, flexible, and (we have been told) argumentative.

We also rooted through books and journals, articles and websites that spanned dozens of different approaches, and spoke to, and observed, experts in many different fields—not least those doctors who consistently achieved exceptional results, and those patients who were equally extraordinary, often recovering their health and wellbeing against all odds.

A lot of what we found on our journey was dross. But we also uncovered pure gold; some of the latter we've shared with you in this book. Substantial additions and revisions have been made for this second edition, and, given the speed with which knowledge expands, we are confident that more will appear in later works.

If we have achieved nothing else, we hope that we have been able to drive home the message that what is most important about any consultation is the patient and the result she gets. More than science, more than research, more than targets, audits, or statistical proof, it is the patient and the uniqueness of her experience that matters most.

Remember, however intelligent you might be, however much you pride yourself on your communication skills, it's not what you know or what you meant that matters, but what the other person understands.

And it is the quality of your relationship with him that can open him to new insight, behavior, and change.

Glossary

A

Abreaction: The sudden and violent release of repressed emotion (see **Silent Abreaction**). Abreaction is to be discouraged to avoid re-anchoring the subject to his distress.

Affect bridging: The linking by anchoring or other means of feeling or response with its original cause.

Alignment: The stage where one enters the patient's model in the Medical NLP Consultation Model.

Allostasis: The process of achieving stability through psychological, physical or behavioral flexibility.

Allostatic Load: Chronic psychological, physical, or emotional stress, preventing allostasis.

Analog: Data presented in continuously variable form, rather than in discrete packages (see **Digital**). The changing volume of speech is Analog, while the words used are Digital.

Anchor: A stimulus or trigger paired with a specific response. Anchors may be set deliberately or inadvertently, openly or covertly.

Anchor collapse: When two different anchors fire simultaneously, the end result is a mixed or neutral state. Neither original anchor will remain intact.

Anchor stack: When two or more anchors are attached to the same trigger, creating a cumulative effect.

Anniversary effect: The tendency of some patients to experience recurrence of symptoms at significant times of their lives.

ANS (Autonomic Nervous System): The division of the peripheral nervous system responsible for the unconscious regulation of organ function.

Associated: Experiencing through one's own senses (seeing through your own eyes, hearing with your own ears, feeling with your own feelings).

Auditory: Representational system pertaining to sense of hearing.

Away-from: Motivational pattern marked by avoidance of an unwanted experience, rather than by accomplishing a desired Outcome (see **Towards**).

B

Biomedical: Biological or physiological process in relation to the field of medicine.

Bonded disconnection: Paradoxical attempt to 'not-have' a symptom or feeling that in practice reinforces the unwanted experience.

Brainwashing: Changing the thoughts, beliefs, behaviors, and responses of a subject without his knowledge and/or consent.

Bridging: Connecting two previously unconnected qualities or states, conversationally or by deliberate anchoring.

Burnout: (See *Compassion Fatigue*).

C

Calibration: Establishing the relevance of non-verbal responses by testing.

Cartesian Dualism: Also known as the 'Mind-Body Split'; suggests mind and body operate independently of each other.

Cause-and-Effect: Real or perceived causal relationship involving two or more events.

Chronopathic: Problems caused by the subject's perception/experience of Time.

Chunking: Altering experience and perception by focusing on large or smaller units of information.

Compassion fatigue: Term used interchangeably with 'Burnout' to describe the adverse effects on the practitioner of over-involvement in the patient's problems. Negative physical and emotional response to stresses experienced in the caring professions.

Conditioning: Used in two senses by Medical NLP: 1. Classical Conditioning, as defined by Behaviorism, and 2. repetition or practice to help the subject create new neural patterns.

Congruence: The alignment of beliefs and other internal experience with behavior.

Consciousness: Everything that is in current awareness.

Content: The 'story', including perceived 'cause', associated with a problem; the product of reflection, interrogation, and psychoanalysis (see also *Pathography*).

D

Description: The first verbal level in the Structural Differential that follows the **Object Level**. The patient's symptoms.

Digital: Data presented in discrete packages, rather than in continuously variable form (see **Analog**). Words, for example, are Digital, whereas the changing volume in which they are spoken is Analog.

Dissipation: The biological discharge of entropy. A requirement for maintaining allostasis.

Dissociation: Experiencing an event as if separated from the self.

E

Ecology/ecological: Used in NLP to emphasize that all interventions and new behaviors should be 'fit for purpose' and will not cause problems in other contexts of the person's life.

Emotional contagion: The tendency to express and feel transferred emotions similar to those of others; burnout.

Engagement: 'Connecting with' the patient; gaining rapport, concordance, etc.

Entropy: The result or waste products of the degradation of energy. Used in Medical NLP to refer to undischarged emotional overload; the unmetabolized chemical residue of systemic stress.

Epigenetics: Effect of psychosocial crises on genetic information. The effects may be hereditary.

Evaluation: Judgments, opinions, inferences (essentially unverifiable) drawn from information.

Event: Pre-verbal level of Korzybski's Structural Differential referring to disturbance of the subject's neurology. The Event or process is *not* within the subject's conscious awareness.

Evidence-based medicine: Use of currently available 'best evidence' in making decisions about patient care. Largely dependent on Randomized Controlled Trial for acceptance.

Exit point: A point in a strategy that allows the subject to know when to stop the processing.

Expectancy: The positive (or negative) anticipation of both patient and practitioner regarding the efficacy of treatment.

Explanatory styles: Term used by Martin Seligman et al to describe subjects' world-view.

Eye-accessing cues: Unconscious eye movements said to reflect the **representational systems** used by the individual to process information.

F

Fact-evaluation spectrum: Process allowing the speaker or listener to differentiate between sensory-specific data and opinion.

Faith effect: The ability to elicit changes in health or wellbeing associated with a sense of connectedness or a strong spiritual belief.

Felt sense: Subjective, internal, non-verbal bodily awareness or sensation linked to a specific experience. (See also: *Kinesthetic* and *Somatic Marker.*)

Flooding: Overwhelming exposure to anxiety-provoking stimulus while preventing or inhibiting the flight component.

Frame: The underlying or supporting scope or schema that imparts meaning to a given set of event, experiences, and behaviors.

Functional Disorder: Condition for which no pathological cause has been identified.

Functional magnetic resonance imaging (fMRI): A process applying Magnetic Resonance Imaging (see *Magnetic Resonance Imaging*) to study neuronal activity.

Future-pace: The act of imagining and 'rehearsing' a future event as if it has already taken place in the future.

G

Gene expression: The process by which the inheritable information from a gene is manifested as a protein, enzyme, or RNA sequence.

General adaptation syndrome (GAS): Term used by Hans Selye to describe the process of adaptation to long-term stressors.

General semantics (Alfred Korzybski): A field pertaining to the study of the relationship of language with neurological function (not to be confused with **Semantics**).

Glyph: A kinesthetic experienced and treated as a three-dimensional object—e.g. a 'red ball' of pain. (see **Kinesthetic** below).

H

Heart rate variability (HRV): Diagnostic tool in cardiology and obstetrics (and Medical NLP), which provides a reliable measure of the functioning of the autonomic nervous system (ANS). This, in turn, reflects the overall psychophysical status of the subject.

Homolateralization: Physical or emotional behavior which results from overdependence on one brain hemisphere over the other.

Host-resistance: Measure of an individual's or group's resistance to illness.

Hyperchronic: Problems caused by the subjective sensation of time moving too rapidly—e.g. stress.

Hypochronic: Problems caused by subjective sensation of time dragging—e.g. depression.

Hypnosis: A method or practice of inducing 'suggestibility' in a subject, sometimes considered to be a normal extension of human consciousness.

Hypnotic Phenomena: See *Trance Phenomena* .

I

Imaginal: Sensory-rich internal creation of an experience or behavior with the intention of creating corresponding neural networks.

Inference: Term used in **General Semantics** to refer to the evaluation of an experience.

K

Kinesthetic: Pertaining to feeling/sensation, both proprioceptive and interoceptive.

Ko Mei: Derived from the Indo-European roots of the word 'communication', a term used in Medical NLP to denote a specific process of communication as a coming together in order to effect change.

L

Layering: Using two or more different techniques towards a given outcome to increase likelihood of success.

Limbic arousal: Increased activity of the limbic system leading to generation of emotions such as rage, elation, fear.

Linear time: The progression of time experienced sequentially.

Linguistic relativity (Also **Sapir-Whorf Hypothesis**)**:** The effect on experience of the language used.

M

Magnetic resonance imaging (MRI): An imaging technique involving powerful magnetic fields rendered by computer software in 3-dimensional images.

Medical NLP: The proprietary development and application of principles and techniques developed out of NLP, together with positive psychology, and solution-oriented therapy, specifically for application within the field of healthcare.

Meta model™: A linguistic model developed by Richard Bandler and John Grinder exploring the transformation of meaning to expression, or Deep Structure to Surface Structure.

Meta-psychology: An explanation of how 'psychology' works.

Meta-state: A state that creates another state—e.g. anxiety that one will have an anxiety attack; fear of fear.

Mirror neurons: Neurons which excite when a subject observes an event or action 'as if' he were experiencing the event or action himself. Believed to be the neurophysiological foundation of empathy.

Modalities: Referring to our five senses, especially when describing how subject experience is 'created'.

Modeling: A process described by Richard Bandler as the act of 'creating a calculus which describes a given system'.

Molecular: Pertaining to molecules—i.e. stable, neutral groups of at least two atoms linked by strong chemical bonds.

N

Negative Frame: A linguistic pattern (e.g. 'isn't it?'; 'wouldn't it?'; 'can't it?') usually employed to increase agreement.

Neuroplasticity: The ability of brain architecture to be changed by experience.

NLP: The study of the structure of subjective experience.

Nominalization: Verb transformed into a noun; a 'process' represented as a 'thing'.

Normalization: Process whereby the practitioner behaves as if events are normal or accepts them to be normal within the context and framework of the subject's own belief-system or cultural reference.

O

Object level: The second pre-verbal level of Korzybski's **structural differential.** At this level the Event or process is within the subject's conscious awareness.

Orientating statement: Information given by physician to patient informing him of what is happening, or is about to happen.

Outcomes: Specific results negotiated and worked towards as a function of the consultation process.

P

Pacing: Matching aspects of the subject's behavior or responses to facilitate rapport.

Pathography: The patient's story about his condition.

Predicates: Words used to describe which representational system someone is using.

Preframing: Setting in advance the boundary conditions of an experience or event.

Premature cognitive closure: Tendency to make decision and initiate action before all available information has been processed.

Presupposition: Information assumed, but not overtly stated, to be present in order for a statement to be understood.

Primary process thinking: A form of relaxed, non-verbal, and receptive mode of mental functioning.

Priming: The use of words covertly to trigger a specific psychological response from the listener.

Process: Strategies or schemas applied in the execution of a feeling, behavior, or response.

Psychotropic: The action of a drug on the central nervous system whereby it alters brain function.

Psychological modulators: Experiences and conditions affecting psychological wellbeing.

R

Randomized control trial (RCT): Statistical tool for measuring a predefined effect of a single drug or medical procedure on a standardized, defined subject population.

Reframing: Changing the meaning of an experience, behavior, or event, by changing its context or interpretation.

Reification: Process of treating an abstraction as a concrete or material object (see also *Nominalization*).

Relaxation response: Antithesis to the fight-or-flight response; invoked by certain 'mindful' meditative techniques, as well as certain breathing techniques (see *Resonant Frequency Breathing*).

Reorientation: Third phase in the Medical NLP Consultation Process in which techniques are applied to bring about change.

Representational systems: Senses through which the brain receives information about the environment—e.g. visual, auditory, kinesthetic.

Resistance: Reason given by some psychologists for why their patients don't respond to treatment.

Restful alertness: A state experienced during meditation characterized by reduced metabolic activity coupled with wakefulness .

Resonant frequency breathing: A specific breathing pattern of approximately six cycles a minute which induces cardiovascular resonance (large changes in blood pressure and heart rate), in turn prompting the autonomic nervous system constantly to regulate, eventually increasing ANS balance or coherence.

S

Safety netting: Giving instructions to a patient as to what action to take in the event of his condition worsening or persisting.

Salutogenesis/Salutogenic: Directed towards achieving healing and health (see **pathogenic/pathogenesis**).

Secondary traumatization: (See *Burnout, Compassion Fatigue* and *Vicarious Traumatization*).

Semantics: The branch of linguistics and logic concerned with meaning.

Shaping/Behavioral shaping: Indirectly guiding and reinforcing 'useful' or desirable behavior, while ignoring or correcting that which is not desired.

Silent abreaction: The gentle, controlled release of repressed emotion. Dissipation of entropy (see also *Abreaction* and *Entropy*).

Single-cause hypothesis: The belief that each illness is caused by a single pathological agent .

Signal-to-noise ratio (SNR or S/N): Derived from engineering, SNR refers to the relationship between meaningful information (the Signal) and background confusion (the Noise).

Solution frame: Construct aimed at orientating the subject towards solutions rather than away from problems.

Solution-orientated thinking: Seeking solutions rather than spending all available time on analyzing problems. Useful in medicine where all 'causes' of a problem have been eliminated.

Somatic marker: Term coined by Antonio Damasio to refer to the internal sensation accompanying a particular emotional experience. (See also *Kinesthetic* and *Felt Sense.*)

Somatoform: Expressed physically by the body.

Split/Splitting: The division of experience into smaller component parts in order to render it more manageable.

State: The integrated sum of mental, physical, and emotional conditions from which the subject is acting.

Strategy: Sequence of internal processes resulting in a specific feeling or behavior.

Stress-enhanced memory: Memory 'fixed' by traumatic events (believed to be a function of increased serum cortisol).

Structural differential: A model created by Alfred Korzybski to demonstrate the process of verbal abstraction used in an attempt to describe subjective experience.

Structure: The way in which a specific behavior functions, as opposed to the reasons it exists (Content).

Sub-modalities: The unique characteristics of the sensory modalities used to create subjective experience—e.g. when we think of a holiday as a picture (Visual Modality), is the picture in color, or black and white (sub-modality of the Visual modality)?

Systematic desensitization: A technique used in behavioral psychology to treat phobias by gradual exposure to the object of fear.

Sympathetic arousal: Arousal of the Sympathetic Nervous System (SNS), giving rise to the fight-or-flight response.

Symptom-solution linkage: A technique in Medical NLP in which a new, resourceful response is attached to the trigger of an older, less resourceful, one.

T

Thought-changing: Term used in psychology in place of the more colloquial 'brain-washing'.

Time distortion: Subjective temporal experience that differs from 'objective' clock time.

Time line: Subjective construct which metaphorically organizes the individual's past, present, and future experience spatially.

Towards: Motivational pattern marked by seeking to accomplish or achieve a particular goal.

Trance: An altered state of consciousness usually marked by reduced awareness of external events and increased focus on specific thoughts or feelings. Often accompanied by increased 'suggestibility', and used interchangeably with **Hypnosis**.

Trance logic: Explanations advanced by the subject to explain behavior induced by post-hypnotic suggestion. These often appear laughable or bizarre to unhypnotized observers.

Trance phenomena: Behaviors usually associated with deep hypnosis (e.g. Amnesia, Arm Levitation, Hallucination, etc).

Transcranial magnetic stimulation (TCMS): The utilization of variable magnetic fields to modulate and map neuronal brain activity.

Transderivational search: Attributing meaning to the statement of another from within one's own experience.

Two-point loop: A self-maintaining repetitive sequence within a strategy.

U

Ultradian rhythms: Biorhythms which occur in 90- to 120-minute cycles.

Unconscious: Everything that is outside present awareness.

Unconscious association: Connections between present and past experience made by the brain on an other-than-conscious level.

Up-time trance: Altered, or hypnotic, state in which the subject maintains contact with the 'external world'.

V

Verifiable data: Sensory-based information (see **Inference**).

Vicarious traumatization: The detrimental effect to the practitioner of exposure to accounts of the client's traumatic experience.

Appendices

In the Eye of the Storm: activating the Relaxation Response

The 'Relaxation Response' is a term coined by Harvard Medical School's Herbert Benson to describe a state that differs significantly from the three states of waking, sleeping and dreaming on which research into consciousness had thus far focused. The state—also known as 'restful alertness'—is marked by dramatically reduced metabolic function, measurably deeper even than deep sleep, coupled with an inner 'wakefulness'.

While considered by some psychologists to be related to a form of relaxed, non-verbal, and receptive mode of mental functioning known as 'primary-process thinking', Benson, and later researchers, including Milton Erickson's research partner, Ernst Rossi, came to regard it as a discrete 'fourth state' of consciousness, naturally occurring, but previously unrecognized in Western culture.

As Rossi elaborates in *The 20-Minute Break*, humans appear to have evolved with the potential to benefit from recognizing and responding to natural mind-body cycles, now known as ultradian rhythms, which occur every 90–120 minutes. The ability simply to observe our thoughts without becoming involved in them appears to have far-reaching effects on the subject's cognitive abilities, health, and longevity.

Nobel Laureate Dr. Elizabeth Blackburn believes that meditation may have salutary effects on telomere length, both by reducing cognitive stress and stress arousal, and by increasing positive states of mind and hormonal factors that may promote 'telomere maintenance'.

Telomeres can be thought of as like the metal tags that prevent your shoelaces from unraveling. These caps of DNA occur at the end of chromosomes, preventing the chromosomes from fusing together. The longer the telomeres, the healthier you are.

Blackburn believes that meditation functions as a kind of 'metacognitive awareness' (an awareness of your thoughts, without becoming involved in them). This could function as a kind of mental housekeeping, by interrupting rumination, allowing one more accurately to evaluate thoughts, and to create greater freedom of choice in responding to thoughts and emotions. This practice, Blackburn and her colleagues point out, differs markedly from cognitive behavioral therapies by changing the relationship to thoughts, rather than trying to change the contents of thinking.[317]

Benson and his colleagues—inspired by research into the Indian technique of Transcendental Meditation®, then newly imported into the West—align completely with the theories and findings of the Blackburn team.

Benson's early research indicated effectiveness in the treatment of hypertension, cardiac irregularities, headaches, anxiety disorders, pre-menstrual syndrome, and mild and moderate depression. Later studies[318] showed benefits to patients suffering from back pain, arthritis, gastrointestinal disorders, including irritable bowel syndrome, angina, infertility, and chemotherapy-induced nausea.[319]

Several researchers believe that the distinctive mix of alpha and theta brainwaves demonstrated during practice of the technique marks specific neurological changes related to psychophysiological self-regulation. Part of its effect is believed to result from the dissipation of accumulated stress, or entropy, thus increasing emotional and physical resilience to day-to-day stressors.[320]

The Relaxation Response differs significantly from more familiar 'relaxation exercises', such as listening to tapes or practicing progressive relaxation, in that it appears to act cumulatively on the functioning of the nervous system's 'alarm system', most notably by down-regulating activity in the reticular formation and thalamus areas of the brain.

Even more significant is the suggestion emanating from the emerging science of epigenetics that experiencing the Relaxation Response on a regular basis can change the expression of more than 1,500 specific genes.[321] This and other studies suggest that purely mental interventions can not only alter people's genetic landscape, but can pass on changes, for better or worse, to their offspring.

Two important characteristics of the Relaxation Response are its essential passivity and its reiterative nature—that is, rather than relying on an external prompt, such as recorded instructions, it repeatedly 'feeds back' into the subject's current level of awareness, progressively deepening his or her state. Several variations of the technique have proved effective, but the essential components include:

- set times to practice undisturbed (preferably twice a day, for approximately 15 minutes each);
- a word or short phrase that acts as an 'anchoring' device (the meaning of the word is less important than its sound. Open vowel sounds, such as those in words like *peace*, *calm* and *relax*, seem to be more suitable than those with hard consonants); and
- a passive attitude towards both the word and any thoughts or distractions that may occur.

Method

1. Sit comfortably, close your eyes, and wait for 20 or 30 seconds for the body to begin to quieten its activity.
2. Silently repeat the word, in time to each out-breath. Do not deliberately change your natural rate or depth of breathing; simply use the exhalation to provide a natural rhythm.
3. Adopt an entirely passive attitude towards thoughts that occur. Do not try to resist them or to force your attention to stay with the word.
4. However, when you 'come to' and realize you have been thinking of something else, gently return to the repetition of the word.
5. When the time is up (feel free to check your watch or a clock), let go of returning to the word, wait for another half-minute or so, and then slowly open your eyes.

Note: Even though you might experience many thoughts, especially when you begin the practice, your heart rate, breathing, and metabolism will slow down automatically. Therefore, avoid getting up too abruptly when the session is over. Also, do not practice for longer than 20 minutes to avoid excessive stress release.

We suggest the practitioner (who should practice the technique him- or herself) guide the patient through the process to ensure full understanding, rather than simply giving instructions. Be sure to emphasize the necessity for regularity of practice.

Alternative methods

For those with visual or kinesthetic sensory preferences, the technique can be adjusted as follows.

Visual

You can pick a simple colored shape that you gently hold in your inner attentional field. Simply observe it without judgment. Each time you become aware that you have drifted off onto thoughts or other distractions, gently brings your attention back to the shape.

Kinesthetic

Place your attention on your nostrils and simply notice the sensation of your breath as it moves in and out. You may silently count each out-breath if you so wish.

Visual-auditory-kinesthetic method

Start at 1, imagining you are breathing in an image of the number itself, seeing and feeling it gently settle in your lower abdomen as you breathe out. You then breathe in 2, visualizing it settling gently on the number 1 as you breathe out again. Your goal should be to reach 10, stacking each number, one on top of the other, before starting again.

B

The On-line Brain: cross-lateral exercises

Cross-lateralization may be used adjunctively to help patients suffering from anxiety, depression, immune disorders, brain injuries, childhood behavioral disorders, and other conditions in which homolateralization (reduced activity of one hemisphere) is suspected. The challenge level of the exercises should be increased progressively to force neural connectivity.

Alternate nostril breathing

Sit comfortably. Place one forefinger on the forehead between the eyebrows, position your thumb on one nostril, and your second finger on the other.

Close one nostril, breathe out, then breathe in through the open nostril, then close it and open the other. Breathe out, then in. Close that nostril and repeat the process for 5–10 minutes.

Note: Ensure that each cycle of breathing begins on the out-breath so that the cross-over takes place after the in-breath.

Basic cross-marching

Stand with the hands at the sides, and then, while looking slightly up, begin to march in place, ensuring that each hand crosses the body's midline to touch the opposite knee.

Complete 10–40 repetitions several times a day.

Cross-marching with eye movements

Follow the instructions for the previous exercise while moving the eyes in large circular movements in both directions, without moving the head.

The challenge level of both cross-marching exercises can be increased by adding an auditory component (counting out loud, reciting the alphabet, etc). When this becomes easy, increase the challenge further: recite the alphabet backwards, count down from 100 in sevens, etc.

Nose-to-ear exercise

Sit comfortably in an upright position. Start with both hands resting on the knees (center position), and then simultaneously touch the tip of nose with the left hand and the left ear with the right hand. Return the hands to the center position, and then the reverse the movement: the tip of the nose with the right hand, and the right ear with the left hand. Repeat 10 to 12 times.

Note: Cross-lateralization may be used even where the patient is immobilized or unconscious. Two people need to work together, gently lifting one knee and moving the opposite hand to touch it, etc.

C

Medical NLP Algorithm: managing pain

Pain is one of the greatest, most enduring, mysteries of medical science and the human condition. While it is broadly described as 'an unpleasant sensory and emotional experience associated with actual or potential tissue damage', chronic pain, as experienced by millions of sufferers, continues to resist the most advanced pharmacological and remedial treatment available.[322]

It is also one of the most widely reported reasons for primary care attendance. According to a World Health Organization 15-country study, pain is the main reason for 22% of patients seeking medical assistance.[323]

The steps to follow in managing pain are:

Acknowledge the patient's discomfort

For example, *'I can understand how this has been disrupting your life/worrying you/stopping you from working'*, etc (pacing patient's subjective experience).

Normalize and re-orientate the patient towards progress and improvement

For example, *'...and that's completely understandable, considering [diagnosis, cause etc], so I'm sure you're looking forward to feeling better/being able to move more easily/be more comfortable... aren't you?'* (Pacing; Leading; Reframing; and Negative Framing: 'aren't you?' invites agreement and concordance).

Encourage toleration of the symptom and detached observation
For example, '*So, just for the moment, let it be the way it is and just stand back and watch it…*'

Gather sensory-based data
For example, '*So, what exactly is it [the pain] like?*'; '*What else is it like?*' (Eliciting the glyph.)

Notes:

1. Avoid labels and interpretations ('bad', 'irritating', 'endless' etc) and encourage sensory-rich descriptions of the kinesthetic—for example, 'tight', 'hot', 'like a knife', 'heavy, red ball', 'gripping' etc.
2. Do not lead the patient by making specific suggestions. If the patient needs help, ask: 'If I were doing it [the pain], how would I know what it was like?' If all else fails, ask: 'If it had a color/shape/weight/size etc [each in turn], what would it be?'

Encourage self-regulation and discharge by deepening experience of tolerance and detached observation
For example, '*So just let [the knife, the tight grip etc] be there and keep standing back and watching.*'

'*Don't actively do anything to change it. Allow it to change by itself—just stay quiet and observe…*' (Dissociation),

Note: Allow sufficient time for the process. Encourage the patient to allow any movement of the kinesthetic to fully continue until it has discharged or shifted to an acceptable level. Encourage to patient to describe whatever is happening out loud by asking: 'So, what's happening now?' from time to time. This helps the patient notice when the symptom begins to move from stuck to moving. Since experiencing the pain and describing it involve different parts of the brain, this also helps to break down the boundary conditions of the condition.

Normalize and encourage any change that takes place. Listen especially for digital changes in sensory channels—for example, from kinesthetic to visual. This suggests dissipation is proceeding spontaneously.

Facilitate process if patient is stuck

Begin with one descriptor and suggest analog changes to test for the most effective direction to pursue

For example, 'So, what would happen if the heavy, black cloud in your head could start to change slightly—maybe to become more of a dark gray?'; 'What would happen if it became a little lighter/more transparent/cooler?', etc (*Sub-modality change.*)

If one or other of the changes reduces the intensity of the experience, suggest, 'So, that can continue happening in that way, and continue watching how it changes…' (*Presuppositions that the subjective experience can change, that change in the direction of greater comfort will continue.*)

D

Strategies: the sequencing of experience

As explained in the body of the book, strategies are chained internal actions (visual, auditory, kinesthetic) that, when run sequentially, result in a specific behavior, feeling, or response. We have internal strategies or 'schemas' for all our behaviors, from making scrambled eggs and buying a shirt to feeling depressed or having an hallucination. In order to achieve the same result, the steps of the sequence will always be repeated in exactly the same order.

In order to assist patients struggling with many chronic psychological and/or physical disorders, it is useful to understand the sequence, or strategy, that their processing follows.

Strategies are most easily elicited by first observing the patient's description of the behavior, noting especially the respective sequences of eye accessing cues and sensory modalities used.

Unpleasant feelings almost inevitably result from an inappropriate coding of a triggering event. Post-Traumatic Stress Disorder results from 'flashbacks' usually experienced as if happening in the present tense (associated). The physiological response is to present-tense threat.

Depression frequently involves melancholic or despairing self-talk (Ad–) or gloomy images (Vi–), which trigger negative feelings (Ki–). These, in turn, result in further pessimistic imagery or internal dialog, leaving the sufferer physically and emotionally depleted.

Anxiety is often a pattern-matching process, transferring a past experience into future possibility, thus setting up a 'meta-state' (the fear that fear will come).

Annotation

In order to be able to analyze a subject's internal processes more easily, they may be annotated as follows:

V = Visual
A = Auditory
K = Kinesthetic
The following superscripts are then added:
i = internal
e = external
r = recalled
c = constructed
d = digital (e.g. auditory digital is annotated as Ad)

The signs + and – may also be incorporated to represent subjectively pleasant or unpleasant feelings, and the sign > signifies a progression from one step to another.

Eliciting strategies

The question, 'How does it happen?' is useful in eliciting a strategy. The answer might be, 'Well, I wake up every morning and the first thing I feel is a weight on my chest (Ki–) and it's like: "I can't go on this way!" (Ad–), and that's when the panic comes (Ki–), and I think: "You're going to have a heart attack!" (Ad–) and the weight just presses down harder and harder, and it just never seems to stop…'

This can be annotated as follows:

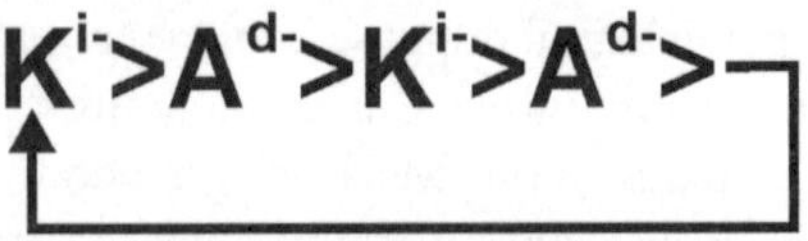

It will be clear from the above that this strategy is a self-maintaining 'two-point loop' (that is, the subjective experience loops from K to A and then back again, repeating endlessly). The practitioner's role is to find an entry point in order to break the loop, provide an appropriate 'exit point', and leverage change.

The sequence of eye accessing cues that patients use when re-accessing their experiences can give the practitioner further clues to the strategy being employed. The above sequence might be:

Eyes down and to the right > across and down to the left > across and down and to the right, etc.

This repeating Ki > Ad pattern, known as a 'two-point loop', is characteristic of people suffering from depressive and anxiety disorders.

References

References: comments on the second edition

1. *NPSA report: Building a memory: preventing harm, reducing risks & improving patient safety*, London July 2005 p53.
2. *The Journal of the American Medical Association (JAMA)* Vol 284, No 4, July 26, 2000.

References: overview

3. Clarke A (1961) Clarke's third law. *In Profiles of the Future*. London: Weidenfeld & Nicolson.
4. Olde Hartman TC, Lucassen PL, van de Lisdonk EH et al (2004) Chronic functional somatic symptoms: a single syndrome? *British Journal of General Practice* **54**: 922–7.
5. Vaillant GE, Mukamal K. Successful Aging. *Am J Psychiatry* (2001) Jun 1; **158(6)**: 839-847.
6. Fraser GE, Shavlik DJ (2001) Ten Years of Life: Is It a Matter of Choice? *Arch Intern Med.* **161**: 1645-1652.
7. Steyn K; Fourie J; Bradshaw D (1992) The impact of chronic diseases of lifestyle and their major risk factors on mortality in South Africa. *S Afr Med J*, Oct, **82**: 4, 227-31.
8. Key TJ, Allen NE, Spencer EA (2002) The effect of diet on risk of cancer. *Lancet.* Sept 14; **360 (9336)**: 861-8.
9. http://hamaralog.com/dev_sc/socialcause.org/getarticlefromdb.php?id=2004
10. European Prospective Investigation into Cancer and Nutrition (EPIC):

study populations and data collection - https://lup.lub.lu.se/search/publication/316426/

11. A-C Vergnaud et al. Adherence to the World Cancer Research Fund/American Institute for Cancer Research guidelines and risk of death in Europe: results from the European Prospective Investigation into Nutrition and Cancer cohort study, *Am J Clin Nutr* May 2013. First published April 3, 2013.
12. Chi Pang Wen, et al (2011) Minimum amount of physical activity for reduced mortality and extended life expectancy: a prospective cohort study, *The Lancet*, Early Online Publication, 16 August—http://www.thelancet.com/journals/lancet/article/PIIS0140-6736%2811%2960749-6/abstract.
13. NPSA report: *Building a memory: preventing harm, reducing risks & improving patient safety*, London July (2005) p53.
14. *The Journal of the American Medical Association (JAMA)* (2000) Vol **284**, No **4**, July 26, 2000
15. Bismark M, Paterson R *No Fault Compensation in New Zealand: Harmonizing Injury Compensation, Provider Accountability & Patient Safety*. Health (Milwood) 200; **25**: 278-83.
16. BMA Health Policy and Economic Research Unit (2000) *Work-related Stress Among Senior Doctors: Review of Research.* London: BMA Health Policy and Economic Research Unit.
17. See www.cfah.org.
18. Adapted from Bakal D (1999) *Minding the Body*. New York: Guildford Press.
19. Bandler R, Grinder J (1975) *The Structure of Magic*. Palo Alto, CA: Science and Behavior Books.
20. Antonovsky A (1979) *Health, Stress and Coping*. San Francisco: Jossey-Bass.
21. Dixon M, Sweeney K (2000) *The Human Effect in Medicine*. Oxfordshire: Radcliffe Medical Press.
22. Lambert MJ (1992) Psychotherapy outcome research: implications for integrative and eclectic therapists. In Norcoss C, Goldfriend M (eds) *Handbook of Psychotherapy Integration*, Ch. 3. New York: Basic Books.
23. Scott KJA (1995) *Dynamic Patterns—the Self-Organization of Brain and Behavior*. Cambridge, MA: MIT Press.
24. Lipton B (2005) *The Biology of Belief*. California: Elite Books.
25. McEwen B (2002) *The End of Stress as We Know It*. Washington DC: Joseph Henry Press.
26. Dixon M, Sweeney K (2000) *The Human Effect in Medicine*. Oxfordshire: Radcliffe Medical Press; Horvath AO (1995) The therapeutic relationship.In Session 1, 7–17; Krupnick JL et al (1996) The role of the therapeutic alliance in psychotherapy pharmacotherapy outcome: findings in the National Institute of Mental Health Treatment of Depression Collaborative Research Project. *Journal of Consulting and Clinical Psychology* **64**: 532-39.
27. Ambady N et al (2002) Surgeons' tone of voice: a clue to malpractice history. *Surgery* 132 (1): 5–9; Levinson W et al (1997) Physician-patient

communication: the relationship with malpractice claims among primary care physicians and surgeons. *Journal of the American Medical Association* **277(7)**: 553–9.

28. Zajicek G (1995) The placebo effect is the healing force of nature. *Cancer Journal* **8(2)**: 44-45.
29. de Craen AJ, Roos PJ, de Vries AL, Kleijnen J. (1996) Effect of color of drugs: systematic review of perceived effect of drugs and of their effectiveness. *BMJ* **313**: 1624-6
30. http://blogs.wsj.com/health/2010/10/18/when-is-a-placebo-not-really-a-placebo-maybe-more-often-than-you-think/
31. Brody H (1997) *The Placebo Response.* New York: HarperCollins.
32. Kirsch I, Saperstein G (1998) Listening to Prozac but hearing placebo: a meta-analysis of antidepressant medication. *Prevention and Treatment* (online journal): http://psycnet.apa.org/psycinfo/1999-11094-001
33. Thompson WG (2005) *The Placebo Effect and Health.* New York: Prometheus Books; Horvath AO (1995) The therapeutic relationship. *In Session* **1**: 7-17.
34. Balint M (2000) *The Doctor, His Patient and the Illness.* London: Churchill Livingstone.

Chapter 1

35. Human Givens: Radical Psychology Today (Spring 2002) *How We Are* **9(1)**: 7.
36. Starfield B (2000) Is US health really the best in the world? *Journal of the American Medical Association* **284(4)**: 483–5; Null G, Dean C (2003) *Death by Medicine.* New York: Nutrition Institute of America.
37. *Journal of the American Medical Association (JAMA)* Vol **284**, No **4**, July 26, 2000.
38. National Audit Office report (3 November 2005) Available from: www.nao.org.uk/publications/nao_reports/05-06/0506456.pdf
39. Greenberg PE, Sisitsky T, Kessler RC et al (1999) The economic burden of anxiety disorders *Journal of Clinical Psychiatry* **60(7)**: 427–35.
40. http://www.centreformentalhealth.org.uk/pdfs/ecomomic_and_social_costs_2010.pdf
41. Ioannidis JPA (2005) Why most published research findings are false. *PLoS Med* **2(8)**: e124
42. Henrich J, Heine SJ and NorenzayanA (2010) The weirdest people in the world? *Behavioral and Brain Sciences* **33**: 61-83.
43. Galsziou P, Chalmers I, Rawlins M, McCulloch P (2007) When are randomized trials unnecessary? Picking signal from noise. *British Medical Journal* **334**: 349–51.
44. Thomas KB (1987) General practice consultations: is there any point in being positive? *British Medical Journal* **294**: 1200–2.

45. Duncan BL, Miller SD, Sparks JA (2004) *A Revolutionary Way to Improve Effectiveness Through Client-directed, Outcome Informed Therapy*. San Francisco: Jossey-Bass.
46. Vase L et al (2003) The contribution of suggestion, desire and expectation to placebo effects in Irritable bowel syndrome patients: an empirical investigation. *Pain* **105(1–2)**: 17–25.
47. Segerstrom SC, Miller GE (2004) Psychological stress and the human immune system: a meta-analytical study of 30 years of inquiry. *Psychological Bulletin* **130(4)**: 601–30.
48. Kopp MS, Rethélyi J (2004) Where psychology meets physiology: chronic stress and premature mortality – the Central-Eastern European health paradox. *Brain Research Bulletin* **62**: 351–67.
49. Bandler R (1993) *Time for a Change*. Capitola, CA: Meta Publications.
50. Benedetti F, Amanzio M, Vighetti S, Asteggiano G (2006) The biochemical and neuroendocrine bases of the hyperalgesic nocebo effect. *Journal of Neuroscience* **26**: 12014–22.
51. Kurtz A, Silverman J (1991) *The Medical Interview: The Three Function Approach.* St Louis, MO: Mosby-Year Book Inc.
52. Usherwood T (1999) *Understanding the Consultation: Evidence, Theory and Practice.* Philadelphia: OUP Buckingham.
53. Dixon M, Sweeney K (2000) *The Human Effect in Medicine*. Oxfordshire: Radcliffe Medical Press; Horvath AO (1995) The therapeutic relationship. *In Session* **1**: 7–17.
54. Krupnick JL et al (1996) The role of the therapeutic alliance in psychotherapy pharmacotherapy outcome: findings in the National Institute of Mental Health Treatment of Depression Collaborative Research Project. *Journal of Consulting and Clinical Psychology* **64**: 532–9.
55. Bandura A (1977) Self efficacy: towards a unifying theory of behavioral change. *Psychological Review* **84**: 191–215.
56. Lipton B (2004) *The Biology of Belief*. Santa Rosa, CA: Elite Books.

Chapter 2

57. Olde Hartman T, Lucasseen P, Van de Lisdonk E, Bor H, Van de Weel C (2004) Chronic functional somatic symptoms: a single syndrome? *British Journal of General Practice* **54**: 922–7.
58. Rosendal M, Olsen F, Fink P (2005) Management of medically unexplained symptoms. *British Medical Journal* **330:** 4–5.
59. Wessley S, Nimnuan C, Sharpe M (1999) Functional somatic syndromes; one or many? *Lancet* **354**: 936–9.
60. Banyard P (1996) *Applying Psychology to Health*. London: Hodder & Stoughton.
61. Selye H (1936) A syndrome produced by diverse nocuous agents. *Nature* **July (138)**: 32.

62. Buchanan TW, Lovallo WR (2001) Enhanced memory for emotional material following stress-level cortisol treatment in humans. *Psychoneuroendocrinology*. **April (3)**: 307–17.
63. For a highly readable, yet scientifically grounded, account of recent developments in this field, we suggest endocrinologist Bruce McEwen's book, *The End of Stress As We Know It* (2002) Washington DC: Joseph Henry Press.
64. Nabi H, et al (2013) Increased risk of coronary heart disease among individuals reporting adverse impact of stress on their health: The Whitehall II prospective cohort study. *European Heart Journal*, 2013.
65. Sterling P, Eyer J (1988) Allostasis: A new paradigm to explain arousal pathology. In: Fisher S, Reason J (Eds.) *Handbook of Life, Stress, Cognition and Health.* New York: John Wiley & Sons.
66. Stanford University's Robert M. Sapolsky, a professor of biology and neurology, has written an entertaining and scholarly book on the effects of chronic stress on health called *Why Zebras Don't Get Ulcers* (3rd edn, 2004, New York: Owl Books). We also recommend Peter A. Levine's rather more populist book, *Waking the Tiger* (1997, Berkeley, CA: North Atlantic Books), which explores our human response to perceived threat.
67. Nesse RM, Williams GC (1966) *Why We get Sick: The New Science of Darwinian Medicine*. New York: Vintage Books.
68. Csíkszentmihályi M (1990) *Flow: The Psychology of Optimal Experience.* New York: Harper and Row.
69. Klieger R, Miller J (1978) Decreased heart rate variability and its association with increased mortality after acute myocardial infarction. *American Journal of Cardiology* **59**: 256–62.
70. Zeigarnik B (1927) Das Behalten erledigter und unerledigter Handlungen. *Psychologische Forschung* **9**: 1–85.
71. For a comprehensive review of the literature on this subject, see Rothschild B (2000) *The Body Remembers: The Psychophysiology of Trauma and Trauma Treatment*. New York: WW Norton & Company.
72. Leader D, Corfield D (2007) *Why Do People Get Ill?* London: Hamish Hamilton.

Chapter 3

73. Avenanti A, Bueti D, Galati G, Aglioti SM (2005) Transcranial magnetic stimulation highlights the sensorimotor side of empathy for pain. *Nature Neuroscience* **8**: 955–60.
74. Ax AA (1964) Goals and methods of psychophysiology. *Psychophysiology* **1**: 8–25.
75. Ramachandran V. http://edge.org/conversation/mirror-neurons-and-imitation-learning-as-the-driving-force-behind-the-great-leap-forward-in-human-evolution

76. Stern D (2002) Attachment: from early childhood through the lifespan. (Conference presentation, audio recording 609–17). Los Angeles: Lifespan Institute.
77. Hatfield E, Cacioppo JT, Rapson RL (1994) *Emotional Contagion: Studies in Emotional and Social Interaction*. Cambridge, UK: Cambridge University Press.
78. Neal DT, Chartrand TL (2011) Embodied Emotion Perception: Amplifying and Dampening Facial Feedback Modulates Emotion Perception Accuracy. *Social Psychological and Personality Science*, April 21.
79. Yue G, Cole KJ (1992) Strength increases from the motor program: comparison of training with maximal voluntary and imagined muscle contractions. *Journal of Neurophysiology* **67(5)**: 114–23.
80. Egolf B, Lasker J, Wolf S, Potvin L (1992) The Roseto effect: a 50-year comparison of mortality rates. *American Journal of Public Health* **82(8)**: 1089–92.
81. Kaiser Permanente, news release, Nov. 9, 2012.
82. Wilson RS et al (2007) Loneliness and Risk of Alzheimer Disease. *Arch Gen Psychiatry*, **64(2)**: 234-240.
83. Holwerda TJ et al (2012) Feelings of loneliness, but not social isolation, predict dementia onset: results from the Amsterdam Study of the Elderly (AMSTEL). *J Neurol Neurosurg Psychiatry*: http://www.ncbi.nlm.nih.gov/pubmed/23232034.
84. Anderson NB, Anderson PE (2003) *Emotional Longevity*. New York: Viking Penguin.
85. House JS, Robbins C, Metzner HL (1982) The association of social relationships and activities with mortality: prospective evidence from the Tecumseh Community Health Study. *American Journal of Epidemiology* **116**: 123–40.
86. Berkman LF, Leo-Summers L, Horwitz RI (1992) Emotional support and survival following myocardial infarction: a prospective, population-based study of the elderly. *Annals of Internal Medicine* **117**: 1003–9.
87. Leserman J et al (2000) Impact of stressful life events, depression, social support, coping and cortisol. *American Journal of Psychiatry* **157**: 1221–28.
88. Cohen S et al (1997) Social ties and susceptibility to the common cold. *Journal of the American Medical Association* **277**: 1940–4.
89. Seeman M, Lewis S (1995) Powerlessness, health and mortality: a longitudinal study of older men and mature women. *Social Science in Medicine* **41**: 517–25.
90. Wolff C, Friedman S, Hofer M, Mason J (1964) Relationship between psychological defences and mean urinary 17-hydroxycorti-costeroid excretion rates. *Psychosomatic Medicine* **26**: 576–91.
91. Chapman C (1989) Giving the patient control of opioid analgesic administration. In Hill C, Field W (eds) *Advances in Pain Research and Therapy*, vol. II. Philadelphia, PA: Lippincott Williams and Wilkins.
92. Rodin J (1986) Ageing and health: effects of the sense of control. *Science* **233**: 1271–6.

93. Melin B, Lunberg U, Soderlund J, Grandqvist M (1999) Psychological and physiological stress reactions of male and female assembly workers: a comparison between two different forms of work organisation. *Journal of Organisational Psychology* **20**: 47–61.
94. Segerstrom S, Sephton S (2010) Optimistic expectancies and cell-mediated immunity: The role of positive affect. *Psychological Science* **21(3)**: 448-55.
95. Schwartz, T. Psychologist and scientist Suzanne Segerstrom 90 studies optimism and the immune system. *Chronicle*. Online at http://legacy.lclark.edu/dept/chron/positives03.html; Goode, E. (2003) Power of Positive Thinking May Have a Health Benefit, Study Says. *The New York Times*. Online at http://psyphz.psych.wisc.edu/web/News/Positive_thinking_NYT_9-03.html.
96. Goleman D (1987) Research affirms power of positive thinking. *The New York Times*. Found online at: http://www.nytimes.com/1987/02/03/science/research-affirms-power-of-positive-thinking.htmll
97. Sapolsky R (2004) *Why Zebras Don't Get Ulcers: The Guide to Stress, Stress-Related Diseases, and Coping*, 3rd ed. New York: Henry Holt.
98. Peterson C, Seligman M, Vaillant G (1988) Pessimistic explanatory style is a risk factor for physical illness: a 35-year longitudinal study. *Journal of Personality and Social Psychology* **55**: 23–27.
99. Kubzansky L et al (2001) Is the glass half empty or half full? A prospective study of optimism and coronary heart disease in the normative ageing study. *Psychosomatic Medicine* **63**: 910–16.
100. McCullough M et al (2000) Religious involvement and mortality: a meta-analytical review. *Health Psychology* **19**: 211–22.
101. Frankl V (2004) *Man's Search for Meaning*. London: Rider & Co.

Chapter 4

102. Sigmund Freud © Copyrights, The Institute of Psycho-Analysis and The Hogarth Press for permission to quote from *The Standard Edition of the Complete Psychological Works of Sigmund Freud*, translated and edited by James Strachey. Reprinted by permission of the Random House Group.
103. Pinker S (new ed 1995) *The Language Instinct: The New Science of Language and Mind*. London: Penguin Books Ltd
104. House JS, Landis KR, Umberson D (1988) Social relations and health. *Science* **241**: 540–5; Hafen Q, Karren KJ, Frandsen KJ, Smith NL (1996) *Mind/Body Health: The Effects of Attitudes, Emotions and Relationships*, Boston: Allyn & Bacon; The GUSTO Investigators (1993) An international randomized trial comparing four thrombolytic studies for acute myocardial infarction. *New England Journal of Medicine* **329**: 673–82.
105. Witthöft M, Rubin GJ (2013) Are media warnings about the adverse health effects of modern life self-fulfilling? An experimental study on idiopathic

environmental intolerance attributed to electromagnetic fields (IEI-EMF) *Journal of Psychosomatic Research* **74**(3): 206-212.
106. Bargh JA, Chartrand TL (1999) The unbearable automaticity of being. *American Psychologist* **54(7)**: 462–79.
107. Ibid.
108. Pert CB, Ruff MR (1985) Neuropeptides and their receptors: a psychosomatic network. *Journal of Immunology* **135(2)**: 820–6.
109. Rosencranz MA et al (2005) Neural circuitry underlying the interaction between emotion and asthma symptom exacerbation. *PNAS* **102(37)**: 13319–24.
110. Thaler Singer M, Lalich J (1996) *Cults in Our Midst.* Hoboken, NJ: Jossey Bass/Wiley.

Chapter 5

111. Pert C (2006) *Everything You Need to Know to Feel Good.* Carlsbad, CA: Hay House.
112. Levy BR (1996) Improving memory in old age through implicit self-stereotyping. *Journal of Personality and Social Psychology* **71(6)**: 1092–107.
113. Levy BR, Hausdorff JM, Hencke R, Wei JY (2000) Reducing cardiovascular stress with positive self-stereotypes of ageing. *Journal of Gerontology Series B: Psychological Sciences and Social Sciences* **55**: 205–13.
114. Langer E, Dillon M, Kurtz R, Katz M (1998) *Believing is Seeing.* Harvard University, Department of Psychology.
115. Langer E (2009) *Counter Clockwise Mindful Health and the Power of Possibility.* New York: Ballantine Books.
116. Ibid.
117. Reisberg D (2007) *Cognition: Exploring the Science of the Mind*, pp 255, 517.
118. Chartrand TL, Bargh JA (1996) Automatic activation of impression formation and memorization goals: Non-conscious goal priming reproduces effects of explicit task instructions. *Journal of Personality and Social Psychology* **71(3)**: 464-478.
119. Social exclusion may make you feel cold. HealthNewsTrack, September 17, 2008, sourced from *Association for Psychological Science* – http://www.psychologicalscience.org/.
120. Bargh JA, Shalev Idit (2012) The Substitutability of Physical and Social Warmth in Daily Life. *Emotion* **12(1)**: 154–162.

Chapter 6

121. Bandler R, Grinder J (1975) *The Structure of Magic*, Palo Alto, CA: Science and Behavior Books.
122. Bradshaw J (1996, 3rd ed.) *The Family: A Revolutionary Way of Self-*

Discovery. Deerfield Beach, FL: Health Communications.

123. Korzybski A (1933; 1994) *Science and Sanity: An Introduction to Non-Aristotelian Systems and General Semantics*. Englewood, NJ: Institute of General Semantics.
124. Miller GA (1956) The magical number seven, plus or minus two: some limits on our capacity for processing information. *Psychological Review* 63: 81–97.
125. McGuire IC (1996) Remembering what the doctor said: organization and older adults' memory. *Experimental Ageing Research* **22**: 403–28.

Chapter 7

126. Libet B (1992) The neural time factor in perception, volition, and free will. *Revue de Métaphysique et de Morale* **97**: 255–72.
127. Wegner DM (2002) *The Illusion of Conscious Will.* Cambridge, MA: Bradford Books.
128. Soon CS, Brass M, Heinze H-J, Haynes J-D (2008) Unconscious determinants of free decisions in the human brain. *Nature Neuroscience* **11**: 543–545.
129. Coskerry P (August 2003) The importance of cognitive errors in diagnosis and strategies to minimize them, *Acad. Med.*, **78**: 775–780.
130. Bolles EB (1991) *A Second Way of Knowing*. New York: Prentice Hall Press.
131. Changing classification of diabetes: *BMJ* (2011); **342**: d3319.
132. *Dorland's Medical Dictionary 32E.*

Chapter 8

133. Gladwell M (2005) *Blink*. London: Allen & Lane.
134. Ekman P, Frieson WV (2003) *Unmasking the Face*. Cambridge, MA: Major Books.
135. Ambady N, Rosenthal R (1993) Half a minute: predicting teacher evaluations from thin slices of nonverbal behaviour and physical attractiveness. *Journal of Personality and Social Psychology* **64(3)**: 431–41.
136. Korsch BM, Gozzi EK, Francis V (1968) Gaps in doctor-patient communication. *Pediatrics* **42**: 855–71.
137. Damasio A (1994) *Descartes' Error*. New York: GP Putnam & Sons.
138. Allen J, Burkin A (2000) Interview by Berkley Rice: How plaintiffs' lawyers pick their targets. *Medical Economics* **77**: 94–96, 99, 103–104.
139. Dixon M, Sweeney K (2000) *The Human Effect in Medicine*. Oxfordshire: Radcliffe Medical Press; Horvath AO (1995) The therapeutic relationship. In *Session* 1: 7–17; Krupnick JL et al (1996) The role of the therapeutic alliance in psychotherapy and pharmacotherapy outcomes: findings in the National Institute of Mental Health Treatment of Depression Collaborative Research

Project. *Journal of Consulting and Clinical Psychology* **64**: 53–9.
140. Laver J (1991) *The Gift of Speech.* Edinburgh: Edinburgh University Press.
141. Pear TH (1931) *Voice and Personality.* London: Chapman & Hall.
142. Linville SE (1998) Acoustic correlates of perceived versus actual sexual orientation in men's speech. *Folia Phoniatrica et Logoapedia* **50**: 35–48.
143. Karpf A (2006) *The Human Voice – the Story of a Remarkable Talent.* London: Bloomsbury.
144. Pennebaker James W (2013) *The Secret Life of Pronouns: What Your Words Say About You.* New York; Bloomsbury Publishing PLC.
145. Langer E (1990) *Mindfulness.* Cambridge, MA: Da Capo Press.

Chapter 9

146. Hunsaker Hawkins A (1999) *Reconstructing Illness: Studies in Pathography.* West Layfayette, Ind: Purdue University Press.
147. Ornstein R (1997) *The Right Mind; Making Sense of the Hemispheres.* Orlando FL: Harcourt Brace.
148. Little M (1995) *Humane Medicine.* Cambridge: Cambridge University Press.
149. Ornstein R (1997) *The Right Mind; Making Sense of the Hemispheres.* Orlando FL: Harcourt Brace.
150. Beckman HB, Frankel RM (1984) The effect of physician behavior on the collection of data. *Annals of Internal Medicine* **101**: 692–6.
151. Ibid.
152. Pennebaker JW, Seagal JD (1999) Forming a Story: The Health Benefits of Narrative. *Journal of Clinical Psychology* **55(10)**: 1243-1254.
153. Pennebaker JW, Kiecolt-Glaser JK, Glaser R (1988) Disclosure of traumas and immune function: Health implications for psychotherapy. *Journal of Consulting and Clinical Psychology* **56**: 239-245.
154. Esterling BA, Antoni MH, Fletcher MA, Margulies S, Schneiderman N (1994) Emotional disclosure through writing and speaking modulates latent Epstein-Barr virus reactivation. *Journal of Consulting and Clinical Psychology* **62**: 130-140.
155. Petrie KJ, Booth RJ, Pennebaker JW, Davison KP, Thomas M (1995) Disclosure of trauma and immune response to Hepatitis B vaccination program. *Journal of Consulting and Clinical Psychology* **63**: 787-792.
156. Pennebaker JW, Seagal JD (1999) Forming a Story: The Health Benefits of Narrative. *Journal of Clinical Psychology* **55(10)**: 1243-1254.
157. Pennebaker JW, Mayne TJ, Francis ME (1997) Linguistic predictors of adaptive bereavement. *Journal of Personality and Social Psychology* **72**: 863-871.
158. Gergen KJ, Gergen MM (1987) Narratives of relationship. In M McGhee, DD Clarke, R Burnett (eds), *Accounting for relationships* (pp. 269-288). Oxford: Blackwell.
159. Gergen KJ, Gergen MM (1988) Narratives and the self as relationship. In L

Berkowitz (ed.), *Advances in experimental social psychology*, Vol. 21 (pp 17-56). New York: Academic.

160. Donnelly DA, Murray EJ (1991) Cognitive and emotional changes in written essays and therapy interviews. *Journal of Social and Clinical Psychology* **10**: 334-350.
161. Murray EJ, Lamnin AD, Carver CS (1981) Emotional expression in written essays and psychotherapy. *Journal of Social and Clinical Psychology* **8**: 414-429.

Chapter 10

162. Kahneman D, Tversky A (1972) Subjective probability: A judgment of representativeness. In Kahneman, Slovic, Tversky. *Judgment under uncertainty: Heuristics and biases.* Cambridge: Cambridge University Press.
163. http://www.wbs.ac.uk/news/the-human-zoo-reveals-women-cant-multi-task-either/.
164. Motluk A (2006) How many things can you do at once? Our flawed talent for multi-tasking. *New Scientist* **7 April**: 28–31.
165. Gazzaniga M (1998) *The Mind's Past.* Berkley, CA: University of California Press.
166. Evans P, Hucklebridge F, Clow A (2000) Cerebral Laterisation and the Immune System, in *Mind, Immunity and Health.* London: Free Association Books.
167. Platt FW, McMath JC (1979) Clinical hypocompetence: the interview. *Annals of Internal Medicine* **91(6)**: 898-902.
168. Desmond J, Copeland L (2000) *Communicating with Today's Patient.* San Francisco: Jossey-Bass.
169. Realni T, Kalet A, Sparling J (1995) Interruptions in the medical interaction. *Archives of Family Medicine* **4**: 1028-33.
170. Marcinowicz L, Chlabicz S, Grebowski R (2007) Open-ended questions in surveys of patients' satisfaction with family doctors. *J Health Serv Res Policy* Apr; **12(2)**: 86-9.
171. Burack R, Carpenter R (1983) The predictive value of the presenting complaint. *Journal of Family Practice* **16(4)**: 749-54.
172. Miller S, Hubble M, Duncan B (1996) *Handbook of Solution Focused Brief Therapy.* San Francisco: Jossey-Bass.

Chapter 11

173. Brody H (2000) *The Placebo Response.* New York, NY: Cliff Street Books.
174. Thomas KB (1987) General practice consultations: is there any point in being positive? *British Medical Journal* **294**: 1200-02.

175. Vase L et al (2003) The contribution of suggestion, desire and expectation to placebo effects in irritable bowel syndrome patients: an empirical investigation. *Pain* **105(1-2)**: 17-25.
176. Lipton B (2005) *The Biology of Belief.* Santa Rosa, CA: Mountain of Love Productions.
177. Balint M (2000) *The Doctor, His Patient and The Illness.* London: Churchill Livingstone.
178. Searle J (1995) *The Mystery of Consciousness.* New York Review of Books. 2 November and 16 November: 60-61.
179. Hoyle F (1983) *The Intelligent Universe.* New York: Holt, Rinehart & Winston.
180. Schroth M (1970) The effect of informative feedback on problem-solving. *Child Development* **41(3)**: 831-7.

Chapter 12

181. From a translation by Rafi Khan. Used by permission.
182. Kopp S (1977) *Back to One.* Palo Alto, CA: Science & Behavior Books.
183. Lakoff G, Johnson M (1980) *Metaphors We Live By.* Chicago, IL: University of Chicago Press.
184. Lakoff G, Johnson M (1999) *Philosophy in the Flesh.* New York: Basic Books.

Chapter 13

185. Wolf IJ (ed.) (1965) *Aphorisms and Facetiae of Bela Schick.* Baltimore: Waverly Press/Knoll Pharmaceutical.
186. Robinson R, West R (1992) A comparison of computer and questionnaire methods of history-taking in a genito-urinary clinic. *Psychology and Health* **6**: 77-84.
187. Engel G (1977) The need for a new medical model: a challenge for biomedicine. *Science* **196**: 129-36.
188. Duncan BL, Miller SD, Sparks JA (2004) *A Revolutionary Way to Improve Effectiveness Through Client-directed, Outcome Informed Therapy.* San Francisco: Jossey-Bass.
189. Vase L et al (2003) The contribution of suggestion, desire and expectation to placebo effects in irritable bowel syndrome patients: an empirical investigation. *Pain* **105(1-2)**: 17-25.
190. In preparation.
191. Bandler R, Grinder J (1982) *Reframing.* Moab, UT: Real People Press.
192. Littlewood R, Lipsedge M (1989) *Aliens and Alienists*, 2nd ed. London: Unwin Hyman.
193. Kubler-Ross E (1969) *On Death and Dying.* New York: Macmillan.

Chapter 14

194. The Disease-Illness Model (1984) of McWhinney et al, University of Western Ontario, suggested the 'transformed clinical method' also be known as 'patient-centered clinical interviewing', to differentiate it from the more traditional 'doctor-centered' method.
195. De Shazer S (1994) *Words Were Originally Magic.* New York: Norton.

Chapter 15

196. Howard RE (2006) *Kull: Exile of Atlantis.* New York: Del Rey Books.
197. See Clark RW (1984) *Einstein: The Life and Times.* New York: Avon, for an entertaining and informative account of an extraordinary life.
198. Jeans, Sir James (2009) *The New Background of Science.* Cambridge, UK: Cambridge University Press.
199. Friedman M, Rosenman R (1974) *Type A Behaviour and Your Heart.* New York: Alfred A Knopf.
200. Csikszentmihalyi M (1991) *Flow: The Psychology of Optimal Experience.* Copenhagen: SOS Free Stock.
201. Whitrow G (1972) *The Nature of Time.* London: Thames & Hudson.
202. Ornstein R (1969) *On the Experience of Time.* New York: Penguin.
203. Benson H (1990) *The Relaxation Response.* New York: Avon Books.

Chapter 16

204. Frankl V (2004) *Man's Search for Meaning.* London: Rider & Co.
205. For an extensive review of research into our human tendency to act out of the rules of group thinking, we know of no better book than David Berreby's *Us and Them—Understanding Your Tribal Mind* (2005) London: Hutchinson.
206. Langer E (1989) *Mindfulness.* Reading, MA: Addison-Wesley.
207. Furedi F (2004) *Therapy Culture: Cultivating Vulnerability in an Uncertain Age.* London: Routledge.
208. Conversation with the author (GT).
209. Gilbert K (2006) The Doctor is Within, *Psychology Today,* September/ October.

Chapter 17

210. Rainville P, Price D (2003) Hypnosis phenomenology and neurobiology of consciousness. *International Journal of Clinical and Experimental Hypnosis*

51(2): 105–29; Ray WJ, De Pascalis V (2003) Temporal aspects of hypnotic processes. *International Journal of Clinical and Experimental Hypnosis* **51(2)**: 147–65; Szechtman H,Woody E, Bowers K, Nahmias C (1998) Where the imaginal appears real: a positron emission tomography study of auditory hallucinations. *Proceedings of the National Academy of Sciences of the United States of America* **95**: 1956–60.

211. Korzybski A (1933) *Science and Sanity: An Introduction to Non-Aristotelian Systems and General Semantics.* Englewood, NJ: Institute of General Semantics.
212. Kershaw CJ (1992) *The Couple's Hypnotic Dance.* New York: Brunner/Mazel.
213. Vaughan AC (1997) *The Talking Cure: The Science behind Psychotherapy.* New York: Grosset/Putnam.
214. Kandel ER (1998) A new intellectual framework for psychiatry. *American Journal of Psychiatry* **155(4)**: 457-69.
215. Deikman J (1982) *The Observing Self: Mysticism and Psychotherapy*. Boston, MA: Beacon Press.
216. Watzlawick P (1974) *Change: Principles of Problem Formation and Problem Resolution.* New York: WW Norton.

Chapter 18

217. Kurisu S, Sato H, Kawagoe T et al (2002) Takotsubo-like left ventricular dysfunction with ST-segment elevation: a novel cardiac syndrome mimicking acute myocardial infarction. *American Heart Journal* **143(3)**: 448-55.
218. Rihal C: (2010) Hearts Can Actually Break, *Wall Street Journal.* http://online.wsj.com/article/SB10001424052748703615904575053443911673752.html.
219. Cavanaugh MA, Boswell W, Roehling MV, Boudreau JW (1998) "Challenge" and "Hindrance" Related Stress Among US Managers, *CAHRS Working Paper Series*: http://digitalcommons.ilr.cornell.edu/cahrswp/126/.
220. Gershon MD (1999) The Enteric Nervous System: A second Brain, *Hospital Practice (Office Edition)* 34, no 7: 31-32, 35-38, 41-42 passim.
221. Armour JA, ed (1991) Anatomy and Function of the Intrathoracic Neurons Regulating the Mammalian Heart, *Reflex Control of the Circulation*, Boca Raton: CRC Press.
222. Keltner D (2009) *Born to be Good—The Science of a Meaningful Life.* London: WW Norton & Company Ltd.
223. Porges SP (1995) Orienting in a Defensive World: Mammalian Modifications of our Evolutionary Heritage: A Polyvagal Theory, *Psychophysiology* **42**: 301-17.
224. Porges SP (1998) Love: an Emergent Property of the Mammalian Autonomic Nervous System, *Psychoendocrinology* **23**: 837-61.
225. Porges SP (April 2009) The polyvagal theory: New insights into adaptive reactions of the autonomic nervous system, *Cleveland Clinic Journal of Medicine* **76(2)**: S86-S90.

226. www.stephenporges.com.
227. Groves DA, Brown VJ (2005) Vagal nerve stimulation: A review of its applications and potential mechanisms that mediate its clinical effects. *Neuroscience & Biobehavioral Reviews* **29(3)**: 493.
228. ClinicaTrials.gov NCT00294281 Vagus Nerve Stimulation for Treating Adults with Severe Fibromyalgia.
229. Tracey K (2007) Physiology and Immunology of the Cholinmergic Anti-Inflammatory Pathway, Stetten Lecture, National Institute of Health, Bethesda.
230. http://www.healthguidance.org/entry/12051/1/Vagal-Nerve-Fainting.html.
231. Liponis M (2008) *Ultra-Longevity*. London: Little Brown and Company.
232. Honkalampi K, et al (2011) Alexithymia and tissue Inflammation. *Journal of Psychotherapy and Psychsomatics* **80(6)**.
233. McCratey R, Atkinson M, Tomasino D, Bradley RT (2009) *The Coherent Heart: Heart-Brain Interactions, Psychophysiological Coherence, and the Emergence of System-Wide Order*. Boulder Creek, CA: The Institute of HeartMath.
234. Sone T, et al (2008) Sense of life worth living (ikigai) and mortality in Japan: Ohsaki Study, *Psychosomatic Medicine* **70**: 709-715.
235. McKeown P (2005) *Asthma-Free Naturally: Everything you need to know about taking control of your asthma*. London: Harper Thorsons.
236. Fried RZ (1986) Hyperventilation Syndrome: Research and Clinical Treatment. *Johns Hopkins Series in Contemporary Medicine and Public Health.*
237. Lum LC (1975) Hyperventilation: the tip and the iceberg, *Journal of Psychosomatic Research* **19**: 375–383, Oxford: Pergamon Press.
238. www.heartmath.org.
239. Hatfield E, Cacioppo JT, Rapson, RL (1993. Emotional contagion. *Current Directions in Psychological Science* **2**: 96-99.

Chapter 19

240. Mihaly Csikszentmihalyi (new ed. 2002) *Flow: The Psychology of Happiness. The Classic Work on How to Achieve Happiness*. London: Rider.
241. Ornstein R (1972) *The Psychology of Consciousness.* San Francisco: WH Freeman.
242. Benson H (1996) *Timeless Healing.* New York: Scribner.
243. Benson H, Stuart E (eds) (1992) *The Wellness Book*. New York: Fireside.
244. http://www.themoralliberal.com/blog/2010/12/20/the-illegitimacy-of-the-%E2%80%9Cpsychiatric-bible%E2%80%9D/.
245. Kirsch I (2009) *The Emperor's New Drugs: Exploding the Anti-Depressant Myth.* London: Bodley Head.
246. *Diagnostic and Statistical Manual of Mental Disorders (DSM)*, Fifth Edition

(May 2013), Arlington VS: American Psychiatric Publishing.

247. Medicine's big new battleground: does mental illness really exist? (May 12, 2013) *The Observer*, London.
248. Hegarty J (1994) 100 Years of Schizophrenia: A Meta-analysis of the Outcome Literature, *American Journal of Psychiatry* **151**:1409-1416.
249. Leff J (1992) The International Pilot Study of Schizophrenia, *Psychological Medicine* **22**: 131-145.
250. Jablensky A (1992) Schizophrenia: Manifestations, Incidents, and Course in Difference Cultures, *Psychological Medicine*, supplement **20**: 1-95.
251. Whitaker R (2010) *Mad in America: Bad Science, Bad Medicine, and the Enduring Mistreatment of the Mentally Ill*. New York: Basic Books.
252. Rosenhan DL (January 1973) 'On being sane in insane places'. *Science* **179** (**4070**): 250-8.
253. http://www.cbsnews.com/stories/2006/12/13/fyi/main2255769.shtml.
254. http://www.theguardian.com/society/2010/jun/11/antidepressant-prescriptions-rise-nhs-recession
255. Watters E (2010) *Crazy Like Us: The Globalization of the Western Mind*. London:Robinson.
256. http://www.youtube.com/watch?v=6vfSFXKlnO0.
257. Valenstein ES (1998) *Blaming the Brain: The Truth about Drugs and Mental Health*. New York: The Free Press.
258. Moncrieff J (2009) *The Myth of the Chemical Cure: A Critique of Psychiatric Drug Treatment*. Basingstoke, Hampshire: Palgrave MacMillan.
259. http://www.mentalhealth.org.uk/help-information/mental-health-a-z/E/exercise-mental-health/.
260. Van de Weller C (2005) Changing diets, changing minds: how food affects mental well being and behavior. In: Longfield J, Ryrie I, Cornah D, eds. *Feeding Minds: The Impact of Food on Mental Health*. London: Sustain, Mental Health Foundation and Food Commision.
261. Sánchez-Villegas A, Henríquez P, Bes-Rastrollo M, Doreste J (2006) Mediterranean diet and depression, *Public Health Nutrition* **9(8A)**: 1104-1109.
262. Perskey H (1979) Pain terms: a list of definitions and notes on usage recommendations by the IASP subcommittee on taxonom. *Pain* **6**: 249-52.
263. Gureje O, Von Korff M, Simon GE, Gater R (1998) Persistent pain and wellbeing. A World Health Organization study in primary care. *JAMA* **280**: 147-51.
264. Smith Blair H (September 2002) Chronic pain: a primary care condition. *In Practice (ARC)* **9**: 1-5.
265. Mcfarlane M, McBeth J, Silman AJ (2001) Widespread body pain and mortality: prospective population based study. *BMJ* **323**: 662-4.
266. Melzack R, Wall PD (1982) *The Challenge of Pain* London: Penguin.
267. Loeser JD (1994) Tic douloureaux and atypical face pain. In Wall PD, Melzack R (eds)*Textbook of Pain*, 3rd edn. Edinburgh: Churchill Livingstone.

268. Scarry E (1985) *The Body in Pain.* New York: Oxford University Press.
269. Evans P, Hucklebridge F, Clow A (2000) *Mind, Immunity and Health: The Science of Psychoneuroimmunology.* London: Free Association Books.

Chapter 20

270. Kermen R, Hickner J, Brody H, Hasham (2010) Family Physicians Believe the Placebo Effect Is Therapeutic But Often Use Real Drugs as Placebos, *Family Medicine* **42(9)**: 636-642.
271. Howick J, Bishop FL, Heneghan C, Wolstenholme J, Stevens S, et al (2013) Placebo Use in the United Kingdom: Results from a National Survey of Primary Care Practitioners. *PLoS One* **8(3)**: e58247.
272. Bohm, David (1980) *Wholeness and the Implicate Order.* London: Routledge.

Chapter 21

273. Ogden P, Minton K, Pain C (2006) *Trauma and the Body.* New York: Norton.
274. Epel E, Blackburn E, Lin J, et al (2004) Accelerated telomere shortening in response to exposure to life stress. *PNAS* **101**: 17312-17315.
275. Jacobs TL et al (2011) Intensive meditation training, immune cell telomerase activity, and psychological mediators. *Psychoneuroendocrinology* **36(5)**: 664-681.
276. For an easily accessible and impressive account of recent developments in research into neuroplasticity, we recommend Norman Doidge's book, *The Brain that Changes Itself* (New York: Viking Penguin, 2007).
277. Feltz DL, Landers DM (1983) The effects of mental practice on motor skill learning and performance: a meta-analysis. *Journal of Sports Psychology* **5**: 25-57.
278. Yue Guang, Cole K (1992) Strength increases from the motor program: comparison of training with maximal voluntary and imagined muscle contractions. *Journal of Neurophysiology* **67(5)**: 1114-23.
279. Moseley GL (2004) Graded motor imagery is effective for long-standing complex regional pain syndrome: a randomized, controlled trial. *Pain* **108**: 192-8.
280. Pascual-Leone A, Hamilton R (2001) The metamodal organization of the brain. *Progress in Brain Research* **134**: 427-45.
281. Henningsen P, Zipfel S, Herzog W (2007) Management of functional somatic syndromes. *Lancet* **369**: 946-55.
282. Scaer RC (2001) *The Body Bears the Burden: Trauma, Dissociation and Disease.* New York: Haworth Medical Press.
283. Bakal D (1999) *Minding the Body: Clinical Uses of Somatic Awareness.* New York: Guilford Press.

284. Koriat A, Goldsmith M, Pansky A (2000) Toward a psychology of memory accuracy. *Annual Review of Psychology* **51**: 481-537.

Chapter 22

285. http://www.iom.edu/Reports/2006/Sleep-Disorders-and-Sleep-Deprivation-An-Unmet-Public-Health-Problem.aspx
286. http://www2.warwick.ac.uk/newsandevents/pressreleases/ne100000021440
287. University of Chicago Medical Center (2008, January 2) Lack Of Deep Sleep May Increase Risk Of Type 2 Diabetes. *ScienceDaily.* Retrieved November 4, 2008, from http://www.sciencedaily.com /releases/2008/01/080101093903.htm.
288. Hall MH et al (2008) Self-Reported Sleep Duration is Associated with the Metabolic Syndrome in Midlife Adults. *Sleep* **31(5)**: 635-643.
289. Liu PY, et al "The Effects of 'Catch-Up' Sleep On Insulin Sensitivity in Men With Lifestyle Driven, Chronic, Intermittent Sleep Restriction." Presented at ENDO 2013, 15-18 June, San Francisco. Link to paper: http://press.endocrine.org/doi/abs/10.1210/endo-meetings.2013.DGM.3.SUN-782
290. American Academy of Sleep Medicine. "Insomnia Linked To Depression In Young Adults." *ScienceDaily*, 3 April 2008.
291. American Academy of Sleep Medicine. "Insomnia May Perpetuate Depression In Some Elderly Patients." *ScienceDaily* 4 April 2008.
292. JAMA and Archives Journals. "Child Sleep Problems Linked To Later Behavioral Difficulties, Study Shows." *ScienceDaily* 10 April 2008.
293. Stanford University Medical Center (2003, October 1). Stanford Research Builds Link Between Sleep, Cancer Progression. *ScienceDaily*. Retrieved November 4, 2008, from http://www.sciencedaily.com / releases/2003/10/031001060734.htm.
294. Verkasalo PK, Lillberg K, Stevens RG, Hublin C, Partinen M, Koskenvuo M, Kaprio J (2005) Sleep duration and breast cancer: a prospective cohort study. *Cancer Res* **65**: 9595-9600.
295. Wu AH, Wang R, Koh WP, Stanczyk FC, Lee HP, Yu MC (2008) Sleep duration, melatonin and breast cancer among Chinese women in Singapore. *Carcinogenesis* **29(6)**: 1244-1248.
296. Pinheiro SP, Schernhammer ES, Tworoger SS, Michels KB (2006) A prospective study on habitual duration of sleep and incidence of breast cancer in a large cohort of women. *Cancer Res* **66**: 5521-5525.

Chapter 23

297. http://www.ehealthserver.com/picis/48-patient-satisfaction-with-healthcare-systems-do-different-funding-models-lead-to-different-results.
298. Royal College of General Practitioners. (1999) *General Practice Workload.* Information Sheet No 3. London: RCGP.

299. Williams, CJ, Calnan M. Key determinants of consumer satisfaction with general practice. *Fam Pract* 1991; **8**: 237-242.
300. Airey C, Erens B (eds.) (1999) *National Surveys of NHS Patients: General Practice 1998*, London: NHS Executive.
301. Pollock K, Grime J (2002) Patients' perception of entitlement to time in general practice consultations for depression: qualitative study. *BMJ*; **325**: 687-698.
302. McGuire LC (1996) Remembering what the doctor said: organization and older adults' memory for medical information. *Experimental Aging Research* **22**: 403-28.
303. Anderson JL, Dodman S, Kopelman M, Fleming A (1979) Patient information recall in a rheumatology clinic. *Rheumatology Rehabilitation* **18**: 245-55.
304. Balint M (2000) *The Doctor, His Patient and the Illness.* London: Livingstone.
305. Beckman HB, Frankel RM (1984) The effect of physician behaviour on the collection of data. *Annals of Internal Medicine* **101**: 692-6.

Chapter 24

306. McGuire LC (1996) Remembering what the doctor said: organization and older adults' memory for medical information. *Experimental Aging Research* **22**: 403-28.
307. Anderson JL, Dodman S, Kopelman M, Fleming A (1979) Patient information recall in a rheumatology clinic. *Rheumatology Rehabilitation* **18**: 245-55.
308. Tuckett D, Boulton M, Olson C, Williams A (1985) *Meetings Between Experts.* London: Tavistock.
309. Bertakis KD (1977) The communication of information from physician to patient: a method for increasing patient retention and satisfaction. *Journal of Family Practice* **5**: 217-22.
310. Thomson AM, Cunningham SJ, Hunt NP (2001) A comparison of information retention at an initial orthodontic consultation. *European Journal of Orthodontics* **23**: 169-78.
311. Blinder D, Rotenberg L, Peleg M, Taicher S (2001) Patient compliance to instructions after oral procedures. *International Journal of Oral and Maxillofacial Surgery* **30**: 216-19.
312. Houts PS, Bachrach R, Witmer JT et al (1998) Using pictographs to enhance recall of spoken medical instructions. *Patient Education and Counseling* **35**: 83-8.
313. Available from: www.nao.org.uk/publications/nao_reports/0607/0607454.pdf.
314. Berg JS et al (1993) Medication compliance: a healthcare problem. *Annals of Pharmacotherapy* **27**: 1-24.

315. Ley P (1979) Memory for medical information. *British Journal of Social and Clinical Psychology* **18**: 245-55.
316. Schramke CJ, Bauer RM (1997) State-dependent learning in older and younger adults. *Psychology of Aging* **12**: 255-62.

Appendix A

317. Blackburn E, Epel E, Daubenmier J, Moskowitz JT, Folkman S . Can meditation slow rate of cellular aging? Cognitive stress, mindfulness, and telomeres. *Ann N Y Acad Sci.* 2009 Aug; **1172**: 34-53.
318. Benson H, Stuart E (eds) (1992) *The Wellness Book*. New York: Fireside.
319. Rossi EL, Nimmons D (1991)*The 20-Minute Break: Using the New Science of Ultradian Rhythms*. Los Angeles: Jeremy O Tracher.
320. For a summary of related research, see Benson H, Klipper MZ (1975). *The Relaxation Response*. New York: HarperTorch.
321. Dusek J (2008), Genomic Counter-Stress Changes Induced by the Relaxation Response, *PLoS One*, Jul; **3(7).**

Appendix C

322. Perskey H (1979) Pain terms: a list of definitions and notes on usage recommendations by the IASP subcommittee on taxonomy. *Pain* **6**: 249–52.
323. Gureje O, Von Korff M, Simon GE, Gater R (1998) Persistent pain and wellbeing. A World Health Organization study in primary care. *JAMA* **280**: 147–51.

Index

Note: page numbers in bold indicate the glossary.

Note: page numbers in bold indicate the glossary.

Note: page numbers in bold indicate the glossary.

Note: page numbers in bold indicate the glossary.

Note: page numbers in bold indicate the glossary.

Note: page numbers in bold indicate the glossary.

Note: page numbers in bold indicate the glossary.

Note: page numbers in bold indicate the glossary.